JUDICIAL DISCRETION IN THE INTERPRETATION OF INTERNATIONAL CRIMES

This book sets out a legality-centred model to better understand the interpretation of crimes in international criminal law.

It offers a new way of understanding the interpretation of crimes as a two-dimensional process: determining what the law is and interpreting whether that law in fact criminalises the conduct in question. This model affects the process and the outcome of judicial interpretation. The book moves beyond the abstract by applying the model to two case studies: (1) organisational policy as a contextual element of crimes against humanity, and (2) the crime of forced marriage. It brings often overlooked criminal law theory into the field of international criminal law, offering a fresh, innovative perspective on interpretation and placing the legality principle back at the centre of crime interpretation.

Volume 105 in the series Studies in International Law

Studies in International Law

RECENT TITLES IN THIS SERIES

The Standard of Review Before the International Court of Justice: Between Principle and Pragmatism Felix Fouchard

Global Lawmaking and Social Change: The Varieties of Customary International Law Gregor Novak

The Effectiveness of the Inter-American Court of Human Rights: The Case of Indigenous Territorial Rights Gabriela CB Navarro

Individuals in International Humanitarian Law: A Historical Analysis Sarina Landefeld

The Pathology of Plenty: Natural Resources in International Law Lys Kulamadayil

The United Nations Security Council and the Authorisation of Force: Form, Character and Nature Marko Svicevic

Protecting the Right to Leave in an Era of Externalised Migration Control Emilie McDonnell

Pluralising Actors and Norms in Human Rights Treaties: Beyond Monolithic States Hinako Takata

Systemic Economic Offences as International Crimes: Theorising a New Paradigm of Mass Criminality Nicole Citeroni

A Central Asian Perspective on International Law Sergey Sayapin

Responsibility for the Crime of Aggression under International Law Nikola Hajdin

Judicial Discretion in the Interpretation of International Crimes: Revisiting the Legality Principle Ligeia Quackelbeen

For a complete list of titles in this series
see www.bloomsbury.com/uk/series/studies-in-international-law/

Acknowledgements

WRITING A BOOK IS often described as a solitary endeavour. Yet I have been fortunate to walk this path accompanied, challenged, supported, and lifted up by many remarkable people. My gratitude to them is far greater than these pages can capture.

This book has its origins in my PhD, yet it has grown and changed in the three years since I defended it. What follows is not simply a thesis in a different cover, but the product of further thinking, discussions, teaching, and the experience that accompanies becoming an academic – and a mother – in those formative years.

First and foremost, my deepest thanks go to my mother. She paved the way for women in academia long before I entered its corridors, and her sharp intellect and unwavering integrity have shaped mine in more ways than I can count. She taught me that small-mindedness and its presence within university walls should never determine my future. Finishing this work is, in many ways, a testament to everything she taught me. Not an *advokwaad* – insider joke, not a typo – but a PhD and now a book which, I hope, will make you proud.

In a similar spirit, I owe immense gratitude to Brianne. Almost eight years ago, at my Utrecht graduation ceremony, you told my parents – while my father was still alive – that I should pursue a PhD. You had no idea how life-altering that sentence would be. It was the first moment I allowed myself to believe that such a path might be within reach. Your steady, intelligent, and generous guidance carried me through the turbulence of changing promotors and the many uncertainties of early academic life. This book, too, owes much to you.

To Yves, who joined as supervisor only in the later stages: thank you for bringing calm, clarity, and confidence into the process. Having you as my thesis supervisor at Ghent University all those years ago, working with you again felt like returning home. Some of my best arguments in this book were made under your guidance.

To Angela, thank you for widening my theoretical horizons and generously engaging with ideas that will surely continue to grow in future collaborations.

To Egon and Levi, thank you for reading, questioning, correcting, and offering the kind of philosophical side notes that improved this work immeasurably.

To Raya and Elisabeth, thank you for helping me through the long, meticulous, and often tiresome process of turning an overly long and methodologically heavy manuscript into a workable book. Your precision and kind discipline made this transformation possible.

To Elies, thank you for making Tilburg my new academic home and becoming a true mentor on my academic journey.

To Jonathan: what a whirlwind the past years have been. Meeting you was the most unexpected gift of the pandemic years, and I still cannot quite believe that our adventure has brought us here, with now two sons we both adore. To Aster, my beautiful firstborn, whose small playdates during the final months of writing my PhD gave me exactly the joy and energy I needed to continue. Watching you grow remains one of the greatest privileges of my life.

To Rûne, my second son, who arrived as this book was taking its final shape. Your arrival has reshaped my days and my understanding of what truly matters. You have added more love and grounding than you will ever know.

And finally, to my father, Julien. I had imagined that you would be here to share this moment and to meet my boys. I miss you deeply. I dedicate this book to you.

Contents

List of Abbreviations

AFRC	Armed Forces Revolutionary Council (SCSL)
ALC	Armée de Libération du Congo
AQIM	Al-Qaeda in the Islamic Maghreb
ASP	Assembly of States Parties (Rome Statute)
CAT	Convention against Torture
CaH	Crimes against Humanity
CPK	Communist Party of Kampuchea (Angkar)
DRC	Democratic Republic of the Congo
ECtHR	European Court of Human Rights
ECCC	Extraordinary Chambers in the Courts of Cambodia
EoC	Elements of Crimes (ICC)
FPLC	Forces Patriotiques pour la Libération du Congo
GCs	Geneva Conventions
GenC	Convention on the Prevention and Punishment of the Crime of Genocide
IHRL	International Human Rights Law
ICC	International Criminal Court
ICJ	International Court of Justice
ICL	International Criminal Law
ICTR	International Criminal Tribunal for Rwanda
ICTY	International Criminal Tribunal for the former Yugoslavia
IMT	International Military Tribunal (Nuremberg)
KSC	Kosovo Specialist Chambers
LRA	Lord's Resistance Army
NMT	Nuremberg Military Tribunals
OTP	Office of the Prosecutor (ICC)
PTC	Pre-Trial Chamber (ICC)
RS	Rome Statute
RUF	Revolutionary United Front (Sierra Leone)
SCSL	Special Court for Sierra Leone
STL	Special Tribunal for Lebanon
TC	Trial Chamber
UPC	Union des Patriotes Congolais
UNSC	United Nations Security Council
UNTOC	United Nations Convention against Transnational Organized Crime
VCLT	Vienna Convention on the Law of Treaties
WCGJ	Women's Caucus for Gender Justice
WIGJ	Women's Initiative for Gender Justice

Table of Cases

International Criminal Tribunals and Courts

Inter-American Court of Human Rights

Human Rights Committee

Other International Courts

International Court of Justice

National Cases

1

Why Legality Matters

> The conundrum for international criminal lawyers [. . .] is how to admit of the diversity and even unpredictability of interpretation and application of certain areas of ICL [. . .], and at the same time maintain legitimacy. The principle of legality is no small character in this drama.[1]

I. INTRODUCTION

THE INTERNATIONAL CRIMINAL COURT (ICC) is the result of monumental effort which many did not think would ever see the light of day. After over 20 years of operating, it has succeeded in being a pivotal player within the global justice system.[2] While it lacks universal jurisdiction, the ICC occupies a central position in the realm of international criminal justice and in many ways aspires to universality.[3]

Yet the international criminal justice project faces persistent challenges. Accusations of neo-colonialism, selective justice, and interpretative divergence have fuelled concerns over its legitimacy. A recurrent criticism is that the ICC is a Western and neo-colonial system targeting African States disproportionately and that interpretations that claim universal applicability in fact only reflect Western perspectives. The ideal of the ICC transcending the dichotomy between the Global North and the Global South, acting as a universal anchor,[4] is as such undermined.[5]

[1] C Steer, 'Legal transplants or legal patchworking? The creation of international criminal law as a pluralistic body of law' in E van Sliedregt and S Vasiliev (eds), *Pluralism and Harmonization in International Criminal Law* (OUP, 2013) 57.

[2] See for a discussion on the Court's track record and highlighting issues central to this introduction: A Heinze and VE Dittrich (eds), *The Past, Present and Future of the International Criminal Court* (Nuremberg Academy Series, 2021).

[3] C Stephen, 'International criminal law: wielding the sword of universal criminal justice?' (2012) 61 *International & Comparative Law Quarterly* 55, 89; See further on jurisdiction: LN Sadat and RS Carden, 'The New International Criminal Court: An Uneasy Revolution' (2000) 88 *Georgetown Law Journal*.

[4] See R Provost, 'Interpretation in International Law as a Transcultural Project' in A Bianchi, D Peat and M Windsor (eds), *Interpretation in International Law* (OUP, 2015) 290–308.

[5] See G Lugano, 'Counter-Shaming the International Criminal Court's Intervention as Neocolonial: Lessons from Kenya' (2017) 11 *IJTJ* 9; see also about the colonial underpinnings of the ICC: AG Kiyani, 'Third world approaches to international criminal law' (2015) 109 *AJIL* 255.

These problems of arbitrariness cannot be understood without a more thorough unravelling of some of the foundational issues underlying the field.[6] What gives the ICC the right to intervene? What is the normative underpinning for this exercise of power (*ius puniendi*)? These questions are relevant to the present study and will be touched upon throughout.

One of these foundational issues central to this book is to understand the limits of the international criminal justice system in terms of judicial interpretation and comprehend why it is important to restrain judicial interpretation in this context. The core idea is that the international criminal justice project needs to come to terms with its limits and, in order to do so, has to curb judicial discretion. This book explores the claim that it is crucial for the international criminal justice project to adhere to the rules of the system, even when these are flawed or when it is considered cumbersome in achieving justice. The law exists to constrain power and prevent arbitrariness. This is not merely a technical requirement. Regardless of who holds power and regardless of what they hold power over, there will be an intolerable amount of subjectivity when the law is not adhered to. As argued by Koskenniemi, the law exists to keep in 'check our own subjectivities'.[7]

Although international criminal courts are primarily judicial institutions, they have adopted constitutional governance structures characterised by a separation of powers and corresponding checks and balances that far exceed those of ordinary courts. Certainly, the ICC's architecture rests on a constitutional division between the legislative, the executive and the judicial branches.[8] Several scholars have observed that, within this institutional framework, judges occupy a paramount position. The international criminal judge enjoys substantial discretion and has significantly shaped the development of the law across a wide range of topics and theories.[9] To the extent that judges usurp legislative authority, a democratic deficit emerges, undermining the legitimacy of these institutions. Next to keeping subjectivity at bay, countering this democratic deficit is therefore a crucial reason to impose meaningful constraints on judicial discretion. The legality principle as such serves to protect the separation of

[6] See K Ambos, 'Punishment without a Sovereign? The *Ius Puniendi* Issue of International Criminal Law: A First Contribution towards a Consistent Theory of International Criminal Law' (2013) 33 *Oxford Journal of Legal Studies* 293; K Ambos, 'The Overall Function of International Criminal Law: Striking the Right Balance Between the Rechtsgut and the Harm Principles A Second Contribution Towards a Consistent Theory of ICL' (2015) 9 *Criminal Law and Philosophy* 301.

[7] M Koskenniemi, *From Apology to Utopia, The Structure of International Legal Argument* (CUP, 2006) 24.

[8] D Raab and H Bevers, 'The International Criminal Court and the Separation of Powers' (2006) 3 *International Organizations Law Review* 93.

[9] S Darcy and J Powderly, *Judicial Creativity at the International Criminal Tribunals* (OUP, 2010); MJ Christensen and NM Orina, 'The International Criminal Court as a Law Laboratory: Professional Battles of Control and the 'Control of the Crime'Theory' (2022) 20 *JICJ* 699; S Vasiliev, 'Judicial Governance Entities as Power-Holders in International Criminal Justice: A Plea for a Socio-Legal Enquiry' in Morten Bergsmo and others (eds), *Power in International Criminal Justice* (Torkel Opsahl Academic EPublisher, 2020).

powers and ensures that legislative authority is in the hands of the legislator and not the judge.[10]

Fitting a liberal theory, this book argues in favour of fundamental constraints through criminal law principles.[11] The key to constraining judicial discretion lies within the principle of legality. The basic idea of this principle can be explained as requiring that there can be no crime without a law (*nullum crimen sine lege*). As a safeguard for the accused, the principle of legality functions as a vital constraint on judicial discretion. Given the crucial importance of protecting individuals in a criminal law setting, this book contends that articulating and steadfastly upholding the boundaries imposed by the legality principle represents a more principled and just approach to adjudication. A system of legal reasoning that loses sight of these deontic constraints of liberal principles risks losing its sense of justice.

The argumentation furthermore proceeds from the underlying assumption that the justification for international prosecutions should be understood in a minimalistic sense.[12] Along that same line, it advocates for International Criminal Law (ICL) being driven by a thin conception of international justice, only intervening with respect to the most heinous crimes and in the absence of other, national or regional, fora stepping in.[13] Delivering international criminal justice is merely delivering one type of justice that, when it wants to be *universally* effective in a *culturally diverse* world, needs to be narrowly defined. This is further substantiated by the idea of complementarity, forcing the international system to play second fiddle to the national systems.

II. ARGUMENTS ON WHY THE PRINCIPLE OF LEGALITY MATTERS

One of the central and foundational arguments in this book is that while ICL draws from elements of public international law, human rights law, and criminal law, it fundamentally remains a branch of criminal law. In criminal law, different elements come into play compared to human rights law and public international law. In conflicts between States, they typically stand as equals,

[10] B Van Schaack, 'Judicial lawmaking the intersection between law and morals' (2008–2009) 97 *Georgetown Law Journal* 119, 121–22.

[11] D Robinson, *Justice in Extreme Cases: Criminal Law Theory meets International Criminal Law* (CUP, 2020) 65ff.

[12] L May, *Normative account of Crimes against Humanity* (Cambridge Studies in Philosophy and Law, CUP, 2004) 8ff: advocating for an 'in-principle, morally minimalist, account of the justification of international prosecutions'.

[13] The notion 'thin conception of international justice' has been partly borrowed from SR Ratner, *The Thin Justice of International Law: A Moral Reckoning of the Law of Nations* (OUP, 2015) and partly inspired by May's account of crimes against humanity. Given that justice means something different across different cultures and multiple stakeholders often want *different* kinds of justice, the pursuit of justice at the international level should be strictly delineated.

even if one State holds more power. However, in human rights law, individuals face a much more formidable entity – the State – and must prove violations. To address this imbalance, the law equips citizens with mechanisms to prove violations, reducing formal obstacles and allowing broader interpretations in favour of citizens. In criminal law, the dynamic is different, and the State, the more potent party, must prove that the individual committed a crime. Criminal law balances this inequality by protecting citizens against the State and imposing rigorous standards, such as a high burden of proof. Also the legality principle is such a legal weapon that protects citizens against the State's potential arbitrariness. Consequently, strict adherence to the law is paramount in the realm of criminal law, as this book will emphasise, as it lies at the core of this legal domain.

Following from this and underpinning the central argumentation of this book, I argue that for the purpose of criminal law, the principle of legality presents a set of devices protecting citizens against the arbitrariness that would otherwise follow from the unchecked exercise of power.[14] As an enlightened idea in the notion of Rechtsstaat or the Rule of Law, it came into existence precisely because of the desire to protect against arbitrariness, also judicial arbitrariness. The *ius puniendi,* or the right to punish, is a form of authority that is particularly sensitive to transgression of authority.[15] Such transgression does not necessarily occur with bad intentions. Quite the contrary, behaviour is often deemed morally repulsive and in need of social control, but there are no or only inadequate legal avenues to punish them. Here, the limits of the law become obvious. From a desire to penalise the conduct, the limits of the law are tested and sometimes transgressed. In response to such a violation, one might argue: 'Do we not agree that this morally reprehensible conduct should not escape punishment?' In this question lies exactly the problem: such agreement is often absent. The consensus lies in the law, and where such law is absent, there is only subjectivity.

That is why it matters to adhere to the legality principle. Otherwise, judges risk falling into traps of unfairness or arbitrariness because of the crimes and the offenders involved. Given the severity of the crimes and the political sphere within which these have occurred, strong sentiment often exists to either convict or acquit the defendants. One's freedom fighter is another's terrorist. The heightened political atmosphere surrounding these trials makes it more difficult to rid the process of political ideology or moral convictions. It is not the blunt contention here that ICC judges are arbitrary. The point is more subtle: the decision-making process is potentially contaminated by considerations for

[14] A Ashworth and J Horder, *Principles of Criminal Law*, 7th edn (OUP, 2013) 116–17; KS Gallant, *The Principle of Legality in International and Comparative Criminal Law* (CUP, 2009) 7; D Robinson, 'The Identity Crisis of International Criminal Law' (2008) 21 *LJIL* 925, 941.

[15] Vasiliev (n 9) 485: 'Traditionally anchored to a sovereign nation State, the punitive power in [ICL] is associated with the (collective) authority of States and, as argued at times, flows from the will of the "international community" or other elusive constituencies such as "victims" or "affected societies"'.

justice or social change or moral considerations – positions with consequentialist tendencies – and choices are made in favour of interpretations perceived as more just, fair or morally defendable. Arguments are made to bend the law *because* it would result in more just outcomes. These interpretations drift away from the law. The consequence of adopting a consequentialist stance is the risk of arbitrariness stemming from interpretative discrepancies.

This book purports to reveal potential dangers that can arise from a consequentialist position focused on doing justice. It proposes a more conservative, principled, and deontic position using the legality principle to defend that position.[16] It does so from the conviction that, in the end, this conservative position will, in fact, better serve justice than will the consequentialist position. It is highly important that the international criminal justice system does not become a system dotted with subjectivities or peppered with arbitrariness. For this to be realised, we need constraints, and in a Kantian sense, we could even contend that the constraint functions as the possibility.[17] In other words, the argument is that the possibility of doing justice begins with the more constraining capacity of a conservative position and not by taking a consequentialist stance. The law, the criminal law and the legality principle, as the system has decided to articulate it, must be followed. If not, we risk delegitimising a project so essential to the Rule of Law.

At the ICC, crimes are often subject to overly broad and divergent interpretations due to judicial misapplication of the law and inappropriate use of interpretative methods. This raises concerns regarding the rights of the accused and calls for an improved interpretative methodology to ensure greater adherence to the legality principle defined by the Rome Statute. Before explaining how the legality principle is articulated at the ICC, the core issues at stake are illustrated by a debate between two philosophers. This debate also serves as an introduction to the theoretical background of this study.

III. THEORETICAL BACKGROUND

The problem examined in the present study is an articulation of a wider theoretical debate on the judicial function in the international criminal justice sphere and the limits set to judicial interpretation. Law is essentially 'a reasoning enterprise'.[18] Each time a case is adjudicated, a problem exists for which a rule offers or should offer a potential legal solution, whereby the judge has to apply that legal rule to that factual problem in order to solve the problem. This involves judgment, recognising something concrete/particular as falling under

[16] Another term used by Robinson which he borrowed from Hart. See Robinson n (11) explaining that a deontic position is a position that does not evaluate the result but takes a principled stance.

[17] I Kant, *Critique of Pure Reason*, trans P Guyer and AW Wood (CUP (first published 1787), 1997). cf G Van de Vijver and E Noé, 'The constraint is the possibility. A dynamical perspective on Kant's theory of objectivity' (2011) 41(1–2) *Idealistic Studies* 95–112.

[18] Robinson (n 11) 11.

something abstract/general. The judge's function is to translate the general legal order to the concrete case, an exercise which entails, by definition, an interpretative activity. Consequently, the problem of interpretation is intrinsic to the legal enterprise. Judges need to tackle questions such as: What is the law, and what sources should be applied to the facts of the case? How should those sources be interpreted, and which interpretative method should be used? But also: Should we evaluate the interpretative solution and see whether it is just or fair and corresponds to certain moral values or an idea of justice? Is the interpretation right or wrong, and how should we meaningfully assess the validity of an interpretation?

Since this book is concerned with judicial interpretation, it draws on hermeneutical insights to deconstruct some of the existing problems. Considering that hermeneutics, as the theory and practice of interpretation, holds a vast body of diverse methodologies,[19] and plays 'a role in a number of disciplines whose subject matter demands interpretative approaches',[20] the choice was made to focus on a specific historical debate in legal philosophy paradigmatic of what is at stake today in the judicial interpretation of crimes, namely between Lon L Fuller,[21] and Herbert L Hart.[22] As this historical debate reveals a disagreement between positivists and naturalists on the relation between Law and Morality, it allows us to identify and distil current issues in criminal law concerning Legality and Justice.

A. The Hart – Fuller Debate on the Radbruch Formula

After World War II, two leading legal philosophers, Hart and Fuller, discussed a jurisprudential problem referred to as the *Radbruch formula*.[23] Radbruch,[24] a German scholar and Minister of Justice in the 1920s, believed the German

[19] J Dyer, 'Hermeneutics' in P Peterson, E Baker and B McGaw (eds), *International Encyclopedia of Education*, 3rd edn (Elsevier, 2010) 63.

[20] G Theodore, 'Hermeneutics' in EN Zalta (ed), *Stanford Encyclopedia of Philosophy* (plato.stanford.edu/archives/win2020/entries/hermeneutics/ 2020).

[21] LL Fuller is viewed as a procedural natural law thinker (see A Keating, *Jurisprudence* (Essential Law Texts, Thomas Reuters, 2011) 7) arguing for the 'inner morality' of legal systems: LL Fuller, *The Morality of Law* (Yale University Press, 1969).

[22] HLA Hart is often referred to as a positivist whose work 'The Concept of Law' was very influential for the field (see A Marmor, *The Routledge companion to philosophy of law* (Routledge, 2012) 5-ff; See also J Raz, *Between Authority and Interpretation* (OUP, 2009) 166ff. HLA Hart, *The Concept of Law*, 2nd edn (Clarendon Press, 1994) 251–54: In his postscript to *The Concept of Law,* Hart agreed with the term of 'soft-positivism' to be applied to him. He was not a 'plain-fact positivist', a term dubbed by Dworkin, as this ignores his 'explicit acknowledgement that the rule of recognition may incorporate as criteria of legal validity conformity with moral principles or substantive values'.

[23] The Radbruch formula in German: 'Der Konflikt zwischen der Gerechtigkeit und der Rechtssicherheit dürfte dahin zu lösen sein, dass das positive, durch Satzung und Macht gesicherte Recht auch dann den Vorrang hat, wenn es inhaltlich ungerecht und unzweckmässige ist, es sei denn, dass der Widerspruch des positiven Gesetzes zur Gerechtigkeit ein so unerträgliches Mass erreicht, dass das Gesetz als "unrichtiges Recht" der Gerechtigkeit zu weichen hat'.

[24] See SL Paulson, 'Radbruch on unjust laws: Competing earlier and later views' (1995) 15 *Oxford Journal of Legal Studies* 489.

judiciary's commitment to Nazi ideals during World War II was, in fact, the result of a blind obedience to legal positivist values and, in denouncing legal positivism, developed the *Radbruch formula* as a solution to the application of the law having an unjust effect.[25] On this solution, Hart and Fuller heavily disagreed.

This discussion unfolded in 1943 and centred around the *Grudge Informer Case*.[26] In this case, which took place in 1934, a woman reported her husband to the Nazi authorities for making insulting comments about Hitler in their home, which led to his prosecution. Initially, he received a death sentence, which was later commuted to forced labour at the battlefront. After World War II, the husband, who against all odds survived his forced labour sentence, filed a complaint against his wife, whom he held responsible for this fate. Confronted with what clearly was a grave injustice, the German court agreed with the husband and qualified his forced labour as a form of illegal deprivation of liberty (*rechtswidrige Freiheitsberauberung*), a crime known to the German legal system since 1871, and held the wife accountable for that deprivation of liberty. For this qualification to pass, the Court nevertheless first had to set aside the statute criminalising insults to Hitler and used the *Radbruch formula* to do so. In the Court of Appeal's view, the statute 'was contrary to the sound conscience and sense of justice of all decent human beings'.[27] In essence, the Statute was considered undeserving of the title 'law'. Only with the disappearance of the legal basis for the forced labour sentence could his fate be qualified as an illegal deprivation of freedom. Based on that reasoning, it became possible to hold the wife responsible. As the judgment clarified, the woman's objection that it was not *her* act that procured her husband's deprivation of liberty but that of the German authorities was not accepted.

This case sparked debate over whether the wife's conviction violated the principle of legality, as her conduct was not criminalised at the time it occurred. Retroactively imposing criminal liability on her was seen as incompatible with the core requirements of legality. Moreover, concerns about retroactivity also arose from the decision not to apply the relevant criminal provision to the husband. It is only by setting the statute criminalising the husband aside that the woman can be held accountable. Otherwise, the deprivation of freedom would not be qualified as illegal. These two aspects reveal a problem of conflict between positive law and justice or a morally acceptable outcome.[28]

[25] G Radbruch, 'Gesetzliches Unrecht und übergesetzliches Recht' (1946) 1 *Süddeutsche Juristen-Zeitung* 105 107; G Radbruch, BL Paulson and SL Paulson, 'Statutory Lawlessness and Supra-Statutory Law' (2006) 26 *Oxford Journal of Legal Studies* 1, 6: 'Positivism, with its principle that "a law is a law", has in fact rendered the German legal profession defenceless against statutes that are arbitrary and criminal'.

[26] See eg D Dyzenhaus, 'The Grudge Informer Case Revisited' (2008) 83 *NYUL Rev* 1000; HO Pappe, 'On the validity of judicial decisions in the Nazi era' (1960) 23 *Mod L Rev.*

[27] As cited in HLA Hart, 'Positivism and the Separation of Law and Morals' (1958) 71 *Harv. L. Rev.* 593, 619: See for the post-World War II reflection of Radbruch (n 25).

[28] The retroactive element in relation to the decriminalisation of the conduct of the husband is not in and of itself in violation with the common conception of the principle of legality. The point made here is that this qualification is needed to allow for the criminalisation of the wife.

This was a common problem in post-World War II society, where judges had to deal with either morally repulsive deeds that were left unpunished in Nazi Germany or morally sound actions that were met with extreme punishment during World War II, but which were no longer criminalised after World War II.[29] Confronted with this problem, judges applied what has throughout the doctrine been referred to as the *Radbruch formula*. Judges in the Third Reich were predominantly positivistically schooled and used the argument that they were merely doing what judges do, namely applying the law (*Gesetz ist Gesetz*). This allowed them to morally justify the most extreme decisions. Any consideration for justice was swept away based on this logic. As a result, Radbruch developed the formula that 'where there is not even an attempt at justice, where equality, the core of justice, is deliberately betrayed in the issuance of positive law, then the statute is not merely 'flawed law', it lacks completely the very nature of law'. He then continued: 'the positive law, secured by legislation and power, takes precedence even when its content is unjust and fails to benefit the people, unless the conflict between statute and justice reaches such an intolerable degree that the statute, as "flawed law", must yield to justice.'[30]

Instead of allowing judges to hide behind the positivist shield of *Gesetz ist Gesetz* (*dura lex sed lex*), the *Radbruch formula* requires that the following hierarchical formula be applied:

> The positive law, secured by legislation and power, takes precedence even when its content is unjust and fails to benefit the people, unless the conflict between statute and justice reaches such an intolerable degree that the statute, as 'flawed law', must yield to justice.[31]

The *Radbruch formula* connects justice and law at the ontological level, depriving a norm of the qualification of law and is in that sense a variation of the *lex injusta non est lex* idea. As a result, the positive law is rendered invalid when in stark contrast with justice. The broader implication of this formula is that it enlarges judicial discretion, allowing certain laws to be set aside or at least giving less weight to them.

When discussing the *Grudge Informer Case,* Hart explained:

> Many of us might applaud the objective – that of punishing a woman for an outrageously immoral act – but this was secured only by declaring a statute established since 1934 not to have the force of law, and at least the wisdom of this course must be doubted. There were, of course, two other choices. One was to let the woman go unpunished; one can sympathise with and endorse the view that this might have

[29] This problem was also central to the Nuremberg proceedings. See I Topalli, 'The Role of Natural Law after World War II (Case of Nuremberg Trial)' (2015) 11 *Acta Universitatis Danubius Juridica* 87.

[30] Radbruch, Paulson and Paulson (n 25); also quoted by: B Bix, 'Radbruch's Formula and Conceptual Analysis' (2011) 6 *Am J Juris* 45, 139.

[31] BH Bix, 'Robert, Alexy, Radbruch's Formula, and the Nature of Legal Theory' (2006) 37 *Rechtstheorie* 139, 140: citing Radbruch (n 25).

> been a bad thing to do. The other was to face the fact that *if the woman were to be punished it must be pursuant to the introduction of a frankly retrospective law* and with a full consciousness of what was sacrificed in securing her punishment in this way. *Odious as retrospective criminal legislation and punishment may be, to have pursued it openly in this case would at least have had the merits of candour.* It would have made plain that in punishing the woman a choice had to be made between two evils, that of leaving her unpunished and that of sacrificing a very precious principle of morality endorsed by most legal systems.[32]

He continued:

> For if we adopt Radbruch's view, and with him and the German courts make our protest against evil law in the form of an assertion that certain rules cannot be law because of their moral iniquity, we confuse one of the most powerful, because it is the simplest, forms of moral criticism. If with the Utilitarians we speak plainly, we say that laws may be law but too evil to be obeyed. This is a moral condemnation which everyone can understand and it makes an immediate and obvious claim to moral attention. If, on the other hand, we formulate our objection as an assertion that these evil things are not law, here is an assertion which many people do not believe, and if they are disposed to consider it at all, it would seem to raise a whole host of philosophical issues before it can be accepted.[33]

Two issues are essential to his argument: (1) when the judge chooses to punish the woman, it should be done straightforwardly on the basis of applying the law retroactively and not based on the argument that the law was not law given on account of its immoral nature which for Hart, is a faulty argument – the validity of a law does not depend on its moral content; (2) the judge can also refuse to apply the rule because, even if an immoral law is in fact a law, this does not mean it has to be obeyed (the judge can feel a moral obligation to refuse to apply the law and as such Hart refuted the argument that positivism was to blame for the German Courts going along with the Nazi regime).

Fuller countered this argument by first addressing the way in which Hart had explained the case and portraying the dilemma with a much fuller account of the laws. His first point was that the law under which the husband was found guilty clearly referred to public statements, and as such, the judges erred in law in finding a violation since the statement was, after all, made in private.[34] Fuller argued:

> I should like to ask the reader whether he can actually share Professor Hart's indignation that, in the perplexities of the postwar reconstruction, the German courts saw fit to declare this thing not a law. Can it be argued seriously that it would have been more beseeming to the judicial process if the postwar courts had undertaken a study

[32] Hart (n 27) 619–20 (emphasis added).
[33] ibid 620 (emphasis added).
[34] L Fuller, 'Positivism and fidelity to law: A reply to Professor Hart' (1958) *Harv. L. Rev.* 630, 653.

> of 'the interpretative principles' in force during Hitler's rule and had then solemnly applied those 'principles' to ascertain the meaning of this statute? On the other hand, would the courts really have been showing respect for Nazi law if they had construed the Nazi statutes by their own, quite different, standards of interpretation?[35]

Fuller refused to accept Hart's argument that a straightforward retroactive application would have helped matters since the difference between the judges saying 'this is not law', or saying 'this is law but it is so evil we will refuse to apply it', is in fact negligible.[36] Restating the dilemma, Fuller stressed that German judges did not reflect on the inner morality of the law. If they had, they would have declared 'the more outrageous Nazi statutes' void. He persisted in his point: the Nazi system might have been an 'order' but not 'a good order' (good order is defined as 'law that corresponds to the demands of justice, or morality, or men's notions of what ought to be'[37]) and that:

> when a system calling itself law is predicated upon a general disregard by judges of the terms of the laws they purport to enforce, when this system habitually cures its legal irregularities, even the grossest, by retroactive statutes, when it has only to resort to forays of terror in the streets, which no one dares challenge, in order to escape even those scant restraints imposed by the pretence of legality – when all these things have become true of a dictatorship, it is not hard for me, at least, to deny to it the name of law.[38]

Given its lack of *inner morality*, Nazi law does not possess the necessary characteristics of law, and therefore, Fuller found no fault in the judges setting aside these statutes based on the *Radbruch formula*.[39]

B. The Positivists – Naturalists Debate on Law and Morality

Fuller's and Hart's readings of the *Grudge Informer* Case uncovers an incongruity in the relationship between law and morality. The *Radbruch formula*'s logic blurs the line between positive law and morality and makes morality a potential source of law. As a result, the entire interpretative space is constituted differently. Using the debate on the *Grudge Informer Case* as a springboard, it is now

[35] ibid 655.
[36] ibid 655.
[37] ibid 644.
[38] ibid 660.
[39] Fuller (n 21) ch 2. See also on the idea of inner morality, G Lamond, 'The Rule of Law' in Marmor (n 22): 'Fuller's account of legality is best known for the claim that it constitutes an "internal morality" (or "inner morality") of law (1969, ch 2). He points out, plausibly enough, that a legal system could not exist if all of its laws lacked any one of the following eight features (or "desiderata"), which could be described as: (1) generality; (2) publicity; (3) prospectiveness; (4) clarity; (5) non-contradiction with other laws; (6) the possibility of conformity to the law; (7) constancy through time; and, finally, (8) congruence between the announced laws and their administration.'

explored how theoretical disagreements between naturalists and positivists on law and morality bring about entirely different ideas on judicial interpretation and its limits.[40]

Before the eighteenth century, all legal thinkers to some extent belonged to the classical natural law family, who found that law was either inherently moral or had to conform to an idea of morality.[41] This connection was first constructed in terms of a divine or natural law.[42] Later, some authors replaced this connection to divine law with a superior idea of morality or Reason. If not compatible with Divine Law or Reason, the law is simply *not* law. In the nineteenth century, philosophers such as Austin, who is considered to be the founding father of legal positivism, started challenging this naturalist conception of law.[43] Positivism introduced the notion of law as a social fact (the Social Thesis),[44] as well as the separation of laws and morals (the Separability or Separation Thesis). Legal positivism means 'the simple contention that it is in no sense a necessary truth that laws reproduce or satisfy certain demands of morality, though in fact they have often done so'.[45] Building further on the insights of Austin, Hart required that the identification of law is a formal test which involves examining to what extent the rule is in fact conforming to the law-ascertaining rules of the system.[46] In a similar regard, the position of the *Grundnorm* in Kelsen's Pure Theory of Law functions as a rule of recognition, which fits a formal and source-based conception of law.[47]

The disagreements between positivists – viewing the law as the result of a social fact – and naturalists – viewing the existence of law as dependent on certain moral values and ideas – led to entirely different approaches to judicial interpretation.[48] On the basis of the Separation Thesis, positivist thinkers

[40] There are more distinctions to be made – the opposition between realists and formalists – but the divide between natural law theory and positivism contrasts best different ideas on interpretation. See also Keating (n 21) 3-83.

[41] See the *Summa Theologiae* (I-II, 94.2) of Thomas Aquinas on this point: 'Because in man there is first of all an inclination to good in accordance with the nature which he has in common with all substances, inasmuch as every substance seeks the preservation of its own being, according to its nature; and by reason of this inclination, whatever is a means of preserving human life and of warding off its own obstacles belongs to the natural law.'

[42] See Blackstone's Commentaries and Austin's critique on this point.

[43] Keating (n 21) 43: Austin is the first to regard the study of law as a science, 'ie the science of what ought to be done towards making good laws together with the skills of doing it'.

[44] Hart (n 22): 'What counts as law in any particular society is fundamentally a matter of social fact'.

[45] ibid 185–86.

[46] J d'Aspremont, 'Herbert Hart in Today's International Legal Scholarship' in J Kammerhofer and J d'Aspremont (eds), *International Legal Positivism in a Post-Modern World* (CUP, 2014).

[47] H Kelsen, *Pure Theory of Law*, 2nd edn (University of California Press, 1970).

[48] J Raz, *The Authority of Law, Essays on Law and Morality* (OUP, 1979) 37ff: 'the positivist social thesis is that what is law and what is not is a matter of social fact (that is, the variety of social theses supported by positivists are various refinements and elaborations of this crude formulation). Their moral thesis is that the moral value of law (both of a particular law and of a whole legal system) or the moral merit it has is a contingent matter dependent on the content of the law and the circumstances of the society to which it applies'.

disconnected the question of the validity of the law from its moral content.[49] The existence of law does not depend on its moral value but on the legal system's sources.[50] Of course, this position still allows for a discussion on what the sources of law are and depends on the way in which the source doctrine is formulated. However, judicial interpretation is much more delineated, and the idea of looking beyond the law in judicial interpretation is much more problematic.[51] Naturalists do not accept the Separation Thesis and find that there is indeed a connection, and even a necessary one, between law and morals (the Connection Thesis).[52] As such, the existence of law depends on its moral value, as is clearly demonstrated by Fuller's position. Consequently, law as it is (*lex lata*) and law as it ought to be (*lex ferenda*), are potentially not necessarily separate, but instead connected, categories. There is no positivist shield that bars drawing on extra-legal principles to remedy unjust outcomes. On top of that, the question of whether the law is moral becomes legally relevant.[53]

The relationship between law and morality thus clearly generates questions on the limits of judicial interpretation. In general terms, naturalists do not take issue with judges referring to 'standards of justice'. A natural law position has a place for morality in adjudication and finds that a judge can take into account extra-legal considerations in the decision-making process.[54] A positivist position will find that this ventures too much into the realm of the legislative and is directed at the question of what ought to be. Morality, therefore, has no place in adjudication according to the positivists.[55]

In relation to this dichotomy in legal theory, a return to Radbruch and the discussion on the *Grudge Informer case* can be highly illuminating. As mentioned before, Radbruch was a positivist before World War II and believed that 'it is the professional duty of the judge to validate the law's claim to validity, to sacrifice his own sense of the right to the authoritative command of the law, to ask only what is legal and not if it is also just'.[56] The naturalist turn he

[49] Hart (n 22) 185ff; See on the separation thesis and the different formulations over time: Hart (n 27); GJ Postema, 'Legal Positivism: Early Foundations' in Marmor (n 22) 31–48, in particular 41.

[50] d'Aspremont (n 46).

[51] Hart's later work has been called 'inclusive positivism' which conceded to certain more naturalist points of views eg (identification of law can also be done on the basis of certain moral criteria, ie incorporation thesis); Raz (n 48) and Shapiro (see SJ Shapiro, *Legality* (The Belknap Press of Harvard University Press, 2011)), the most known Hartian scholars, did not agree with this watered-down concept of positivism. See also d'Aspremont (n 46).

[52] See Alexy arguing that the existence of human rights is evidence of the existence of pre-existing moral values and arguing for a traditional naturalist point of view, ie the connection thesis: R Alexy, 'Law, morality, and the Existence of Human Rights' (2012) 25 *Ratio Juris* 2.

[53] G Duke and RP George, *The Cambridge Companion to Natural Law Jurisprudence* (CUP, 2017) 1–3.

[54] MS Moore, 'The Various Relations between Law and Morality in Contemporary Legal Philosophy' (2012) 25 *Ratio Juris* 435.

[55] The discussion is much more complex than portrayed here and ideas such as Rawl's veil of ignorance could shed another light. For delineation purposes, selection was necessary. See, eg, 'Two Concepts of Rules' (1955) 64 *Philosophical Review* 3.

[56] Bix (n 30) 48.

took after World War II was underpinned by his departure from a strict separation between law and morality. Radbruch found that whether something accords with the concept of law can only be determined 'by the standard of purported justice'.[57] He thereby endorsed the view that morality (or justice) has a place in adjudication. By fading the separation between law and morality, the judge is no longer restricted in depending on extra-legal considerations. The judge is liberated from the positivist straitjacket and can also rely on moral or social values as a source of law.

Lastly, this debate demonstrates that although the principle of legality serves a function in naturalist theories as well, it has a much less constraining capacity.[58] To the extent that the boundary between law and non-law fades, the legality principle has an entirely different expression. As Fuller's account illustrated, the judge is allocated a much more liberated role in relation to which law or legal source to apply or which interpretative methods to use. The next section addresses the implications of the debate between naturalists and positivists within the field of criminal law.

C. The Criminal Law Debate on Legality and Justice

In criminal law, the above-sketched disagreement between naturalists and positivists also exists. Furthermore, several parallels can be drawn between the discussions that arose in post-World War II case law and the current struggles and debates in ICL. It is by no means the intention to argue that the choice of applying an *evil* law or *no* law, as was the case in the *Grudge Informer Case*, is the choice with which ICC judges are today confronted. However, when confronted with an indeterminate, incomplete, or inconsistent text, a dilemma presents itself akin to the one demonstrated by Fuller and Hart. The struggle lies in the positive law having limits as to what justice it can achieve. As such, it might be questioned whether decisions are always taken solely based on positive law or whether principles external to the law influence judicial interpretation as well. Much of these discussions boil down to what one considers to be (positive) law and whether decision-making is allowed to be dependent on principles external to positive law, the latter again depending on what is considered positive law.

On the one hand, the embodiment of the idea of law in criminal law is the principle of legality, which, in its most widely accepted form, is a principle against the retroactive application of the law. As the Latin adagio *nullum crimen sine lege* expresses, only a law can set forth a crime. In essence, this principle

[57] Radbruch quoted by T Spaak, 'Meta-Ethics and Legal Theory: The Case of Gustav Radbruch' (2009) 28 *Law and Philosophy* 261, 278.

[58] See for a modern naturalist position: JM Finnis, *Natural Law and Natural Rights* (Clarendon Law Series, OUP, 2011); JM Finnis, 'Natural Law and Legal Reasoning' (1990) 38 *Cleveland State Law Review* 1; JM Finnis, 'Law, morality, and sexual orientation' (1993) 69 *Notre Dame Law Review*.

forces the judge to place the law at the centre and work within its confines when interpreting. It is a principle that forms an essential protection for the accused as it sets limits to the judge's power.

On the other hand, there is the notion of seeking justice, a notion that, according to Raz, must be qualified as a moral consideration.[59] Justice is, similar to the notion of morals, an elusive concept. It would be a study in itself to try to define and comprehend the position of justice at the ICC in all its aspects.[60] Furthermore, different conceptions exist, such as legal justice, transformative justice, formal or substantive justice, and the concept has also been approached from particular perspectives, eg victims' justice.[61] This concept is purposefully left open in order to encompass both legal and extra-legal justice and include many perspectives. Judges evidently want to see justice prevail, and consequently, for the purpose of achieving justice and because a given application of the law would have an *unwanted* effect, interpretations potentially stretch the law.[62] In the context of criminal law, the issue of morality is in fact an issue of justice, and opposite to legality stands the question of how far considerations of justice can bring the judge outside the ambit of the law.

Reliance on justice is often overly simplistic. At first glance, the word seems to be used as an antonym of impunity.[63] In that sense, the realisation of a conviction is considered to serve the goals of justice.[64] Adhering to legality requirements can entail, however, that the requirements for justice as one would wish them fulfilled in an ideal world are not achieved or fulfilled. For example, acquittals based on insufficient evidence or convictions under a lesser charge based on the same reasons are often perceived as an injustice, certainly in relation to crimes of such a grave nature as are being prosecuted at the ICC. A criminal trial entails some principled (ie, non-consequentialist) constraints on the pursuit of justice, the legality principle being one of the most important.[65] Understood in this way, it is clear that these requirements can pull in different directions, and faced with the risk of an *injustice*, judges put aside the law or interpret it more loosely in order to see justice done or remedy a perceived injustice. Given the limited scope

[59] Raz (n 48) 45–46. See also Hart (n 22) 167ff.

[60] See on the perspective on justice of the ICC Prosecutor: CJ Davis, 'Doing "Justice" at the Office of the Prosecutor: Portrayals of a cultural value' in JA Fraser and BM Leyh (eds), *Intersections of Law and Culture at the International Criminal Court* (Edward Elgar, 2020).

[61] See, eg, Leila Ulrich has studied how the ICC's conception of justice has been very much formed around the notion of justice for victims: L Ullrich and C Hoyle, 'New court, new justice? The evolution of "justice for victims" at domestic courts and at the International Criminal Court' (2014) 12 *JICJ* 681.

[62] See, eg, *Jurisdictional Immunities of the State (Germany v Italy, Greece intervening)* (Dissenting Opinion Cançado Trindade) [2012] ICJ Rep para 125: the opinion clearly demonstrates great respect for natural law thinking and following this allows for and even considers it essential that ideas of justice are taken into account. As such, 'the universal juridical conscience' is even 'understood as the ultimate material source of all Law'.

[63] Robinson (n 11) 12.

[64] See CJ Davis, 'Doing "Justice" at the Office of the Prosecutor: Portrayals of a cultural value' arguing that the OTP has established a culture of framing justice in terms of justice to victims.

[65] D Robinson, 'A cosmopolitan liberal account of international criminal law' (2013) 26 *LJIL* 127, 133.

of a criminal trial, the question is whether such a consequentialist pull, hoping to achieve more justice and extensive claims or interpretations made in the name of justice, has a legitimate place in a criminal trial.[66] This result-oriented idea of justice creates the risk of stepping outside of the law in the hopes of achieving a certain aim and, as such, comes to be at odds with the limits of positive law. An international criminal trial aspires to achieve many goals, and goals that do not always mutually support one another but rather pull in opposite directions and thus should be balanced against each other.

Since the Nuremberg trials, judges have undertaken such a balancing effort and have struggled to strike the right balance between, on the one hand, serving justice by holding perpetrators accountable for the gravest of crimes and thereby bringing justice to victims and the international community, and on the other hand ensuring fair proceedings for these perpetrators by adhering to (well-established) principles of criminal law. While performing this exercise, the strive for justice pulls the consequentialist to interpret the rules more loosely if necessary to achieve justice, whereas a principled and non-consequentialist thinker adheres strictly to the rules, regardless of the consequences of applying this rule. If judicial interpretation becomes framed in terms of justice, humanity or other vague values which in themselves do not constitute independent sources of law but are relied upon as such, concerns arise. It is essential to understand the dangers of a consequentialist pull, hoping to achieve more justice.[67]

How the legality principle constrains this exercise depends on what is considered to be positive law and which sources of law can be relied on, on what methods can be used in the interpretation of crimes, on what scope the legality principle carries and on what discretion is afforded to the judge in interpreting these crimes. Moreover, the discussion on balancing the requirements of legality and justice can no longer be held in the same way as at the time of Nuremberg. Back then, the principle of legality was a soft principle of justice, not restraining the judge much and leaving room for extra-legal considerations. The law is much more well-established today, crimes are much better defined, the interpretative legal framework and methods of the ICC are better refined, with the legality principle now statutorily enshrined in the Rome Statute. Scholars agree that the constraining capacity of the legality principle in ICL is much more extensive in scope.[68] The legality principle now clearly constrains the judge to strictly construe a crime and thereby protects the accused from a judge who

[66] S Trechsel, *Human Rights in Criminal Proceedings* (The Collected Courses of the Academy of European Law, OUP, 2005) 83; WJordash, 'Joint Criminal Enterprise Liability: Result Orientated Justice' in W Schabas and Y McDermott (eds), *The Ashgate Research Companion to International Criminal Law: Critical Perspectives* (Routledge, 2013).

[67] MR Damaska, *The Faces of Justice and State Authority: A Comparative Approach to the Legal Process* (Yale University Press, 1986) contrasts a traditional, legalistic model (judicial decisions are judged by fidelity to established standards) with a consequentialist model that evaluates decisions by their outcomes.

[68] See, eg, WA Schabas, 'Strict Construction and the Rome Statute' in S Dewulf (ed), *Liber Amicorum Chris Van den Wyngaert* (Maklu, 2017).

oversteps the principle by broadly interpreting. As a result, a theory that corresponds to this legality principle is needed. The next section responds to that need and sets out this study's developed theory on interpretation.

IV. A HARTIAN CRIMINAL LAW THEORY OF INTERPRETATION

This book focuses on interpretation and thereby requires a hermeneutical understanding of what constitutes interpretation and, more specifically, what constitutes judicial interpretation. The study of interpretation has a long scientific tradition. Philosophers, sociologists, psychologists and linguists have sought answers to the question: what is the nature of interpretation?[69] For centuries, going back as early as Aristotle,[70] this issue has triggered debate. It is therefore not easy to situate the issue of crime interpretation in this vast scientific landscape. A first entry point is the observation that many legal theorists were influenced by Wittgenstein and his insights into the philosophy of language.[71] Leaving aside whether the transposition of his insights to the legal tradition always happens correctly, it is certainly so that many theories have advanced to new insights through his work.[72] It is therefore interesting to start by understanding interpretation as 'the imposition of meaning on an object'.[73] As most theorists agree that language is by nature indeterminate, the object can be interpreted in more than one way. This does not imply, however, that anything goes. The challenge is indeed to determine how words and utterances relate to objects and *vice versa*, allowing us to consider certain utterances as more adequate than others.[74] This idea of indeterminacy is very well captured by the German concept *Wortlautgrenze*.[75] A word might have more than one meaning, but it cannot mean everything.

In order to go further in formulating answers to the problems of interpretation under examination, this book, in the first order, draws from Hartian Positivism, which is highly influenced, particularly by the developments in

[69] P Allott, 'Interpretation-An Exact Art' in A Bianchi, D Peat and M Windsor (eds), *Interpretation in International Law* (OUP, 2015): provides a concise overview of the study of interpretation in philosophy and fields relevant to the legal domain.

[70] The second book of the *Organon*, '*De interpretation*' deals with the issue of language and is one of the oldest philosophical texts on the topic.

[71] L Wittgenstein, *Philosophical Investigations* (Blackwell Publishing, 1986); see also: DG Stern, *Wittgenstein's Philosophical Investigations: An Introduction*, vol 2 (CUP, 2004).

[72] Both naturalists and positivists drew from the work of Wittgenstein: eg Fuller (n 21) 186 quoting Wittgenstein: 'The limits of my language are the limits of my world'; and Hart (n 22) 280.

[73] A Marmor, *Interpretation and Legal Theory* (Clarendon Law Series, Clarendon Press, 2005) 11: providing this definition also finds its origin in the works of L Wittgenstein and HLA Hart. See also L Siliquini-Cinelli, What is Legal Reasoning? (2025) 38 *Int J Semiot Law* 143, 147.

[74] Here the issue of objectivity already shines through. A known disagreement in philosophy exists between realists and conventionalists. Conventionalists see the meaning of this to be a matter of convention, whereas for realists the meaning of a thing lies in the thing itself.

[75] See further on this concept of Wortlautgrenze: M Klatt, *Making the Law Explicit: The Normativity of Legal Argumentation* (European Academy of Legal Theory Monograph Series, Oxford and Portland, Oregon, 2008).

language philosophy. In *The Concept of Law*, Hart developed a theory of law setting out the basis for the further development of theories of legal reasoning that were influential in my understanding of the process of interpretation.[76] He understood the legal system as a union of primary and secondary rules.[77] The secondary rules are those that enable us to know the primary rules. Without this type of structure, a legal system, according to Hart, does not exist. The most crucial secondary rule is the Rule of Recognition, which Raz described as:

> [A] rule arising out of the behaviour of law-enforcing officials through a period of time. The rest of the laws of the system are valid because they fulfil the conditions set out in the rule of recognition. The general criterion of identity of all legal systems is that each contains a rule of recognition and all those laws satisfying the conditions it stipulates.[78]

Legal validity, therefore, rests entirely with the rule of recognition and what it identifies as law.[79] This rule of recognition can be very rudimentary and does not even need to be in written form. A social rule that sets out these conditions, pointing to the legal rules, suffices.[80] In essence, Hart looks to the legal system for answers of validity and thereby puts forward a source-based conception of law.[81] This study similarly adopts such a source-based conception of the law.

This book is furthermore influenced by the analytical approach of Hartian positivism.[82] It is the intention to inquire into whether the interpretation conforms with the law. The normative stretch of this book is therefore somewhat limited as it refrains from taking a position in relation to what should be criminalised at the international level,[83] it does not assess the merit or demerit

[76] Hart himself is sometimes said to not have formulated a theory of adjudication. Some of his followers, such as J Raz, however, focused more on the position of the judge.

[77] Hart (n 22) 80-ff, 94.

[78] J Raz, 'Legal Principles and the Limits of Law' (1972) 81 *Y.L.J.* 823.

[79] Shapiro (n 51) 80: 'Hart claims that at the foundation of every legal system lies a social rule that sets out the criteria of legal validity. This master rule, which Hart calls "the rule of recognition," determines which power-conferring and duty-imposing rules are valid in the system.'; Hart considered that international law had no rule of recognition but this position is no longer attainable given the considerable evolution of the field: S Besson and J Tasioulas, *The Philosophy of International Law* (OUP, 2010) 180.

[80] Hart (n 22) 89.

[81] Marmor (n 73) 7: 'An additional thesis of legal positivism is that the law is essentially source based. This means that a norm cannot be legally valid unless it derives its validity from one of the sources identified by the pertinent conventional rules.' (footnotes omitted).

[82] Hart (n 22) v: 'it is concerned with the clarification of the general framework of legal thought, rather than with the criticism of law or legal policy'; JG Murphey and J Coleman, *Philosophy Of Law: An Introduction To Jurisprudence* (Dimensions of Philosophy Series, Revised edn, Routledge, 2013) 1: 'Analytical jurisprudence is concerned with the logical analysis of the basic concepts that arise in law, eg duty, responsibility, excuse, negligence, and the concept of law itself.' See also S Coyle, *Modern Jurisprudence. A Philosophical Guide* (Hart Publishing, 2014) 11; Shapiro (n 51) 3–4.

[83] M Van Hoecke, 'Legal Doctrine: Which Method(s) for What Kind of Discipline?' in M Van Hoecke (ed), *Methodologies of Legal Research: Which Kind of Method for What Kind of Discipline?* (Hart Publishing, 2011).

of the existence of a certain criminalisation,[84] and does not look for 'the right adjudicative truth'.[85] This book aims to isolate and analyse specific legal factors in judicial decision-making rather than exploring the impact of external factors and understand when interpretations overstep the boundaries of the law.

Despite Hart not formulating a general legal theory of interpretation, he laid the groundwork for further interpretative theories by explaining the necessary *open-textured* nature of rules:

> Whichever device, precedent or legislation, is chosen for the communication of standards of behaviour, these, however smoothly they work over the great mass of ordinary cases, will, at some point where their application is in question, prove indeterminate; they will have what has been termed an *open texture*. [. . .] [A]s a general feature of human language; uncertainty at the borderline is the price to be paid for the use of general classifying terms in any form of communication concerning matters of fact. Natural languages like English are when so used irreducibly open-textured.[86]

Hart comprehended that there is a necessary compromise to be made between 'the need for certain rules' that can be applied simply to a great area of conduct and 'the need to leave open, for later settlement' other rules which may need further judicial elaboration.[87] When the choice is made for the latter type of rules, judicial discretion is necessary, and penumbra cases will inevitably arise.[88] The idea that the mechanical application of rules not allowing for any judicial discretion is possible, draws on the incorrect assumption that one can predict, before a particular case arises, what interest or values will be at stake. Hart correctly clarifies that this is not possible and even unfruitful to try to circumvent this moment of judgment in which judicial discretion is paramount.

With these insights, he set the outer limits of judicial interpretation, allowing other theorists, such as Raz, Marmor and Shapiro, to develop more specific theories of adjudication and interpretation. On the basis of their work and in particular that of Raz, interpretation can be better understood in terms of four dimensions. First, the act of interpretation relates to an *object,* referred to by Raz as 'the original'.[89] Interpretation is always *about* something – it says something *about* that object. Second, an interpretation states or shows *the meaning* of the original.[90] Hartian positivists describe the process of interpretation as 'attaching meaning to a word', thereby qualifying the object as meaningful. Third, interpretation is an intentional act, a 'performative and constitutive activity',

[84] B Bix, 'HLA Hart and the Hermeneutic Turn in Legal Theory' (1999) 52 *SMU Law Review*: The existence of the law is one thing; its merit or demerit is another. Whether it be or not is one enquiry; whether it be or be not conformable to an assumed standard, is a different enquiry.

[85] d'Aspremont (n 46) 115.

[86] Hart (n 22) 127–28.

[87] ibid 130.

[88] ibid 136ff.

[89] Raz (n 22) 278.

[90] ibid 278.

a 'deliberate action', and can thereby be distinguished from 'understanding'. Interpretation requires the initiation of a determinate process in the sense that it obliges us to advance a certain position, to invoke certain arguments, to make certain claims or to set aside certain options in favour of others.[91] Fourth, interpretations are subject to assessment as right or wrong (correct or incorrect), or as good or bad (or some approximations of these, such as 'almost right').[92] Interpretations are considered to be successful when they illuminate the meaning of their objects and are supported by 'constitutive reasons'.[93]

As mentioned before, law *as* language 'carries with it a certain degree of indeterminacy'.[94] Furthermore, if rules want to provide for a meaningful sense of direction and function as an instrument of social control, it cannot be that rules are formulated at the level of the individual.[95] Consequently, legal rules have to be characterised by a certain degree of *generality,* which results in an added level of indeterminacy. Despite acknowledging that there is indeterminacy, it is unacceptable to say that there is an 'unlimited choice in how interpretation shapes and constructs the meaning of a text'.[96] Raz's understanding of interpretation presented above also concedes to the fact that there can be more than one acceptable interpretation and allows for legal pluralism.[97] Hart, in this regard, also held:

> The open texture of the law means that there are, indeed, areas of conduct which must be left to be developed by courts or officials striking a balance, in the light of circumstances, between competing interests which vary in weight from case to case.

Considering that this study is similar to the research conducted by MacCormick & Summers does not seek to reveal what precise moral or political reasons exist for making an interpretative choice,[98] but wants to see when interpretations are made *within* the ambit of the law and which ones fall *outside* the ambit of the law, it adopts a similar focus on operative interpretation. Based on a differentiation made by Wróblewski between interpretation *sensu largissimo, sensu largo* and *sensu stricto,* MacCormick views 'operative interpretation' as falling within the category of interpretation in the narrow sense – 'interpretation that occurs where there are doubts in the understanding of a language when it is used, in a particular context, in an act of communication'. Interpretation *sensu stricto* occurs when the interpreter is confronted with interpretative choices or

[91] Marmor (n 73).

[92] A Marmor, *The Language of Law* (OUP, 2014) 108.

[93] ibid 230.

[94] GI Hernández, 'Interpretative Authority and the International Judiciary' in A Bianchi, D Peat and M Windsor (eds), *Interpretation in International Law* (OUP, 2015) 166.

[95] Hart (n 22) 124.

[96] GI Hernández, 'Interpretation' in J Kammerhofer and J D'Aspremont (eds), *International Legal Positivism in a Post-Modern World* (CUP, 2014) 321; Hernández (n 94) 170; see also Hart (n 27) 629.

[97] J Raz, 'Why Interpret?' (1996) 9 *Ratio Juris* 349, 353–56.

[98] N MacCormick and RS Summers, *Interpreting Statutes, A Comparative Study* (Darmouth Publishing Company Limited, 1991) 16–17.

alternatives. Operative interpretation is a subcategory of interpretation and occurs 'only when there is an act of interpretation *sensu stricto* performed by a [judge] for the purpose of making a binding legal decision in an actual trial or litigated controversy'. It takes place when a judge 'has to determine the meaning of legal language in a way sufficiently precise to make a decision in the case and to provide a justification for the decision on the ground of the interpreted meaning of the provision in issue'.[99]

Besides the influence of Hartian positivism, this book, in the second order, adopts a criminal law approach. ICL is a field that is legally multidisciplinary and consists of multiple branches of law and has traditionally drawn from a range of legal disciplines.[100] The ICL project is an international project firmly embedded in public international law (PIL).[101] Different moments in history have demonstrated that the question of holding individuals criminally accountable at the international level is intertwined with interstate relations and PIL matters.[102] And even today, the ICL project is not possible without traditional interstate cooperation and involves issues such as head of state immunity to be resolved.[103] Furthermore, the issue of holding individuals responsible internationally traditionally arose in connection to the desire of ending conflict or establishing peace and as such, international humanitarian law (IHL) similarly is intertwined with ICL. In order to define war crimes, humanitarian conventions were very influential.[104] As a result, the ICC has frequently drawn from IHL to understand certain crime definitions. Another branch of law relevant to ICL is international human rights law (IHRL). IHRL has developed simultaneously with ICL and also experienced its greatest development after World War II. It is therefore no surprise that these fields have influenced each other and that human rights play a crucial role in criminal proceedings.[105] The importance of IHRL cannot be

[99] ibid 13.

[100] See AKA Greenawalt, 'The pluralism of international criminal law' (2011) 86 *Indiana Law Journal* 1036; C Stahn and L van den Herik, '"Fragmentation", Diversification and "3D" Legal Pluralism: International Criminal Law as the Jack-in-The-Box?' in C Stahn and L van den Herik (eds), *The Diversification and Fragmentation of International Criminal Law* (Martinus Nijhoff, 2012); E van Sliedregt, 'Pluralism in International Criminal Law' (2012) 25 *LJIL* 847.

[101] D Akande, 'Sources of International Criminal Law' in A Cassese (ed), *Oxford Companion to International Criminal Justice* (OUP, 2005) 41: ICL 'is a part of public international law and its sources are to be found in the sources of international law.'

[102] See for the discussion of several cooperation issues: O Bekou and D Birkett (eds), *Cooperation and the International Criminal Court: Perspectives from Theory and Practice* (Brill, 2016).

[103] See the issue of head of state immunity that arose in the context of the *Al Bashir case*: P Gaeta, 'Does President Al Bashir enjoy immunity from arrest?' (2009) 7 *JICJ* 315.

[104] See on the importance of humanitarian law: T Meron, 'The Humanization of Humanitarian Law' (2000) 94 *AJIL* 239.

[105] See for a comprehensive study on human rights in ICL: K Zeegers, *International Criminal Tribunals and Human Rights Law, Adherence and Contextualization*, vol 5 (International Criminal Justice Series, Springer, 2016); See also R Bartels, *The Interplay between International Human Rights Law and International Humanitarian Law during International Criminal Trials* (Amsterdam Law School Legal Studies Research Paper, 2018); AS Galand, 'The Systemic Effect of International Human Rights Law on International Criminal Law' in M Scheinin (ed), *Human Rights Norms in 'Other' International Courts* (CUP, 2019).

underestimated in both procedural as well as substantive criminal law and has, in conformity with article 21(3), influenced interpretation throughout.[106]

But considering that ICL's most prominent feature is criminal law,[107] this study draws mostly from criminal law theory. It is its *penal* characteristic that sets ICL apart from other branches of law. This focus is moreover warranted, given that this is a study of crime interpretation. In conclusion, criminal law theory has been hugely influential in the key understandings discussed in this study. Much is owed to the insights of Robinson, who similarly uses criminal law theory to develop his work. He, for example, stresses the need for adherence to deontic principles such as the legality principle in order to enhance legitimacy. This work comes to a conclusion along the same line and uses a criminal law theory lens to understand the main developments in relation to the principle of legality and crime interpretation in international criminal justice.[108]

This combination of a Hartian analytical analysis and a criminal law theory approach provides a unique perspective that led to the development of a legality-centred evaluation tool introduced in the next section.

V. A LEGALITY-CENTRED EVALUATION OF CRIME INTERPRETATION

The theoretical approach developed above unfolds as a legality-centred evaluation. The legality principle is understood to involve and limit the interpretative process as well as the result. Crime interpretation requires a judge to determine what the law is and interpret whether that law, in fact, criminalises the conduct with which the judge is confronted. Importantly, this principle affects both the process and outcome of the interpretation.

A. Evaluating the Interpretative Process

In the *interpretative process*, the judge faces a dimension of law determination and needs to discover the applicable law while applying it in conformity with the source doctrine. This process intrinsically involves a judge calling upon methods of interpretation in order to understand these sources. This means that the evaluation of the process entails an evaluation of the dimension of law determination and accompanying source doctrine, and a dimension of interpretation and accompanying interpretative methods.

[106] See E Irving, 'The Other Side of the Article 21(3) Coin: Human rights in the Rome Statute and the Limits of Article 21(3)' (2019) 32 *LJIL* 837.

[107] CM Bassiouni, 'The Penal Characteristics of Conventional International Criminal Law' (1983) 15 *Case Western Reserve Journal of International Law* 27, 27.

[108] See Robinson (n 11).

At the ICC, Article 21 Rome Statute outlines the applicable law. This article firstly states that the Court should apply the Statute, the Elements of Crimes and its Rules of Procedure and Evidence. Secondly, 'where appropriate, applicable treaties and the principles and rules of international law, including the established principles of the international law of armed conflict' should be applied. Thirdly, 'the Court shall apply general principles of law derived by the Court from national laws of legal systems of the world, including, as appropriate, the national laws of States that would normally exercise jurisdiction over the crime, provided that those principles are consistent with this Statute and with international law and internationally recognised norms and standards'. The Court may also apply principles and rules of law as interpreted in its previous decisions. On the basis of Article 21(3), interpretation must be consistent with internationally recognised human rights.

This unique interpretative framework marks the first instance of an international criminal court with a detailed source doctrine outlined in a statutory provision. Furthermore, as a relatively young institution, the ICC is still delineating the parameters of its source doctrine. Article 21's complex hierarchy has not yet been afforded a fixed meaning. While research in relation to parts of this hierarchy has been conducted, the field is far from saturated and a systematic analysis of the ICC's case law is highly needed.[109]

Where the sources of law are defined, the Rome Statute remains silent as to the modes or canons of interpretation. This begs the question of which methods are to be used in relation to the interpretation of the crimes listed in the Rome Statute. The common practice in ICL is to draw upon the Vienna Convention on the Law of Treaties (VCLT), which provides for a set of provisions outlining methods of interpretation. Article 31(1) puts forward as a general rule of interpretation: 'a treaty shall be interpreted in good faith in accordance with the ordinary meaning to be given to the terms of the treaty in their context and in

[109] Some studies focused on the legality principle in general (see, eg, S Lamb, '*Nullum crimen, nulla poena sine lege* in International Criminal Law' in A Cassese, P Gaeta and JRWDS Jones (eds), *The Rome Statute of the International Criminal Court*, vol 1 (OUP, 2002); K Gallant, *The Principle of Legality in International and Comparative Criminal Law*); or as part of a ICL study (see, eg, A Cassese, *International Criminal Law*, 3rd edn (OUP, 2013)), others have focused on certain sources (eg, N Arajärvi, 'Between Lex Lata and Lex Ferenda. Customary International (Criminal) Law and the Principle of Legality' (2010–2011) 15 *Tilburg Law Review* 163); others have considered the implications of crimes with a customary basis (eg, N Arajärvi, *The changing nature of customary international law: methods of interpreting the concept of custom in international criminal tribunals* (Routledge, 2014)) and others study the role of judges in the creation of crimes (eg, Van Schaack (n 10)); M Swart, 'Judicial Lawmaking at the ad hoc Tribunals: The Creative Use of the Sources of International Law and "Adventurous Interpretation"' (2010) *ZaöRV*); others generally reflected on interpretative methodology (LN Sadat and JM Jolly, 'Seven Canons of ICC treaty Interpretation, Making Sense of Article 25's Rorschach Blot' (2014) 27 *LJIL*); others have addressed more interpretative tendencies in light of the philosophy of ICL (eg, R Cryer, 'Royalism and the King: Article 21 of the Rome Statute and the Politics of Sources' (2009) 12 *New Criminal Law Review: In International and Interdisciplinary Journal* 390).

light of its object and purpose'. Article 31(2) and (3) further proclaim how such a context should be established, and Article 31(4) specifies how a special meaning may be afforded 'if it is established that the parties so intended'. Article 32 adds supplementary means of interpretation, including the preparatory works of the treaty and the circumstances of its conclusion. Article 33 provides guidance when the treaties have multiple authentic languages.

Although some scholars highlighted the problematic nature of some interpretative methods in the criminal justice context[110] or have tried to modify these methods to fit the specific nature of criminal law,[111] these canons remain the authoritative point of reference.[112] Considering that these canons are widely recognised as customary international law, the question of whether the VCLT should apply in the first place is often dismissed as irrelevant. A very underdeveloped side of this discussion has been to critically examine the application of the VCLT. This book delves into the intriguing question of whether and to what extent VCLT can be applied in the context of crime interpretation. This analysis also encompasses an examination of how interpretative methods set out in Article 22(2) of the Rome Statute, holding three legality principles: (1) the principle of strict construction, (2) the prohibition on analogy and (3) the *in dubio pro reo* principle, affect the interpretative process.

B. Evaluating the Interpretative Result

The legality principle also affects the *interpretative result*. The legality principle under the Rome Statute requires a strict construction of the crime, meaning that an interpretation of the crime must adhere to a specific rigour and does not permit an overly expansive interpretation. In addition, there have been calls for labels of crimes to be fair, and although not statutorily enshrined, the principle of fair labelling has been put forward as a general principle affecting crime interpretation. This principle works towards the construction and labelling that conform to a certain idea of fairness. These principles thereby necessitate that the interpretative result be tested in terms of strict construction as well as the fairness of the label. On top of providing a hierarchical outline of the sources for the judges to apply, Article 22(2) of the Rome Statute curtails the judges' *espace interprétatif* in that it requires the judge to apply the law strictly. The principle of strict construction goes further than the general notion of

[110] See, eg, Akande (n 101).

[111] See, eg, L Grover, 'A Call for Arms: Fundamental Dilemmas confronting the Interpretation of Crimes in the Rome Statute of the International Criminal Court' (2010) 21 *European Journal of International Law* 543.

[112] An exception to this majority view is D Jacobs, *Why the Vienna Convention should not be applied to the ICC Rome Statute: a plea for respecting the principle of legality* (2013); and to a certain extent: N Jain, 'Interpretive Divergence' (2017) 57 *Virginia Journal of International Law* 45.

legality and non-retroactivity, as it mandates a narrow interpretation of crime definitions.

Many examinations demonstrate that the scope afforded to the legality principle by the ICC judges – and also the criminal tribunals before it – is often found to be too 'light' in terms of restricting judicial discretion. Several authors have advocated for a sounder interpretative methodology with a more solid position for the principle of legality, restricting judicial discretion more adequately.[113] In light of the often rudimentary assessment in the ICC's case law, further scrutiny of the legality principle and its constraining capacity on the interpretation of crimes is needed.

Experts have highlighted that considerations not strictly part of the legality principle are equally at play in the judicial interpretation of crimes.[114] Recently, the principle of fair labelling has been introduced to the debate on crime interpretation.[115] The principle of fair labelling is generally understood as requiring that the label signals 'the essence and the totality of the criminal conduct'.[116] Judges should label conduct adequately in order to fairly represent 'the moral gravity' of the conduct.[117] This principle has, in a similar fashion to the legality principle, been framed as a principle central to the rights of the accused.[118] What matters is not merely that people are convicted, but what they are convicted of.[119]

The principle of fair labelling is a bridge to considerations outside of the strictly legal realm. When fair labelling means fair to the accused, then the principle has similar objectives as the legality principle. Understood in this way, both principles will favour the stricter crime definitions. Fair labelling has a different objective than the legality principle when it is approached from the perspective of the victim. To the extent that it favours broad victim-oriented definitions and wants to guarantee fairness to victims, it opposes the legality principle. The principle of strict construction pulls the interpreter to interpret strictly in favour of the accused. Contrary hereto, the principle of fair labelling is an argument to interpret broadly. Interpreted this way, these two principles may, though not necessarily, lead to conflicting crime interpretations. So far, no study has considered the principle of strict construction and the principle of fair labelling as two potentially conflicting principles in the interpretation of crimes. This book,

[113] See, eg, J Powderly, 'The Rome Statute and the Attempted Corseting of the Interpretative Judicial Function: Reflections on Sources of Law and Interpretative Technique' in C Stahn (ed), *The Law and Practice of the International Criminal Court* (OUP, 2015); A Appazov, 'International Criminal Court and the Decision-Making Heritage of the Ad Hoc Tribunals: A Study of Judicial Activism' (2016) 3 *Journal of Global Justice & Public Policy* 1.

[114] See, eg, C Roberts, 'On the Definition of Crimes against Humanity and Other Widespread or Systematic Human Rights Violations' (2017) 20 *University of Pennsylvania Journal of Law and Social* Change 1.

[115] T de Souza Dias, 'Recharacterisation of Crimes and the Principle of Fair Labelling in International Criminal Law' (2018) 18 *International Criminal Law Review* 788.

[116] DL Nersessian, 'Comparative Approaches to Punishing Hate: The Intersection of Genocide and Crimes Against Humanity' (2007) 43 *Stanford Journal of International Law* 221, 255.

[117] V Tadros, 'Fair labelling and social solidarity' in L Zedner and JV Roberts (eds), *Principles and Values in Criminal Law and Criminal Justice: Essays in Honour of Andrew Ashworth* (OUP, 2012) 67–68.

[118] J Chalmers and F Leverick, 'Fair Labelling in Criminal Law' (2008) 71 *Modern Law Review* 217, 225–26.

[119] J Horder, 'Rethinking Non-Fatal Offences against the Person' (1994) 14 *Oxford Journal of Legal Studies* 335.

therefore, seeks to fill that gap and to evaluate how that divide between these principles should be addressed.

C. A Two-dimensional Evaluation Model

This book proposes an analysis of the interpretative space constituted by a two-dimensional functional relationship between the applicable law and methods of interpretation (see Table I below). Article 21 of the Rome Statute sets out the applicable law, and as such, this study seeks to understand the workings of that provision. In terms of methods of interpretation, the methods used in international law, namely those presented in Articles 31–33 of the Vienna Convention on the Law of Treaties (VCLT), are traditionally used in ICL. As a result, this study analyses these methods but debunks their use in the context of crime interpretation, after which an alternative is presented on the basis of Article 22 of the Rome Statute, involving the principle of legality.

This categorisation is not a suggestion to see the interpretative outcomes as always neatly broad or strict, or clearly fair or unfair. The purpose is to assess the outcomes and identify those outcomes that are normatively unacceptable in light of the boundaries set by the legality principle. Outcomes in the bottom-left quadrant are broadly constructed and unfairly labelled and are self-evidently both in violation of the principle of legality as well as the principle of fair labelling. The upper right quadrant is the most desired outcome, offering both an interpretation that is strict and fair. The two remaining quadrants are where it becomes more difficult because the outcome is either in tension with the principle of fair labelling or strict construction. As the figure below demonstrates, the outcomes can be categorised under one of the four quadrants. These quadrants are categorical tools in terms of which practical cases are examined.

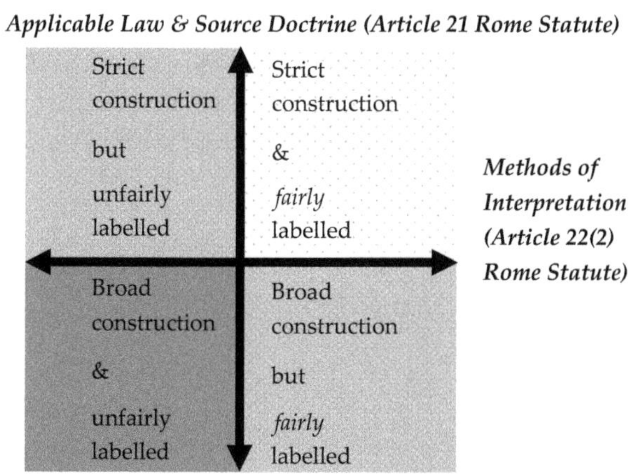

Table I A two-dimensional approach to the interpretative process with quadrantal categorisation of the interpretative outcomes

Taking this two-dimensional functional approach into account, this book provides a case law analysis of the ICC's jurisprudence that studies both the interpretative process as well as the interpretative result in light of the legality principle. These two dimensions of the legality principle are explored through two case studies.

VI. BOOK OUTLINE

This book is divided into six chapters, two case studies and a conclusion. Following this introductory chapter, chapter two provides a roadmap on how the principle of legality evolved into a complex interpretative principle. It explains how this study arrived at viewing crime interpretation as a two-dimensional process consisting of the applicable law and corresponding source doctrine and the interpretative methods. Chapter three examines the first dimension of the interpretative process and provides a legality-centred analysis of the applicable law and source doctrine. This primarily entails an assessment of the applicable law provision in the Rome Statute, ie, Article 21. Chapter four analyses the methods of interpretation in ICL and those used at the ICC. This entails a critical analysis of the use of the methods of interpretation in Articles 31–33 VCLT for the purpose of crime interpretation. Chapter five evaluates the interpretative result based on Article 22 and the principle of fair labelling. Chapter six sets out an alternative legality-centred approach to crime interpretation.

The second part of this book evaluates the ICC's approach to crime interpretation by means of two case studies: one on the contextual element of organisational policy and one on the categorisation of fact patterns called 'forced marriages'. These case studies assess how the ICC judges have applied the interpretational framework. Based on the two-dimensional model, the flaws and strengths in the ICC's approach in terms of interpretative process and result are evaluated.

The concluding chapter brings together the conceptual analysis of the legality principle and how it affects the decision-making process, and connects these to the findings of the case studies. It holds recommendations on how to improve the interpretative methodology in light of the legality principle and reflects on the future of ICL and how its liberal philosophy is best served.

2

A Roadmap Towards a Legality-Centred, Two-Dimensional Model

> [N]ullum crimen sine lege is more than only a protection against arbitrary governance. It 'provides the rationale [. . .] for a system of justice rather than administrative elimination of wrongdoers by command of those in power. It is the reason why we are ruled by law and not by police.'[1]

I. INTRODUCTION

THIS CHAPTER HAS AS a main purpose to justify how this study came to the two-dimensional understanding of the principle by examining the historical, doctrinal and theoretical underpinnings of the legality principle in international criminal law (ICL). The legality principle can no longer be viewed as a monolithic principle,[2] but rather developed into a complex set of sub-principles, each impacting on the activity of crime interpretation.[3] The seemingly basic philosophy underlying the legality principle has rather broad implications and, as a consequence, the principle has been dissected into multiple sub-principles linked to its core and derived from its underlying philosophy.[4] Therefore, most authors do not mention a single legality principle but multiple principles, or a 'bundle of maxims'.[5] In order to grasp these complex sets of principles, this chapter offers a selective roadmap through legal history, doctrines, fields and theories.

[1] C Stahn, *A Critical Introduction to International Criminal Law* (CUP, 2019) 11.

[2] Borrowing the term monolithic from: WT Worster, 'On the Purposes of Legality and its Applicability to International Law' (2011) 9 *JICJ* 973, 974.

[3] A Ashworth and J Horder, *Principles of Criminal Law*, 7th edn (OUP, 2013) 57; KS Gallant, *The Principle of Legality in International and Comparative Criminal Law* (CUP, 2009) 12–14.

[4] This chapter underscores that the legality principle's purpose is to protect citizens from arbitrary interference of their freedom. The principle is a manifestation of the idea that we are ruled by law and not simply commanded by those in power. See Gallant (n 3) 15; B Van Schaack, 'Judicial lawmaking the intersection between law and morals' (2008-2009) 97 *Georgetown Law Journal* 119, 121–22.

[5] M Dubber, 'The Legality Principle in American and German Criminal Law: An Essay in Comparative Legal History' in G Martyn, A Musson and H Pihlajamäki (eds), *From the Judge's Arbitrium to the Legality Principle: Legislation as a Source of Law in Criminal Trials* (2013) 373.

The exploration begins with the legality principle's roots in criminal law doctrine, delves into insights from the Positivist School of Criminology and the New Social Defence School, and then shifts to its understanding within international human rights law (IHRL). The discussion further extends to its development in ICL, particularly highlighting its evolution during the Nuremberg proceedings and ad hoc tribunals. The focus is on international law development, with national jurisdictions referenced as illustrative examples. This chapter does not represent a clean chronological overview but rather focuses on certain shifts and examines interpretations by understanding their historical footing. The most significant shift examined is the move from viewing the legality principle solely as a prohibition on retroactive legislation to understanding it as the central principle guiding crime interpretation. Another important shift is the evolution from understanding the legality principle as a principle of justice having little constraining impact on judicial discretion to a principle requiring strict construction and thereby setting clear limits to judicial discretion. Stemming from the desire to soften the application of strict construction, calls to include the principle of fair labelling under the legality principle emerged alongside this final shift.

This chapter concludes by explaining the two-dimensional model and the identification of the four quadrantal outcomes. More specifically, it clarifies how the two-dimensional functional approach was developed and how the legality principle evolved into a set of interrelated principles impacting, in a complex way, the judicial interpretation of crimes.

II. THE DOCTRINAL AND NATIONAL DEVELOPMENT OF THE LEGALITY PRINCIPLE

The roots of the legality principle trace back to Beccaria, who, inspired by Montesquieu's political theory,[6] penned the treatise *On Crimes and Punishments* in 1764.[7] Beccaria aimed to humanise the criminal justice system and counter the unchecked power of judges, advocating for certainty and established guarantees. Aligned with the enlightened idea of the separation of powers, he opposed judges enacting laws, reserving that authority for the legislative power. Distrust in the judiciary led Beccaria to advocate against almost any form of judicial interpretation. Very close to Montesquieu's idea of *La bouche de la loi,* Beccaria stated:

> The judge should construct a perfect syllogism about every criminal case: the major premise should be the general law; the minor, the conformity or otherwise of the

[6] C de S Montesquieu, *L'Espirit des Lois* (1748) Livre XI Chap VI, 136.

[7] C Beccaria, *On Crimes and Punishments and Other Writings* (Cambridge Texts in the History of Political Thought, CUP, 1764).

action with the law; and the conclusion, freedom or punishment. Whenever the judge is forced, or takes it upon himself, to construct even as few as two syllogisms, the door is opened to uncertainty.[8]

Beccaria thereby laid out the philosophical foundation of the legality principle and identified it as essential in the judicial interpretation of crimes. Feuerbach later coined the well-known Latin adagio *nullum crimen, nulla poena sine lege.*[9] And although these authors suggest a civil law origin of the principle, traces of the principle have equally been found in the writings of common law writers such as Blackstone.[10] It nevertheless remains controversial to what extent *lex* also entails common law developed *lex* and whether judges can also construct law. Regardless, the common law understanding of the principle stands in sharp contrast to the understanding of Beccaria, who only viewed statutory law as *lex*. Common law doctrines focus more on non-retroactivity and foreseeability.[11]

Despite the different viewpoints, the emergence of the legality principle is indicative of an enlightened movement concerned with the rationalisation and humanisation of criminal law. The eighteenth century's liberalism in penal theory found its expression in what has been called Classicism or the Classical School.[12] This School succeeded in the spread of the principle across the globe. By the beginning of the twentieth century, most legal systems recognised the principle, be it in varying forms.[13] From the first enactment of the principle in Austrian Law in the late eighteenth century to the early beginnings of the twentieth century, this Classical School dominated the penal codes.[14] The legality principle set rational limits to the exercise of power and afforded rights to the individual. In both civil and common law systems, the core rationale of the principle was to protect against arbitrary power. From this, a second rationale grew, namely to provide the individual with notice and require that the consequences of conduct should be foreseeable. The rationales of the principle are not unimportant in considering its later interpretation.

[8] ibid 14.

[9] PJA von Feuerbach, *Lehrbuch des gemeinen in Deutschland gültigen Peinlichen Rechts* (Georg Friedrich Heyers' Verlag, 1832); Gallant (n 3); S Glaser, 'Nullum Crimen Sine Lege, a contribution' (1942) 24 *Journal of Comparative Legislation & International Law* 29.

[10] W Blackstone, *Commentaries on the Laws of England in Four Books* (Routledge–Cavendish, 1753) Vol I, 46: 'There is still a more unreasonable method than this, which is called making of laws ex post facto; when after an action [. . .] is committed, the legislator then for the first time declares it to have been a crime, [. . .]. Here it is impossible that the party could foresee that an action, innocent when it was done, should be afterwards converted to guilt.'

[11] J Hall, *Principles of Criminal Law* (The Bobbs-Merrill Company Publisher, 1947); see also Ashworth and Horder (n 3) 62.

[12] JM Canals, 'Classicism, Positivism and Social Defense' (1960) 50 *The Journal of Criminal Law, Criminology, and Police Science* 541.

[13] B Broomhall, 'Nullum crimen sine lege' in K Ambos and O Trifferer (eds), *The Rome Statute of the International Criminal Court, A Commentary* (Beck – Hart – Nomos, 2016) 957.

[14] See, eg, paragraph I of the 1787 Austrian Law; Article 8 of the Declaration of the Rights of Man and the Citizen of August 26, 1789; paragraph 9 of the Prussian law of February 5, 1794; See further: Glaser (n 9); Canals (n 12) 542–45.

At the beginning of the twentieth century, the Classical School was criticised by proponents of the Positivist School of Criminology and the School of Social Defence.[15] Where Classicism was primarily driven by protecting the individual versus the state, the concern that now entered the debate was that the State could not deal with criminal behaviour effectively. New insights in biology and psychology led the Positivist school to conclude that some criminals are more dangerous than others, and thus, sentences had to be adopted depending on how big the danger of the convict was vis-à-vis society.[16] Motivated by a desire to better protect society, Positivism advocated for a wider differentiation of penalties and sought to enable the judge to model the sanction after the offender's specific characteristics.[17]

Legality was too rigid, and in order to respond effectively to crime, Positivists called for an adaptation of some of the core principles that had become deeply enshrined in the criminal law of most European countries. The more radical the Positivist Theory, the less there is a link between the conduct and the legal consequence connected thereto, and the more focus there is on the offender's personality.[18] Furthermore, the idea of having to prevent crime emerged, which directly impacted the idea of retroactivity. Legality was no longer to function as a straitjacket, stripping the judge of the ability to respond to a specific case, and although most Positivists did not advocate for a full departure from the principle, some came very close.[19]

The Positivist School did not yield as much legislative transformation as the Classical School, but one particular legislative example is worth mentioning, as it demonstrates the change in vision on legality. The *Nationalsozialistische Deutsche Arbeiterpartei* (NSDAP) in 1933 conducted a Penal Reform in which

[15] Legal Positivism in legal theory and jurisprudence should be differentiated from Criminological Positivism as a penal theory. Legal Positivism is understood as the counterpart of Natural Law Theory as discussed in this study's introduction. Criminological Positivism is a response to classical penal theory and was specifically concerned with how to adequately respond to crime. See further P Garfinkel, *Criminal Law in liberal and fascist Italy* (Studies in Legal History, CUP, 2019) 17–18: Positivist criminology 'initially emerged from the writings of [Lombroso, Ferri and Garofalo], [. . .] who cofounded the Positivist "school" of criminology in the 1880s'. The criteria for identifying criminologists as Positivists: 'that the offender's biopsychological constitution represented a – if not the – primary cause of criminal behavior; that an illegal act was a symptom of an organically pathological and thus a socially dangerous person, not a misdeed perpetrated by a rational, morally aware agent; that moral responsibility [. . .] must be replaced with legal responsibility [..] that punishing the criminal rather than the crime represented the true object of penal law'. Punishment was 'no longer repressive and proportional to the crime, but instead preventative, indefinite, and individualised in order to defend society against dangerous offenders'.

[16] For example Lombroso linked certain biological features (shape of the skull) to a predisposition to commit crime. See C Lombroso, *Criminal man* (Duke University Press, 2006).

[17] See on sentencing theory: A Ashworth and M Wasik (eds), *Fundamentals of Sentencing Theory: Essays in honour of Andrew von Hirsch* (Oxford Monographs on Criminal Law and Criminal Justice, Clarendon Press, 1998).

[18] Canals (n 12); Garfinkel (n 15); E Ferri, *La sociologie criminelle*, 2nd edn (Alcan, 1914). See for a Belgian Positivist position: A Prins, *Science pénale et droit positif* (Bruylant, 1899) 40.

[19] G Battaglini, 'Fascist Reform of the Penal Law in Italy' (1933–1934) *Am Inst Crim L & Criminology* 278.

the abolition of the *nullum crimen sine lege principle* served a prime role. Acts found morally reprehensible according to the sound perception of the people were now punishable without there being a written law:

> Whoever commits an action which the law declares to be punishable or which is deserving of punishment *according to the fundamental idea of a penal law and the sound perception of the people*, shall be punished. If no determinate penal law is directly applicable to the action, it shall be punished according to the law, the basic idea of which fits it best.[20]

Since there had been cases in which the *Reichsgericht* could not find an act punishable because the law did not provide for a precise criminalisation, the idea of substantive justice now provided for the possibility of interpretation by analogy.[21] Based on the above-cited formulation of analogy, mixed marriages between non-Aryans and Aryans were punishable without explicit written law. Judges could justify criminalising such acts as contrary to 'the legal order of the national-racial state (*völkischer Staat*)'.

The theories of the Positivist School of Criminology resulted in a severe absence of safeguards against abuse of power. Post-World War II, the New Social Defence School emerged to address and rectify these aberrations of Positivism. The New Social Defence movement tried to reconcile the differences between the Classical and Positivist Schools and balance the rights of the accused protected by the legality principle with the right of society to be protected against socially dangerous behaviour.[22] Having the horrors of World War II fresh in their memories, Filippo Gramatica and Marc Ancel, founders of the International Society of Social Defence (ISSD),[23] rephrased the theory of social defence.[24] Rejecting the legacy of the Classic School, and in line with the Positivists, the idea of moral responsibility was not accepted, nor was a retributive philosophy of criminal law.[25] The intention was nonetheless not to depart from 'pure law' as much as the Positivist criminologists. Ancel clarified that the criminal judge should decide cases according to the law and apply the penalty laid down. He nevertheless doubted 'that the human and social problem presented by a particular criminal act can be wholly resolved by the abstract working of a distributive conception of justice'.[26]

[20] Gesetz zur Änderung des Strafgesetzbuchs (1933) *Reichsgesetzblatt*, I, 839, Art 1 (emphasis added) and translation from: L Preuss, 'Punishment by Analogy in National Socialistic Penal Law' (1935) 26 *Am Inst Crim L & Criminology* 847.

[21] ibid 851.

[22] C Kreß, 'Nulla poena nullum crimen sine lege', *Max Planck Encyclopedia of Public International Law* (OUP, 2010): discussing the German as well as the Russian example of abolishing the legality principle.

[23] The organisation was originally called *Société internationale de défense sociale*. Still active today, it has been renamed to International Society of Social Defence and Humane Criminal Policy.

[24] M Ancel, *Social Defence: A Modern Approach to Criminal Problems*, vol 14 (The Sociology of Law and Criminology, Routledge, 1998) 17–18.

[25] ibid 2.

[26] ibid 99–100.

In some sense, this movement signalled a return to the Classical principles of criminal law and was very much driven by a humanisation of criminal law. Beccaria's legacy was not disposed of, and his principles were still considered essential to criminal law.[27] This movement was very influential in the development of human rights as a limit to penal action. Consequently, although a flexible sanction system was a sign of a good social defence policy, the principle of legality as a human right was preserved as a safeguard against excessive governmental interference. In line with this reasoning, the dangerousness of the offender, although a factor for sentence adaptation, was conceptually subjected to the legality principle. As such, this theory does not *per se* reject judicial decision-making to be policy-driven. The judge, in that sense, can take into consideration extra-legal elements as long as adherence to positive law is guaranteed.[28]

One of the most important takeaways from these theoretical insights is that disagreements in relation to the legality principle are, in essence, disagreements about judicial discretion. Where, for a Classicist, the principle means that the judge is required to stick to positive law, the Positivist criminologist is not primarily concerned with setting limits to the judge's arbitrium. Quite the contrary, the judge is seen as an actor in the fight against crime and one of the key players in protecting society from crime. Although the New Social Defence School finds the judge to be limited by positive law, policy-driven decision-making within the limits of that positive law is accepted and even encouraged.

The following section assesses how the principle has been translated to the international level at Nuremberg, a place where different schools and legal systems came together. This moment was meaningful given that Nuremberg was situated at a time when a purely classically conceived criminal justice system was deemed unable to tackle crime effectively, but the Positivist conception had also shown the consequences of unfettered state power. As the New Social Defence movement indicated, a more balanced system was vital.

III. NUREMBERG AND TOKYO: LEGALITY AS A PRINCIPLE OF SUBSTANTIVE JUSTICE

The first traces of the legality principle being transplanted to the international plane arose at the International Military Tribunal in Nuremberg (IMT),[29] the International Military Tribunal for the Far East (IMTFE)[30] and the subsequent

[27] ibid 3–4.

[28] ibid.

[29] Agreement for the Prosecution and Punishment of the Major War Criminals of the European Axis (London Charter) (8 August 1945) UNTS No 251.

[30] Special Proclamation by the Supreme Commanderfor the Allied Powers at Tokyo (Tokyo Charter) (19 January 1946) Treaties and Other International Acts Series 1589.

trials at the Nuremberg Military Tribunals (NMTs).[31] This section discusses some of the key interpretations of legality in the case law of these tribunals.[32]

The IMT, IMTFE and the NMTs came into being under immense political pressure of the trials to take place, but with little positive law to rely on. There was no international court or forum available, and the international legal instruments were insufficient to respond to a large part of criminal behaviour. The Hague Regulation, for example, set out a range of war crimes, but did not include crimes such as waging an illegal war or committing atrocities against a state's own civilian population.[33] As a result, the genocide against the Jewish People with German citizenship would potentially remain unpunished. Unmistakably, this was felt to be unacceptable, and so legal solutions were sought. The IMT was established with the London Charter, which included novel categories of crimes: crimes against humanity and crimes against peace.[34]

With the legal solution of newly established crime categories, however, came a new legal problem, and that was the problem of retroactivity. The introduction of these crime categories to address past conduct was argued to be in violation of the legality principle. Probably realising objections of retroactivity could be raised successfully,[35] the drafters decided not to incorporate the legality principle in the London Charter, which meant that the different viewpoints articulated on the principle thus far,[36] were tested and discussed in court. Reevaluating certain arguments related to this principle is valuable for comprehending the judges' preference for a theory of substantive justice over strict legality.

When the defendants argued that the crimes against humanity and crimes against peace violated the principle of legality given their retroactive application, the counter-argument raised was that the legality principle could not extensively curb judicial interpretation. The signboard phrase that became well-known in legal literature was:

> [T]he maxim *nullum crimen sine lege* is not a limitation of sovereignty, but is in general a principle of justice.[37]

[31] Control Council Law No. 10 Punishment of Persons Guilty of War Crimes, Crimes against Peace and against Humanity (December 20, 1945) 3 *Official Gazette*.

[32] See also J Descheemaeker, 'Le tribunal militaire international des grands criminels de guerre' (1946) 1 *Revue générale de droit international public* 210, 226–33; HD de Vabres, 'Le jugement de Nuremberg et le principe de légalité des délits et des peines' (1946–47) *Revue de droit pénal et de criminologie*; H Ehard, 'The Nuremberg Trial Against the Major War Criminals and International Law' (1949) 43 *AJIL* 223; GA Finch, 'The Nuremberg trial and international law' (1947) 20 *AJIL* 20; H Kelsen, 'The Rule Against Ex Post Facto Laws and the Prosecution of the Axis War Criminals' (1945) *The Judge Advocate Journal*.

[33] See, eg, Hague Convention (II) on the Laws and Customs of War on Land (adopted on 29 July 1899, entered into force 4 September 1890).

[34] Art 6(c) London Charter.

[35] CM Bassiouni, *Crimes Against Humanity: Historical Evolution and Contemporary Application*, 2nd edn (CUP, 2013) 137.

[36] See S Garibian, 'Crimes against humanity and international legality in legal theory after Nuremberg' (2007) 9 *Journal of Genocide Research* 93.

[37] *France et al v Göring et al* (Judgment and Sentence) Trial of the Major War Criminals before the International Military Tribunal (1 October 1946) 219.

The Court thus put forward a natural law theory of substantive justice rather than a theory of strict legality.[38] The principle was not understood as limiting the sovereign's power to legislate retroactively.[39] The underpinning reasoning can be broken down into several sub-arguments.

The first argument was that the London Charter cannot be qualified as *ex post facto* law, given that the charter was a codification of customary international law. For crimes against humanity, the customary status was, for example, proven by reliance on political declarations condemning certain atrocities as violations of the laws of humanity.[40] The origin of the crime was connected to the Martens Clause of the 1907 Hague Convention, since it refers to 'the laws of humanity'.[41] This argument of customary origin did not reach so far as to also include crimes committed during peacetime – it still required a war nexus – but it did succeed in extending the scope of international crimes to crimes against the German civilian population. As a result, the Nazis' extermination of their own population was not left unpunished.

The second argument was strongly connected to the first argument and reinforced it. It held that the category of war crimes never excluded crimes committed against a state's own population and regarded crimes against humanity as a type of war crime.[42] Human rights terminology did not yet dominate the international legal domain, and legal thinking had not yet developed to the point of recognising a general protection of human rights violations against a state's own population. As a result, in order to grasp these acts, a connection was sought with war crimes.

The third argument focused on the connection between national and international criminalisation. According to this reasoning, extermination could not be an *ex post facto* criminalisation under the London Charter, given that every developed legal system, even the Nazi system, held a criminal provision against murder or theft.[43] Arguing that extermination was an unforeseeable criminalisation,[44] this reasoning is based on the idea that the legality principle is sufficiently fulfilled if it is foreseeable that the behaviour is criminal. There were no signs at that time of considering the label to be a relevant factor in the legality test. Whether criminal under national or international law, or as a war crime or a crime against humanity, such legal categorisation was of no importance in the assessment.

[38] Gallant (n 3), 2; G Acquaviva, 'At the Origins of Crimes against Humanity: Clues to a Proper Understanding of the Nullum Crimen Principle in the Nuremberg Judgement' (2011) 9 *JICJ* 811.

[39] See also Kelsen (n 32).

[40] Joint Declaration from France, Great Britain, and Russia (24 May 1915) R.G. 59, 867.4016/67 (Telegram Sent From Department of State, Washington to American Embassy Constantinople).

[41] See Bassiouni (n 35), 87ff; RS Clark, 'History of Efforts to Codify Crimes Against Humanity From the Charter of Nuremberg to the Statute of Rome' in LN Sadat (ed), *Forging a Convention for Crimes Against Humanity* (CUP 2011) 8; N Geras, *Crimes Against Humanity: Birth of a Concept* (Manchester University Press, 2011) 12ff.

[42] Gallant (n 3) 123 indicated that the French Judge Donnedieu de Vabres, and the French Prosecutor Merthon, found no legality problem to exist in relation to crimes against humanity, which were war crimes under a different name; see also A Cassese, 'The Martens Clause: half a loaf or simply pie in the sky?' (2000) 11 *EJIL* 187.

[43] Kelsen (n 32) 9.

[44] Bassiouni (n 35) 338; E Schwelb, 'Crimes against humanity' (1946) 23 *BYIL* 178, 196ff.

The fourth argument was that the German defendants could not reasonably invoke the protection of a principle they themselves had abolished.[45] The NSDAP in 1933 articulated a statute according to which any act found morally reprehensible according to the sound perception of the people was punishable without there being a written law.[46] With this law, any protection offered by the legality principle was swept away.[47]

With these arguments, the new crime category was argued not to go against the principle of legality. Today, many disagree with this conclusion and find the birth and origin of crimes against humanity to have been created *ex post facto* at Nuremberg and not earlier in the Martens Clause or other sources.[48]

The discussion on the retroactive creation of the category of crimes against humanity also arose at the NMTs. An interesting difference is that Control Council Law No. 10 no longer held a war nexus.[49] This broader definition of crimes against humanity, distancing it from the old war crimes category, created complications regarding retroactivity. Moreover, at the NMTs, the complexity of deciding which law to apply arose, with disagreement over whether national (German or American) law, international law, or both should be considered. Consequently, the opinions on legality were more divergent, as Heller has demonstrated.[50] In some cases, it was also found necessary to adapt the scope of the legality principle to the international context.[51]

In different passages of the NMTs' case law, the legality principle is explained as requiring that the defendant should have known his act was wrongful.[52] Given that the acts under examination 'were long known and understood as criminal under the general principles of criminal law',[53] or under national law,[54] legality cannot be violated by qualifying these acts as crimes against humanity. Similar

[45] J Nicholson, *Strengthening the Validity of International Criminal Tribunals* (Brill, 2017) 106–107; H Kelsen, 'Will the Judgement in the Nuremberg Trial Constitute a Precedent in International Law?' (1947) 1 *International Law Quarterly* 153, 164–65.

[46] Gesetz zur Änderung des Strafgesetzbuchs (1933) *Reichsgesetzblatt*, I, 839, Art 1. See also Preuss (n 20).

[47] Kelsen (n 32) 11–12.

[48] See M Milanovic, 'Was Nuremberg a Violation of the Principle of Legality?' (2010) www.ejiltalk.org/was-nuremberg-a-violation-of-the-principle-of-legality/ EJIL:Talk!: discussing how the ECtHR's GC in the *Kononov v Latvia* judgment revealed that many are of the opinion that NMT was an articulation of *ex post facto* law; see also A Cassese, 'From Nuremberg to Rome: international military tribunals to the International Criminal Court' in An Cassese, P Gaeta and JRWD Jones (eds), *The Rome Statute of the International Criminal Court*, vol 1 (OUP, 2002) 22ff.

[49] Article II(1)(c) Control Council Law No 10.

[50] KJ Heller, *The Nuremberg Military Tribunals and the Origins of International Criminal Law* (OUP, 2011) 126ff.

[51] *United States v Alstötter et al (the Justice Case)* Trials of War Criminals before the Nuremberg Military Tribunal under Control Council Law No 10, Vol III, 974–75.

[52] *United States v von Weizaecker et al (Ministries Case)* Trials of War Criminals before the Nuremberg Military Tribunal under Control Council Law No 10, Vol XIV, 1103.

[53] *United States v Ohlendorf et al (Einsatzgruppen case)* Trials of War Criminals before the Nuremberg Military Tribunal under Control Council Law No 10, Vol IV, 499.

[54] ibid 459: 'In the main, the defendants in this case are charged with murder. Certainly no one can claim with the slightest pretense at reasoning that there is any taint of *ex post factoism* in the law of murder.'

to the IMT, the label is not yet considered to be of relevance to the legality analysis. When retroactivity is assessed, it suffices that *a* legal source holds the conduct criminal. It seems that it does not matter whether it is the law applicable before that institution. The dissenting opinion of Judge Power indicates that the view was not unanimous, as he found that the legal question should be 'whether it is a crime under the rules applicable here, always keeping in mind that we have no right to extend these rules by construction'. He relied on the notion of strict construction and *in dubio pro reo* to make his argument.[55]

Other judgments held a more stringent view on legality and found that 'crimes against humanity as defined in CCL 10 must be strictly construed to exclude isolated cases of atrocity or persecution, whether committed by private individuals or by governmental authority'. That section only 'provides for punishment of crimes committed against German nationals [. . .] where there is proof of conscious participation in systematic government-organised or approved procedures'.[56]

Taking this phrase separately, one would almost conclude that a doctrine of strict legality, more in line with a positivist view, was adopted at Nuremberg. Ultimately, however, a doctrine of substantive justice prevailed. A doctrine of strict legality would have impeded the liability of the Nazi.[57] In the words of Gallant, at least this theory of substantive justice 'saved them for another day'.[58]

The IMTFE judgment, in general terms, concurred with the IMT and reflected the same reasoning. The majority understood the principle of legality to be a principle of substantive justice under international law. Nevertheless, many judges dissented and offered separate opinions, which created a slightly more dispersed picture.

Some judges bluntly found that international law did not have a principle of legality.[59] Others rejected the notion of the principle as a principle of justice and found that this interpretation would require the exclusion of every crime in the Charter because these were all *ex post facto* created.

The Dutch judge, Judge Röling, wrote that the legality principle is rather 'a rule of policy, valid only if expressly adopted, so as to protect citizens against arbitrariness of courts'.[60] As the principle did not appear in the law applied by the tribunal, it was simply not applicable. Judge Pal used the insights of Kelsen to substantiate the lack of a legal basis for criminal responsibility at the international level and argued that the Nuremberg Charter was indeed a retroactive law

[55] Dissenting Opinion Judge Powers to the *Ministries Case* 871ff.

[56] *United States v Alstötter et al* (n 51) 982.

[57] H Van der Wilt, 'Nullum Crimen and International Criminal Law: The Relevance of the Foreseeability Test' (2015) 84 *Nordic Journal of International Law* 515, 516.

[58] Gallant (n 3) 155.

[59] *United States et al v Araki et al* (Concurring Opinion by the Honorable Mr Justice Delfin Jaranilla Member for the Republic of the Philippines) IMTFE Records (1 November 1948) 17–19.

[60] *United States et al v Araki et al* (Opinion of Mr Justice Röling, Member for the Netherlands) IMTFE Records (12 November 1948) 44.

establishing criminal responsibility. In his view, however, no international legality principle precluded this kind of *ex post facto* creation of criminal responsibility.[61]

All these discussions at the IMT, NMT and NMTFE have in common that they were dominated by the questions of whether the law prescribed the crime and thus whether there was no *ex post facto* crime creation. It was not yet on the agenda to assess whether extensive interpretative methods can result in retroactive expansion of crime categories and whether that would violate the legality principle. And although strict construction and *in dubio pro reo* were mentioned a few times, the Nuremberg and Tokyo case law did not address how the broadness of the interpretation of a crime could be problematic.

In general terms, the theory of substantive justice prevailed, and a strict view of legality did not break through. After Nuremberg, the legality principle at the international level was further developed in IHRL, the milestones of which are set out in the next section.

IV. THE LEGALITY PRINCIPLE AS A HUMAN RIGHT

Due to the Cold War, projects for the establishment of a permanent international court came to a halt. For an understanding of the scope of the international legality principle in the post-World War II period, one can therefore only look at IHRL.[62] The subsequent examination is directed at revealing how the substantive justice theory was transplanted to IHRL and also became influential at the level of the international criminal tribunals (ICTs).[63] In that regard, this IHRL examination serves as a bridge between the previous Nuremberg analysis and the subsequent examination of the ICTs' case law. Another reason for including a discussion on the legality principle under IHRL is that Article 21(3) Rome Statute requires consistency of interpretation with internationally recognised human rights. Furthermore, the general interconnection of ICL and IHRL necessitates a human rights assessment.

The first IHRL instrument, including the legality principle, was the Universal Declaration on Human Rights (UDHR).[64] Article 11(2) holds:

> No one shall be held guilty of any penal offence on account of any act or omission which did not constitute a penal offence, under national or international law, at the time when it was committed . . .[65]

[61] Kelsen (n 32).

[62] Van Schaack (n 4) 122–23.

[63] S Darcy, 'The Principle of Legality at the Crossroads of Human Rights and International Criminal Law' in MM deGuzman and D Amman (eds), *Arcs of Global Justice, Essays in Honor of William A Schabas* (OUP, 2016): arguing that the cross-fertilization of the legality approach is noticeable among the ECtHR, the criminal tribunals and the ICC.

[64] Universal Declaration of Human Rights (adopted 10 December 1948 UNGA Res 217 A(III)).

[65] As the discussion on *nulla poena sine lege* is omitted, the second part of the provision is not included.

This provision is basically a prohibition of retroactive law and thereby installs non-retroactivity as the core of the principle of legality (*lex praevia*). This non-binding declaration was adopted shortly after the IMT judgment, and traces of the IMT experience appear in the provision.[66] The concern was that the legality principle would cast doubt on the legitimacy of Nuremberg.[67] As a result, the provision refers to criminalisation by both national and international law.[68] Furthermore, the *lex praevia* principle is not formulated to require written law and, in that sense, does not *a priori* oppose common law criminalisation or customary law crimes.[69] Recalling that at Nuremberg, the crimes against humanity category was argued to exist under customary law, it is quite understandable that customary law creation could not be opposed by the UDHR drafters.

Article 15 of the International Covenant on Civil and Political Rights (ICCPR)[70] mirrors the UDHR provision's first paragraph and adds a second paragraph:

> 2. Nothing in this article shall prejudice the trial and punishment of any person for any act or omission which, at the time when it was committed, was criminal according to the general principles of law recognized by the community of nations.

The principle of non-retroactivity was not the contentious issue. There was wide acceptance that a pre-existing law had to exist.[71] A more debated issue was what source of law fulfilled the *lex praevia* requirement. Some drafts demonstrated that apart from non-retroactivity, any source could fulfil this requirement.[72] This was in start contrast with civil law inspired proposals demanding statutory crimes.[73] The general position of the Human Rights Committee (HRC), the Covenant's treaty monitoring body, has been that 'the author's acts, at the material time of commission, constituted sufficiently defined criminal offences' under the national or international law. The legal basis is thus not strictly defined

[66] See on the drafters' positions: J Morsink, *The Universal Declaration of Human Rights: Origins, Drafting, and Intent* (Pennsylvania Studies In Human Rights, University of Pennsylvania Press, 1999) 52–58.

[67] ibid 54: 'Since these international trials were set up to combat the same horrors that led to the writing of the Declaration these delegations wanted to avoid creating even the appearance of conflict between the Nuremberg judgements and the Declaration. They therefore proposed to add the following paragraph: "Nothing in this Article shall prejudice the trial and punishment of any person for the commission of any act which, at the time it was committed, was criminal according to the general principles of law recognised by civilized nations"'.

[68] ibid 55: 'A subcommittee [. . .] was set up to decide the text of the article. That committee decided to drop the Nuremberg clause as a whole and to subsume that problem under the word "international," which it put into the text of this second paragraph'.

[69] For a more elaborate examination of the UDHR's legality principle see Gallant (n 3) 158ff.

[70] International Covenant on Civil and Political Rights (adopted 16 December 1966, entered into force 23 March 1976) 999 UNTS 171.

[71] Gallant (n 3) 160–75.

[72] See the example used by Gallant of the UK delegation not requiring a statute: ibid 166.

[73] See the example used by Gallant of the French Delegation requiring a statute: ibid 165.

and can be found in either national or international law.[74] The HRC at one point permitted a State Party 'to employ retroactive criminal statutes [. . .] when the acts were criminal according to the general principles of law recognized by the community of nations at the time when they were committed'.[75]

As stated, the second paragraph of Article 15 introduced a novelty not included in the UDHR,[76] and introduced criminalisation through 'the general principles of law recognized by the community of nations'. This phrase, called the Nuremberg Clause, was contentious partly because of the lack of clarity on what constituted a general principle.[77] Some found that this source of law, also referred to in articles 38 of the Statutes of the Permanent Court of International Justice and the International Court of Justice, should be understood broadly and referred to principles of natural law or 'objective justice'.[78] Others found this approach to be a dangerous free pass for judges and had a much narrower idea of source doctrine.[79] Moreover, some experts view the two paragraphs as one single principle of non-retroactivity, while others interpret the Nuremberg Clause as an exception to the general prohibition against retroactivity.[80]

The HRC had the opportunity to explain the Nuremberg Clause in the *Baumgarten case,* known as the German Border Guard case, but settled the issue mostly within the first paragraph in finding that GDR law had a sufficient legal basis to criminalise the killing of fleeing citizens through its provisions on homicide.[81] It thus remained unclear whether general principles were allowed as a source of criminalisation.[82] The HRC only indicated that it requires criminal offences to be sufficiently defined 'under the criminal law of the GDR or under international law'.[83]

[74] See, eg, *Baumgarten v Germany* (Communication No 960/2000) UN Doc CCPR/C/78/D/960/2000 (31 July 2003).

[75] *Concluding observations on the initial report of Montenegro* CCPR/C/MNE/CO/1 (21 November 2014).

[76] Gallant (n 3) 170–73.

[77] On the discussions and different positions see PM Taylor, *A Commentary on the International Covenant on Civil and Political Rights* (CUP 2020) 442; see RB Schlesinger, 'Research on the General Principles of Law Recognised by Civilized Nations' (1957) 51 *AJIL* 734.

[78] See, eg, Baron Descamps, the Belgian representative and president of the Advisory Committee of Jurists, was a known proponent of this broad conception of general principles. See on the drafting history and the different positions on the issue of general principle: Special Rapporteur M Vázquez-Bermúdez, *First report on general principles of law*, 2019) 25ff.

[79] See, eg, Lord Phillimore (United Kingdom) and Elihu Root (United States) were against Baron Descamps approach and viewed this as giving quasi-legislative power to the judge. See also ibid 25ff.

[80] T Rauter, *Judicial Practice, Customary International Law and Nullum Crimen Sine Lege* (Springer, 2017) 32–35.

[81] *Baumgarten v Germany* (n 74) paras 9.1–9.4; see also S Joseph and M Castan, *The International Covenant on Civil and Political Rights: Cases, Materials and Commentary*, 3rd edn (OUP, 2013) 529–32.

[82] A Baets, 'The United Nations Human Rights Committee's View of the Past' (2017) 8 Compare 29, 34.

[83] *Baumgarten v Germany* (n 74) para 9.3.

The other instruments with legality principle provisions are the regional human rights instruments.[84] Article 7 of the European Convention on Human Rights (ECHR),[85] Article 9 of the American Convention on Human Rights (ACHR),[86] and Article 7.2 of the African Charter of Human and Peoples' Rights (ACHPR) stipulate the legality principle.[87] After the adoption of the Rome Statute, the Charter of Fundamental Rights of the European Union was established, and the Arab Charter on Human Rights adopted, both incorporating a legality principle.[88] Given that the EU Charter holds a copy of the ECHR, and this book, found no evidence of the Arab Charter producing case law, these two Charters were excluded from this analysis. Instead, our focus is on the European Human Rights system.

The focus on the ECtHR is justified, even if it is perceived as Eurocentric, given the link between the ECHR's legality principle and its development at Nuremberg. On top of that, the cross-fertilisation between the ECtHR and

[84] There are also two declarations holding a legality principle: See Art 20(2) of the ASEAN Human Rights declaration (19 November 2012); Article XXV American Declaration of the Rights and Duties of Man (Adopted by the Ninth International Conference of American States, Bogotá, Colombia, 1948)

[85] Adopted in 1950, Art 7 of this instrument holds: 1. No one shall be held guilty of any criminal offence on account of any act or omission which did not constitute a criminal offence under national or international law at the time when it was committed. Nor shall a heavier penalty be imposed than the one that was applicable at the time the criminal offence was committed. 2. This Article shall not prejudice the trial and punishment of any person for any act or omission which, at the time when it was committed, was criminal according to the general principles of law recognised by civilised nations. See also the legality principle in Article 49 of the EU Charter on Fundamental Rights. See for further analysis: C Peristeridou, *The principle of legality in European criminal law* (Intersentia, 2015).

[86] Adopted in 1969, Art 9 of this instrument holds: No one shall be convicted of any act or omission that did not constitute a criminal offense, under the applicable law, at the time it was committed. A heavier penalty shall not be imposed than the one that was applicable at the time the criminal offense was committed. If subsequent to the commission of the offense the law provides for the imposition of a lighter punishment, the guilty person shall benefit therefrom. Note that also article 7 has a principle of non-retroactivity. See for further analysis: MM Rosique, 'The Principle of Legality in Criminal Law in the Inter-American System for the Protection of Human Rights' in MP Manzano, JAL Sánchez and MM Rosique (eds), *Multilevel Protection of the Principle of Legality in Criminal Law* (Springer, 2018).

[87] Adopted in 1981, Art 7.2 of this instrument holds: No one may be condemned for an act or omission which did not constitute a legally punishable offence at the time it was committed. No penalty may be inflicted for an offence for which no provision was made at the time it was committed. Punishment is personal and can be imposed only on the offender. See for further analysis: R Murray, *The African Charter on Human and Peoples' Rights: A Commentary* (OUP, 2019) 242ff.

[88] Adopted in 2004, Art 15 of the Revised Arab Charter holds: 'No crime and no penalty can be established without a prior provision of the law. In all circumstances, the law most favorable to the defendant shall be applied; Adopted in 2016, Art 49 of the Fundamental Charter holds: 1. No one shall be held guilty of any criminal offence on account of any act or omission which did not constitute a criminal offence under national law or international law at the time when it was committed. Nor shall a heavier penalty be imposed than the one that was applicable at the time the criminal offence was committed. If, subsequent to the commission of a criminal offence, the law provides for a lighter penalty, that shall be applicable. 2. This Article shall not prejudice the trial and punishment of any person for any act or omission which, at the time when it was committed, was criminal according to the general principles recognized by the community of nations.'

ICTs,[89] the fact that the ECtHR has been influential in the ICTs' case law, and has addressed the scope of this principle in relation to international crimes,[90] justify this focus.

The ECtHR's case law has to be understood taking into account its role as a human rights court. For instance, while it understandably allows certain elements to fall within the State's margin of appreciation, the absence of explicit rejection for a particular theory doesn't imply that it is the optimal choice from a human rights perspective. What is meant by this is that the ECtHR might not oppose a criminalisation by an unwritten source, as this is a choice the states have to make and falls within their competence.[91] The inquiry of the ECtHR is only marginal to the extent that it checks, *a posteriori*, whether a violation occurred. It does not set out the best option in terms of criminal policy. Hence, when the ECtHR neither finds a violation nor addresses an issue, it doesn't necessarily imply, from a criminal policy standpoint, that alternative state choices would not better ensure human rights.

In general terms, the ECtHR requires crimes to be *prescribed by law* and that this prescription is both *accessible* and *foreseeable*. From the beginning, the ECtHR evaluated whether the crime is defined by law by using the notions of foreseeability and accessibility.[92] Faced with diverse legal systems and affording states a margin of appreciation, the ECtHR has approached the definition of law without intruding on the national choice of source doctrine. The Court did not want to reject the common law crime creation.[93] Although Article 7 ECHR

[89] See for further analysis on cross-fertilization: T Mariniello and P Lobba, 'The Cross Fertilisation Rhetoric in Question: Use and Abuse of the European Court's Jurisprudence by International Criminal Tribunals' (2015) 84 *Nordic Journal of International Law* 363. The principle of legality is identified as one of the areas in which the influence of the ECtHR cannot be underestimated. See also T Mariniello, 'The "Nuremberg Clause" and Beyond: Legality Principle and Sources of International Criminal Law in the European Court's Jurisprudence' (2013) 82 *Nordic Journal of International Law* 221.

[90] For a critical voice on the issue: S Vasiliev, 'International Criminal Tribunals in the Shadow of Strasbourg and Politics of Cross-fertilisation' (2015) 84 *Nordic Journal of International Law* 371; See also WA Schabas, 'Synergy or Fragmentation?: International Criminal Law and the European Convention on Human Rights' (2011) 9 *JICJ* 609.

[91] See on the margin of appreciation: SC Greer, *The margin of appreciation: interpretation and discretion under the European Convention on Human Rights*, vol 17 (Human rights files, Council of Europe, 2000) 15–17.

[92] See these cases for the notions of foreseeability and accessibility: *Sunday Times v United Kingdom*, App no 6538/74 Judgment (27 April 1979) 14 EHRR 123, paras 46–53; *Cantoni v France*, App no 17862/91 (Judgment) (Grand Chamber) (15 November 1996) ECHR 52, para 29; *Jorgic v Germany*, App no 74613/01, Judgment (12 July 2007) paras 100–116; *Korbely v Hungary*, App no 9174/02, Judgment (Grand Chamber) (5 July 2007) ECHR 5554, paras 69–77; *Kafkaris v Cyprus*, App no 21906/04, Judgment (Grand Chamber) (12 February 2008) 49 EHRR 35, para 140; *Del Río Prada v Spain*, Application no 42750/09, Judgment (Grand Chamber) (21 October 2013) ECHR 1004, para 79; *Vasiliauskas v Lithuania*, App no 35343/05, Judgment (Grand Chamber) (20 October 2015) ECHR 923, paras 153–169.

[93] See, eg, *Norman v United Kingdom*, App no 41387/17, Judgment (6 July 2021) para 62: 'the common law nature of the offence [. . .] does not in itself give rise to any particular concerns under Article 7. The Court's case-law makes clear that Article 7 does not require a criminal offence to be placed on a statutory footing [. . .]. What is important is that, whatever the basis for the offence, the substantive guarantees of legal certainty are satisfied'.

makes no mention of foreseeability or accessibility, the concepts were used in order to identify what could be considered as 'prescribed by law'. The ECtHR developed the following approach:

> Firstly, the law must be adequately accessible: the citizen must be able to have an indication that is adequate in the circumstances of the legal rules applicable to a given case. Secondly, a norm cannot be regarded as a 'law' unless it is formulated with sufficient precision to enable the citizen to regulate his conduct: he must be able – if need be with appropriate advice – to foresee, to a degree that is reasonable in the circumstances, the consequences which a given action may entail. Those consequences need not be foreseeable with absolute certainty: experience shows this to be unattainable. Again, whilst certainty is highly desirable, it may bring in its train excessive rigidity and the law must be able to keep pace with changing circumstances. Accordingly, many laws are inevitably couched in terms which, to a greater or lesser extent, are vague and whose interpretation and application are questions of practice.[94]

The *German Border Guard cases* explain what it means that crimes must be prescribed by law. In the 1990s, after the unification of Germany, the *Bundesgerichtshof* was confronted with a series of cases concerning German Democratic Republic (GDR) border guards shooting people attempting to flee from East to West Germany. The border guards were under the explicit order to defend the border at all costs. A common practice was developed to shoot fleeing subjects, even when these were unarmed and posed no threat. These manifestly immoral deeds were punished after the unification of Germany, and this punishment was justified by relying on the *Radbruch formula* as described and explained in the introductory chapter. On the basis of this formula,[95] a statutory injustice (*gesetzliches Unrecht*), namely the law allowing for 'the intentional killing of persons who sought nothing more than to cross the intra-German border unarmed', had to be set aside. Given that this statute was considered invalid, the Court could prosecute the guards for violations of the right to life, as these were self-evidently a crime (murder) at the time when the acts were committed.[96] In a similar way to the *Grudge Informer Case*, the *Radbruch formula* made it possible to hold someone responsible who would otherwise be protected by the principle of non-retroactivity.

In the *Streletz, Kessler and Krenz* case, the ECtHR's Grand Chamber unanimously decided that the convictions of the border guards' superiors for incitement to murder were not a violation of the principle of legality. The majority opinion did not reflect on whether it was justified to use the *Radbruch formula*. The Grand Chamber only held that it was 'not for the Court to express

[94] ibid para 49.

[95] *Streletz, Kessler and Krenz v Germany*, App Nos 34044/96, 35532/97 and 44801/98, Judgment (Grand Chamber) (22 March 2001) 33 EHRR 31, para 22.

[96] The formula reads: 'Positive law must be considered contrary to justice where the contradiction between statute law and justice is so intolerable that the former must give way to the latter'; see also R Geiger, 'The German border guard cases and international human rights' (1998) 9 *EJIL* 540.

an opinion on these different approaches.'[97] The judges explained that the use of firearms on the basis of GDR law was only justified 'to prevent the imminent commission or continuation of an offence which appears in the circumstances to constitute a serious crime or in order to arrest a person strongly suspected of having committed a serious crime'.[98] Mere border crossing, in which no firearms or dangerous means were involved, did not qualify as a serious crime, as a result of which the shootings were not justified, and prosecution for these acts was not barred.[99]

Next, the Grand Chamber tackled the issue of whether state practice could be relied on as a way of justifying their conduct. It first acknowledged the existence of a practice 'to protect the State border at all costs'.[100] Given that the superiors were government officials, the court did not allow the defendants to rely on the order they had themselves given.[101] According 'to the general principles of law, defendants are not entitled to justify the conduct' simply by showing that it formed a practice.[102] The applicants could not claim unforeseeability in the prosecution, as the lack of prosecution for the lethal use of force was a state practice violating both domestic legislation and internationally recognised human rights. This judgment is evidence of the fact that preference was given to argue that the positive law allows for prosecution rather than to let justice pierce through the positive law veil.

When the ECtHR was confronted with another border shooting case, but this time by a 20-year-old border guard,[103] the Court found that the GDR law, and the right to life enshrined therein, was accessible, and he could have known the practice was in sharp contradiction with the GDR law. Furthermore, given his voluntary enrolment, he had acquiesced to this cruel practice. Although not unanimously, the Court found his conviction not to be in contradiction with the principle of non-retroactivity.[104]

Some of the ECtHR's case law on the principle of legality, and the former European Commission of Human Rights' (ECommHR) case law, are particularly interesting in the context of ICL because they deal with international crimes, beginning with the core crimes in the Nuremberg Charter and later expanding to others under the Nuremberg Clause. When confronted with the question whether the Nuremberg crimes were prescribed by law, often still being absent from national criminal law at the time of the occurrence of the facts, the EcommHR and ECtHR initially used the Nuremberg Clause

[97] *Streletz, Kessler and Krenz v Germany*, paras 65–66.
[98] ibid para 59 (citation marks omitted).
[99] ibid para 59 (citation marks omitted); See also J Arnold, N Karsten and H Kreicker, 'The German border guard cases before the European Court of Human Rights' (2003) 11 *Eur J Crime Cr L Cr J* 67.
[100] *Streletz, Kessler and Krenz v Germany*, para 69.
[101] ibid para 74.
[102] ibid para 74.
[103] *K-H W v Germany*, App no 37201/97 Judgment (Grand Chamber) (22 March 2001) ECHR 229.
[104] ibid paras 44–106.

to argue for criminalisation under general principles. Retroactivity could not be invoked as the criminalisation occurred through international law. In the *Touvier* case, the ECommHR held that the Nuremberg Clause means that Article 7 does not affect laws which were passed, 'in the wholly exceptional circumstances at the end of the Second World War'.[105] This clause was later also used in relation to international crimes not necessarily covered by the Nuremberg Charter.[106]

It is not until the *Kononov* case that the prescription of international crimes is assessed under Article 7(1).[107] The case concerned a Red Partisan unit attacking a village and killing men and women, one of whom was pregnant, in what they argued was a reprisal action against a group of villagers collaborating with the Nazi's.[108] In large parts, the decision revolved around the scope of civilian protection in 1944 according to IHL and whether or not the villagers, even when considered combatants, were at that time *hors combat* and thus deserving of protection.[109] If not covered by civilian protection, the second legal issue was whether these acts constituted a war crime or an ordinary crime. That qualification, in turn, would answer whether the crime was statute-barred. There is no need to go into every legal detail or interpretation. It suffices to explain why the ECtHR's Chamber and the Grand Chamber came to different conclusions.

The Chamber, in essence, found a violation of Article 7 because the Latvian Criminal Court had retroactively applied the principle of distinction in Article 50 of the Additional Protocol I to the Geneva Conventions[110] and wrongfully afforded civilian status to the villagers.[111] The killing of the villagers did not constitute a war crime, and 'it would thus be contrary to the principle of foreseeability to punish the applicant almost half a century after the expiry of that limitation period'.[112] This decision was criticised because it failed to make a distinction between retroactively applying the law and resorting to instruments enacted later in time in order to clarify and spell out a notion that already existed

[105] *Touvier v France*, App No 29420/95, Decision on the admissibility of the application (13 January 1997) 88-B Eur Comm'n HR Dec & Rep 148, 161.

[106] See, eg, *Kolk and Kislyiy v Estonia,* App Nos 23052/04 and 24018/04, Decision on Admissibility (17 January 2006) see also A Cassese, 'Balancing the Prosecution of Crimes against Humanity and Non-Retroactivity of Criminal Law' (2006) 4 *JICJ* 410 arguing that invoking the Nuremberg clause has its limits considering that peace time crimes against humanities were not criminalised under international law and not considered by the IMT, a point which was not addresses by the ECtHR.

[107] *Kononov v Latvia*, App no 36376/04, Judgment (24 July 2008); see also Van der Wilt (n 57) 519.

[108] See for a clear case summary and analysis: L Mälksoo, 'Kononov v. Latvia' (2011) 105 *AJIL* 101.

[109] WA Schabas, 'General Principles, Nullum Crimen and Accountability for International Crimes' in P Acconci and others (eds), *International Law and the Protection of Humanity, Essays in honour of Flavia Lattanzi* (Brill | Nijhoff, 2017) 500ff.

[110] Additional Protocol I of 8 June 1977 to the Geneva Conventions of 12 August 1949 and relating to the Protection of Victims of International Armed Conflicts.

[111] See for a more detailed analysis of the Chamber's decision: G Pinzauti, 'The European Court of Human Rights' Incidental Application of International Criminal Law and Humanitarian Law, A Critical Discussion of Kononov v. Latvia' (2008) 6 *JICJ* 1043.

[112] *Kononov Chamber Judgment* (n 107) para 146.

at the time when the facts occurred. The civilian protection already existed under the 1907 Hague Regulation[113] and therefore could have been used.[114]

The Grand Chamber argued the opposite of the Chamber and found a violation of the legality principle. It used the Hague Regulation as the source of criminalisation. Even when accepting that the villagers were combatants, they deserved protection since they were *hors combat*.[115] In relation to foreseeability, the Grand Chamber held that:

> having regard to the flagrantly unlawful nature of the ill-treatment and killing of the nine villagers in the established circumstances of the operation on 27 May 1944, even the most cursory reflection by the applicant, would have indicated that, at the very least, the impugned acts risked being counter to the laws and customs of war as understood at that time and, notably, risked constituting war crimes for which, as commander, he could be held individually and criminally accountable.[116]

Given that Kononov was a commander, the Grand Chamber concluded that he 'must have been aware' that his actions would result in criminal liability. '[I]t was clearly objectively foreseeable in 1944 that the applicant's acts were criminal and it was unnecessary to show that he was aware of each element of the precise legal qualification of his acts'.[117]

As the many separate opinions – a joint concurring opinion of four judges, and the dissenting opinion of one judge, joined by two other judges – demonstrated, this case was controversial and far from easy.[118] That is why the language of the Grand Chamber that the conduct was 'flagrantly unlawful' is difficult to swallow. Although one can argue about whether or not the conduct was lawful, whether or not civilian protection covered the villagers, to argue that this issue was straightforward is questionable.

The Grand Chamber acknowledged that the Nuremberg Clause was drafted 'to eliminate any doubt about the validity of the post-Second World War prosecutions by the IMTs' and 'universal validity of the IMTs and their principles'.[119] It nonetheless did not operationalise Article 7(2) as an exception but rather, as the use of the standard of foreseeability demonstrates, treated it as part of the principle. It is regrettable that the Grand Chamber saw this foreseeability standard so easily fulfilled. Many commentators now seem to be of the opinion that Nuremberg was retroactive and not merely declaratory of custom, as a result of which arguing for foreseeability in 1944 is a position not easily defendable.[120]

[113] Hague Convention (IV) respecting the Laws and Customs of War on Land: Regulations concerning the Laws and Customs of War on Land (18 October 1907).

[114] Pinzauti (n 111) 1054.

[115] *Kononov v Latvia*, App no 36376/04, Judgment (Grand Chamber) (17 May 2010) para 216.

[116] ibid para 236.

[117] ibid para 158.

[118] Van der Wilt (n 57) 525.

[119] *Kononov Grand Chamber Judgment* (n 115) para 159.

[120] *Kononov v Latvia*, App no 36376/04, Dissenting Opinion of Judge Costa joined by Judges Kalaydjieva and Poalelungi (17 May 2010); *Kononov v Latvia*, App no 36376/04, Concurring Opinion of Judge Myjer (24 July 2008); see Schabas (n 90); See as discussed by Milanovic (n 48).

The ECtHR's case law has now developed the foreseeability test, which in the context of this book, is more important than the accessibility standard, in relation to crimes exclusively based on international treaty law[121] and/or customary international law.[122] The prime reason is that the ICTs have taken this standard and imported it into their case law.[123] The evaluation of the foreseeability of a law is made dependent upon whether or not one can reasonably know that the conduct is criminalised. This standard is not as strict as to require a law prescribing everything neatly. It might be needed for one to seek legal advice or explanation through judicial interpretation.[124]

Since the beginning, the ECtHR has adopted qualitative requirements to test the foreseeability of a criminal provision. In large part, the ECtHR has opted for a subjective interpretation of the legality principle and assessed primarily from the perspective of the accused whether the acts were foreseeably criminalised. Concerns of crime provisions being strictly construed and the necessity of having interpretations in favour of the accused emerged, but have not yet been fully embraced by the ECtHR. The ECtHR does not require that the label of the offence be foreseeable. To date, the principle of fair labelling, explicitly recognising the requirement for legal categorisation or labels to be foreseeable, has not been acknowledged within the context of legality. It could, however, be argued that the label given to a certain conduct becomes relevant when considering the position of victims. Victims have become central to human rights thinking, an evolution that has been documented by a number of authors.[125] Furthermore, these victims have not only been provided a set of procedural rights in a criminal law context, but a doctrine has developed towards granting substantive rights as well.[126] IHRL has recognised that victims have the right to have a crime committed against them investigated, prosecuted and punished.[127]

Absent from the above analysis is the issue of the extent to which an extensive interpretation can give rise to legality concerns. The field of human rights law has generally supported broad interpretative methods such as the purposive

[121] *Streletz, Kessler and Krenz v Germany* paras 90-106; *Jorgic v Germany* para 106

[122] *Van Anraat v the Netherlands* App no 65389/09, Admissibility Decision (6 July 2010) para 92.

[123] Van der Wilt (n 57): also focusing more on the notion of foreseeability and assessing the evaluative concept in relation to international crimes.

[124] *Kafkaris v Cyprus* para 141.

[125] See, eg, CM Bassiouni, 'International Recognition of Victims' Rights' (2006) 6 *HRLRev* 203.

[126] M Pinto, *Historical Trends of Human Rights Gone Criminal* (2020) providing insights into this evolution; and as critically assessed in relation to ICL: BM Leyh, *Procedural justice? Victim Participation in International Criminal Proceedings* (Intersentia, 2011)

[127] The IACtHR has a very broad take on this and has held that 'States must prevent, investigate and punish any violation of the rights recognised by the Convention' (see: *Case of Velasquez Rodriguez v Honduras* (Judgment) Inter-American Court of Human Rights Series C No 4 (29 July 1988) para 166), the ECtHR has a slightly narrower understanding of positive obligations and although it recognised the duty to investigate and prosecute (see *Rantsev v Cyprus and Russia*, App no 25965/04, Judgment (7 January 2010) paras 232–247), it has not fully underscored the duty to punish. See also A Mowbray, *The Development of Positive Obligations under the European Convention on Human Rights by the European Court of Human Rights* (Hart Publishing, 2004).

or teleological approach.[128] When the source of the criminal prohibition is identified, and there is an applicable law prohibiting certain conduct, can there still be a foreseeability problem given the broadness of a judicial interpretation? A question raised in relation hereto is what discretion is given to the judge to interpret and clarify the crime. The ECtHR standard approach has been that the requirement of an offence being defined in the law is fulfilled 'where the individual can know from the wording of the relevant provision and, if need be, with the assistance of the courts' interpretation of it, what acts and omissions will make him criminally liable'.[129]

This issue came up in the *Jorgic* case. The case revolved around the interpretation of genocide by the German Courts, which found that genocide encompassed 'destroying the group in question as a social unit'.[130] Building on previous case law, the court held that the legality principle goes beyond the prohibition of *ex post facto,* considering that the law 'must not be extensively construed to the detriment of an accused'.[131] The ECtHR stressed the role of courts 'in the gradual clarification of the rules of criminal liability, provided that the development is consistent with the essence of the offence and could reasonably be foreseen'.[132] It found the widening of genocidal intent with an aim to destroy a social unit rather than aim for its physical or biological destruction, to be a permissible clarification.[133]

Particularly interesting about this case for the purpose of this study is that the ECtHR's judgment goes completely against the ICTY interpretation, limiting the definition of genocide to those acts seeking physical or biological destruction.[134] It is acknowledged without any hesitation that many authorities have given a narrower interpretation,[135] but the ECtHR found the broader interpretation to be 'consistent with the essence of the offence' and reasonably foreseeable.[136] The ECtHR thereby revealed that no method of interpretation is *a priori* dismissed. Extensively construing a crime is not considered to be to the detriment of the accused when it remains foreseeable.

V. THE AD HOC TRIBUNALS' RELAXED STANDARD OF LEGALITY

For understanding the legality principle, the next relevant fora are the Ad Hoc tribunals.[137] This section's examination of a selection of cases reveals that certain

[128] *Svinarenko and Slyadnev v Russia*, App nos 32541/08 and 43441/08, Judgment (Grand Chamber) (17 July 2014) para 118.

[129] *Veeber v Estonia* Appl no 45771/99, Judgment, (21 January 2003) para 31; *K-H W v Germany* para 85.

[130] *Jorgic v Germany* para 104.

[131] ibid para 100.

[132] ibid para 101.

[133] ibid para 101.

[134] ibid para 112; see, eg, *Prosecutor v Krstic* (Judgment) IT-98-33-T (2 Augustus 2001).

[135] ibid para 113.

[136] ibid para 114.

[137] See, eg, N Arajärvi, 'Between Lex Lata and Lex Ferenda. Customary International (Criminal) Law and the Principle of Legality' (2010–2011) 15 *Tilburg Law Review* 163.

theories developed at the ECtHR influenced the ICT judges in their approach to crime interpretation and subsequently inspired the ICC's legality approach.

From the onset, the creators of the tribunals were concerned with challenges of retroactivity that could potentially undermine their efforts to bring perpetrators to justice. Identical to the concerns at Nuremberg, the Statutes' drafters were confronted with a legislative exercise after the facts.[138] Also identical is that the tribunals had no statutory principle of legality.[139] Consequently, the core issue of this legality discussion centred around the applicable law.[140] The drafters wanted to avoid judges making law, and so the consensus was pre-existing legal basis had to be found in custom.

Both the ICTY and the ICTR responded to this issue differently. The ICTY adopted a narrower approach and stated that 'the principle *nullum crimen sine lege* requires that the international tribunal should apply rules of international humanitarian law which are beyond any doubt part of customary law'.[141] The ICTR had a broader subject-matter jurisdiction in the sense that customary law more generally could be relied on.[142] Both approaches clearly did away with the principle of *lex scripta,* as specifically custom, an unwritten source, is specified as the applicable law.[143] Given the often indeterminate nature of custom, the legality issues logically ensued.[144]

At first sight, the ICTY's subject-matter jurisdiction of customary law had to be firmly established and introduced a high standard for the construction of custom.[145] Aräjarvi indicated, however, that multiple views on the construction of custom were articulated at the ICTY.[146] Some judges underscored the traditional formula of customary construction relying on state practice and *opinio juris*.[147] But even in relation to this well-established standard, conflicting views

[138] Taking note of the fact that both tribunals were established by Security council resolutions: UNSC Res 808 (1993) UN Doc S/Res/808; UNSC Res 955 (1995) UN Doc S/RES/955.

[139] See also Gallant (n 3) 304ff.

[140] As was even recognised in the case law: *Prosecutor v Rutaganda* (Judgment and Sentence) ICTR-96-3-T (6 December 1999) para 86.

[141] Report of the Secretary-General pursuant to Paragraph 2 of Security Council Resolution 808 (1993), 3 May 1993, S/25704, para 34.

[142] Some have stated however that custom played a less impactful role in the ICTRs case law: T Meron, 'Revival of Customary Humanitarian Law' (2005) 99 *AJIL* 817; See also T Hoffmann, 'The Gentle Civilizer of Humanitarian Law' in C Stahn and L van den Herik (eds), *Future Perspectives on International Criminal Justice* (TMC Asser Press, 2010) 67.

[143] S Lamb, '*Nullum crimen, nulla poena sine lege* in International Criminal Law' in Cassese, Gaeta and Jones (n 48) 741.

[144] J d'Aspremont, *Formalism and the Sources of International Law, A Theory of the Ascertainment of Legal Rules* (OUP, 2011) 162ff.

[145] M Swart, 'Judicial Lawmaking at the ad hoc Tribunals: The Creative Use of the Sources of International Law and "Adventurous Interpretation"' (2010) *ZaöRV* 461.

[146] N Arajärvi, *The changing nature of customary international law: methods of interpreting the concept of custom in international criminal tribunals* (Routledge, 2014) 1; see also Swart (n 145) 461.

[147] See, eg, *Prosecutor v Hadzihasanovic* (Decision on Interlocutory Appeal Challenging Jurisdiction in Relation to Command Responsibility) IT-01-47-AR72 (16 July 2003) para 12.

existed on the weight given to *opinio juris*,[148] or on 'how much practice is needed to make a custom'.[149] In this context, it was held that the Rome Statute was 'an authoritative expression of the legal views of a great number of States'.[150] Other decisions used nothing of the traditional vocabulary of customary formation.[151] At other times, custom was very loosely established. For example, the theory of joint criminal enterprise liability (JCE) was established without a clear Nuremberg precedent and was underscored by a liberal understanding of custom.[152]

The tension between custom, a source not so easily grasped through formal ascertainment of rules and potentially unspecified and dynamic in nature, and the legality principle, which requires certainty rather than flexibility, became clear. This tension is further illustrated by discussing the ICTY case law in relation to the definition of rape. The choice for focusing on this example is motivated by the fact that sexual violence is the focus of the second case study.

The *Furundžija* Trial Chamber had to decide whether rape encompassed acts of oral penetration or whether these acts should be classified as sexual assault, the less grave crime. The Chamber analysed whether there was a customary basis for enlarging the *actus reus* of the crime of rape. To 'arrive at an accurate definition of rape based on the criminal law principle of specificity', the Chamber found it 'necessary to look for principles of criminal law common to the major legal systems of the world'.[153] National laws showed differences; some countries qualify it as rape, while other national jurisdictions only qualify it as sexual assault. The divergence in national law was solved by relying on broad general principles of human dignity, which were found not to encroach upon legality.[154] The Chamber reasoned that 'since forcible oral sex is in any event a crime, and indeed an extremely serious crime,' the difference between these two qualifications can be resolved through sentencing.[155]

[148] *Prosecutor v Kupreškić et al* (Trial Judgment) IT 95-16 (14 January 2000) para 527: 'This is however an area where *opinio juris sive necessitatis* may play a much greater role than *usus*, as a result of the [. . .] Martens Clause. [It] may emerge through a customary process under the pressure of the demands of humanity or the dictates of public conscience, even where State practice is scant or inconsistent. The other element, [. . .] *opinio necessitatis*, crystallising as a result of the imperatives of humanity or public conscience, may turn out to be the decisive element heralding the emergence of a general rule [. . .]'.

[149] L Gradoni, *Nullum Crimen Sine Consuetudine: A Few Observations on How the International Criminal Tribunal for the Former Yugoslavia Has Been Identifying Custom* (2004) 4.

[150] *Prosecutor v Furundžija* (Judgment) IT-95-17/1 (10 December 1998) para 227.

[151] See: AS Galand, 'Approaching Custom Identification as a Conflict Avoidance Technique: Tadić and Kupreškić Revisited' (2018) 31 *LJIL* 403.

[152] L van den Herik, 'Using Custom to Reconceptualize Crimes Against Humanity' in S Darcy and J Powderly (eds), *Judicial Creativity: The International Criminal Tribunals* (OUP, 2010): explaining the role of the Presiding Judge Cassese in the *Kupreškić* Trial Judgment adopting a looser standard of state practice. See also N Arajärvi, 'The Role of the International Criminal Judge in the Formation of Customary International Law' (2007) 1 *European Journal of Legal Studies* 1.

[153] *Furundžija* para 177.

[154] Rauter (n 80) 61.

[155] *Furundžija* para 177.

From this reasoning, two points can be taken. The first point is that the Chamber connected the retroactivity to the criminality of an act and not to the label. The difference between sexual assault as a crime under national law and rape as a crime against humanity had to be counterweighed entirely by sentencing. This is quite a questionable jump, and whether this label is a fair representation of the wrongfulness of the act might be open to critique.[156] The second point is that the Chamber's take on the applicable law is so broad that defending this position from a legality perspective becomes difficult. Although not much is specified on how to arrive at a customary status – there is no reference to state practice or *opinio juris* – the reliance on general principles seemed to be motivated by a lack of conformity in state practice. Also, the notion of 'general principle of respect for human dignity' is a very broad conception, which makes the expansion of the *actus reus* even weaker.[157]

In the *Furundžija case*, there are no signs of the ICTY considering the ECtHR standards of foreseeability and accessibility. Only in later cases did the Tribunal rely on those standards when considering a customary legal basis.[158] The judges held that 'if customary international law does not provide for a sufficiently precise definition of a crime listed in the Statute, the Trial Chamber would have no choice but to refrain from exercising its jurisdiction over it, regardless of the fact that the crime is listed [. . .] in the Statute.'[159]

At the Tribunals, the first hints of a discussion on whether all interpretative methods are suitable in terms of the legality principle also arose. For example, in the *Čelebići* case, the analysis of the legality principle was quite extensive.[160] The Chamber addressed the analysis of the construction of criminal statutes, separately from the general aids of interpretation,[161] suggesting that criminal statutes, even of an international character, require different methods of interpretation. It also reflected on what the mixed civil and common law heritage means for the methods of interpretation. In time, a diversity in approaches appeared in relation to (1) the purposive approach; (2) the *in dubio pro reo* principle; and (3) the ban on analogy.

In discussing the teleological approach, the ICTY Trial Chamber explained that the common law understanding of the principle is to look into a legislative historical approach,[162] whereas the civil law approach attaches

[156] See also N Hayes, 'Creating a Definition of Rape in International Law: The Contribution of the International Criminal Tribunals' in S Darcy and J Powderly (eds), *Judicial Creativity at the International Criminal Tribunals* (2010) 149–50; D Akande, 'Sources of International Criminal Law' in A Cassese (ed), *Oxford Companion to International Criminal Justice* (OUP, 2005) 52.

[157] Van Schaack (n 4) 166–67.

[158] *Prosecutor v Vasiljevic* (Judgment) IT-98-32-T (29 November 2002) para 193.

[159] ibid para 202.

[160] *Prosecutor v Delalic et al (Čelebići case)* (Appeals Judgment) IT-96-21-A (20 February 2001) para 402.

[161] ibid paras 402–18; paras 158–71.

[162] *Čelebići case* para 164.

greater weight to the progressive and gap-filling function of this approach.[163] Unfortunately, the Chamber did not explain the teleological approach under international law.[164] In answering what weight should be given to it, the Chamber concluded that the interpretation must 'take into consideration the objects of the Statute and the social and political considerations which gave rise to its creation'. It held that '[t]he international community can only come to grips with the hydra-headed elusiveness of human conduct through a reasonable as well as a purposive interpretation of [. . .] customary law'.[165] The Chamber specified that it is for the legislature and not the judge to define a crime.[166] It continued 'that the language of a particular provision shall be construed' to only include conduct which fits 'within the reasonable meaning of its terms and within the spirit and scope of the enactment'.[167] The conduct should 'comprise all the elements which, whether morally material or not, are in fact made to constitute the offence as defined by the statute'.[168] Accidental legislative omissions should be rectified by ascertaining the legislative intent. The Chamber concluded by holding that 'strict construction is not violated by giving the expression its full meaning or the alternative meaning which is more consonant with the legislative intent.'[169] This excerpt clarifies that strict construction is not irreconcilable with a purposive approach. Although stricter positions on legality existed,[170] '[l]awmaking under the guise of purposive interpretation' became a common practice at the ICTY.[171] A known example of this approach is the definition of protected persons in the *Tadic* case.[172] Also, ICTR judges used purposive approaches to substantiate broad crime interpretations and embraced the notion of progressive development through judicial interpretation.[173]

The principle of *in dubio pro reo* was, for the first time, accepted as a true interpretative principle in the *Akayesu case*. The judges held that the understanding of killing and *meurtre*, pursuant to the presumption of innocence of

[163] ibid para 165.

[164] The Chamber does refer to article 31 VCLT and stipulates that it is established jurisprudence to rely on the VCLT in para 1161. It does however not reiterate its position on the purposive approach.

[165] ibid para 170.

[166] *Prosecutor v Delalic et al (Čelebići Case)* (Trial Chamber Judgment) IT-96-21-T (16 November 1998) para 408.

[167] ibid para 410.

[168] ibid para 411.

[169] ibid para 412.

[170] *Prosecutor v Milutinovic et al* (Decision on Dragoljub Ojdanic's motion challenging jurisdiction -joint criminal enterprise) IT-99-37-AR72 (21 May 2003) para 42.

[171] Swart (n 145) 484; see also Kreß (n 22) para 31.

[172] *Prosecutor v Tadić* para. 168; see also WA Schabas, 'Interpreting the Statutes of the Ad Hoc Tribunals' in Lal Chand Vohran and others (eds), *Man's Inhumanity to Man: Essays on International Law in Honour of Antonio Cassese* (Brill-Nijhoff, 2003).

[173] *Prosecutor v Akayesu* (Trial Chamber Judgment) ICTR-96-4-T (2 September 1998) para 575; *Milutinovic et al* para 38; see also M Shahabuddeen, 'Does the Principle of Legality Stand in the Way of Progressive Development of Law' (2004) 2 *J Int'l Crim Just* 1007.

the accused, and pursuant to the general principles of criminal law, required the Chamber to uphold the version more favourable to the accused.[174] The *Stakic case* produced evidence of the opposite viewpoint: the ICTY Trial Chamber held that the principle is not 'a principle for the interpretation of the substantive criminal law' and is only 'applicable to findings of fact and not of law'.[175] It is true that the idea of an ambiguity being solved in favour of the accused has mostly been applied in relation to evidence.[176] As a corollary principle to the presumption of innocence, it primarily has a procedural relevance. Whether it also applies to matters of substantive law remained a point of disagreement.[177] In some cases, the *in dubio pro reo* reasoning in relation to substantive law was embraced as part of the principle of strict construction: 'where an equivocal word or ambiguous sentence leaves a reasonable doubt of its meaning which the canons of construction fail to solve, the benefit of the doubt should be given to the subject and against the legislature which has failed to explain itself'.[178] This was the prime reason 'why ambiguous criminal statutes are to be construed *contra proferentem*'.[179]

Reasoning by analogy is a method of interpretation whereby conduct that is not *strictu senso* encompassed under a criminal provision is argued to fall under it because of its resemblance to the prohibited conduct.[180] It extends the scope of the statute to similar conduct, and in civil law systems is generally limited as strict construction requires the inclusion of only acts strictly covered by a provision.[181] Some of the tribunals' decisions do not consider it necessary to ban all analogy in light of the legality principle.[182] Further supported by the fact that not all national systems know a strict prohibition against analogy, some judges found that such a principle does not exist in ICL. The extension of war crime provisions applicable in IACs to NIACs is a known example of the use of analogy in the ICTY, which, although it evidently entailed an expansion of a substantive crime definition, was not found contrary to legality.[183] Another form of analogy exists in the *ejusdem generis* canon, which means 'things of the same kind'. On the basis of this canon, the judge considers acts analogous to the one

[174] *Akayesu* paras 500–501.

[175] *Prosecutor v Stakic* (Trial Chamber Judgment) IT-97-24-T (31 July 2003) para 416; *Prosecutor v Limaj et al* (Partially Dissenting and Separate Opinion and Declaration of Judge Schomburg to the Appeals Chamber Judgment) IT-03-66-A (17 September 2007) paras 15–20.

[176] D Robinson, 'The Identity Crisis of International Criminal Law' (2008) 21 *LJIL* 925, fn 37.

[177] *Prosecutor v Limaj et al* (Declarations of Judge Shahabuddeen to Appeals Chamber Judgment) IT-03-66-A (17 September 2007) para 2.

[178] *Čelebići Case* para 413.

[179] ibid para 413.

[180] Gallant (n 3) 36–37.

[181] K Langenbucher, 'Argument by Analogy in European Law' (1998) 57 The *CLJ* 481, 481.

[182] See on this issue: Broomhall (n 13) 961–62.

[183] *Prosecutor v Tadić* (Decision on the Defence Motion for Interlocutory Appeal on Jurisdiction) IT-94-1 (2 October 1995) para 199.

described in the provision.[184] The crime category of 'other inhumane acts', which was included in the ICTY, ICTR and SCSL Statutes, has been understood as an *ejusdem generis* provision requiring the judge to assess whether the conduct is of a similar gravity or seriousness.[185] When answered affirmatively, the judge may include the conduct that is analogously grave to the other listed crimes against humanity. One of the most well-known examples of the residual crime category being interpreted is the *Tadic* case. The Trial Chamber had to decide whether the mutilation of a corpse with a fire extinguisher could be qualified as another inhumane act. A corpse could not be qualified as 'a thing of the same kind', and as a result, this act was not included as another inhumane act.[186]

In conclusion, allowing these broad methods of interpretations fitted within the ICTY's 'relaxed attitude' towards legality, a position that became untenable at the ICC.[187]

VI. THE ROME STATUTE'S COMPLEX LEGALITY PRINCIPLE

This section discusses the Rome Statute's developments on the principle of legality by following a chronological approach, tracing the influence of the tribunals' advancements running through the attempts at establishing an international criminal court.

In 1994, the Draft Statute of the International Law Commission (ILC) formulated a legality principle as a prohibition against retroactive law.[188] It, furthermore, presented a two-pronged applicable law provision differentiating between, on the one hand, crimes under general international law – notably genocide, aggression, serious violations of the laws and customs applicable in armed conflict and crimes against humanity – and on the other hand, other treaty crimes. In relation to the first set of crimes, it was deemed unnecessary to confer jurisdiction by more than a mere reference. The Statute was merely an 'adjectival and procedural instrument', not having the 'function to define new crimes'.[189] Of course, the ILC recognised that this approach carried more risk in relation to some crimes, having,

[184] *Black's Law Dictionary*, 8th edn (2004): 'A canon of construction that when a general word or phrase follows a list of specifics, the general word or phrase will be interpreted to include only items of the same type as those listed. For example, in the phrase horses, cattle, sheep, pigs, goats, or any other farm animal, the general language or any other farm animal [. . .] would probably be held to include only four-legged, hoofed mammals typically found on farms, and thus would exclude chickens.'

[185] See, eg, on this category of crimes: *Prosecutor v Rutaganda* para 77.

[186] *Prosecutor v Tadić* (Opinion and Judgment) IT-94-1-T (7 May 1997) para 748; see also Broomhall (n 13) 961.

[187] WA Schabas, 'Commentary on Judgment, Prosecutor v Furundžija' in André Klip and Göran Sluiter (eds), *Annotated Leading Cases of International Criminal Tribunals, Vol III, The International Criminal Tribunal for the Former Yugoslavia, 1997–1999* (Intersentia, 2001) 753–57.

[188] Art 39 of the Draft Statute for an International Criminal Court with Commentaries (YBILC 1994, Vol II, Part 2).

[189] ibid 38.

for example, the lack of definition for the crime of aggression in mind, than in relation to other crimes, such as genocide as defined in the Genocide Convention. In relation to crimes against humanity, the report explicitly recognised that there were unresolved definitional issues, as a result of which it was doubted whether a mere reference to this category would be sufficient in clarifying which crimes could be tried as international crimes.[190] These concerns certainly motivated a change in attitude, as was also concluded by Broomhall, and resulted in thinking more about delineating the jurisdiction of the court.[191]

In 1996, delegates in the Ad Hoc Committee discussed concerns about specifying crimes, considering various approaches such as incorporating treaty provisions or using existing statutes. There was a shared aim to balance flexibility and certainty, emphasising the need for clear, precise definitions aligned with the principle of legality. However, the exact scope of the principle of legality remained unspecified at that time.

By 1997, the approach started to change. Contrary to what had been done before, it was now considered necessary to separate the provisions on jurisdiction *ratione temporis* from the idea of non-retroactivity. Second, the provision on non-retroactivity, now renamed Article A, was structured differently.[192] At the level of content, the principle of retroactivity underwent no substantial changes.[193] The text transmitted in 1998 by the Drafting Committee to the Committee of the Whole still formulated a principle of non-retroactivity as follows:

> Article 22
>
> Non-retroactivity
>
> 1. No person shall be criminally responsible under this Statute for conduct prior to the entry into force of the Statute.
> 2. In the event of a change in the law applicable to a given case prior to a final judgment, the law more favourable to the person being investigated, prosecuted or convicted shall apply.[194]

It was not until the Rome Conference that another shift occurred in relation to this principle.

[190] ibid 38–40: see also Art 20 setting out the crimes under the jurisdiction of the Court.

[191] Broomhall (n 13) 950–51.

[192] Preparatory Committee, Decisions taken by the Preparatory Committee (Sessions from 11 to 21 February 1997) A/AC.249/1997/L.5 (1997) Art A (Nullum crimen) and A bis (Jurisdiction ratione temporis)

[193] See the Zutphen Draft (Report of the Inter-Sessional Meeting from 19 to 30 January 1998 in Zutphen, the Netherlands) A/AC.249/1998/L.13 (1998) and the Preparatory Committee, Draft Statute for the International Criminal Court (Part 1 of the Addendum to the Report of the Preparatory Committee on the Establishment of an International Criminal Court) A/CONF.183/2/Add.1 (1998). See also C Bassiouni and WA Schabas, *The legislative history of the international criminal court*, vol 2 (International Criminal Law Series, Brill, 2016) 244–45.

[194] Preparatory Committee, Draft Statute for the International Criminal Court (Part 1 of the Addendum to the Report of the Preparatory Committee on the Establishment of an International Criminal Court) A/CONF.183/2/Add.1 (1998). See for an overview of the different drafts on legality: Bassiouni and Schabas (n 193) 236–43.

The Rome Conference brought more substantial changes to the legality principle. As is quite clear from this chapter's historical account, there was no longer anything contentious about the principle of non-retroactivity, and its inclusion into Article 22(1) was rather unproblematic.[195] The novelty is found in Article 22(2) that, with the introduction of a second paragraph, specifies three principles of interpretation.

In a report of the Preparatory Committee, the first traces of this novelty can be found in a footnoted comment to the applicable law provision, which by then already included a reference to the interpretation having to be consistent with internationally recognised human rights. The view was that the *nullum crimen sine lege* principle, as a human right, should be more explicitly stated, and a suggestion was made to reformulate it as follows: 'The provisions of article 5 shall be strictly construed and shall not be extended by analogy to, or be interpreted to proscribe, conduct not clearly criminal under it.'[196] Two of the three new interpretative principles are introduced: the principle of strict construction and the prohibition on analogy. The issue was taken up again by the Working Group on General Principles of Criminal Law, which agreed upon a paragraph that resembles the current provision.[197] Some technical changes were implemented, which eventually resulted in Article 22 in its final form being concluded upon. The second paragraph of Article 22 now reads:

> The definition of a crime shall be strictly construed and shall not be extended by analogy. In case of ambiguity, the definition shall be interpreted in favour of the person being investigated, prosecuted or convicted.[198]

This constitutes an essential turning point as Article 22 no longer only reflected the traditional principle on non-retroactivity but articulated three interpretative principles: (1) the principle of strict construction; (2) the prohibition against analogy and (3) the *in dubio pro reo* principle. This can also be pinpointed as the moment in which the principle, as later incorporated into the Rome Statute, departed from its traditional understanding in international law.[199]

Not every articulation of the legality principle embraces the principle of strict construction and requires that there be a *lex stricta*. The drafting history only reveals that the principle was introduced with a view to limiting judicial discretion. No exact boundaries were agreed upon. Furthermore, the national counterparts do not offer a fixed solution, and also at the international level,

[195] P Saland, 'Chapter 7 International Criminal Law Principles' in RS Lee (ed), *The International Criminal Court: the making of the Rome Statute: issues, negotiations, results* (Kluwer Law International, 1999) 194–95.

[196] Preparatory Committee, Report of the Preparatory Committee on the Establishment of an International Criminal Court, A/CONF.183/2/Add.1 (14 April 1998) fn 61.

[197] Preparatory Committee, Report of the Working group on General Principles of Criminal Law, A/CONF.183/C.1/WGGP/L.4 (18 June 1998): 'The definition of a crime shall be strictly construed and shall not be extended by analogy. In case of ambiguity, it shall be interpreted in favour of the person being investigated or prosecuted'.

[198] Note that there is a third paragraph to this article which is of lesser importance to this study.

[199] Broomhall (n 13) 953–54.

the rule is so 'variously and unpredictably' invoked.[200] The principle is 'so often conflated with inconsistencies, that it is hard to discern widespread adherence to any general policy of statutory construction'.[201] Despite the lack of guidance of the statutory works and the principle's unsettled scope, the principle, in any event, must be understood as opposing extensive interpretation. The structure of Article 22(2) further clarifies that, whereas the *in dubio pro reo* principle is triggered by the existence of an ambiguity, the principle of strict construction requires no such trigger. Contrary to what some of the ICTY decisions might have suggested, the principle of strict construction functions independently. What can be settled is that the strict construction entails an examination of the methods of interpretation and has made the principle of legality mature into a true principle of interpretation.

Whereas the principle of strict construction opposes an extensive interpretation of a provision, the prohibition against interpretation by analogy restricts the interpretation of a case not regulated by the Statute is interpreted through the application of a Statute which, strictly speaking, was not designed to be applied to the case at hand.[202] The two notions are very closely related and, in most cases, an analogical interpretation will violate the principle of strict construction.[203] Some authors find analogy a valuable tool in interpretation and do not bar all forms of analogical reasoning.[204] Even the express statutory inclusion of the prohibition does not lead these authors to exclude analogy.[205] It is argued that, similar to the principle of strict construction, this interpretative technique is useful to encompass conduct which, although not expressly covered by the Statute, was nevertheless intended to be included by the drafters. This justification makes noticeable a tension between adhering to the prohibition of analogy and invoking legislative intention as a basis for an extension of a crime definition.

The extension by analogy engages the concept of resemblance, and in that context, it is interesting to note that while interpretation by analogy is forbidden, the Rome Statute is not free from analogical reasoning. The question thus remains whether anything has changed with the express inclusion of the prohibition in the statute or whether analogy is still possible. It is key that the use of analogical reasoning is handled with care. This means that extension of a crime definition by analogy violates the principle of legality when extending the listed crime to more than what a textual analysis allows for.

Another novelty incorporated into the Rome Statute is the principle of *in dubio pro reo*. Sometimes, the principle is referred to as interpretation *contra proferentem*, a concept that has been transplanted from contract law and means

[200] Ashworth and Horder (n 3) 67–69.
[201] ibid 67–69.
[202] Gallant (n 3), 36; see also H Silving, 'Analogy and Extensive Interpretation' (1967) 36, 311.
[203] Broomhall (n 13) 961.
[204] P Cugat, *Les crimes contre l'humanité dans le statut de la Cour internationale* (Schulthess, 2006) 152–53.
[205] Broomhall (n 13) 961–62.

that a contractual obligation has to be explained in favour of the one bound by the obligation.[206] Others link the origin of the principle to 'the presumption of common law judges in *favorem vitae,* used to ameliorate the effect of statutes requiring the death penalty'.[207] The national counterparts of the principle differ greatly, and so it is impossible to draw on a uniform understanding of the principle.[208] Similar to the other discussed legality novelties, it is also not clear what scope the drafters of the Rome Statute had in mind with the introduction of this principle.

ICL's history has primarily produced evidence of a narrow reading of the principle. It limits it to an evidentiary or factual scope and states that the idea is that a defendant may not be convicted when doubts about guilt remain. This narrow reading is not reconcilable with the articulation in the Statute. Given the explicit incorporation into the legality provision, it must be seen as a proper interpretative technique. A more acceptable reading is that ambiguities in the crime's definition must be solved in favour of the accused.[209]

VII. CONCLUSION: LEGALITY'S OPERATIONALISATION INTO A TWO-DIMENSIONAL PROCESS WITH FOUR QUADRANTAL OUTCOMES

This chapter has undertaken a comprehensive examination of the legality principle, tracing its evolution from a simple concept of non-retroactivity to a multifaceted set of interpretative principles that influence judicial crime interpretation. The analysis has revealed that legality is not confined to non-retroactivity but extends into a complex web of interpretative considerations and has several international and national strands as well.

The historical analysis of these intertwined strands of legality serves as a backdrop for the dimensions of the legality principle explored in the upcoming chapters. Unfortunately, the drafters of the Rome Statute did not provide a detailed guidebook for understanding the intricate legality principle. The only clear directive is that Article 22 serves the purpose of restraining and confining judicial creativity.

This chapter illuminated the process of crime interpretation as a two-dimensional endeavour. It hinges on two fundamental dimensions: (1) the sources and applicable law, and (2) the methods of interpretation. These two dimensions interplay and give rise to four distinct quadrantal outcomes, as outlined in the model below:

[206] L Grover, *Interpreting Crimes in the Rome Statute of the International Criminal Court* (CUP, 2014) 59.

[207] Broomhall (n 13) 962.

[208] See, eg, C Davidson, 'How to Read International Criminal Law: Strict Construction and the Rome Statute of the International Criminal Court' (2017) 91 *John's L Rev* 37, 45–46.

[209] ibid.

A. Applicable Law & Source Doctrine (Article 21 Rome Statute)

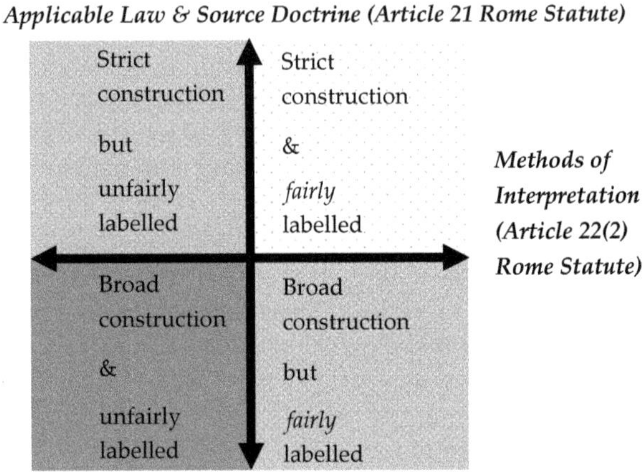

Historically, discussions surrounding the legality principle have revolved around the issue of retroactivity. From debates about the Grudge Informer to contemporary matters adjudicated by the ECtHR, the core concern has been whether criminal provisions were established retroactively. However, to determine retroactivity, one must first define what constitutes applicable law. The next chapter will delve into the concept of applicable law under the ICC system, examining Article 21 of the Rome Statute as the cornerstone of this framework. Despite the codification of sources of law in the statute, concerns persist regarding the reconciliation of strict construction and sources of law provisions. Therefore, a focused examination of applicable law from a legality perspective remains imperative, as offered in chapter three.

B. The Legality Principle and Methods of Interpretation

While not historically central to legality principle debates, ICTs' case law has shown that interpretative methods can also clash with legality concerns. Certain methods, like a teleological approach, have been labelled as inherently risky in terms of legality. Justifications for broad interpretations are often linked to specific interpretative methods, necessitating an in-depth analysis of their application.

Unlike applicable law, the Rome Statute lacks an explicit article dedicated to interpretative methods. Consequently, international law's interpretative framework, particularly Article 31 of the Vienna Convention on the Law of Treaties (VCLT), serves as the default. In Chapter 4, these methods will undergo scrutiny and assessment in the context of criminal law. The chapter will explore the extent to which these methods can be harmonised with Article 22 and whether adjustments are necessary to align with the legality principle. A substantial portion of this chapter aims to debunk the use of VCLT methods in crime interpretation.

Despite the absence of a specific article on interpretative methods, the Rome Statute introduces three novel principles of interpretation: strict construction, ban on analogy, and *in dubio pro reo*. Chapter 4 will conduct a detailed analysis of these principles, aiming to establish an interpretative methodology based on them.

C. The Legality Principle and the Interpretative Result: the Principle of Strict Construction and Fair Labelling

Article 22(2) of the Statute introduces the principle of strict construction, which has evolved into an independent element of the legality principle. It impacts both the interpretative process and the need to ensure definitions are sufficiently narrow. Chapter five will explore how strict construction imposes limits on interpretative outcomes.

This chapter has also highlighted the growing significance of correctly labelling crimes in ICL. Furthermore, the introduction of strict construction has prompted a discussion on the necessary balance between a strict definition and fairness in labelling. This tension has been explored throughout this chapter and will also be the central theme of chapter five.

3

Evaluating Crime Interpretation in Terms of Law Determination: Applicable Law and Source Doctrine

[W]e imagine tracing a river to its sources from whence spring its waters, flow downhill and eventually unite to form a broad stream.[1]

I. INTRODUCING A LEGALITY-CENTRED EVALUATION OF LAW DETERMINATION

ADJUDICATION CONCERNS A MULTIFACETED PROCESS that comprises elements of law determination, ascertainment, interpretation, and application. There are multiple viewpoints on the differentiation between these steps as well as the meaning of each step.[2] As such, the interpretative process is

[1] J Kammerhofer, 'Sources in Legal Positivist Theories: The Pure Theory's Structural Analysis of the Law' in S Besson and J d'Aspremont (eds), *The Oxford Handbook of the Sources of International Law* (OUP, 2017) 343.

[2] See on judicial discretion and interpretation in the realm of legal theory: A Barak, *Judicial discretion* (Yale University Press, 1989); R Dworkin, 'Judicial Discretion' (1963) 60 *The Journal of Philosophy* 624; MS Moore, 'A Natural Law Theory of Interpretation' (1985) *Southern California Law Review* 277; SE Fish, *Is There a Text in This Class? The Authority of Interpretive Communities* (Harvard University Press, 1980); OM Fiss, 'Objectivity and Interpretation' (1981–82) 34 *Stanford Law Review* 739; A Vermeule, *Judging under Uncertainty: An Institutional Theory of Legal Interpretation* (Harvard University Press, 2006); for a more comparative angle: MR Damaska, *The Faces of Justice and State Authority: A Comparative Approach to the Legal Process* (Yale University Press, 1986); N MacCormick and RS Summers, *Interpreting Statutes, A Comparative Study* (Darmouth Publishing Company Limited, 1991); specific to the field of international law: J d'Aspremont, *Formalism and the Sources of International Law, A Theory of the Ascertainment of Legal Rules* (OUP, 2011); M Bos, 'Theory and Practice of Treaty Interpretation' (1980) 27 *Netherlands International Law Review* 3; T Ginsburg, *International judicial lawmaking* (Mohr Siebeck, 2006); L Lo Giacco, *Judicial Decisions in International Law Argumentation: Between Entrapment and Creativity* (Hart Publishing, 2022); I Johnston, 'Treaty Interpretation: The Authority of Interpretative Communities' (1991) 12 *Michigan Journal of International Law* 371 and specific to the field of ICL: L Grover, *Interpreting Crimes in the Rome Statute of the International Criminal Court* (CUP, 2014); N Jain, 'Interpretive Divergence' (2017) 57 *Virginia Journal of International Law* 45.

sometimes understood as having a preceding phase of law-determination before turning to the phase of interpretation.[3] Rather than focusing on the specifics of the differentiation between law-ascertainment and content-determination,[4] this study adopts a positivist and source-based conception of law which understands tracing the sources of law as one of the essential features of judicial interpretation.[5] This chapter focuses solely on the role played by legal sources in decision-making, setting aside an examination of extra-legal influences.[6]

Following this source-based conception of the law, this chapter examines the source doctrine at the ICC through the lens of Hart's concept of the rule of recognition.[7] Hart starts by conceptualising a legal system as a union of primary and secondary rules, with the latter making the former knowable. The rule of recognition, which is required for a legal system to exist,[8] is a type of secondary rule that identifies the primary rules.[9] Source doctrine, understood as a rule

[3] A difference has been made between identifying the law, applying it and finally interpreting it: N MacCormick, 'Argumentation and interpretation in law' (1993) 6 *Ratio Juris* 16; d'Aspremont (n 2) 157ff. Other distinctions are between fact determination, law application and law determination: A Barak, 'The Role of a Supreme Court in a Democracy' (2001) 53 *Hastings Law Journal* 1205.

[4] J d'Aspremont, 'The Multidimensional Process of Interpretation: Content-Determination and Law-Ascertainment Distinguished' in A Bianchi, D Peat and M Windsor (eds), *Interpretation in International Law* (OUP, 2015) 111ff.

[5] J Raz, *The Authority of Law, Essays on Law and Morality* (OUP, 1979) 49–52; D Lefkowitz, 'Sources in Legal Positivist Theories: Law as Necessarily Posited and the Challenge of Customary Law Creation' in S Besson and J d'Aspremont (eds), *The Oxford Handbook of the Sources of International Law* (OUP, 2017) 323–24: '"legal positivism", is the view that a norm's status as law, its membership in a legal order or system, is solely a matter of its social source without regard for its merit. [. . .]), all legal positivists maintain that law is necessarily posited, made, or created, not discerned in the natural order of things or deduced from principles knowable a priori'.

[6] For a similar way of studying ICL's source doctrine: SR Ratner, 'Sources of International Humanitarian Law and International Criminal Law: War/Crimes and the Limits of the Doctrine of Sources' in S Besson and J d'Aspremont (eds), *The Oxford Handbook of the Sources of International Law* (OUP, 2017); R Van Steenberghe, 'Sources of International Humanitarian Law and International Criminal Law: Specific Features' in S Besson and J d'Aspremont (eds), *The Oxford Handbook of the Sources of International Law* (OUP, 2017).

[7] SJ Shapiro, 'What Is the Rule of Recognition (and Does It Exist)?' (2009) Public Law & Legal Theory Research Paper Series, Research Paper No 181: discussing disagreement on the scope of the rule of recognition and whether it should be understood in a narrow – 'as the test of legal validity for a particular legal system' – or broad sense – 'as a duty-imposing convention among officials'.

[8] HLA Hart, *The Concept of Law*, 2nd edn (Clarendon Press, 1994) 79–99; SJ Shapiro, *Legality* (Cambridge, The Belknap Press of Harvard University Press, 2011) 80: 'at the foundation of every legal system lies a social rule that sets out the criteria of legal validity. This master rule, which Hart calls "the rule of recognition," determines which power-conferring and duty-imposing rules are valid in the system'. Hart did not qualify the international system as a proper legal system since it lacked, in his view, secondary rules such as a proper rule of recognition (see Hart, *The Concept of Law*, 236). However, several scholars nowadays admit that Hart's analysis of the international system was underdeveloped and is no longer accurate: see D Kritsiotis, 'Public International Law and the Concept of Law Applied' (2012) 3 *Transnational Legal Theory* 189; S Besson, Theorizing Sources of International Law in S Besson and J Tasioulas (eds), *The Philosophy of International Law* (OUP, 2010) 163ff.

[9] One objection to Hart's approach is that Article 21 does not fulfil the criteria of the rule of recognition as a social, supreme and ultimate rule (see Hart (n 8) 105ff. In my view, incorporating Article 21 in the Statute does not change the fact that it *ultimately* tells us which legal rules and sources are *valid* and, in that sense, corresponds to the core idea of a rule of recognition.

of recognition, identifies the valid law within a system.[10] A judicial decision's formal validity thus depends on whether it can be justified by reference to recognised legal sources.

This chapter identifies Article 21 of the Rome Statute as the prime rule of recognition in the context of the ICC.[11] It first clarifies its workings to then evaluate whether the sources used in crime interpretation abide by Article 21, affording it formal validity.[12] This entails making sense of the hierarchy of sources presented in this provision, as well as clarifying the meaning of each of the sources outlined. It also encompasses the question of whether Article 21 lists sources exhaustively or whether sources outside its scope can have a bearing on the interpretation of crimes. The core point of this chapter is to assess the source doctrine in crime interpretation and examine the effects of the legality principle on it. Therefore, particular attention is given to the relationship between Article 21 and the legality principle under Article 22.

II. THE ICC'S HIERARCHICAL RULE OF RECOGNITION ON LAW DETERMINATION

Despite the dynamic nature of international law, source doctrine in this context has been approached in a highly formal way, developing around Article 38 of the ICJ Statute.[13] This provision presents a list of sources,[14] which, although being the applicable law of the International Court of Justice, have been relied on by many national and international actors and courts.[15] It is now considered the epicentre of source doctrine in international law.[16] Even in ICL, the ICTs

[10] S Besson, 'Theorizing the Sources of International Law' in S Besson and J Tasioulas (eds), *The Philosophy of International Law* (OUP, 2010) 180ff; A Marmor, *Interpretation and Legal Theory*, Clarendon Law Series (Clarendon Press, 2005) 7–8.

[11] See N Arajärvi, 'Between *Lex Lata* and *Lex Ferenda*: Customary International (Criminal) Law and the Principle of Legality' (2010–11) 15 *Tilburg Law Review* 163; J Verhoeven, 'Article 21 of the Rome Statute and the Ambiguities of Applicable Law' (2002) 33 *Netherlands Yearbook of International Law* 2.

[12] R Kolb, *Theory of International Law* (Hart Publishing, 2016) 155–56.

[13] d'Aspremont (n 2) 70.

[14] '1. The Court [. . .] shall apply: (a) international conventions, [. . .]; (b) international custom,[. . .]; (c) the general principles of law [. . .]; (d) [. . .] judicial decisions and the teachings of the most highly qualified publicists [. . .]'.

[15] See *Mursic v Croatia*, App no 7334/13, Partly dissenting opinion of Judge Pinto de Albuquerque (20 October 2016) paras 3–7; *Prosecutor v Mucić et al* (Judgment) IT-96-21-T (16 November 1998) para 414; and also national courts: L Lo Giacco, 'Swinging Between Finding and Justification: Judicial Citation and International Law-Making' (2017) 6 *Cambridge International Law Journal* 27, 32.

[16] MN Shaw, *International Law*, 6th edn (CUP, 2008) 70–71; M Fitzmaurice, 'The History of Article 38 of the Statute of the International Court of Justice: The Journey from the Past to the Present' in S Besson and J d'Aspremont (eds), *The Oxford Handbook of the Sources of International Law* (OUP, 2017) 198; D Akande, 'Sources of International Criminal Law' in A Cassese (ed), *Oxford Companion to International Criminal Justice* (OUP, 2005) 33; AZ Borda, 'A Formal Approach to Article 38(1)(d) of the ICJ Statute from the Perspective of the International Criminal Courts and Tribunals' (2013) 24 *EJIL* 649.

which had no rule comparable to that of article 38 in its statutes, have referred to this provision.[17] This practice shifted with the introduction of Article 21 of the Rome Statute. Like Article 38, it formalises a rule of recognition; however, it differs by establishing a hierarchy of sources rather than merely listing them. Although both articles reflect a formalisation of source doctrine, debates persist on whether they provide binding and exhaustive instructions or act more as guidelines.[18]

Article 21 represents the first codification of sources in international criminal justice and is the product of extensive negotiations and political compromise.[19] The final text reflects competing views: some sought strict judicial restraint under the legality principle, while others advocated judicial flexibility to address inevitable gaps in the law. This tension led to a complex and confusing formulation, which, given the lack of official negotiation records and clear preparatory works, is not always easy to comprehend.[20]

Early drafts of the ICC's applicable law, such as the 1994 ILC Draft, presented a simple list of sources,[21] with debates showing limited concern for legality constraints and primarily dealing with which particular sources, such as national law, would make the list.[22] Over time, discussions at the ILC and Preparatory Committees,[23] and during the 1998 Rome Conference, gradually

[17] H Thirlway, 'The Sources of International Law' in MD Evans (ed), *International Law* (OUP, 2003); H Thirlway, *The Sources of International Law*, 2nd edn (OUP, 2019) 8ff; D Lefkowitz, 'The Sources of International Law: Some Philosophical Reflections' in S Besson and J Tasioulas (eds), *The Philosophy of International Law* (OUP, 2010).

[18] Thirlway (n 17) 138–42; R Cryer, 'Royalism and the King: Article 21 of the Rome Statute and the Politics of Sources' (2009) 12 *New Criminal Law Review: An International and Interdisciplinary Journal* 390, 393.

[19] See I Caracciolo, 'Applicable Law' in W Schabas and F Lattanzi (eds), *Essays on the Rome Statute*, vol 1 (1999).

[20] See A Cassese, 'The Statute of the International Criminal Court: Some Preliminary Reflections' (1999) 10 *EJIL* 145: attesting to the lack of formal preparatory works reflecting the debates and negotiations that took place at the Rome Diplomatic Conference; see also S Rosenne, 'Poor Drafting and Imperfect Organization: Flaws to Overcome in the Rome Statute' (2000) 41 *Virginia Journal of International Law* 164; WA Schabas, 'The Dynamics of the Rome Conference' in MM deGuzman and V Oosterveld (eds), *The Elgar Companion to the International Criminal Court* (Edward Elgar, 2020).

[21] Draft Statute for an International Criminal Court with Commentaries (YBILC 1994, Vol II, Part 2) 51–52; see also WA Schabas, 'General Principles of Criminal Law in the International Criminal Court Statute (Part III)' (1998) 6 *European Journal of Crime, Criminal Law and Criminal Justice* 400, 402–404.

[22] Draft Statute for an International Criminal Court with Commentaries (YBILC 1994, Vol II, Part 2) Art 33: 'The Court shall apply: (a) This Statute; (b) Applicable treaties and the principles and rules of general international law; (c) To the extent applicable, any rule of national law'. See also J Crawford, 'The ILC's Draft Statute for an International Criminal Tribunal' (1994) 88 *AJIL* 140; WA Schabas, *The International Criminal Court: A Commentary on the Rome Statute*, Oxford Commentaries on International Law (OUP, 2010) 381ff.

[23] For an overview of proposals: MC Bassiouni and WA Schabas, *The Legislative History of the International Criminal Court*, vol 2, International Criminal Law Series (Brill, 2016) 230–33 and in particular: Preparatory Committee, *Report of the Preparatory Committee on the Establishment of an International Criminal Court: Proceedings of the Preparatory Committee during March–April and August 1996*, UN Doc A/51/22, 51st Session, Supp No 22, 103ff.

moved towards recognising the need to limit judicial discretion while allowing sufficient flexibility to address unforeseen issues.[24] This culminated in the hierarchical structure we find today.[25] In its final form, Article 21 states:

1. The Court shall apply:
   (a) In the first place, this Statute, Elements of Crimes and its Rules of Procedure and Evidence;
   (b) In the second place, where appropriate, applicable treaties and the principles and rules of international law, including the established principles of the international law of armed conflict;
   (c) Failing that, general principles of law derived by the Court from national laws of legal systems of the world, including, as appropriate, the national laws of States that would normally exercise jurisdiction over the crime, provided that those principles are not inconsistent with this Statute and with international law and internationally recognized norms and standards.
2. The Court may apply principles and rules of law as interpreted in its previous decisions.
3. The application and interpretation of law under this article must be consistent with internationally recognized human rights, and be without any adverse distinction founded on grounds such as gender as defined in article 7, paragraph 3, age, race, colour, language, religion or belief, political or other opinion, national, ethnic or social origin, wealth, birth or other status.

Some argue that Article 21 offers a complex hierarchy with 'imperfectly defined sources'.[26] Others have referred to it as a 'strict hierarchy'.[27] A commonly heard criticism is that the provision is idiosyncratic in nature.[28] The application of the set of sources is, in any event, not straightforward, and several approaches to its functioning have been formulated. Furthermore, not every source is clearly delineated, and each of the paragraphs has led to discussion on their exact scope. The only thing clear is the general rationale for such a complex and formalised system of sources, and that is to limit the judges' interpretative space.[29]

The sources in Article 21 can be divided into two main categories: on the one hand, the 'proper law'[30] or 'internal sources of law'[31] and on the other hand,

[24] MM deGuzman, 'Article 21 Applicable Law' in O Triffterer and K Ambos (eds), *The Rome Statute of the International Criminal Court*, 3rd edn (Verlag CH Beck oHG, 2016) 933.

[25] MH Arsanjani, 'The Rome Statute of the International Criminal Court' (1999) 93 *AJIL* 22, 25: reporting that the applicable law provision was one of the most difficult to negotiate.

[26] A Pellet, 'Applicable Law' in A Cassese, P Gaeta and JRWD Jones (eds), *The Rome Statute of the International Criminal Court: A Commentary*, vol 2 (OUP, 2002) 1053ff.

[27] Arsanjani (n 25) 28.

[28] J Powderly, *Judges and the Making of International Criminal Law* (Brill Nijhoff, 2020) 466.

[29] J Powderly, 'The Rome Statute and the Attempted Corseting of the Interpretative Judicial Function: Reflections on Sources of Law and Interpretative Technique' in C Stahn (ed), *The Law and Practice of the International Criminal Court* (OUP, 2015).

[30] Pellet (n 26) 1054–67.

[31] G Bitti, 'Article 21 and the Hierarchy of Sources of Law before the ICC' in C Stahn (ed), *The Law and Practice of the International Criminal Court* (OUP, 2015) 414–25.

sources external thereto. The sources of interest within the first category are the Rome Statute and the Elements of Crimes.[32] The external sources category breaks down into different types of sources. As this division does not add to the understanding of the functioning of Article 21, a more useful division is used in this chapter, and that is to differentiate between three steps in the application of the sources that reflect the 'multiplicity of hierarchies' better.[33]

First, there is the hierarchy of sources in the first paragraph, which breaks down into three layers: primary sources (Rome Statute and Elements of Crimes); secondary sources (applicable treaties and principles, rules of international law) and tertiary sources (general principles of law derived from national laws). This hierarchy is a mandatory step in the application of sources. Second, Article 21(2) formulates an optional step in the source doctrine by specifying that the court may apply principles and rules of law as interpreted in its previous decisions. This optional step makes it possible to examine the position of precedent as a source.[34] Third, the last paragraph formulates that the interpretation has to be consistent with internationally recognised human rights. This inserts again a mandatory step in the interpretative process that requires human rights to be taken into consideration as an overarching source.

III. PRIMARY SOURCES: THE ROME STATUTE AND THE ELEMENTS OF CRIMES

The Rome Statute, the Elements of Crimes (EoC), and the Rules of Procedure and Evidence constitute the ICC's primary sources under Article 21(1)(a). Their mandatory application is emphasised by the use of shall, distinguishing them from the optional sources listed later in Article 21. Among these, the Rome Statute and the EoC are particularly central to crime interpretation.[35]

Unlike the tribunals established based on UNSC Resolutions, the ICC is based on a treaty, enhancing legal certainty. This statutory basis furthermore triggers the application of the Vienna Convention on the Law of Treaties (VCLT).[36] Next to the Rome Statute, the adjacent document of the EoC was introduced to appease the concerns of the drafters that judges would be able to 'legislate principles of criminal law.'[37] Although Article 21(1)(a) places the EoC

[32] The present book disregards the following documents: the Rules of Procedure and Evidence, Regulations of the Court, Regulations of the Registry, the Code of Professional Conduct for Counsel, the Regulations of the Trust Fund for Victims, and the Regulations of the Office of the Prosecutor because they have little to no bearing on the interpretation of crime provisions.

[33] Bitti (n 31) 413.

[34] See also Pellet (n 26) 1067–76; Bitti (n 31) 425–43.

[35] G Hochmayr, 'Applicable Law in Practice and Theory: Interpreting Article 21 of the ICC Statute' (2014) 12 *JICJ* 655.

[36] See ch 4.

[37] Preparatory Committee, *Report of the Preparatory Committee on the Establishment of an International Criminal Court*, vol II, Compilation of Proposals, 51st Session, Supp No 22A, UN Doc A/51/22, 104–05.

alongside the Statute, Article 9 clarifies that the EoC 'shall assist' in interpreting Articles 6, 7, and 8.[38] This article furthermore states that the EoC 'shall be consistent with this Statute.'[39]

A. Understanding the Elements of Crimes

During the 1998 Rome Conference, the United States proposed attaching a document with crime definitions to the Statute.[40] This proposal, which was met with quite some opposition,[41] ultimately led to a compromise between proponents of a full codification and those who feared that rigid definitions would overly constrain judges.[42] A Preparatory Commission was tasked to draft the EoC after the conclusion of the Rome Conference.[43] It took the US proposal as a basis, but modified the wording so that the EoC would *only assist* in the interpretation of crimes.[44] The compromise language in Articles 9 and 21 has been attributed to the imperfections of diplomatic drafting.[45]

These provisions' formulations have given rise to debates on three interconnected issues:[46] the nature of the EoC, the uncertainty surrounding its binding force, and its unclear positioning within the hierarchy of sources. The ICC has developed a solution to these interpretative difficulties called the *irreconcilable contradiction test*.

The first problem is that there seems to be disagreement on the EoC's nature and how to qualify this document. Both judges and scholars have sought to qualify the EoC using the VCLT, identifying it either as a subsequent agreement or subsequent practice under Article 31(2) and (3).[47] This qualification triggers questions on whether these sources can bring about an interpretation that modifies

[38] *Rome Statute of the International Criminal Court* (adopted 17 July 1998, entered into force 1 July 2002) 2187 UNTS 90, Art 9(1).

[39] ibid Art 9(3).

[40] United States, *Proposal Submitted by the United States Concerning the Bureau Proposal on Article XX* (UN Diplomatic Conference of Plenipotentiaries on the Establishment of an International Criminal Court) UN Doc A/CONF.183/C.1/L.69 (19 June 1998); see also RS Lee, *The International Criminal Court: The Making of the Rome Statute – Issues, Negotiations and Results* (Kluwer Law International, 1999) 87.

[41] *Summary Records of the Plenary Meetings and of the Meetings of the Committee of the Whole (Rome, 15 June–17 July 1998)*, UN Doc A/CONF.183/13 (UN Diplomatic Conference of Plenipotentiaries on the Establishment of an International Criminal Court), vol II E.g. Sweden, 271, para 43'; Sierra Leonne, 271, para 56; Azerbaijan, 272, para 60.

[42] Arsanjani (n 25) 35.

[43] Final Act of the United Nations Diplomatic Conference of Plenipotentiaries on the Establishment of an International Criminal Court, Resolution F, UN Doc A/CONF.183/10 (17 July 1998) paras 5, 9 and 10.

[44] *Summary Records of the Plenary Meetings and of the Meetings of the Committee of the Whole (Rome, 15 June–17 July 1998)*, UN Doc A/CONF.183/13 (UN Diplomatic Conference of Plenipotentiaries on the Establishment of an International Criminal Court), vol II, 152 paras 50, 139 and 159.

[45] S Rosenne, 'Poor Drafting and Imperfect Organisation: Flaws to Overcome in the Rome Statute' (2000) 41 *Virginia Journal of International Law* 164, 167–68.

[46] Akande (n 16) 47.

[47] I Buga, 'Subsequent Practice and Treaty Modificiation' in Michael J Bowman and Dino Kritsiotis (eds), *Conceptual and Contextual Perspectives on the Modern Law of Treaties* (CUP, 2018) 363.

the corresponding treaty.[48] Despite the VCLT not setting explicit limits to modification through interpretation, and much depending on how one defines interpretation and modification,[49] scholars have nonetheless warned that there are limits to far-reaching interpretations that could alter the treaty.[50] The extent to which interpretations proposed by subsequent agreement or practice broaden the scope of a crime may be at odds with the legality principle, in particular, non-retroactivity. Legality concerns arise when the EoC is qualified as a subsequent agreement or practice, opening the door to modifications of the Rome Statute crimes *ex post facto*. Despite most authors treating the application of the VCLT as a *fait accompli*,[51] legality concerns offer strong reasons to bar this qualification and to search for alternative ways to understand the EoC.[52] Both qualifying it as an agreement – which is difficult given the non-binding nature of the EoC – or a practice[53] – which is difficult to reconcile with the EoC's subsidiary nature[54] – is neither satisfactory nor useful.[55] As clarified further, it is preferable to focus on the structure of the Rome Statute itself to make sense of the EoC's role.

A second problem concerns the uncertainty regarding the binding force of the EoC. Unfortunately, Articles 21(1)(a) and 9 of the Statute are terminologically inconsistent: the former suggests a mandatory application ('shall apply'), whereas the latter only requires that the EoC assist interpretation. This ambiguity has led to diverging views. Cryer argues that by using the term assist, the drafters indicated that the EoC is non-binding, criticising the *Al Bashir* decision for wrongly suggesting an obligation to apply the EoC.[56] DeGuzman, in contrast, proposes reading the two provisions together, suggesting that 'the Court shall apply the Elements for the purpose of assisting the Court', thereby establishing

[48] See for two positions on this issue: JE Alvarez, 'Limits of Change by Way of Subsequent Agreements and Practice' in G Nolte (ed), *Treaties and Subsequent Practice* (OUP, 2013); G Hafner, 'Subsequent Agreements and Practice: Between Interpretation, Informal Modification, and Formal Amendment' in RK Gardiner (ed), *Treaties and Subsequent Practice* (OUP, 2013).

[49] See the ILC's project on 'Subsequent Agreements and Subsequent Practice in Relation to Interpretation of Treaties' legal.un.org/ilc/guide/1_11.shtml, in particular: G Nolte, *Second Report on Subsequent Agreements and Subsequent Practice in Relation to the Interpretation of Treaties* (Sixty sixth session, 2014): 'Subsequent agreements and subsequent practice [. . .] can contribute to the clarification of the meaning of a treaty, in particular by narrowing or *widening* the range of possible interpretations'.

[50] Hafner (n 48) 114–17. See also J Arato, 'Subsequent Practice and Evolutive Interpretation: Techniques of Treaty Interpretation over Time and Their Diverse Consequences' (2010) 9 *The Law & Practice of International Courts and Tribunals* 443.

[51] See how Security Resolutions understood as subsequent agreements have broadened the interpretation of genocide: M Ramsden, 'The Crime of Genocide in General Assembly Resolutions: Legal Foundations and Effects' (2021) 21 *Human Rights Law Review* 671.

[52] See for a critical take on the VCLT: Alvarez (n 48) 124.

[53] C Kreß, 'The ICC's First Encounter with the Crime of Genocide: The Case against Al-Bashir' in C Stahn (ed), *The Law and Practice of the International Criminal Court* (OUP, 2015) 677.

[54] This position of the subsequent practice being authoritative is more unsettled than reflected here.

[55] RK Gardiner, *Treaty Interpretation* (OUP, 2008) 484–85.

[56] Cryer (n 18) 400.

at least an obligation to consider the EoC in interpretation.[57] Although this proposal has the merit of ensuring that judges cannot entirely disregard the EoC, it still leaves considerable uncertainty about the precise weight and authority of the EoC in crime interpretation.

A third and connected problem concerns the position of the EoC in the hierarchy and how to understand its relationship to the Rome Statute. When can we legitimately resort to the EoC? This question is answered in the next section.

B. The Irreconcilable Contradiction Test

To resolve conflicts between the Rome Statute and the EoC, the ICC has developed the so-called irreconcilable contradiction test. According to this test, the EoC must be applied unless a direct and irreconcilable contradiction with the Statute is found, in which case the Statute prevails.[58] This approach was applied in the *Al Bashir* case, where the Court determined that the EoC's additional requirement to the definition of genocide – that genocidal acts occur in the context of a manifest pattern – did not contradict the Statute's definition of genocide, but merely clarified it.[59] The contextual element added by the EoC[60] was an *addition* rather than a *contradiction* of the Statute. The judges found such an addition unproblematic from the perspective of the legality principle.[61]

The most problematic part of this test is that it narrowly focuses on identifying contradictions while ignoring other potential forms of conflict between the Statute and the EoC. Everything depends on what is considered an 'irreconcilable contradiction', a concept that appears unduly restrictive given the complexity of interpretative conflicts. The choice of this terminology is furthermore surprising given its lack of legal basis. No provision expressly addresses how to solve conflicts between the Statute and the EoC. Article 9 merely prescribes that the EoC shall be consistent with the Statute, without offering conflict-resolution guidance. A conflict-resolution provision does exist for a conflict between the Rules of Procedure and the Statute. Using entirely different language, this provision could offer insights into a more appropriate method of reconciliation.

The irreconcilable contradiction solution is insufficient in resolving the full range of interpretational conflicts. Furthermore, it has been argued that by permitting the EoC to add elements to crimes without recognising inconsistencies, the Court risks subordinating the Statute's authority to the EoC, despite

[57] deGuzman (n 24) 936.

[58] *Situation in Darfur, Sudan* (Decision on the Prosecution's Application for a Warrant of Arrest against Omar Hassan Ahmad Al Bashir) ICC-02/05-01/09-3 (4 March 2009) para 128.

[59] ibid.

[60] *Elements of Crimes*, Art. 6, 'conduct took place in the context of a manifest pattern of similar conduct directed against the targeted group or must have had such a nature so as to itself effect, the total or partial destruction of the targeted group'.

[61] *Situation in Darfur, Sudan* (n 58) paras 123–26.

its assertion of the Statute's primacy. Efforts by scholars such as Cryer[62] and DeGuzman[63] to reconcile these difficulties is valuable, but ultimately falls short of providing a fully satisfactory framework. Conscious of the fact that no methodology can prevent all future interpretative challenges, this study proposes refinements that aim to better uphold the legality principle.

A crucial preliminary point is the binding force of the EoC. Although debates over whether the EoC is binding or merely persuasive have produced divergent views,[64] it is the proposition here that the EoC can be qualified as nothing less than a binding instrument. Adopted by the Assembly of States Parties, the body competent to approve statutory revisions, the EoC carries legislative authority. However, recognising its binding nature does not elevate it above the Rome Statute.[65] The formulation 'shall assist' in Article 9 confirms that the EoC operates subordinately to the Statute. It is thus binding in the sense that judges must incorporate it into their interpretation of crimes, but subordinate in that it cannot override the Statute where inconsistencies arise. The essential point is that while binding, the EoC's role remains limited: it assists interpretation without modifying the Statute's content. This understanding lays the foundation for developing a more legality-conscious way of dealing with inconsistency.

C. A Legality-Centred Alternative: The Inconsistency Test?

The limitations of the irreconcilable contradiction test necessitate an alternative methodology that better aligns with the legality principle. This study proposes such an alternative, breaking down into three elements:

First, there needs to be *mandatory consideration* of the EoC. This means that judges must meaningfully engage with the EoC when interpreting crimes. The EoC cannot be ignored or marginalised. Its binding nature, confirmed by its adoption through the ASP, requires that judges consult and incorporate its content into their interpretative reasoning, even if it remains subordinate to the Statute.

Second, the judge needs to deal with each *inconsistency* explicitly and offer a motivated way out of this conflict. This broader concept of inconsistency, derived from Article 9's requirement of consistency and inspired by Article

[62] Cryer (n 18) 400–401.

[63] deGuzman (n 24) 936; A Aarnio, R Alexy and A Peczenik, 'The foundation of legal reasoning' (1981) 12 *Rechtstheorie* 133.

[64] L Grover, 'A Call for Arms: Fundamental Dilemmas Confronting the Interpretation of Crimes in the Rome Statute of the International Criminal Court' (2010) 21 *EJIL* 543, 536: referring to the EoC as 'a key authoritative non-binding interpretive aid'; L McKay, 'Characterising the System of the International Criminal Court: An Exploration of the Role of the Court through the Elements of Crimes and the Crime of Genocide' (2006) 6 *International Criminal Law Review* 257, 269: calling the EoC 'clearly non-binding in nature'; M Politi, 'Elements of Crimes' in A Cassese, P Gaeta and JRWD Jones (eds), *The Rome Statute of the International Criminal Court: A Commentary*, vol 1 (OUP, 2002) 443–73: 'the elements are meant to be used by the judges as simple guidelines in reaching determinations as to individual criminal responsibility'.

[65] Cryer (n 18) 400.

51(4), provides a more appropriate standard than the overly narrow notion of irreconcilable contradiction. Inconsistencies include additions or clarifications by the EoC that depart from the Statute's definitions in a way that threatens the clarity or foreseeability required under the legality principle.

Third, the judge needs to test this solution against the legality principle and understand the EoC as an instrument meant to 'give teeth' to the legality principle.[66] The EoC must be used to clarify, not expand, the scope of crimes. Judges should examine whether reliance on a specific element of the EoC maintains strict construction. Where an interpretation supported by the EoC risks expanding the contours of a crime beyond what the Statute prescribes, that element must be set aside in favour of the Statute's more restrictive wording.

Taken together, these elements offer a more legality-centred reconciliation method. Rather than waiting for an outright contradiction, judges must actively assess whether the EoC's provisions are consistent with the Statute's text and the overarching guarantees of the legality principle. Only where an inconsistency arises that affects these guarantees should recourse to the EoC be limited.

IV. SECONDARY SOURCES: TREATIES AND CUSTOMARY INTERNATIONAL LAW

Article 21(1)(b) provides that the Court shall apply, '[i]n the second place, where appropriate, applicable treaties and the principles and rules of international law, including the established principles of the international law of armed conflict.' These sources represent the second layer of the hierarchy after the primary sources.

While treaties are relatively straightforward to identify, the clause 'where appropriate' complicates their application. It indicates that judges must assess whether a treaty is truly applicable in the specific interpretative context. Contrary to what some authors have suggested that this is intended to 'permit(s) judges considerable leeway in considering which sources of international law could be appropriately applied in a particular case',[67] the suggestion is to keep in mind Article 21's overall purpose to limit judicial discretion and ensure that resort to external sources does not undermine the Statute's primacy.

A. Applicable Treaties

Applicable treaties are listed first under Article 21(1)(b) and, as a concept, seem quite unproblematic to understand. As Pellet observed, treaties played an important role in the drafting history, where earlier versions even contemplated direct inclusion

[66] Proposal submitted by the United States on Elements of offences for the International Criminal Court, A/AC.249/1998/DP.11 (2 April 1998).

[67] L N Sadat, *The International Criminal Court and the Transformation of International Law: Justice for the New Millennium* (Transnational Publisher, 2002) 177.

of treaty crimes under ICC jurisdiction.[68] Three distinct situations illustrate how treaties may influence the interpretation of crimes within primary sources.

The first situation arises when the Rome Statute explicitly incorporates treaty crimes, such as the grave breaches of the Geneva Conventions listed in Article 8(2). As Pellet notes, where the Statute expressly refers to a treaty, judges are obligated to apply it.[69] Some of the IHL crimes were not absorbed under the war crimes provisions (eg, apartheid) and a reference to other well established IHL conventions is lacking (eg, Additional Protocols to the Geneva Conventions). This piecemeal absorption complicates interpretation. Where discrepancies exist between the treaty and the Statute (or the Elements of Crimes), the primacy of the internal sources must prevail. Any element that departs from the definitions elaborated within the primary sources must be excluded to uphold the legality principle.

A second situation arises where a crime in the Rome Statute mirrors a crime in a treaty without explicitly referencing it, such as genocide under the Genocide Convention (GenC)[70] or torture under the UN Convention against Torture (CAT).[71] Here, differences between definitions create interpretative challenges. Difficulties arise when treaties add elements where the Statute is silent. For instance, CAT requires torture to be inflicted by a public official,[72] while the Rome Statute and EoC omit this element, thereby broadening the definition.[73] Although an accused might advocate for applying the narrower CAT definition under Article 21(1)(b), legality concerns do not necessarily require this. External treaties cannot automatically override statutory definitions, but neither should they be sidelined merely because they are not perfect copies. As discussed in relation to methods of interpretation, the existence of a mirroring crime does not itself create an ambiguity triggering the *in dubio pro reo* principle. Instead, a more thorough analysis of the internal sources – including teleological interpretation and reference to the preparatory works – reveals that certain omissions, like the public official requirement in the definition of torture, were deliberate.[74] Therefore, legality does not not require the rigid adoption of the most restrictive external definition, but rather respecting the carefully negotiated scope of the Statute.[75]

[68] Pellet (n 26) 1068.

[69] ibid 1069–70.

[70] *Convention on the Prevention and Punishment of the Crime of Genocide* (adopted 9 December 1948, entered into force 12 January 1951) 78 UNTS 277.

[71] *Convention against Torture and Other Cruel, Inhuman or Degrading Treatment or Punishment* (adopted 10 December 1984, entered into force 26 June 1987) 1465 UNTS 113.

[72] See P Gaeta, 'When is the Involvement of State Officials a Requirement for the Crime of Torture?' (2008) 6 *JICJ* 183.

[73] See NS Rodley, 'The Definition(s) of Torture in International Law' (2002) 55 *Current Legal Problems* 467.

[74] See, eg, Preparatory Committee, *Decisions Taken by the Preparatory Committee (Sessions from 11 to 21 February 1997)* A/AC.249/1997/L.5 (1997) where the definition of CAT was considered for inclusion into the Rome Statute.

[75] P Saland, 'Chapter 7: International Criminal Law Principles' in RS Lee (ed), *The International Criminal Court: The Making of the Rome Statute: Issues, Negotiations, Results* (Kluwer Law International, 1999) 215.

A third situation arises where a treaty does not mirror a crime but may still inform crime interpretation. For instance, is the Convention on the Rights of the Child applicable in cases involving child soldiers, or merely relevant?[76] The wording of Article 21(1)(b) differentiates between 'applicable' and merely 'relevant' treaties, suggesting that not every relevant treaty automatically applies. Often, arguments can be made for either position. However, because treaties deemed only relevant would also qualify as 'principles and rules of international law,' resolving this distinction is of limited practical importance.[77] Accordingly, treaties such as the Additional Protocols, though not explicitly absorbed, can still be considered under Article 21(1)(b)'s broader framework.

In conclusion, the primacy of the internal sources should be held to a high standard. In terms of legality, this can potentially mean that a definition less favourable to the accused is chosen over a more stringent definition of a mirroring crime found in an external treaty. Treaties can nonetheless be informative as to certain statutory concepts, and an ambiguity should not be invoked too easily.

B. Customary International Law

The phrase 'principles and rules of international law' in Article 21(1)(b) has generated significant debate. Three main issues arise: (1) the meaning of 'principle' in both paragraphs (b) and (c); (2) the ambiguity as to whether Article 21(1)(b) refers to customary international law; and (3) the question of whether the jurisprudence of the *ad hoc* tribunals can be considered under this provision.

First, the meaning of 'principles and rules' must be clarified to differentiate paragraphs (b) and (c). The Preparatory Committee proposals from 1996 already revealed confusion, producing varied formulations like 'principles and rules of general international law',[78] 'general principles of criminal law',[79] and 'principles of law developed by the Court from national law'.[80] At the Rome Conference, the phrase 'principles and rules of general international law'[81]

[76] The *Lubanga* Appeals Chamber has held that the Convention on the Rights of the Child is applicable under Article 21(1)(b): see *The Prosecutor v Thomas Lubanga Dyilo*, Case No. ICC-01/04 -01/06 A5, Judgment on the appeal of Mr Thomas Lubanga Dyilo against his conviction, 1 December 2014, para 277.

[77] deGuzman (n 24) 938–39.

[78] Preparatory Committee, Report of the Preparatory Committee on the Establishment of an International Criminal Court, vol II, Compilation of Proposals, Fifty-first Session Supplement No 22A (A/51/22) 151.

[79] ibid 106.

[80] ibid 151.

[81] *Report of the Preparatory Committee on the Establishment of an International Criminal Court to the United Nations Diplomatic Conference of Plenipotentiaries on the Establishment of an International Criminal Court* A/CONF.183/2/Add.1 46.

was initially favoured but ultimately dropped, probably to ensure inclusion of criminal law principles.[82] As a result, the preparatory works do not resolve how principles and rules should be understood or distinguish paragraph (b) from (c).

The core of the confusion lies in whether a principle necessarily means a general principle. Schabas interpreted 'principles and rules' as encompassing the sources listed in Article 38(1) of the ICJ Statute, thus comprising treaties, custom, and general principles of law,[83] while Schachter's typology distinguished different types of general principles.[84] Following this, Jain has suggested that Article 21 refers to two types: international principles under (b) and domestic general principles under (c).[85] Thus, the distinction would be based on whether the principle derives from international or national law.[86]

Furthermore, ICL scholarship has often sidestepped the fundamental difference between a rule and a principle. In legal theory, this issue has been widely commented on from various perspectives. Dworkin, for example, tackled Hart's conception of the law as missing the concept of principles, which differ in nature and weight from rules. Two differences exist: (1) principles conflict, whereas legal rules do not, and (2) principles have a relative weight.[87] Raz understood the difference as one of degree and argued that rules prescribe acts, while principles are directed at more general actions.[88] Principles are more abstract notions than rules. Building further on these insights, Petersen characterised principles 'by a balancing of goods in cases of conflict, they always serve the purpose of protecting a common or an individual good and are thus value-related. Rules, on the other hand, are in general conduct-related'.[89] Petersen further notes that principles aim to protect values and thus differ qualitatively from rules, which govern conduct. Importantly, general principles do not require proof of state practice, unlike customary law, making them subsidiary by nature.[90]

[82] Draft Statute for an International Criminal Court with Commentaries (1994) II (2) Yearbook of the International Law Commission; Report of the International Law Commission on the Work of Its Forty-Sixth Session (2 May–22 July 1994), UN Doc A/49/10, 51.

[83] Schabas (n 22) 391.

[84] N Jain, 'Judicial Lawmaking and General Principles of Law in International Criminal Law' (2016) 57 *Harvard International Law Journal* 111, 117–18: using Schachter's types of general principles to address the question of their formal and material validity.

[85] ibid 130.

[86] Pellet (n 26) 1070.

[87] R Dworkin, *Taking Rights Seriously* (Bloomsbury Academic Publisher, 1978) 22ff; 24.

[88] J Raz, 'Legal Principles and the Limits of Law' (1972) 81 *Yale Law Journal* 823, 838: Rules prescribe relatively specific acts; principles prescribe highly unspecific actions. Generic acts, types of acts, are of various degrees of specificity.

[89] N Petersen, 'Customary Law without Custom – Rules, Principles, and the Role of State Practice in International Norm Creation' (2008) 23 *American University International Law Review* 275, 288.

[90] T Schneider, 'Customary International Law' in R Bernhardt (ed), *Encyclopedia of Public International Law: History of International Law, Foundations and Principles of International Law, Sources of International Law, Law of Treaties, vol 7* (North-Holland Publishing Co, 1984) 62.

Building on these insights and consistent with scholarly commentary,[91] and ICC case law,[92] this study concludes that general principles are not included under Article 21(1)(b). They are more appropriately addressed under paragraph (c), as they lack the formal requirements associated with custom. Both legality concerns and structural considerations within the Statute support this reading.

The second issue concerns whether Article 21(1)(b) refers to customary international law. Although not expressly mentioned, most scholars agree that it does.[93] In relation to crime interpretation, Grover asserted that 'for crimes in the Rome Statute derived from custom, custom is arguably both relevant and applicable'.[94] So what lies at the basis of the conclusion that custom is covered by the reference to principles and rules of international law? Pocar warns against this reasoning and argues that the only thing that can be concluded is that the 'Statute itself expressly recognizes that customary international law has a role to play, albeit an ancillary one. How ancillary, however, may be a matter of debate'.[95]

Custom ascertainment presents further difficulties. While traditional doctrine requires state practice and *opinio juris*,[96] it is widely recognised that judicial influence on custom formation has increased.[97] While this study cannot resolve that debate, it emphasises that the legality principle sets high standards in the ascertainment of custom. In the context of crime interpretation, customary rules must be based on convincing evidence of state practice, not merely *opinio juris*.[98] The ICC judges must rigorously ascertain custom rather than assume its existence based on precedent.

[91] S Bailey, 'Article 21(3) of the Rome Statute: A Plea for Clarity' (2014) 14 *International Criminal Law Review* 513, 521; deGuzman (n 24) 706–707; Grover (n 64) 572; Hochmayr (n 35) 668; Pellet (n 26) 1071; S Vasiliev, 'General Rules and Principles of International Criminal Procedure: Definition, Legal Nature, and Identification' in G Sluiter and S Vasiliev (eds), *International Criminal Procedure: Towards a Coherent Body of Law* (2009); LN Sadat and JM Jolly, 'Seven Canons of ICC treaty Interpretation, Making Sense of Article 25's Rorschach Blot' (2014) 27 *Leiden Journal of International Law* 64.

[92] *Prosecutor v Bemba* (Judgment pursuant to Article 74 of the Statute) ICC-01/05-01/08 (21 March 2016) para 71-75: The Trial Chamber considers general principles to come into play after the sources in article 21(1)(a), (b) and (c) are exhausted.

[93] Bailey (n 91) 521; deGuzman (n 24) 939–40; Grover (n 64) 572; Hochmayr (n 35) 668; Pellet (n 26) 1071; Vasiliev (n 91) 64.

[94] Grover (n 64) 572; see also Y Tan, 'The Identification of Customary Rules in International Criminal Law' (2018) 34 *Utrecht Journal of International and European Law* 92–100.

[95] F Pocar, 'Transformation of Customary Law through ICC Practice' in *Symposium on the Rome Statute at Twenty* (CUP, 2018) 183.

[96] Thirlway (n 17) 121–27; *North Sea Continental Shelf (Federal Republic of Germany/Denmark; Federal Republic of Germany/Netherlands) (Judgment)* [1969] ICJ Rep 3, para 74; *Military and Paramilitary Activities in and against Nicaragua (Nicaragua v United States of America) (Judgment)* [1986] ICJ Rep 14, para 186.

[97] N Arajärvi, *The Changing Nature of Customary International Law: Methods of Interpreting the Concept of Custom in International Criminal Tribunals* (Routledge, 2014) 1–2.

[98] It is precisely for this reason that the ICTY jurisdiction was limited to crimes which are beyond any doubt part of customary law. See Report of the Secretary General Pursuant to Paragraph 2 of UNSC Res 808, UN Doc S/25704, para 34.

The third issue creating confusion in the interpretation of Article 21(1)(b) is to what extent the ICTs' jurisprudence interpreting the rules and principles of international law can also be drawn in at this level of the hierarchy. This issue ties in with the previous point. The growing importance of jurisprudence in custom formation is no longer doubted. At the same time, it is difficult to assess exactly how much influence they exactly have.[99] Studies by Terris et al. and Borda highlight the absence of consistent use of external precedent.[100] Some judges have problematically called for a relaxed standard of custom formation and indicated that state practice is less important in this field,[101] while others underscore more rigorous standards for custom ascertainment.[102] Judge Kaul, dissenting in the Kenya investigation, warned against overreliance on tribunal case law, emphasising that the ICC must independently assess the existence of custom.[103] The Court does not exist 'in autistic isolation',[104] but nonetheless requires a sound approach, ascertaining for itself in a given instance whether the constitutive elements of custom are met.[105] Jurisprudence may serve as persuasive evidence but not as a direct source.[106] In the context of crime interpretation, this is even more so the case. Given customs' unwritten nature, the principle of legality requires an even more diligent assessment.[107]

Another point of debate is whether human rights norms can be invoked under Article 21(1)(b). As Vasiliev notes, there is uncertainty as to what human rights standards apply qua customary law and general principles of law'.[108] Given the

[99] R Cryer, 'Of Custom, Treaties, Scholars and the Gavel: The Influence of the International Criminal Tribunals on the ICRC Customary Law Study' (2006) 11 *Journal of Conflict and Security Law* 239, 239.

[100] D Terris, CPR Romano and L Swigart, *The International Judge: An Introduction to the Men and Women Who Decide the World's Cases* (2007). AZ Borda, 'Precedent in International Criminal Courts and Tribunals' (2013) 2 *Cambridge Journal of International and Comparative Law* 287, 293.

[101] See T Meron, 'The Martens Clause, Principles of Humanity, and Dictates of Public Conscience' (2000) 94 *AJIL*; A Cassese, 'The Martens Clause: half a loaf or simply pie in the sky?' (2000) 11 *EJIL* 187.

[102] See *Situation in the Republic of Kenya* (Dissenting Opinion of Judge Hans-Peter Kaul to the Decision Pursuant to Article 15 of the Rome Statute on the Authorization of an Investigation Into the Situation in the Republic of Kenya) ICC-01/09 (31 March 2010) para 29; See further: Y Tan, *The Rome Statute as Evidence of Customary International Law* (Brill | Nijhoff, 2021); V Nerlich, 'The status of ICTY and ICTR precedent in proceedings before the ICC' in C Stahn and G Sluiter (eds), *The Emerging Practice of the International Criminal Court* (Martinus Nijhoff, 2009) 320.

[103] *Situation in the Republic of Kenya* (Dissenting Opinion of Judge Hans-Peter Kaul to the Decision Pursuant to Article 15 of the Rome Statute on the Authorization of an Investigation Into the Situation in the Republic of Kenya) ICC-01/09 (31 March 2010) para 29.

[104] ibid para 30.

[105] *Bemba* para 75: Article 31(3)(c) of the VCLT empowers the Chamber to consider the case law of other international courts and tribunals as a means of interpretation of the applicable law [and] is to assist the Judges in identifying rules of customary law [...] [or] interpreting the applicable law referred to in Article 21(1)(a). [Judges] must not use the concept of treaty interpretation to replace the applicable law.

[106] Nerlich (n 102) 313.

[107] Tan (n 94) 93–94.

[108] S Vasiliev, '*International Criminal Trials: A Normative Theory*', Universiteit van Amsterdam (2014) 107.

challenges in establishing the customary status of international human rights law IHRL norms, applying them under paragraph (b) risks undermining the Statute's carefully constructed hierarchy.[109] While the hierarchy may at times feel restrictive, it serves a deliberate purpose and should not be circumvented.

In conclusion, the reference to 'rules and principles of international law' in Article 21(1)(b) should be understood as referring to customary international law, not general principles, which more appropriately fall under Article 21(1)(c). The principle of legality forces custom to play a less prominent role at the ICC than at the tribunals.[110] And when applied, judges need to ascertain custom by relying on a demonstrable basis in state practice and not by overrelying on *opinio juris* or tribunal jurisprudence. Otherwise, they risk undermining legality and elevating tribunal jurisprudence above the ICC's case law.

C. Article 21(1)(b)'s Trigger: the Appropriateness Standard

In order to understand the methodology on Article 21(1)(b) developed at the ICC and grasp how the subsidiary sources weigh in on the interpretative process, the phrase 'where appropriate' needs to be understood.[111] This section first assesses and evaluates the appropriateness standard and finally proposes an alternative approach.

Over the years, the ICC has developed its appropriateness standard according to which resort to subsidiary sources is only appropriate when: (i) there is a *lacuna* in the written law contained in the Statute, the Elements of Crimes and the Rules; and (ii) such *lacuna* cannot be filled by the application of the criteria of interpretation provided in Articles 31 and 32 VCLT and Article 21(3) of the Statute. A *lacuna* has been defined as 'an area or subject not covered by any law, a gap in the law'.[112] The Appeals Chamber has further held that not every silence in the law is a *lacuna*.[113]

[109] See also G Sluiter, 'The Surrender of War Criminals to the International Criminal Court' (2003) 15 *Loyola of Los Angeles International and Comparative Law Review* 605, 938.

[110] Akande (n 16) 50; K Ambos, *Treatise on International Criminal Law, vol 1: Foundations and General Part* (OUP, 2013) 74.

[111] See also *Situation in Uganda* (Decision on the Prosecutor's Position on the Decision of Pre-Trial Chamber II to Redact Factual Descriptions of Crimes from the Warrants of Arrest, Motion for Reconsideration, and Motion for Clarification) ICC-02/0401/05-60 (28 October 2005) para 19; *Prosecutor v Lubanga* (Judgment on the Appeal of Mr. Thomas Lubanga Dyilo against the Decision on the Defence Challenge to the Jurisdiction of the Court pursuant to Article 19(2)(a) of the Statute of 3 October 2006) ICC-01/04-01/06-772 (14 December 2006) para 34.

[112] V Condé, *A Handbook of International Human Rights Terminology* (Human Rights in International Perspective, University of Nebraska Press, 2004) 145.

[113] *Situation in the Central Republic of Africa* (Judgment on the appeals of the Prosecutor, Mr Jean-Pierre Bemba Gombo, Mr Fidèle Babala and Mr Narcisse Arido against the decision of Trial Chamber VII entitled "Decision on Sentence pursuant to Article 76 of the Statute") ICC-01/05-01/13 (8 March 2018) para 76.

This two-step approach was applied in the *Al Bashir Arrest Warrant Decision* for the purpose of crime interpretation.[114] To interpret genocide, this approach was supplemented with a reference to Article 10 of the Statute, according to which 'the definition of the crimes in the Statute and the Elements of Crimes shall not be interpreted as limiting or prejudicing in any way existing or developing rules of international law for purposes other than this Statute'.[115] This approach required that the genocide definition under customary law be reviewed, which necessitated a look at the definition as stipulated in the 1948 Genocide Convention.

The Rome Statute specifies that the genocidal conduct 'took place in the context of a manifest pattern of similar conduct'.[116] This article introduced a contextual element to the definition of genocide, which is absent from the definition in the Genocide Convention.[117] In relation to his contextual element, the EoC holds two clarifications:

> The term 'in the context of' would include the initial acts in an emerging pattern;
> The term 'manifest' is an objective qualification.[118]

The Court found there to be no irreconcilable contradiction between the EoC and the Statute. But apart from that, the question still left unanswered was whether secondary sources needed to be considered for the interpretation of genocide in the primary sources. The Pre-Trial Chamber recognised that this contextual element introduced a controversy, as neither the Genocide Convention nor the ICTY or ICTR Statutes formulated such a requirement.[119] In light of the absence of such an element in international law, how do we then interpret this addition by the EoC? Is it appropriate to let the absence of a contextual element weigh in the interpretation of a statutory crime? The Pre-Trial Chamber found that the contextual element does not 'amend the crime's definition but provides for a welcome clarification of the latter'.[120] To support its conclusion, it relied heavily on the ICTY's and ICTR's case law.[121] Whereas the PTC in general terms requires there to be a *lacuna* before the secondary sources should be applied, in relation to this specific interpretative problem, it does not identify nor discuss the *lacuna*.

[114] *Prosecutor v Bashir* (Decision on the Prosecution's Application for a Warrant of Arrest against Omar Hassan Ahmad Al Bashir) ICC-02/05-01/09-3 (4 March 2009) paras 44 and 126.

[115] ibid para 127.

[116] *Rome Statute* (n 38) art 6.

[117] *Convention on the Prevention and Punishment of the Crime of Genocide* (adopted 9 December 1948, entered into force 12 January 1951) 78 UNTS 277, art II.

[118] *Official Records of the Assembly of States Parties to the Rome Statute*, First session, UN doc E.03.V.2 (2002), *Elements of Crimes*, Introduction to Article 6.

[119] *Prosecutor v Bashir* (Decision on the Prosecution's Application for a Warrant of Arrest against Omar Hassan Ahmad Al Bashir) ICC-02/05-01/09-3 (4 March 2009) para 125.

[120] Kreß (n 53) 674.

[121] *Bashir* Decision on Arrest Warrant (n 119) para 120, fn 139.

From a methodological point of view, the non-application of the formulated test is seriously flawed. That being said, the threshold of having to identify a *lacuna* is quite high. One can wonder whether it would not have been better to develop a more realistic standard based on the wording 'where appropriate'. In relation to crime interpretation, this appropriateness standard should be tailored to the principle of legality. This primarily means that the custom ascertainment has to be sound and should not escape the requirement of also proving state practice. When external jurisprudence is relied on to assert such custom, there should be a clear and consistent line of jurisprudence, realistically foreseeable for the accused. But even better, judges should conduct an independent examination of state practice and *opinio juris*, which only subsidiarily uses external jurisprudence. In relation to some procedural aspects, the ICC judges have refused to take into account external sources because of their inappropriateness.[122] Trial Chamber I, for example, found that although the practice of witness proofing was well established at the tribunals, it was not appropriate to be applied at the ICC.[123] Similar clarity is sorely missed in relation to crime interpretation. This was again demonstrated by the more recent reference of the Trial Chamber in the *Al Hassan Judgment* to article 21(1)(b). Using the jurisprudence of other courts to understand which acts constitute outrages upon personal dignity, the judges simply mention article 21(1)(b) in a footnote without assessing the appropriateness of invoking the jurisprudence of these courts.[124]

V. TERTIARY SOURCES: GENERAL PRINCIPLES

Building on the distinction established in the previous section – Article 21(1)(b) referring to custom and Article 21(1)(c) to general principles – this section addresses the nature and function of general principles in the ICC's hierarchy of sources. Some commentators have understood Article 21(b) to refer to principles derived from international law, whereas Article 21(1)(c) holds general principles derived from national systems. But for the reasons presented in section IV, this position cannot be supported, and Article 21(b) should be limited to customary law.

A. Principles Derived from National Systems

Article 21(1)(c) permits the Court to apply 'general principles of law derived by the Court from national laws of legal systems of the world . . . provided that

[122] *Prosecutor v Lubanga* (Decision Regarding the Practices Used to Prepare and Familiarise Witnesses for Giving Testimony at Trial) ICC-01/04-01/06-1049 (30 November 2007) para 44.
[123] ibid para 45.
[124] *Prosecutor v Al Hassan* (Trial Judgment) ICC-01/12-01/18-2594-Red (26 June 2024) fn 3859.

those principles are not inconsistent with this Statute and with international law and internationally recognized norms and standards.'[125] It can be understood as a default source ('Failing that').[126] The provision reflects a compromise: some States wished to prioritise national law, particularly the law of the State that would normally exercise jurisdiction, while others resisted this. The final wording still requires engagement with national law, but is not as far-reaching as to simply apply national law.[127]

Building further on this understanding, the most fitting reading of 21(1)(c) aligns with Schachter's first category of general principles – principles of domestic law that are recognised by civilised nations.[128] Does this classification mean that other types (eg, universalist principles or principles of justice) are excluded from the scope of Article 21(1)(c)? Not necessarily, but paragraph (c) does hold an instruction to the judge to distil principles from national systems and undertake a comparative exercise. This interpretation is reinforced by Cassese and Ambos, who stress the need for a genuine comparative exercise.[129] This entails that judges should avoid solely relying on familiar systems or easily accessible sources,[130] but must engage in a pluralist (including multiple legal systems and families) comparative analysis.

Even when the instructions in Article 21(c) are followed, the question remains whether general principles are useful in crime interpretation. The problems with general principles can be illustrated by discussing the definition of rape in the *Furundzija* case and whether it should include forcible oral penetration. In order to answer this question, the Trial Chamber stated that neither customary law and treaty law nor general principles of international criminal law or international law were of any avail.[131] Without examining any particular state practice, it found in subsequent order that principles of criminal law common to the majority of the world's legal systems had to be examined. After a survey, it was found that there was a discrepancy between states that qualified forcible oral penetration as sexual assault and states qualifying it as rape. The Chamber then returned to consider, having dismissed these a couple of paragraphs earlier, the general principles of international criminal law and international law.[132] The Trial Chamber found 'the forced penetration

[125] *Situation in the Democratic Republic of the Congo* (Judgment on the Prosecutor's Application for Extraordinary Review of Pre-Trial Chamber I's 31 March 2006 Decision Denying Leave to Appeal) ICC-01/04-168 (24 July 2006) para 24.

[126] Ambos (n 110) 74.

[127] Saland (n 75) 214–15; Schabas (n 21) 403–404. See also *Summary records of the plenary meetings and of the meetings of the Committee of the Whole* (United Nations Diplomatic Conference of Plenipotentiaries on the Establishment of an International Criminal Court) A/CONF. 183/13 (Rome, 15 June–17 July 1998), vol II, 221–24.

[128] Jain (n 84) 7: discussing the five identified types of Schachter.

[129] Ambos (n 110) 76-78; A Cassese, *International Criminal Law*, 3rd edn (OUP, 2013).

[130] M Delmas-Marty, 'The Contribution of Comparative Law to a Pluralist Conception of International Criminal Law' (2003) 1 *JICJ* 13.

[131] *Prosecutor v Furundžija* (Judgment) IT-95-17/1 (10 December 1998) para 177.

[132] ibid para 182.

of the mouth by the male sexual organ [. . .] a most humiliating and degrading attack upon human dignity'.[133] The judges continued that '[t]he *general principle of respect for human dignity* is the basic underpinning and indeed the very *raison d'être* of international humanitarian law and human rights law' and has become so paramount 'as to permeate the whole body of international law'. It shields 'human beings from outrages upon their personal dignity, whether such outrages are carried out by unlawfully attacking the body or by humiliating and debasing the honour, the self-respect or the mental wellbeing of a person'. The judges concluded, therefore that 'oral penetration should be classified as rape'.[134]

This Trial Judgment portrays a highly problematic approach. The Chamber's comparative analysis lacked depth, and its reliance on a broad, value-laden principle of human dignity did not provide a sufficiently concrete legal basis. Furthermore, the Trial Chamber's articulation of 'the fundamental principle of protecting human dignity', which favours a broad definition of rape, was understood to override legality concerns.[135] Under Schachter's typology, dignity qualifies as a 'principle of justice'– a type that risks enabling expansive judicial interpretation. While the outcome in Furundžija may be normatively desirable, the methodology represents a form of judge-made law and raises serious legality concerns. General principles of this kind cannot be regarded as sufficiently specific legal norms in defining the objective elements of crimes.

B. Article 21(1)(c)'s Trigger: the Appropriateness Standard

So far, the ICC judges have used general principles for the interpretation of several procedural matters, such as the scope of review of earlier decisions[136] and witness proofing.[137] On the issue of witness proofing, for example, the Chamber refused to recognise that a sufficient legal basis existed, given that the cited sources were solely from common law systems. No civil law systems were cited, and it seemed no tradition of witness proofing in the Romano-Germanic legal system existed.[138] It was furthermore held that the fact that the tribunals had a practice of witness proofing did not constitute binding precedent.[139] In relation to substantive matters and crime definitions, the conducted case law review has not found evidence of the ICC judges applying Article 21(1)(c) to crime interpretation. It would be premature to conclude from this that general principles will never be used for this purpose. Given that the tribunals have done

[133] ibid para 183.
[134] ibid.
[135] ibid para 184.
[136] *Situation in the Democratic Republic of the Congo* (Appeal on Extraordinary Review) (n 125).
[137] *Lubanga* (Decision on Familiarizing Witnesses) (n 122).
[138] ibid para 41.
[139] ibid paras 43–44.

so, it is likely that the ICC judges will also use them to assist in the interpretation of the crimes.

If and when general principles are used for crime interpretation, certain safeguards must apply. First, as with Article 21(1)(b), their application should not be triggered solely by a perceived gap. While the Appeals Chamber has held that paragraph (c) is subject to the same precondition as paragraph (b), namely the existence of a lacuna, this study maintains that such gaps are unlikely to be meaningfully filled by general principles, especially when custom has already proven unhelpful. Second, the general and abstract nature of these principles threatens the principle of strict construction. Particularly when relying on broader 'principles of justice', it is difficult to satisfy the legality requirements of specificity and foreseeability. General principles should only be used when appropriate, when custom has failed, and only to support the interpretation of crimes, and never as an independent basis for extending definitions.[140]

VI. IMPLICIT SOURCES: INTERNAL PRECEDENTS

Article 21(2) holds that '[t]he Court may apply principles and rules of law as interpreted in its previous decisions'. Compared to the first paragraph of Article 21, the language shifts in the second paragraph. The fact that these sources *may* apply, instead of *shall* apply, means that it lies entirely within the judges' discretion to follow previous decisions. This optional and non-mandatory step is a compromise between the common law system of *stare decisis*, requiring judges to follow precedent, and the civil law system, which is unfamiliar with the binding nature of precedent. Despite international courts not generally incorporating the principle of *stare decisis*,[141] they tend to ensure their decisions are not at odds with previous case law in order to enhance legal certainty.[142] Therefore, it is advisable that judges follow the decisions of higher chambers and use internal precedent to promote consistency and coherence in the development of the law. It is indeed good practice for the Pre-Trial and Trial Chambers to follow the Appeals Chamber when there are no good reasons to depart from their decisions. This solidification of a certain direction in judicial reasoning enhances legitimacy and foreseeability. The fact that the system of *stare decisis* is not embedded in the Rome Statute system leaves room for the judges to diverge from a certain development in the case law. There can be good reasons to do so, and thus, this built-in flexibility is useful. However, when such

[140] Jain (n 84) 22–23.

[141] At the ICTY and ICTR, the Trial Chambers are bound by the decisions of the Appeals Chamber.

[142] *Prosecutor v Gbagbo & Blé Goudé* (Separate Concurring Opinion of Judge Eboe-Osuji) ICC-02/11-01/15-1400 (31 March 2021) para 60: '[The] better administration of justice [. . .] strongly recommends that even courts of final jurisdiction should follow past precedents for the sake of stability and predictability; while remaining free to depart from them for cogent reasons in the interest of justice and socio-legal development.'

a diversion occurs, the reasons for that diversion should be well explained. So far, some scholars have indicated that the case law of the Appeals Chamber 'does not seem to be placed on a higher level' and warn that this can create instability.[143] From a legality perspective, there is a need for more explicit solidification of judicial practice.

As discussed in relation to Article 21(1)(b) and (c), it has become common practice at the ICC to distil from the jurisprudence of other courts or to determine through the ICT jurisprudence whether custom or general principles exist.[144] As a result, external precedent potentially finds entrance at a higher step in the hierarchy than internal precedent. Manley has, for instance, demonstrated that national precedent has played an 'unanticipated' role before the ICC,[145] and has also concluded that reliance on ICT precedent is frequent despite it not being applicable law.[146] It is therefore necessary to recall that external precedent should be handled with care, as the effect of not doing so might be that the ICC is less influenced by its own legal history than it is by that of other courts.

VII. OVERARCHING SOURCES: HUMAN RIGHTS

Article 21(3) requires that all interpretation and application of law be consistent with internationally recognised human rights.[147] This paragraph has undoubtedly attracted the most scholarly attention out of all the paragraphs of Article 21, with several authors trying to bring clarity to its unclear terms.[148] This section focuses on the first part of Article 21(3) and on how the interpretation of crimes can be in conformity with human rights.

A. The Concept of Human Rights

First to discuss is the scope of 'internationally recognized human rights'. While the phrase was introduced late in the drafting process and preparatory works offer limited guidance,[149] the clause seems designed to reflect 'certain

[143] Bitti (n 31) 292–93.

[144] A Cassese, 'The Influence of the European Court of Human Rights on International Criminal Tribunals – Some Methodological Remarks' in M Bergsmo (ed), *Human Rights and Criminal Justice For the Downtrodden: Essays in Honour of Asbjorn Eide* (Brill Nijhoff, 2003) 20.

[145] S Manley, 'Citation Practices of the International Criminal Court: The Situation in Darfur, Sudan' (2017) 30 *Leiden Journal of International Law* 1003, 1019.

[146] S Manley, 'Referencing Patterns at the International Criminal Court' (2016) 27 *EJIL* 191, 195.

[147] The second half of art 21(3) will not be discussed.

[148] Pellet (n 26) 1079; D Sheppard, 'International Criminal Court and Internationally Recognized Human Rights: Understanding Article 21(3) of the Rome Statute' (2010) 10 *International Criminal Law Review* 43, 44.

[149] G Hafner and C Binder, 'The Interpretation of Article 21 (3) ICC Statute: Opinion Reviewed' (2004) 9 *Austrian Review of International and European Law* 163.

internationally recognized values', not to replace or override the Statute.[150] Apart from the delegate of Iran expressing concern over the concept of human rights,[151] there was not much discussion on this point. It seems that the drafters did not anticipate difficulty in understanding its application.

The phrase 'internationally recognized' suggests broad, though not necessarily universal acceptance.[152] As Judge Pikis once observed: such rights may be those 'acknowledged by customary international law and international treaties and conventions'.[153] This interpretation allows some flexibility while excluding norms confined to regional or highly contested frameworks. Although many rights appear in both regional and global instruments, judges should be cautious when relying solely on regional jurisprudence, especially where international consensus is lacking.[154]

The Appeals Chamber held that '[h]uman rights underpin the Statute; every aspect of it'.[155] This is, for example, demonstrated by Article 36(b)(ii) requiring that judicial candidates have competence in fields such as 'the law of human rights', as well as Article 69(7), which discusses the need for evidence to be gathered in coherence with 'internationally recognized human rights'.[156] Also, the definition of persecution allows for expansion of grounds to those 'that are universally recognized as impermissible under international law'.[157]

Another aspect is that Article 21(3) does not utilize the concept of 'international human rights law'. Most experts do not elaborate on the potential difference between 'human rights' and 'human rights law', despite the first concept being more restrictive and not necessarily including the entire body of law. The choice for human rights supports the opinion that case law interpreting human rights should not necessarily be included under Article 21(3). So, despite the previous elements leading to the conclusion that 'internationally recognized

[150] *Summary records of the plenary meetings and of the meetings of the Committee of the Whole* (United Nations Diplomatic Conference of Plenipotentiaries on the Establishment of an International Criminal Court) A/CONF. 183/13 (Rome, 15 June-17 July 1998), vol II, 221–22, para 52; see also Saland (n 75) 214.

[151] *Summary records of the plenary meetings and of the meetings of the Committee of the Whole* (United Nations Diplomatic Conference of Plenipotentiaries on the Establishment of an International Criminal Court) A/CONF. 183/13 (Rome, 15 June–17 July 1998), vol II, 223: 'human rights norms recognized by the international community or recognized by the main legal systems'.

[152] R Young, 'Internationally Recognized Human Rights Before the International Criminal Court' (2011) 60 *International and Comparative Law Quarterly* 189, 194; Bitti (n 31) 301.

[153] *Prosecutor v Lubanga* (Separate opinion of Judge Pikis to the Decision on the Prosecutor's'Application for Leave to Reply to "Conclusions de la défense en réponse au mémoire d'appel du Procureur"') ICC-01/04-01/06 (12 September 2006) para 3.

[154] A Davidson, 'Human Rights Protection before the International Criminal Court' (2016) 18 *International Community Law Review* 72, 77.

[155] *Lubanga* (Judgment on the Appeal against the Decision on the Defence Challenge to the Jurisdiction of the Court) (n 111) para 37.

[156] *Rome Statute* (n 38) art 69(7): Evidence obtained by means of a violation of this Statute or internationally recognized human rights shall not be admissible if: (a) [. . .] & (b) [. . .].

[157] ibid art 7(1)(h).

human rights' is fairly broad, the fact that the choice was made for human rights instead of IHRL provides a restricting twist.

The *raison d'être* of adding this last paragraph to Article 21 was to constrain the judges' discretion.[158] In that regard, the idea behind the paragraph is the same as the general purpose of the article. In line with this, some authors predicted shortly after establishing the Rome Statute that Article 21(3) would 'have little concrete impact on the implementation of the applicable law'.[159] Again, this shows that there was little awareness of how difficult this paragraph would fit the structure of Article 21. According to Arsanjani, this paragraph could potentially have 'the opposite effect and broaden the competence of the court' instead of limiting the court's power. Given that it 'provides a standard against which all the law applied by the court should be tested', it could be used to set aside other sources.[160]

B. Human Rights in the Context of Crime Interpretation

There have been multiple positions on the functioning of this paragraph. Some experts have called it a quasi-constitutional provision,[161] while others have called it 'a very important safeguard, guaranteeing the respect for human rights throughout the proceedings'.[162] The paragraph has likewise been introduced as a notion of a super legality[163] that trumps any other source listed. Hafner and Binder disagree and find that the structure of Article 21 does not allow for this idea of super legality.[164] Nonetheless, even a conservative interpretation of paragraph (3) 'could support the proposition that, in the case of a conflict between the Statute and a human rights norm, the court could decline to apply the statutory rule'.[165] Similarly, Zeegers understands Article 21(3) as requiring 'a mandatory test of consistency'.[166] Lastly, this paragraph has also been argued to function as a principle of systemic integration in the sense of Article 31(3)(c) VCLT.[167]

The reason for these different understandings of Article 21(3) can be partly attributed to the fact that it mentions both the interpretation and application

[158] Arsanjani (n 25) 28.
[159] Pellet (n 26) 1082.
[160] Arsanjani (n 25) 29.
[161] Sheppard (n 148) 46; see also Schabas (n 22).
[162] A Bos, '1948–1998: The Universal Declaration of Human Rights and the Statute of the International Criminal Court' (1998) 22 *Fordham International Law Journal* 229.
[163] Pellet (n 26) 1080–81.
[164] G Hafner and C Binder, 'The Interpretation of Article 21 (3) ICC Statute: Opinion Reviewed' (2004) 9 *Austrian Review of International and European Law* 163, 173–74.
[165] Sheppard (n 148) 46.
[166] K Zeegers, *International Criminal Tribunals and Human Rights Law: Adherence and Contextualization*, vol 5 (International Criminal Justice Series, Springer, 2016) 76ff.
[167] Bailey (n 91) 527.

of human rights. As a result, the discussion has arisen on whether Article 21(3) can be seen as a direct source or merely as an interpretative principle assisting the judge. Although some authors would wish to afford a limited role to human rights in the interpretative process, the fact that application is also mentioned makes it more difficult to see this paragraph as a mere interpretative principle. The Appeals Chamber has furthermore held that the Statute must be interpreted and, more importantly, applied in accordance with internationally recognised human rights.[168] Nevertheless, the approach taken by the Court in the application of Article 21(3) has differed depending on the context, and some authors have questioned whether the court sufficiently weighs the use of Article 21(3) against other criminal law principles.[169] In relation to several procedural matters, there are decisions at the ICC that are evidence of the fact that limits have been set on applying human rights.[170]

Some scholars argue that international crimes are the criminalisation of human rights violations.[171] This type of reasoning is a slippery slope towards legality violations, as it seems to suggest Article 21(3) operating as a legal basis for a crime. It is therefore important to stress the difference as well as the interconnectedness of ICL and IHR.[172] The ICC is not a human rights court.[173] And although there is no need to unnecessarily limit the way in which Article 21(3) operates, it has to be carefully examined whether the role of human rights is in conformity with the principle of legality. So, despite the Rome Statute also being 'an instrument for augmenting the protection of human rights',[174] the legality principle opposes a criminalisation on the basis of Article 21(3).[175] This being clear, however, the overall relationship between Article 21(3) and Article

[168] *Situation in the Democratic Republic of the Congo, Prosecutor v Lubanga* (Judgment on the Appeal of Mr Thomas Lubanga Dyilo against the Decision on the Defence Challenge to the Jurisdiction of the Court pursuant to article 19(2)(a) of the Statute of 3 October 2006) ICC-01/04-01/06 (OA4) (14 December 2006) paras 36–37.

[169] B McGonigle Leyh, 'Pragmatism over Principles: The International Criminal Court and a Human Rights-Based Approach to Judicial Interpretation' (2018) 41 *Fordham International Law Journal* 734ff.

[170] See G Irving, 'The other side of the Article 21(3) coin: Human rights in the Rome Statute and the limits of Article 21(3)' (2018) 31 *Leiden Journal of International Law* 641–65: analysing three more conservative positions.

[171] *Prosecutor v Nahimana* (Judgment and Sentence) ICTR-99-52-T (3 December 2003) para 1078.

[172] McGonigle Leyh (n 169) 699.

[173] *Prosecutor v Katanga* (Decision on the application for the interim release of detained Witnesses DRCD02-P-0236, DRC-D02-P-0228 and DRC-D02-P-0350) CC-01/04-01/07 (1 October 2013) para 27; *Prosecutor v Gaddafi and Al-Senuss* (Judgment on the Appeal of Mr Abdullah Al-Senussi against the Decision of Pre-Trial Chamber I of 11 October 2013 entitled, 'Decision on the admissibility of the case against Abdullah Al-Senussi') ICC-01/11-01/11565 (May 24, 2014) para 219; *Prosecutor v Gaddafi and Al-Senuss* (Dissenting opinion of Judge Separate Opinion of Judge Anita Usacka to the Judgment on the Appeal of Mr Abdullah Al-Senussi against the Decision of Pre-Trial Chamber I of 11 October 2013) ICC-01/11-01/11565 (May 24, 2014) para 10; see also Emma Irving, 'The other side of the Article 21(3) coin: Human rights in the Rome Statute and the limits of Article 21(3)' (2019) 32 *LJIL* 845; McGonigle Leyh (n 169) 724.

[174] Bailey (n 91) 546.

[175] Davidson (n 154) 94.

22 remains particularly contentious. The only passage clarifying their relation states 'that consistency with internationally recognized human rights would require that interpretation by the Court be consistent with the principle of nullum crimen sine lege'.[176]

The ICTR's judgment in *Nahimana* illustrates the overall legality concerns.[177] Faced with the interpretation of incitement to genocide, the ICTR Trial Chamber bypassed the Genocide Convention and, in the absence of case law from the ICT, relied heavily on human rights jurisprudence concerning hate speech. This led to a departure from the requirement of a causal link between incitement and genocide.[178] Orentlicher criticised this approach because it did not take into account the *travaux préparatoires* of the Genocide Convention.[179] Furthermore, had the same reasoning been applied at the ICC, it would have placed Article 21(3) in direct conflict with Article 22(2). *Nahimana* demonstrates the risk of using expansive human rights norms to reshape crime definitions.

The Appeals Chamber in the *Abd-Al-Rahman* case, addressing a jurisdictional challenge related to the Security Council referral on Darfur, explicitly confirmed that the principle of legality falls within the scope of Article 21(3) and analysed it alongside Article 22(2).[180] While the Chamber relied on human rights jurisprudence to articulate the legality standard, it did so without addressing the standard demanded by the Rome Statute. Despite acknowledging that 'the precise language of the principle differs across jurisdiction',[181] the judges still adopted a human rights-based understanding of legality. This overlooked the higher threshold embedded in Article 22(2), which codifies three interpretive sub-principles: strict construction, the prohibition of analogy, and in dubio pro reo. These legality requirements limit the extent to which human rights can be used. As Galand notes, 'even if IHRL is superior to other norms enshrined in the Rome Statute, IHRL obligations must also be contextualised'.[182]

Even if one were to accept the absolute primacy of IHRL over other sources and allow provisions of the Statute or the EoC to be set aside in the face of conflicting norms, such application would still be constrained by the requirements of Article 22(2). Human rights norms used in crime interpretation must

[176] *Report of the Preparatory Committee on the Establishment of an International Criminal Court to the United Nations Diplomatic Conference of Plenipotentiaries on the Establishment of an International Criminal Court* A/CONF.183/2/Add.1.

[177] see DF Orentlicher, 'Criminalizing hate speech: a comment on the ICTR's judgment in the prosecutor v. Nahimana et al.' (2005) 13 *Human Rights Brief* 1–5.

[178] *The Prosecutor v Ferdinand Nahimana, Jean-Bosco Barayagwiza, and Hassan Ngeze* (Judgment and Sentence) ICTR-99-52-T (3 December 2003) paras 983–99.

[179] Orentlicher (n 177) 2.

[180] *Prosecutor v Abd-Al-Rahman* (Judgment on the appeal of Mr Abd-Al-Rahman against the Pre-Trial Chamber II's 'Decision on the Defence '*Exception d'incompétence*') ICC-02/05-01/20-302 (1 November 2021) para 83.

[181] ibid para 85.

[182] AS Galand, 'The Systemic Effect of International Human Rights Law on International Criminal Law' in M Scheinin (ed), *Human Rights Norms in 'Other' International Courts* (CUP, 2019).

pass the legality test set by this provision. As the case studies will show, there are examples where crime interpretation has relied on human rights reasoning, even if not explicitly invoking Article 21(3). In such cases, the challenge remains to rigorously assess whether legality safeguards have been respected.

VIII. SOURCES OUTSIDE THE SCOPE OF ARTICLE 21: ACADEMIC WRITINGS

As the introduction has shown, the positivistic direction of this study requires that judicial decision-making is grounded in the law. Achieving formal validity of a decision is not possible without a decision being justified by *legal* sources. However, an issue that so far has been unaddressed is the extent to which Article 21 is designed to be an exhaustive provision or whether it leaves room for other sources to be taken into account.

One additional source, not listed in Article 21 but often referenced, is scholarly writing. Unlike Article 38(1)(d) of the ICJ Statute – which explicitly includes 'the teachings of the most highly qualified publicists' – Article 21 omits such mention. An empirical study of Stappert, which analysed references to academic writings in the case law of several ICTs, came to the conclusion that 'academic writings overall seem to play a more influential role in the judicial interpretative process than its characterization as a subsidiary means indicates'.[183] She argued that 'the use of academic articles and monographs - also vis-a-vis treaty commentaries – is even more pronounced at the ICC', despite the lack of explicit inclusion in Article 21.[184]

This study finds it unhealthy to propose that judges refrain from consulting academic debates or disregard scholarly writings, as academic insights can certainly improve judicial reasoning. It is nonetheless important to consider a sound and transparent methodology. First, judges should clearly present academic writings as subsidiary aids to interpreting law, not as independent sources. It serves legal certainty when judges illuminate how the scholarly work fits the sources as outlined in the Statute. Second, and inspired by Article 38 ICJ Statute, the scholarly works cited by the Court should convey a certain authority. When renowned and well-established experts of ICL are cited, this is much more authoritative than when academic sources appear in judgments that are from experts with no pedigree in ICL. Third, where possible, judges should avoid relying on isolated or marginal academic views. As the case studies will demonstrate, some references to academic sources are more adequate than others.

[183] N Stappert, 'A New Influence of Legal Scholars? The Use of Academic Writings at International Criminal Courts and Tribunals' (2018) 31 *Leiden Journal of International Law* 963, 975.

[184] ibid 972.

IX. CONCLUSION: A LEGALITY-CENTRED METHODOLOGY OF APPLICABLE LAW

This chapter examined Article 21, understanding it as the ICC's rule of recognition. It showed how its hierarchical structure must be strictly upheld but should be fine-tuned in the context of crime interpretation, which requires a source doctrine shaped by the principle of legality. Some key observations can be made.

First, in the context of crime interpretation, the ICC judges should particularly clarify when relying on sources beyond the Rome Statute and the Elements of Crimes is necessary, underscoring the primacy of the primary sources and how they align with Article 21. This chapter has criticised the *irreconcilable difference* test and proposed an appropriateness test to deal with conflicts between the primary sources. Second, in relation to Article 21(1)(b), this study has explained that, next to treaties, the paragraph is understood to encompass customary law. Customary law, given its often unwritten nature, holds an inherent legality risk. It is crucial that the judges motivate relying on this source and, more importantly, conduct a full and independent custom ascertainment which involves an examination of both state practice and *opinio juris* and not merely an assessment of precedent. Third, this study rejects including general principles under paragraph (b) and presents convincing reasons to place them under paragraph (c). Their broad nature opposes being used as a sole basis of criminalisation. Moreover, the judge cannot bypass the stricter requirements of custom formation and rely directly on general principles, as these are more easily established. Fourth, as for Article 21(2), convincing arguments were discussed to not exclude precedent from the interpretative process and allow for external precedent to aid in contextualising interpretation. The Rome Statute's system of precedent, which is not as strict as *stare decisis* but nevertheless affords a position to internal precedent, should be used to the advantage of the court. The Chambers should make explicit when precedent is followed and when it is not, and why. However, the misuse of precedent to sidestep the finding of the constituent elements in custom formation is a development that is highly problematic. Solely relying on precedent, certainly external precedent, for the conclusion that a crime exists in customary law, is not allowed in light of Article 21. Article 21(3) is, despite its overall importance and non-subsidiary nature, a source that should be handled with care in the context of crime interpretation. This study does not afford a superior position to this source and finds that, particularly in relation to crime interpretation, limits should be set. Despite the interconnectedness between IHRL and ICL, IHRL cannot serve as a basis for criminalisation or cannot be used by the judge to extend crime definitions. The primacy of the Rome Statute does not allow for this, and the choice for 'human rights' rather than IHRL in this paragraph further underscores such a position.

Lastly, this study finds convincing reasons to conclude that Article 21 is non-exhaustive and allows judges to consult and use sources external to this article. It nonetheless has to be made explicit that these sources are only used to inform decision-making and not as a way to circumvent the hierarchy of sources. For instance, with academic sources, the court can certainly use them and even refer to them, but the latter should be handled with moderation and a clear reason why their use is necessary.

To conclude, in the words of Vasiliev: 'Article 21 was included in the ICC Statute to create a solid, transparent and predictable legal regime equipped to deal with legal collisions and lacunae, while at the same time avoiding or diminishing the risk of judicial lawmaking.'[185] This chapter has, in the run-up to the case studies, made several propositions on how Article 21's mandate can be fulfilled and addressed how the meandering of the river of sources can be better guided to adhere to the principle of legality.

[185] S Vasiliev, 'Proofing the Ban on Witness Proofing: Did the ICC Get it Right?' (2009) 20 *Criminal Law Forum* 193, 212.

4

Evaluating Crime Interpretation in Terms of Methods of Interpretation

There is no part of the law of treaties which the text writer approaches with more trepidation than the question of interpretation[1]

I. INTRODUCTION

THIS CHAPTER BUILDS UPON the general introduction's discussion of interpretation, drawing from MacCormick's insight that a norm must first be understood before it can be applied.[2] Without delving again into the specific distinctions between law-ascertainment, law-determination and law interpretation,[3] this chapter focuses on the last element: the methods used to interpret sources once they have been identified. In the same way that the previous chapter identified Article 21 of the Rome Statute as a rule of recognition for determining sources, this chapter argues that, in the absence of a dedicated rule on interpretative methods within the Rome Statute, Article 22 of that Statute should similarly function as a rule of recognition for methods of interpretation.[4] Before substantiating this claim, it first critically evaluates the default reliance in international law on the methods set out in Articles 31 to 33 of the Vienna Convention on the Law of Treaties (VCLT).[5] While the VCLT formally applies only to 'treaties between states',[6] its methods are routinely used for a

[1] A McNair, *The Law of Treaties* (OUP, 1961) 361.

[2] N MacCormick, 'Argumentation and interpretation in law' (1993) 6 *Ratio Juris* 16, 19.

[3] See ch 3 and J d'Aspremont, 'The Multidimensional Process of Interpretation: Content-Determination and Law-Ascertainment Distinguished' in A Bianchi, D Peat and M Windsor (eds), *Interpretation in International Law* (OUP, 2015).

[4] See ch 3 and see on the rule of recognition: SJ Shapiro, 'What is the Rule of Recognition (and does it exist)?' (2009) *Public Law & Legal Theory Research Paper Series* No. 181.

[5] Vienna Convention on the Law of Treaties (adopted 23 May 1969, entered into force 27 January 1980) 1155 UNTS 331 (VCLT).

[6] Article 1 VCLT: 'The present Convention applies to treaties between States'.

far wider range of legal instruments,[7] including international investment treaties,[8] and bilateral agreements,[9] regional human rights instruments,[10] constituent treaties of international organisations,[11] Security Council resolutions,[12] and even non-binding instruments[13] and national law.[14] Furthermore, a vast array of actors have relied on them.[15] Moreover, not only written treaties but also customary and unwritten norms have been interpreted according to the VCLT rules.[16] These rules have acquired clear and unequivocal customary status,[17] and this practice has entrenched a dominant paradigm that the VCLT should serve as the central reference point for all interpretative activity.

This chapter critically examines and challenges the ICC judges' adoption of this paradigm. It highlights that the VCLT rules, which have been applied uncritically to various interpretative activities – including the interpretation of crimes – have largely escaped scrutiny in ICL. While most scholarship assumes their applicability, only Dov Jacobs has explicitly questioned their suitability for

[7] O Dörr and K Schmalenbach, *Vienna convention on the Law of Treaties: A commentary* (Springer, 2012) 536–37; RK Gardiner, *Treaty Interpretation* (OUP, 2008) 478.

[8] See, eg, *Murphy International v Ecuador*, ICSID Case No. ARB/08/4, Award on Jurisdiction (15 December 2010) para 71; *Giovanni Alemanni and Others v The Argentine Republic*, ICSID Case No. ARB/07/8, Decision on Jurisdiction and Admissibility (17 November 2014) para 270; T Gazzini, *Interpretation of International Investment Treaties* (Hart Publishing, 2016).

[9] See, eg, *Sempra Energy International v Argentina*, ICSID Case No. ARB/02/16, Award (28 September 2007) para 3; See further T Gazzini, 'Interpretation of (Allegedly) Self-judging Clauses in Bilateral Investment Treaties' in M Fitzmaurice, O Elias and P Merkouris (eds), *Treaty Interpretation and the Vienna Convention on the Law of Treaties: 30 years on* (Martinus Nijhoff, 2010).

[10] See, eg, *Demir and Baykara v Turkey*, 48 EHRR (2009) 54, paras 65–68; see further G Letsas, 'Strasbourg's Interpretive Ethic: Lessons for the International Lawyer' (2010) 21 *EJIL* 509; G Letsas, *A theory of interpretation of the European Convention on Human Rights* (OUP, 2007); *Case of the 'Mapiripán Massacre' v Colombia* (Merits, Reparations, and Costs, Judgment) Inter-American Court of Human Rights Series C No 134 (15 September 2005), para 106; see further L Lixinski, 'Treaty interpretation by the Inter-American Court of Human Rights: expansionism at the service of the unity of international law' (2010) 21 *EJIL* 585.

[11] See, eg, *Legality of the Threat or Use by a State of Nuclear Weapons*, Advisory Opinion, 1996 ICJ Reports 226, 237–38, para 19; see further HG Schermers and NM Blokker, *International Institutional Law, Unity within diversity*, 4th edn (Martinus Nijhoff, 2003) para 1148, paras 1346–50.

[12] See, eg, Case T-315/01 *Kadi and Al Barakaat International Foundation v Council and Commission* ECLI:EU:T:2005:332, 21 September 2005; see further M Wood, 'The Interpretation of Security Council Resolutions, Revisited' (2017) 20 *Max Planck Yearbook of United Nations Law Online* 1, 7–8.

[13] See, eg, *Access to Information under OSPAR (Ireland v United Kingdom)*, 23 RIAA 59 (2003); see further R Cryer, 'Royalism and the King: Article 21 of the Rome Statute and the Politics of Sources' (2009) 12 *New Criminal Law Review: An International and Interdisciplinary Journal* 390.

[14] See further on applying the VCLT to national law and M Waibel, 'Principles of Treaty Interpretation Developed for and Applied by National Courts?' in HP Aust and G Nolte (eds), *The Interpretation of International Law by Domestic Courts: Uniformity, Diversity, Convergence* (OUP, 2016).

[15] See A Aust, *Modern Treaty Law and Practice*, 2nd edn (CUP, 2007) 233; M Durkee, 'Interpretive Entrepreneurs' (2021) 107 *Virginia Law Review* 431, 445–47.

[16] See further on applying the VCLT to the customary definition of terrorism.

[17] Case concerning the *Territorial Dispute (Libya v Chad)* (Judgment) [1994] ICJ Reports 6, 26–27, para 41; *Nuclear Weapons* Advisory Opinion (n 11) para 19; Case concerning *Oil Platforms (Iran v United States)* (Preliminary Objections, Judgment) [1996] ICJ Reports 812, para 23; *Kasikili/Sedudu Island (Botswana v Namibia)* (Judgment) [1999] ICJ rep 1045, para 18.

criminal law.[18] Drawing from his critique and extending it, this chapter investigates whether there is truly an obligation to apply the VCLT to all international legal interpretation, examining in particular whether such an obligation exists in the context of crime interpretation. Beyond the question of obligation, this chapter also reassesses whether efforts to reconcile the VCLT rules with criminal law rules of interpretation – particularly those articulated in Article 22 of the Rome Statute – are helpful.

This chapter first discusses the interpretative methods in the field of public international law (section II) and then examines how these methods were transplanted to international criminal law (ICL) (section III). Section IV scrutinises this transplant and evaluates arguments in favour of and against the VCLT application. This chapter concludes with an assessment of the usefulness and limitations of this transplant.

II. THE VCLT RULES OF INTERPRETATION IN PUBLIC INTERNATIONAL LAW

Articles 31 to 33 VCLT stipulate the rules of interpretation that apply to the interpretation of treaties. Article 31 VCLT sets out a general rule of interpretation:

> A treaty shall be interpreted in good faith in accordance with the ordinary meaning to be given to the terms of the treaty in their context and in the light of its object and purpose.

Article 31(2) specifies that the context shall comprise primarily the text, including its preamble, as well as any agreement[19] or other instrument[20] made in connection with it. Furthermore, Article 31(3) stipulates instruments that make up the context.[21]

Article 31(4) holds that: 'A special meaning shall be given to a term if it is established that the parties so intended'.

Article 32 specifies that recourse may be had to *supplementary means of interpretation*, including the preparatory work of the treaty and the circumstances of its conclusion, in order to confirm the meaning resulting from the

[18] D Jacobs, *Why the Vienna Convention should not be applied to the ICC Rome Statute: a plea for respecting the principle of legality* (2013) dovjacobs.com/2013/08/24/why-the-vienna-convention-should-not-be-applied-to-the-icc-rome-statute-a-plea-for-respecting-the-principle-of-legality/; D Jacobs, 'Positivism and International Criminal Law: the Principle of Legality as a Rule of Conflict of Theories' in J d'Aspremont and J Kammerhofer (eds), *International Legal Positivism in a Post-Modern World* (CUP, 2014).

[19] (a) any agreement relating to the treaty which was made between all the parties in connexion with the conclusion of the treaty.

[20] (b) any instrument which was made by one or more parties in connexion with the conclusion of the treaty and accepted by the other parties as an instrument related to the treaty.

[21] (a) any subsequent agreement [. . .]; (b) any subsequent practice [. . .]; (c) any relevant rules of international law applicable in the relations between the parties.

application of Article 31, or to determine the meaning when the interpretation according to Article 31:

(a) leaves the meaning ambiguous or obscure; or
(b) leads to a result which is manifestly absurd or unreasonable.

Article 33 addresses the interpretation of treaties authenticated in two or more languages, which are presumed to have the same meaning. In case of doubt, 'the meaning which best reconciles the texts, having regard to the object and purpose of the treaty, shall be adopted.'

The International Law Commission (ILC) spent nearly two decades debating interpretative methods. During this drafting process, many expressed doubts about the usefulness of codifying interpretative methods and whether such an enterprise could meaningfully guide interpretation in practice.[22] Some experts expressed the view that legal interpretation could not be captured in rules,[23] while others supported the idea that there is a logic, not void of objectivity, inherent to the process of legal interpretation.[24]

The negotiation process showed that the drafters struggled in formulating one fixed point of reference for all legal interpretation in an international landscape with multiple legal cultures, multiple languages and a wide variety of regional and doctrinal schools about interpretation.[25] Eventually, the idea prevailed that a formalist and 'predominantly rule-based approach to interpretation'[26] would bring these differences together.[27] The dominant internationalist paradigm nowadays sees these rules as an effective tool against the fragmentation

[22] See, eg, ILC, 'Summary Records Of the Sixteenth Session, 726th Meeting: Law of Treaties, E/CN.4/167' (1964) vol I para 15; ILC, 'Third Report on the law of treaties, by Sir Humphrey Waldock, Special Rapporteur, A/CN.4/167 and Add.1-3' (1964) vol II *YBILC* 52–54; see also P Merkouris, 'Introduction: Interpretation is a science, is an art, is a science' in M Fitzmaurice, O Elias and P Merkouris (eds), *Treaty Interpretation and the Vienna Convention on the Law of Treaties: 30 years on* (Martinus Nijhoff, 2010) 9; J Klabbers, 'Virtuous Interpretation' in M Fitzmaurice, O Elias and P Merkouris (eds), *Treaty Interpretation and the Vienna Convention on the Law of Treaties: 30 years on* (Martinus Nijhoff, 2010) 17–25; Gardiner (n 7) 69–72.

[23] D Peat and M Windsor, 'Playing the Game of Interpretation, On Meaning and Metaphor in International Law' in A Bianchi, D Peat and M Windsor (eds), *Interpretation in International Law* (OUP, 2015) 16; See also P Allott, 'Interpretation-An Exact Art' in A Bianchi, D Peat and M Windsor (eds), *Interpretation in International Law* (OUP, 2015).

[24] See, eg, U Linderfalk, 'Is Treaty Interpretation an Art or a Science? International Law and Rational Decision Making' (2015) 26 *EJIL* 169; See for more elaborate discussions on the issue of objectivity: OM Fiss, 'Objectivity and Interpretation' (1981–1982) 34 *Stanford Law Review* 739; J Husa and M Van Hoecke (eds), *Objectivity in Law and Legal Reasoning* (European Academy of Legal Theory Series, Hart Publishing, 2012).

[25] Peat and Windsor (n 23) 7–9.

[26] J d'Aspremont, *Epistemic Forces in International Law* (Edward Elgar, 2015) 214.

[27] C Djeffal, 'Establishing the Argumentative DNA of International Law: A Cubistic View on the Rule of Treaty Interpretation and its Underlying Legal Culture(s)' (2014) 5 *Transnational Legal Theory* 128, 137; see also M Fitzmaurice, 'The Practical Workings of the Law of Treaties' in MD Evans (ed), *International Law* (OUP, 2003) 186.

of international law.[28] Particularly, the principle of systematic integration in Article 31(1)(c) VCLT, according to which interpretation should occur 'against the background of the general principles of international law',[29] functions as the glue that holds international law, with all its specialised regimes, together.[30]

Since their adoption, the VCLT methods have been widely used across courts, reinforcing the perception that their application is self-evident.[31] Article 31(1) sets out four elements: interpretation must occur (1) in good faith, (2) in accordance with the ordinary meaning, (3) within the context of the treaty, and (4) in light of its object and purpose.[32] These elements are not applied sequentially or hierarchically but rather operate as part of a 'single combined operation', whereby 'various elements, as they were present in any given case, would be thrown into the crucible and their interaction would give the legally relevant interpretation'.[33] This so-called crucible approach reflects a deliberate choice for interpretative flexibility over a rigid hierarchy of methods,[34] enabling either a textual, contextual, or teleological emphasis, depending on the case.[35]

The first element in Article 31(1) of the VCLT is the requirement to interpret treaties in good faith. This concept is familiar in most legal systems as a principle of contract law, and has been transplanted to international law, where it is seen as useful for treaties that resemble contracts between states.[36] Often associated with the idea of reasonableness, the principle's operation in the context of contractual or treaty obligations is relatively straightforward. However, its contours in treaty interpretation are much less clear, and it remains a rather

[28] M Koskenniemi and P Leino, 'Fragmentation of International Law? Postmodern Anxieties' (2002) 15 *LJIL* 553–79; M Koskenniemi, Fragmentation of international law: difficulties arising from the diversification and expansion of international law: Report of the study group of the international law commission' (2006) para 37.

[29] AD McNair, *The Law of Treaties* (OUP, 1986) 466.

[30] C Stahn and L van den Herik, '"Fragmentation", Diversification and "3D" Legal Pluralism: International Criminal Law as the Jack-in-The-Box?' in C Stahn and L van den Herik (eds), *The Diversification and Fragmentation of International Criminal Law* (Martinus Nijhoff, 2012) 25–26.

[31] See the sources in fns 6–18; J-M Sorel and V Boré Eveno, 'Article 31. Convention of 1969. Article 31 Convention of 1986' in O Corten and P Klein (eds), *The Vienna Conventions on the Law of Treaties: a Commentary*, vol 1 (OUP, 2011) 817.

[32] See ME Villiger, 'The rules on interpretation: misgivings, misunderstandings, miscarriage? The "crucible" intended by the International Law Commission' in E Cannizzaro (ed), *The Law of Treaties Beyond the Vienna Convention* (OUP, 2011).

[33] ILC, 'Reports of the International Law Commission on the second part of its seventeenth session and on its eighteenth session' (1966) vol II *YBILC* 219–20; see also Gardiner (n 7) 10. ILC, 'Reports of the International Law Commission on the second part of its seventeenth session and on its eighteenth session' (1966) vol II *YBILC* 219–20; see also Gardiner (n 7) 10.

[34] Gardiner (n 7) 481; GI Hernández, 'Interpretation' in J Kammerhofer and J d'Aspremont (eds), *International Legal Positivism in a Post-Modern World* (CUP, 2014) 329; ME Villiger, *Commentary on the 1969 Vienna Convention on the Law of Treaties* (Martinus Nijhoff, 2009) 436.

[35] ILC, 'Summary Records of the Sixteenth Session, 726th Meeting: Law of Treaties, E/CN.4/167' (1964) vol I para 4.

[36] S Reinhold, 'Good Faith in International Law' (2013) 2 *UCL Journal of Law and Jurisprudence* 40; see also M Waibel, *The Origins of Interpretive Canons in Domestic Legal Systems* (Research Paper Series, 2018) 4–5.

elusive concept in that setting. Therefore, good faith is sometimes linked to the principle of effectiveness,[37] expressed in the Latin maxim *ut res magis valeat quam pereat*[38] – it is better for a thing to have effect than to be rendered void. This principle supports choosing interpretations that allow a treaty to function effectively and aligns with teleological reasoning. When two interpretations are possible, the one that enables the treaty to produce appropriate effects should be preferred, in line with good faith and the treaty's object and purpose.[39]

ILC's Rapporteur proposed enshrining the principle of effectiveness in a separate provision. He suggested that treaties be interpreted to give them the 'fullest weight and effect'.[40] However, the proposal was unanimously rejected, largely because it was seen as too expansive.[41] There is a significant difference between avoiding interpretations that render treaties ineffective and requiring interpretations that give them the greatest possible effect. The ILC's rejection of Waldock's formulation signals a preference for the former, narrower reading.[42] Linderfalk's reading of the principle of effectiveness as articulated by Rapporteurs Thirlway and Amerasinghe states that it comprises two sub-rules: (1) *la règle de l'effet utile* – every treaty provision must be presumed to have meaning – and (2) *la règle de l'efficacité* – the treaty should be interpreted so that it achieves its intended end.[43] This approach suggests that effectiveness is best understood in negative terms: interpretations should not render a treaty or its provisions without legal effect.

The ICJ regards good faith as a cornerstone principle inherent to international co-operation,[44] and has furthermore embraced it as a principle of interpretation.[45] Time and time again, the ICJ has used the principle of effectiveness as part of a teleological interpretation of treaty provisions.[46] This principle has at times led to very extensive interpretations.[47] As will be argued in the section dealing with the transposition of these principles to ICL, the principle of effectiveness stands diametrically opposed to the principle of restrictive interpretation and could even be considered mutually incompatible.[48]

[37] Waibel (n 36) 4–5.

[38] Gardiner (n 7) 148.

[39] ILC, 'Reports of the International Law Commission on the second part of its seventeenth session and on its eighteenth session' (1966) vol II *YBILC* 219.

[40] ILC, 'Third Report on the law of treaties, by Sir Humphrey Waldock, Special Rapporteur, A/CN.4/167 and Add.1-3' (1964) vol II *YBILC* 53.

[41] U Linderfalk, *On the Interpretation of Treaties: The Modern International Law as Expressed in the 1969 Vienna Convention on the Law of Treaties* (Springer, 2007) 218–20.

[42] ibid 218–20.

[43] ibid 229, fn 64.

[44] See, eg, *Nuclear Test Case (Australia v France)* (Judgment) [1974] ICJ Rep 253, para 46.

[45] See, eg, *The Fisheries Jurisdiction Case (Spain v Canada)* (Judgment) [1998] ICJ Rep 432, para 52.

[46] See, eg, *Case concerning the Territorial Dispute (Libya v Chad)* (Judgment) (n 17) para 47.

[47] See, eg, *Application of the International Convention on the Elimination of All Forms of Racial Discrimination (Georgia v Russian Federation)* (Joint Dissenting Opinion of President Owada, Judges Simma Abraham and Donoghue and Judge Ad Hoc Gaja) [2011] ICJ Rep 70, para 21.

[48] H Lauterpacht, 'Restrictive interpretation and the Principle of effectiveness in the Interpretation of Treaties' (1949) 26 *British Yearbook of International Law* 48.

The second ingredient articulated in Article 31 VCLT is that a rule shall be given a clear, plain, ordinary or unambiguous meaning. This method is often seen as the foundation of legal interpretation.[49] While it does not trump other means of interpretation, it is often seen as the starting point.[50] The merits of the textualist approach are that 'it urges judges to interpret the law according to what the legislature has actually communicated', avoids overreliance on external factors, and eliminates interpretative choices that find no ground in the text.[51] Whereas the crucible approach in theory attaches equal weight to each interpretative ingredient, at times, the ICJ seems to afford a more prominent role in the interpretative process to the textual ingredient.[52]

A textual approach can operate across different levels. At the micro-level, the analysis focuses on understanding a concept or a word. This can entail consulting a dictionary to clarify a term.[53] In most instances, this is too simplistic to offer an in-depth understanding,[54] and a more technical or legal understanding is more adequate.[55] The textual approach can also function at the meso-level, which includes taking into account grammar (eg, issues of punctuation can be relevant or the syntax can reveal the meaning).[56] The textual approach can adopt a broader/systemic focus (eg, looking at that subsection of the treaty or the treaty as a whole).[57] The reference to the 'terms of the treaty' in that general rule reflects a compromise linking the text of the provision to the treaty as a whole. Accordingly, textual analysis extends into contextual analysis when terms are situated within the treaty's broader structure and purpose.[58] The wider our understanding of a textual approach, the closer it gets to a contextual approach. There is, in that regard, a certain overlap between these two methods. Of course, the object and purpose can also be found in the ordinary meaning of the text, and in that regard, there is also an overlap between a textual and teleological approach. A textual approach nonetheless attaches a higher importance to the text and seeks 'what the text would reasonably be understood to mean, rather

[49] MS Moore, 'A Natural Law Theory of Interpretation' (1985) *Southern California Law Review* 277; BG Slocum, *Ordinary Meaning: A Theory of the Most Fundamental Principle of Legal Interpretation* (University of Chicago Press, 2015) 4.

[50] Aust (n 15) 235.

[51] A Marmor, *The Language of Law* (OUP, 2014) 107.

[52] *Legality of the Use of Force Case (Serbia and Montenegro v Belgium)* (Preliminary Objections) [2004] ICJ Rep 279, para 100.

[53] See, eg, *Oil Platforms* Judgment (n 17) para 45; see also Gardiner (n 7) 495.

[54] H Lauterpacht, 'Restrictive interpretation and the principle of effectiveness in the interpretation of treaties' (1949) 26 *British Yearbook of International Law* 48.

[55] See, eg, *Kasikili/Sedudu Island (Botswana v Namibia)* (n 17) para 28.

[56] See, eg, *Aegean Sea Continental Shelf case (Greece v Turkey)* (Judgment) [1978] ICJ Rep 3, paras 50–55.

[57] See, eg, *Helvering v Gregory Revenue (US Court of Appeals, 2nd Circuit)* Opinion Judge Learned Hand [1934] 69 F 2d 809, 810–11.

[58] IM Sinclair, *The Vienna Convention on the Law of Treaties* (Melland Schill monographs in international law, 2nd edn (MUP, 1984) 121.

than upon what it was intended to mean'.[59] These approaches differ, but the dividing line between them is not so clear-cut.[60]

Textualism should be understood as an inclusive method, leaving room for other methods of interpretation. Based on a misunderstanding of textualism as an exclusionist vision on treaty interpretation, it is often misunderstood as the best way of adhering to the principle of strict construction. Quite the contrary, textualism neither supports nor contradicts a strict interpretation. There is a misconception amongst scholars that a literal meaning necessarily guarantees a strict construction,[61] an issue which is further fleshed out when discussing the ICL practice.[62]

The third interpretative ingredient is the context. The focus here is on the *legal context* not captured by textual analysis, even though extra-legal elements can also be included.[63]

Article 31(2) VCLT defines the relevant context as including the treaty's text, preamble, annexes, and agreements or instruments related to the treaty's conclusion. However, ambiguity remains as to what qualifies as being 'in connection to the conclusion of the treaty', and views diverge on whether this paragraph only includes agreements drawn up at the same time as the conclusion of the treaty. The central debate is whether the specifications in the second paragraph are merely exemplary or exhaustive.[64]

Article 31(3)(c) stipulates that 'any relevant rules of international law applicable in the relations between parties' need to be considered. This subparagraph is said to include the doctrine of systemic integration. Although rarely used before 2003, the ICJ's *Oil Platforms* case revived interest,[65] and systemic integration has since evolved beyond a mere principle of interpretation into a broad anti-fragmentation tool.[66] It results in the international legal order being understood as 'one single system' in which the doctrine of systemic integration allows us to 'transgress the borders of specialised sub-regimes of international law', and 'find a meaning for the terms in question that reflects the common basis of legal rules in an integrated system of international law'.[67] The VCLT's anti-fragmentation paradigm is what keeps the system of international law unified.

This principle of systemic integration has, however, sparked debate.[68] The debate is roughly divided between those who see the diversity of systems and the

[59] C Nelson, 'What is Textualism?' (2005) 91 *Virginia Law Review* 347, 352.

[60] ibid 349.

[61] J Powderly, 'The Rome Statute and the Attempted Corseting of the Interpretative Judicial Function: Reflections on Sources of Law and Interpretative Technique' in C Stahn (ed), *The Law and Practice of the International Criminal Court* (OUP, 2015) 465.

[62] See below.

[63] See, eg, *Kasikili/Sedudu Island (Botswana v Namibia)* (n 17) para 20.

[64] See Linderfalk (n 41) 133ff.

[65] See *Oil Platforms* Judgment (n 17).

[66] C McLachlan, 'The Principle of Systemic Integration and Article 31(3)(C) of the Vienna Convention' (2005) 54 *International and Comparative Law Quarterly* 279, 279–80.

[67] Dörr and Schmalenbach (n 7) 561.

[68] See P Webb, *International Judicial Integration and Fragmentation* (OUP, 2013).

proliferation of courts as a richness and those who fear too much fragmentation and regard it as the downfall of international law.[69] Depending on the point of view, a treaty system is categorised as a 'separate, autonomous, and self-contained system',[70] a self-sustained system,[71] or a closed system – even if the latter is difficult to perceive as possible.[72] Scholars like Simma and Koskenniemi offer differing visions. Simma sees self-contained regimes as having their own exhaustive set of secondary rules.[73] Koskenniemi, by contrast, acknowledges the special character of certain regimes but maintains that international law continues to provide the overarching normative framework.[74] This means that the understanding of this principle has a far-reaching effect on how the relationship between the subsystem of law and the general body of international law is understood.

Conflicts between specific ICL rules and broader international norms are typically managed through the *lex specialis* principle, granting priority to the more specific rule.[75] Yet the more one views the Rome Statute as a standalone regime, the less persuasive *lex specialis* becomes.[76] Therefore, when a problem of interpretation arises or when the more specific rule at hand does not immediately provide a solution, there are reasons to look more broadly at the system and not immediately turn to PIL to solve the issue. The notion of a self-contained regime offers a way out of this interpretative problem and means that not every single departure from interpretation in line with PIL has to be justified with reference to *lex specialis*.[77]

The last interpretative ingredient is 'the object and purpose'. This ingredient introduces a teleological or purpose-oriented technique of interpretation.[78] This approach comes in two forms. The first is the subjective-teleological approach that looks at the intention of the drafters, which involves a historical inquiry into the intention of the original lawmaker. Article 31 does not explicitly refer to intention, leaving the inclusion of this form debated.[79] The second is the objective-teleological approach, which seeks to discover the purpose 'assigned to the law by the legal community'.[80]

[69] McLachlan (n 66) 287ff.

[70] A Zammit Borda, 'Decision-making Patterns at the first trial of the ICC: A Perspective on the ICC' (2011) 2 *Creighton International and Comparative Law Journal* 30, 43.

[71] R Bellelli, *International Criminal Justice: Law and Practice from the Rome Statute to its Review* (Ashgate, 2010) 20.

[72] B Simma, 'Self-contained regimes' (1985) 16 *Netherlands Yearbook of International Law* 111, 111.

[73] ibid 493.

[74] Koskenniemi (n 28) paras 192–93.

[75] See further A Lindroos, 'Addressing norm conflicts in a fragmented legal system: the doctrine of *lex specialis*' (2005) 74 *Nordic Journal of International Law* 27; Koskenniemi (n 28) paras 35–65.

[76] ibid paras 65–67.

[77] B Simma and D Pulkowski, 'Of planets and the universe: self-contained regimes in international law' (2006) 17 *EJIL* 483, 488.

[78] C Gall, 'Coming to terms with a new role: The approach of the international court of justice to the interpretation of human rights treaties' (2014) 21 *Australian International Law Journal* 55, 56.

[79] A Bianchi, D Peat and M Windsor, *Interpretation in International Law* (OUP, 2015) 9.

[80] Linderfalk (n 41) 203.

As mentioned, this interpretative method connects to the *principle of effectiveness*, which promotes interpretations that best fulfil a treaty's purpose.[81] It is questionable whether reaching the object and purpose can always be formulated as a matter of effectiveness. Treaties may serve multiple or even conflicting purposes, complicating interpretative choices. Where two readings are possible, one furthering the treaty's purpose and the other undermining it, the former is typically preferred. However, the real challenge arises when both interpretations advance different purposes, making it challenging to frame the choice in terms of effectiveness.

Seeking a treaty's object and purpose is often done through the instrument's text.[82] For example, the object and purpose can be discovered through the *travaux préparatoires* of a treaty, which, in the case of a multilateral treaty, necessitates revealing the common intention of drafters.[83] Regularly, the *raison d'être* of a treaty is explained in its preamble.[84]

The ICJ frequently employs the teleological approach, often to support expansive readings.[85] This is not necessarily problematic in relation to human rights treaties, which generally aim to afford the highest degree of protection possible to individuals.[86] However, in ICL, this method carries significant risks as broad interpretations may clash with the principle of legality. This tension – and the dangers of importing teleological methods into ICL – are examined further in this chapter.[87]

III. THE VCLT'S TRANSPLANT TO ICL

The Nuremberg trials, which predate the VCLT, offer little in terms of explicit reflection on interpretative methodology. Interpretative methods were not openly debated. This absence can be partly explained by the urgency of other legal concerns – chiefly how to deflect charges of retroactivity – and by the diversity

[81] Dörr and Schmalenbach (n 7) 545.

[82] Linderfalk (n 41) 203.

[83] E Bjørge, *The Evolutionary Interpretation of Treaties* (OUP, 2014) 61; JD Mortenson, 'The Travaux of Travaux: Is the Vienna Convention Hostile to Drafting History?' (2013) 107 *American Journal of International Law* 780, 780; D Akande, 'Sources of International Criminal Law' in A Cassese (ed), *Oxford Companion to International Criminal Justice* (OUP, 2005) 44.

[84] MH Hulme, 'Preamble in Treaty Interpretation' (2015) 164 *University of Pennsylvania Law Review* 1281, 1300–1302.

[85] Application of the Convention on the Prevention and Punishment of the Crime of Genocide (*Bosnia and Herzegovina v Serbia and Montenegro*) (Judgment) [2007] ICJ Reports 43, para 161; Case concerning Sovereignty over Pulau Ligitan and Pulau Sipadan (*Indonesia v Malaysia*) (Judgment) [2002] ICJ Reports 625, para 51; *Abaclat and Others v Argentina* (Dissenting Opinion of Georges Abi-Saab to Decision on Jurisdiction and Admissibility) [2011] ICSID Case No ARB/07/5, para 159; see also M H Hulme, 'Preamble in Treaty Interpretation' (2015) 164 *University of Pennsylvania Law Review* 1281, 1324–30.

[86] C Gall, 'Coming to terms with a new role: The approach of the international court of justice to the interpretation of human rights treaties' (2014) 21 *Australian International Law Journal* 55, 56.

[87] See s IV below.

of interpretative traditions among the international bench. Still, interpretative reasoning did occur, often implicitly.

A well-known example is the controversy over Article 6(c) of the Nuremberg Charter, which was formulated differently across different authoritative language versions of the text – a semi-colon in the English version and a colon in the French and Russian versions. In the English text, the semi-colon suggested that only the crime of persecution required a nexus to war ("before or during the war; or persecution . . .), while in the French and Russian texts, the colon implied that all crimes against humanity were subject to the war nexus requirement. This discrepancy, common in multilingual treaty interpretation, posed a challenge which was eventually resolved through an official protocol amending the English version to align with the others, removing the semi-colon and thereby extending the war nexus to all crimes listed in Article 6(c).[88]

Another example pertains more generally to the interpretation of crimes against humanity. As a novel category, it was vulnerable to retroactivity claims.[89] The requirement that such crimes be committed 'in execution of or in connection with' other crimes introduced an indirect war nexus to bolster their legal basis. It enabled judges to argue that this crime category was not really novel but had always been included under the body of war crimes. Additionally, judges drew on the Martens Clause to support expansive readings tapping into a 'reservoir of uncodified law' that serves to protect humanity.[90] This clause held:

> Until a more complete code of the laws of war is issued, [. . .] populations and belligerents *remain under the protection and empire of the principles of international law*, as they result from the usages established between civilized nations, from the *laws of humanity* and the *requirements of the public conscience*.[91]

While the use of this clause potentially comes at odds with the legality principle, the judges in the *Krupp* case held that the clause was 'much more than a pious declaration', allowing recourse to it when written rules fell short and showing little concern over legality violations.[92] In a similar regard, the *Hostage case* shows the judges explicitly prioritised effectiveness over formal legality, warning

[88] IMT (Nuremberg), Judgment and Sentence (1 October 1946), Trial of the Major War Criminals before the International Military Tribunal, 919–20.

[89] See H Kelsen, 'The Rule Against Ex Post Facto Laws and the Prosecution of the Axis War Criminals' (1945) *The Judge Advocate Journal* 1; G Acquaviva, 'At the Origins of Crimes against Humanity: Clues to a Proper Understanding of the *Nullum Crimen* Principle in the Nuremberg Judgment' (2011) 9 *JICJ* 811.

[90] B Van Schaack, 'Judicial lawmaking the intersection between law and morals' (2008-2009) 97 *Georgetown Law Journal* 119, 148–49; see also A Cassese, 'The Martens Clause: half a loaf or simply pie in the sky?' (2000) 11 *EJIL* 187.

[91] Preamble to the 1899 Hague Convention (II) ('Laws and Customs of War on Land').

[92] United States v Krupp (the Krupp Case) (1948) 9 Trials of War Criminals before the Nuremberg Military Tribunals under Control Council Law No 10 1341.

that placing international law in a 'formalistic strait-jacket would ultimately destroy any effectiveness that it has acquired'.[93]

These examples reveal a tension between certain methods of interpretation and the principle of legality. While not yet the subject of systematic or explicit debate, the tendency was to resolve this tension in favour of flexibility.

It is only at the later International Criminal Tribunals (ICTs), which served as a testing ground for the interpretation of criminal statutes using the VCLT rules, that legality-based concerns would move to the foreground.[94] The ICTY's first challenge was justifying the application of the VCLT, a treaty-interpretation tool, to its Statute, a Security Council resolution.[95] The justification was surprisingly brief. The Statute was recognised as *sui generis*, legally distinct from a treaty, yet the VCLT was still considered relevant.[96] In contrast, the ICJ's Kosovo advisory opinion addressed the limits of applying VCLT canons to SC resolutions, stressing the need to consider factors like statements by Security Council members and relevant practice–an analysis that might have strengthened the ICTY judges' arguments.[97]

The first discussion of interpretative principles appeared in the 1998 *Čelebići* case. The Chamber emphasised the tribunal's hybrid nature and drew on both civil and common law traditions.[98] The essence of interpretation, it argued, was to reveal 'the purpose and intent of the statute'.[99] Interestingly, while the judges might have been inspired by the VCLT rules,[100] they did not mention it and instead relied on statutory interpretation principles.[101] This trend continued in early judgments that did not routinely refer to the VCLT.[102]

[93] ibid 1235.

[94] See also L Grover, *Interpreting Crimes in the Rome Statute of the International Criminal Court* (CUP, 2014); Powderly (n 61) 465.

[95] UNSC Res 827 (1993) UN Doc S/RES/827 establishing the ICTY; UNSC Res 955 (1995) UN Doc S/RES/955 establishing the ICTR.

[96] *Prosecutor v Tadić* (Appeals Chamber Judgment) IT-94-1-A (15 July 1999) para 282; *Prosecutor v Tadić* (Trial Chamber Decision on the Prosecutor's Motion Requesting Protective Measures for Victims and Witnesses) IT-94-1-T (10 August 1995) para 18; *Prosecutor v Delalić et al (Čelebići case)* (Appeals Judgment) IT-96-21-A (20 February 2001) paras 64ff; N Jain, 'Interpretive Divergence' (2017) 57 *Virginia Journal of International Law* 45, 55; C Lister, 'What's in a Name? Labels and the Statute of the International Criminal Tribunal for the Former Yugoslavia' (2005) 18 *LJIL* 77, 77; KAA Khan, C Buisman and C Gosnell, *Principles of evidence in international criminal justice* (OUP, 2010) 192; J Powderly, 'Judicial Interpretation at the Ad Hoc Tribunals: Method from Chaos?' in S Darcy and J Powderly (eds), *Judicial Creativity at the International Criminal Tribunals* (OUP, 2010) 20; see further Wood (n 12).

[97] *Accordance with International Law of the Unilateral Declaration of Independence in respect of Kosovo* (Advisory Opinion) [2010] ICJ Reports 403, para 94; see WA Schabas, 'Interpreting the Statutes of the Ad Hoc Tribunals' in LC Vohran and others (eds), *Man's Inhumanity to Man: Essays on International Law in Honour of Antonio Cassese* (Brill-Nijhoff, 2003) 849–52.

[98] *Prosecutor v Delalić et al (Čelebići Case)* (Trial Chamber Judgment) IT-96-21-T (16 November 1998) paras 158–59.

[99] ibid para 159.

[100] See J Powderly, *Judges and the Making of International Criminal Law* (Brill Nijhoff, 2020) 369.

[101] *Čelebići Case* (TC Judgment) (n 99) paras 160–71.

[102] *Prosecutor v Tadić* (Opinion and Judgment) IT-94-1-T (7 May 1997); *Prosecutor v Furundžija* (Judgment) IT-95-17/1 (10 December 1998) para 180. *Prosecutor v Aleksovski* (Trial Judgment) IT-95-14/1-T (25 June 1999).

In 1999, the VCLT began to surface more clearly, with the *Tadić* Appeals Chamber citing it in interpreting a crime,[103] and shortly after, the *Jelisić* Trial Chamber applying it to the genocide definition in the Genocide Convention.[104] Some scholars noted the oddity of interpreting the genocide definition – understood as customary law – in treaty interpretation.[105] Despite many judgments making no mention of the VCLT,[106] it still gradually became the standard interpretative tool.[107]

The ICTY, in most cases, found the VCLT methods unproblematic in terms of legality. Even a purposive method pushing for broad interpretations was not incompatible with legality. As Appazov observed, the ICTY judges often (1) adopted a purposive approach; (2) assumed the Statute's main object was to maximize victim protection; and (3) allowed this purpose to override other considerations, even text.[108]

This approach was taken in the interpretation of the Appeals Chamber, stressing the purpose of the Geneva Conventions (GCs),[109] is to 'ensure [the] protection of civilians to the maximum extent possible' and adopting a broad understanding of national groups, ensuring Bosnian Muslims were protected.[110] While the interpretative outcome might be normatively desirable, the process is undoubtedly motivated by a one-sided and broad purpose.[111] If such broad maxims become the sole guiding aim, few interpretative boundaries remain.

Hybrid tribunals have continued the trend of using the VCLT in a very far-reaching manner.[112] The Special Tribunal for Lebanon (STL) even considered it relevant for the interpretation of the crime of terrorism in domestic law.[113] The STL's approach was widely criticised as judicial activism, although the academic focus was largely on its source doctrine, not the broad application of the VCLT

[103] *Prosecutor v Tadić* (Appeals Chamber Judgment) (n 97) paras 300–302.

[104] *Prosecutor v Jelisić* (Trial Chamber Judgment) T-95-10-T (14 December 1999) para 61.

[105] M Swart, 'Judicial Lawmaking at the ad hoc Tribunals: The Creative Use of the Sources of International Law and "Adventurous Interpretation"' (2010) 70 *ZaöRV* 474.

[106] See, eg, *Prosecutor v Kordić & Čerkez* (Trial Chamber Judgment) IT-95-14/2-T (27 February 2001).

[107] See, eg, *Prosecutor v Blaškić* (Judgment) IT-95-14-T (3 March 2000) paras 326–27; See also M Swart, 'Is There a Text in This Court? The Purposive Method of Interpretation and the ad hoc Tribunals' (2010) *ZaöRV* 772.

[108] A Appazov, 'International Criminal Court and the Decision-Making Heritage of the Ad Hoc Tribunals: A Study of Judicial Activism' (2016) 3 *Journal of Global Justice & Public Policy* 1, 13.

[109] Geneva Convention IV Relative to the Protection of Civilian Persons in Time of War (adopted 12 August 1949, entered into force 21 October 1950) 75 UNTS 287 (Fourth Geneva Convention).

[110] *Prosecutor v Aleksovski* (Appeals Chamber Judgment) IT-95-14/1-A (24 March 2000) paras 147–52.

[111] Appazov (n 108) 14.

[112] See also eg *Case 001* (Appeal Judgment) 001/18-07-2007-ECCC/SC (3 February 2012) para 59; and the SCSL's use of the VCLT for crime interpretation: *Prosecutor v Brima et al (AFRC Case)* (Trial Judgment) SCSL-04-16-T (20 June 2007) para 650.

[113] *Case STL-ll-Oll1* (Interlocutory Decision on the Applicable Law: Terrorism, Conspiracy, Homicide, Perpetration, Cumulative Charging) STL-11-01/I/AC/R176bis (16 February 2011) para 26.

itself.[114] A similar trajectory may emerge at the Kosovo Specialist Chambers, where national and international legal hierarchies are blended.[115] The future will show to what extent these judicial bodies, when faced with interpretative challenges, will also rely on the VCLT in the same unlimited fashion

IV. THE ICC PRACTICE: A FIRMLY ESTABLISHED VCLT FRAMEWORK

A systematic case law review,[116] revealed how the VCLT came to be entrenched in the ICC's case law. From the Confirmation of Charges Decisions[117] to the judgments,[118] the judges have very regularly taken the position that the VCLT methods apply.[119] In particular, the general rule in 31(1) VCLT appears frequently in the decisions of the Court.[120] Notably, while the general rule of interpretation in Article 31(1) VCLT is regularly invoked, other VCLT rules receive less attention. For example, the *Katanga* Trial Judgment omits any reference to Article 31(2), without explaining whether this reflects a deliberate limitation of the VCLT's scope.[121] The Court has also extended VCLT methods beyond treaties, applying them to instruments such as the Rules of Procedure and the Elements of Crimes, without clarifying how this transposition operates. While this expansive use has long gone unquestioned, a notable shift occurred from 2019 onwards: the *Ntaganda*, *Ongwen* and *Al Hassan* Trial Judgments do not refer to the VCLT. Whether this reflects a change in interpretative approach or simply oversight

[114] See, eg, K Ambos, 'Judicial creativity at the Special Tribunal for Lebanon: Is there a crime of terrorism under international law?' (2011) 24 *LJIL* 655, 655.

[115] See Article 3 Law on Specialist Chambers and Specialist Prosecutor's Office (05/L-053) 3 August 2015.

[116] The presented analysis is based on data collected between June 2018 and December 2021. It covers a total of 18 COC decisions, 8 trial chamber judgments, and 1 acquittal on appeal, representing all relevant ICC decisions rendered between 29 January 2007 and 9 December 2021. Additional decisions were identified and included through a snowball method to ensure completeness.

[117] See, eg, *Prosecutor v Ruto, Kosgey & Sang* (Decision on the Confirmation of Charges) ICC-01/09-01/11 (23 January 2012) para 289; *Prosecutor v Yekatom & Ngaïssona* (Decision on the confirmation of charges against Alfred Yekatom and Patrice-Edouard Ngaïssona) ICC-01/14-01/18 (20 December 2019) paras 49–52.

[118] *Prosecutor v Lubanga* (Judgment pursuant to Article 74 of the Statute) ICC-01/04-01/06 (14 March 2012) paras 601–602; *Prosecutor v Katanga* (Judgment pursuant to Article 74 of the Statute) ICC-01/04-01/07 (7 March 2014) para 41; *Prosecutor v Bemba* (Judgment pursuant to Article 74 of the Statute) ICC-01/05-01/08 (21 March 2016) paras 75–86; *Prosecutor v Ruto, Kosgey & Sang* (Decision on Defence Applications for Judgments of Acquittal) ICC-01/09-01/11 (05 April 2016) para 303.

[119] See *Situation in the Democratic Republic of the Congo* (Judgment on the Prosecutor's Application for Extraordinary Review of Pre-Trial Chamber I's 31 March 2006 Decision Denying Leave to Appeal) ICC-01/04-168 (13 July 2006) para 33; *Situation in the State of Palestine* (Decision on the 'Prosecution request pursuant to Article 19(3) for a ruling on the Court's territorial jurisdiction in Palestine') ICC-01/18 (5 February 2021) para 91.

[120] See, eg, *Bemba* (TC Judgment) (n 118) para 75; *Ruto, Kosgey & Sang* (Acquittal Decision) (n 118) para 303.

[121] ibid paras 43–47.

remains unclear. This selective engagement, in any event, weakens the methodological consistency of the Court's interpretative practice.

Furthermore, the applicability of the VCLT has rarely been contested, and some judges have even categorically rejected the idea that any of its rules could conflict with the legality principle.[122] Other ICC decisions represented a position more sensitive to the need for adherence to criminal law principles.[123] Even these more critical decisions, however, do not question the VCLT's formal relevance.[124] Although these decisions hold very divergent opinions on how the interpretative framework of the Rome Statute should be reconciled with the VCLT, they remain reconciliation efforts nevertheless.[125] This means that the overarching paradigm – that the VCLT applies – has been upheld across ICC case law.

A striking example of the lack of critical engagement is found in the *Bemba* Confirmation of Charges Decision, which simply states: 'The Statute, being a multilateral treaty, is governed by the principles of treaty interpretation set out in Articles 31 and 32 VCLT.'[126] This reasoning is flawed: the multilateral character of a treaty is not a criterion triggering the VLCT's application. That an irrelevant factor is cited as a basis for applying the VCLT suggests that the underlying justification has not been rigorously thought through.

A. The Crucible Approach and a Hierarchical Source Doctrine

The ICC's Trial and Appeal Chambers have largely embraced the crucible approach, treating interpretation as a holistic process.[127] Interpretation involves reading a provision's wording 'in context and in light of its object and purpose', with context understood as defined by 'the particular sub-section of the law read as a whole in conjunction with the section of an enactment in its entirety'.[128] The purpose can be 'gathered from the chapter of the law in which the particular

[122] See, eg, *Prosecutor v Katanga & Ngudjolo Chui* (Judgment on the Appeal Against the Decision on Joinder rendered on 10 March 2008 by the Pre-Trial Chamber in the Germain Katanga and Mathieu Ngudjolo Chui Cases) ICC-01/04-01/07 OA 6 (9 June 2008) paras 2–4.

[123] See, eg, *Prosecutor v Ngudjolo Chui* (Judgment pursuant to Article 74 of the Statute) ICC-01/04-02/12 (18 December 2012) paras 10–11, 52.

[124] See, eg, *Prosecutor v Lubanga* (Separate Opinion of Judge Fulford to the Judgment pursuant to Article 74 of the Statute) ICC-01/04-01/06 (14 March 2012) para 13.

[125] See, eg, *Prosecutor v Ngudjolo Chui* (Concurring Opinion of Judge Christine Van den Wyngaert to the Judgment pursuant to Article 74 of the Statute) ICC-01/04-02/12 (18 December 2012) paras 11, 18–19 and in particular para 18: 'Article 22(2) of the Statute [. . .] obliges the Court to interpret the definition of crimes strictly and prohibits any extension by analogy'. '[It] overrides the conventional methods of treaty interpretation, [. . .], particularly the teleological method.'

[126] *Prosecutor v Bemba* (Decision on the Confirmation of Charges) ICC-01/05-01/08 (15 June 2009) para 361.

[127] *Katanga* (TC Judgment) (n 118) para 45.

[128] *Prosecutor v Lubanga* (Decision on the Confirmation of Charges) ICC-01/04-01/06 (29 January 2007) para 601; *Situation in Congo* (AC Judgment) (n 120) para 33; similar to the *Bemba* (TC Judgment) (n 118) para 77.

section is included' and 'its preamble and general tenor of the treaty'.[129] The interpretative ingredients – good faith, the ordinary meaning, the context and object and purpose – should all be used simultaneously in one single process.[130] Although slicing up the interpretative methods or inserting a hierarchy between them would be contrary to the nature of interpretation,[131] it is unclear what to do with the Rome Statute's source doctrine in Article 21, which provides for a 'multiplicity of hierarchies'.[132] The ICC's case law has not provided more guidance on this matter, apart from the Pre-Trial Chamber finding that 'recourse to article 31(3)(c) [VCLT], being a rule of interpretation, cannot in any way set aside the hierarchy of sources of law'.[133]

B. Good Faith and the Principle of Effectiveness

The concept of good faith also played a role in ICL. As discussed earlier, it is a broad and fluid notion, capable of supporting a wide range of interpretative techniques and outcomes. Its vagueness makes it difficult to pin down. Still, some attempts have been made to concretise it in ICL. The ICC Appeals Chamber, for instance, linked good faith to the wording of the Statute but declined to define it further.[134] In other instances, the ICC judges associate it with the principle of effectiveness.[135] The Trial Chamber has held that good faith encompasses effectiveness, rejecting interpretations that 'disregard or render any other of [a law's] provisions void'.[136] This links the principle to teleological reasoning, as the following passage illustrates:

> [T]he judge is often confronted with a choice between conflicting and equally legitimate principles of interpretation. [. . .] [H]e is bound to interpret that intention in accordance with the paramount principle of good faith which demands that [. . .] the *maximum effect* must be given to the instrument.[137]

This statement highlights both the value and the limits of effectiveness. In criminal law, these limits are crucial. Lauterpacht noted that effectiveness is difficult to reconcile with restrictive interpretation – a cornerstone of criminal justice.

[129] ibid.
[130] ibid para 45.
[131] ibid para 44; *Bemba* (TC Judgment) (n 118) para 77; See also L Grover, 'A Call for Arms: Fundamental Dilemmas confronting the Interpretation of Crimes in the Rome Statute of the International Criminal Court' (2010) 21 *EJIL* 543, 548; see also Villiger (n 32).
[132] G Bitti, 'Article 21 and the Hierarchy of Sources of Law before the ICC' in C Stahn (ed), *The Law and Practice of the International Criminal Court* (OUP, 2015) 413.
[133] *Situation in Palestine* (Decision on Territorial Jurisdiction) (n 119) para 88.
[134] *Situation in Congo* (AC Judgment) (n 119) para 33.
[135] See, eg, *Situation in the People's Republic of Bangladesh/Republic of the Union of Myanmar* (Decision Pursuant to Article 15 of the Rome Statute on the Authorisation of an Investigation) ICC-01/19-27 (14 November 2019) para 59; see also Gardiner (n 7) 148.
[136] *Bemba* (TC Judgment) (n 118) para 77.
[137] *Ruto, Kosgey & Sang* (Acquittal Decision) (n 118) – reasons of Judge Eboe-Osuji, para 381.

The issue is not about choosing between effective and ineffective readings, but between different kinds of effectiveness.[138] For example, an interpretation effectively protecting victims might be ineffective in guaranteeing the rights of the accused. Particularly in crime interpretation, invoking maximum effect raises normative and methodological concerns. This can be illustrated by the *Katanga case* in which the judges wanted to give full effect to 'each of the contextual elements of crimes against humanity'.[139] The principle of effectiveness was the basis for a restrictive interpretation requiring proof of an organisation.[140] Although this particular use of effectiveness resulted in a restrictive interpretation, the danger of maximisation makes the principle problematic, particularly when the victims are the intended beneficiaries.[141] This is exemplified by the interpretation of forced pregnancy in the *Ongwen Judgment*. The Trial Chamber formulated that 'the rule against surplusage, a basic principle of statutory interpretation that presumes that the legislator does nothing in vain and that the court must endeavour to give significance to every word of a statutory instrument,' should result in an 'independent meaning from the other sexual and gender based violence crimes' being given to forced pregnancy.[142] This idea is very similar to the principle of effectiveness: not to read a provision in a way that loses effect. It is debatable whether this was of value to the interpretation.

The principle of effectiveness should assume only a limited role in the interpretation of crimes. Its tendency for broad, often victim-centred readings sits uneasily with the principle of strict construction enshrined in Article 22(2). Accordingly, the concept of good faith should be confined to preventing interpretations that lead to absurd results or render provisions void of legal effect. Beyond this negative function, the principle of effectiveness risks introducing expansive tendencies incompatible with the principle of legality.[143]

C. The Ordinary Meaning and the Textual Approach

A textual approach is frequently relied upon by ICC judges, particularly in cases where the meaning of a provision appears settled. In such instances, the Court can adopt a textual method to support its interpretation with little controversy. This was, for example, the case for the crime of 'murder', which requires minimal

[138] H Lauterpacht, 'Restrictive Interpretation and the Principle of Effectiveness in the Interpretation of Treaties' (1949) 26 *British Yearbook of International Law* 67–74.

[139] *Katanga* (TC Judgment) (n 119) para 1069; see also paras 46–47.

[140] See Case Study 1.

[141] *Prosecutor v Al-Bashir* (Joint Concurring Opinion of Judges Eboe-Osuji, Morrison, Hofmański and Bossa) ICC-02/05-01/09-397-Anx1-Corr (6 May 2019) para 419.

[142] *Prosecutor v Ongwen* (Trial Judgment) ICC-02/04-01/15 (4 February 2021) para 2722.

[143] *A contrario*: *Prosecutor v Lubanga* (Separate Opinion of Judge Luz Del Carmen Ibáñez Carranza to the Reparations Judgment) ICC-01/04-01/06-3466-AnxII (16 September 2019) para 69.

elaboration given its settled interpretation under domestic legal systems.[144] Similarly, when addressing the phrase 'in the context of and associated with an armed conflict' in Article 8(2)(e)(vii), the ordinary meaning of the provision was deemed sufficient.[145] In some cases, it suffices to consult a dictionary.[146]

In other cases, arriving at an ordinary meaning is not so easily done. Text must often be read in its grammatical and syntactical context, with meaning shaped by its placement within a phrase or provision. This was the approach taken to the phrase 'in the ordinary course of events' in Article 30, where context informed the interpretation.[147]

This also illustrates that the ordinary meaning is mostly used in combination with other methods. For instance, in interpreting 'enlistment' and 'conscription', the *Lubanga* Trial Chamber began by analysing these terms in the Additional Protocols, before turning to the Statute to apply their 'plain and ordinary meaning'.[148] This approach was both textual and contextual in nature. A combination of a textual and teleological approach was adopted with regard to *dolus eventualis* and whether or not co-perpetration liability could be met with this *mens rea* standard. The Trial Chamber overturned the Pre-Trial Chamber's view, finding that both the drafting history and the text of Article 30 excluded *dolus eventualis*.[149] In other cases, the Court interpreted the drafters' omissions, combined with the provision's plain language, as grounds for a more restrictive reading.[150]

However, a purely textual approach does not always curtail interpretative choices. For example, Article 25(3)(a)'s disjunction has been read inclusively, despite the Chambers acknowledging that both inclusive and exclusive readings are possible based on a strict textualist interpretation.[151] Similarly, the case law on indirect co-perpetration shows how textual methods can support broad interpretations. While scholars have criticised the extension of Article 25 to accommodate this liability mode, the Court maintained that its interpretation was 'captured by the language of Article 25(3)(a)', without recourse to external sources.[152]

As the case law currently stands, it would be premature to conclude that textual interpretation is the prevailing method at the ICC. While the Court frequently relies on textual reasoning, it does so primarily in conjunction with

[144] *Prosecutor v Katanga & Ngudjolo Chui* (Decision on the Confirmation of Charges) ICC-01/04-01/07 (30 September 2008) fn 563.

[145] *Lubanga* (TC Judgment) (n 118) para 571.

[146] ibid para 1012.

[147] *Bemba* (CoC Decision) (n 126) para 362.

[148] *Lubanga* (CoC Decision) (n 128) para 608.

[149] *Lubanga* (TC Judgment) (n 118) paras 352–54; See further: JD Ohlin, 'Co-Perpetration: German Dogmatik or German Invasion?' in C Stahn (ed), *The Law and Practice of the International Criminal Court* (OUP, 2016) 517–38. See also *Bemba* (CoC Decision) (n 126) para 364.

[150] *Prosecutor v Al Mahdi* (Judgment and Sentence) ICC-01/12-01/15 (27 September 2016) para 15.

[151] *Katanga* (CoC Decision) (n 144) para 491; *Ruto, Kosgey & Sang* (CoC Decision) (n 117) para 287.

[152] *Ruto, Kosgey & Sang* (CoC Decision) (n 117) para 287.

other interpretative approaches. In *Kenyatta*, Trial Chamber V emphasised that the search for the 'general and ordinary meaning' does not preclude deeper inquiry: it 'is merely a starting-point, a prima facie guide, and cannot be allowed to obstruct the essential quest in the application of treaties, namely to search for the real intention of the contracting parties in using the language employed by them'.[153] This reflects what appears to be the ICC's overarching position – namely, that textual interpretation offers an entry point, but not the final word.[154]

This understanding corresponds to the position taken by Grover, who rightly observes that a literal reading does not resolve whether an interpretation should be broad or strict.[155] In line with this view, it is argued here that textualism alone cannot satisfy the requirements of the principle of strict construction and additional safeguards are needed to respect the threshold set by Article 22(2).

D. The Context, a Contextual Approach and the Principle of Systemic Integration

A contextual approach takes various forms depending on how the notion of context is defined – whether it remains internal to the Statute's structure and focuses on, for example, a particular section of the Statute, or extends externally to include broader legal frameworks, systemic features, or related sources of law.[156] This section traces how ICC Chambers have drawn on both internal and external context in their interpretation of crimes.

At its narrowest, the context concerns the provision's internal structure. For example, interpreting sexual crimes listed under Article 7(1)(g) requires reading crimes such as 'sexual slavery' and 'enforced prostitution' enumerated in that provision together. Because double qualification or concurrence of crimes is prohibited where crimes lack materially distinct elements, their definitions must be understood relationally.[157] The same holds for residual categories like 'other inhumane acts' or 'other forms of sexual violence', which must be of similar gravity. Such contextual readings must be carefully constrained, however, as they risk sliding into prohibited analogy. It is a fine line between a legitimate contextual reading requiring analogical argumentation and a forbidden extension by analogy of a crime.[158]

[153] *Prosecutor v Kenyatta* (Decision on Defence Request for Conditional Excusal from Continuous Presence at Trial) ICC-01/09-02/11 (18 October 2013) para 68.

[154] See also *Prosecutor vs. William Samoei Ruto and Joshua Arap Sang* (Public redacted version of Separate, Partly Concurring Opinion of Judge Eboe-Osuji on the 'Decision on Prosecution Request for Admission of Prior Recorded Testimony') ICC-01/09-01/11 (19 August 2015); *Kenyatta* (Excusal Decision) (n 153) paras 68–75.

[155] Grover (n 94) 49.

[156] *Lubanga* (TC Judgment) (n 118) para 601.

[157] See, eg, *Katanga* (TC Judgment) (n 118) para 1696. See Case Study 2.

[158] See Case Study 2.

The context can also be determined by the subsection or the chapter of the provision. For example, the division between Part 2 (applicable law) and Part 3 (general principles of criminal law) has interpretative implications. The fact that Article 21 (applicable law) is placed outside the general principles section (Articles 22–33), while Article 22 is included, may be read contextually as supporting the primacy of the principle of legality in the interpretation of crimes – and as indicating that this principle governs that interpretative activity.[159]

Chambers have also used the internal context to interpret terms across provisions. In the *Myanmar* decision, the Pre-Trial Chamber considered the terms 'crime' and 'conduct' in Article 12(2)(a).[160] Since the *travaux préparatoires* provided no explanation for their differential use,[161] the Chamber interpreted them in light of related provisions – particularly Article 20 – which uses 'conduct' to refer to acts underlying crimes. The Chamber concluded that both terms serve similar functions, supporting a unified reading.[162]

Beyond internal context, interpretations can invoke external context, which may include related legal instruments. In this sense, a contextual reading can serve as a bridge between the Statute and other sources. This type of reasoning is particularly relevant where statutory labels mirror customary international law.[163] For instance, the ICC has considered customary definitions – such as that of genocide under the Genocide Convention – when interpreting statutory crimes. Although Article 21(1)(b) governs the use of custom and should only be used when sources higher in the hierarchy fail, Chambers have at times bypassed this provision by embedding custom into contextual analysis. While Article 21 requires a stepwise approach to sources, contextual reasoning risks circumventing that order. A broader reading of context might allow custom to inform interpretation even where the statutory provision is not ambiguous or incomplete. This approach raises legality concerns, particularly where customary definitions are broader than those in the Statute.[164]

Article 31(2) and (3) VCLT extend context to include 'subsequent agreements' and 'subsequent practice'. The term 'subsequent' already reveals a tension with the idea of non-retroactivity, which opposes subsequently altering the meaning in a treaty by another instrument.[165] But instead of discussing in depth all possible

[159] K Ambos, 'General principles of criminal law in the Rome Statute' (1999) 10 *Criminal Law Forum* 1; WA Schabas, 'General Principles of Criminal Law in the International Criminal Court Statute (Part III)' (1998) 6 *European Journal of Crime, Criminal Law and Criminal Justice* 400, 402.

[160] *Bangladesh/Myanmar Situation* (n 135) para 47.

[161] ibid para 48.

[162] ibid para 49.

[163] Preparatory Committee, Report of the Preparatory Committee on the Establishment of an International Criminal Court (Proceedings of the Preparatory Committee during March–April and August 1996) A/51/22 Fifty-first Session, Supplement No. 22, para 54: 'Several delegations held the view that the Statute should codify customary international law and not extend to the progressive development of international law'.

[164] See s II above.

[165] Jacobs (n 18) 467.

instruments that fall under Article 31(2) and (3) VCLT, it is most useful to examine Article 31(3)(c) and its inclusion of the principle of systemic integration, which allows referral to 'any relevant rules of international law applicable in the relations between the parties'. This principle, which is understood to mitigate fragmentation in international law,[166] presumes a harmony between specialised regimes and general international law and finds that whatever the particular field might be, the normative reference point is PIL. If something is regulated within a particular subfield, then *lex specialis* requires that the more specific rule be applied above the general rule.[167] But when something is 'not regulated' or included under 'the normative environment', the principle of systemic integration requires a solution with reference to PIL.[168] While *lex specialis* should prevail where specific rules exist, systemic integration might be used to justify the opposite – substituting general principles for the particular rules of ICL.

The ICC's case law on systemic integration is limited but telling. In *Bemba*, the Trial Chamber used Article 31(3)(c) to justify referring to the jurisprudence of other international courts as interpretative support and to identify customary law where gaps existed.[169] It stressed that while such a reference could inform the interpretation of Article 21(1)(a) sources, it must not override applicable law.[170] This reasoning opened the door to indirect use of custom without observing Article 21's structure. This type of use of systemic integration has been used on other occasions as well.[171] The logic underpinning of systemic integration – interpretative coherence – conflicts with the logic of interpretative constraint required in criminal law. Whereas a strict contextual interpretation with reliance on the internal context is acceptable, these broad contextual methods relying on external context are a slippery slope towards violations of the legality principle.

Another layer of contextual reasoning considers the nature of the legal system to which the interpreted norm belongs. In this view, ICL's hybrid foundations – drawing from IHRL, IHL, PIL, and domestic criminal law – necessitate deliberate choices about which field to prioritise. When interpreting crimes, the logic and constraints of criminal law should guide the process. As will be argued in the next section, a human rights–oriented reading risks broadening definitions in ways incompatible with strict construction.[172]

Finally, while context may include extra-legal considerations, the principle of legality and strict construction leave little for policy considerations to weigh in

[166] M Bos, 'Theory and Practice of Treaty Interpretation' (1980) 27 *Netherlands International Law Review* 3, 29ff.

[167] Jacobs (n 18) 469.

[168] McLachlan (n 66) 279.

[169] *Bemba* (TC Judgment) (n 118) para 78.

[170] *Prosecutor v Bemba* (Separate opinion of Kuniko Ozaki to the Judgment pursuant to Article 74 of the Statute) ICC-01/05 -01/08 (21 March 2016) para 74.

[171] *Bangladesh/Myanmar Situation* (n 135) para 55 and fn 93.

[172] See s IV(E) below.

on the decision-making process. In conclusion, the broader the context invoked, the more difficult it becomes to maintain interpretative strictness. It is for this reason that a broad contextual approach is difficult to reconcile with the legality principle. Furthermore, the principle of strict construction favours an application of the principle of *lex specialis* and finds that the normative environment for provisions setting out individual criminal responsibility has to be shaped by the dictates of criminal law, and as such must be directed towards the specific rules of ICL. Any role for systemic integration must be narrowly defined and limited to procedural or institutional matters. Reference to general international law in the context of crime interpretation should be rejected.

E. The Object and Purpose and the Teleological Approach

This section explores how the ICC judges have applied the teleological approach embedded in Article 31 VCLT, supporting broad and narrow interpretations and approaching it both subjectively (based on the drafters' intent) as well as objectively (based on the text at hand).[173]

Two contrasting opinions illustrate the method's flexibility. In his dissent in the Kenya investigation decision, Judge Kaul used a teleological approach to support a restrictive reading of the policy element in crimes against humanity.[174] He argued that the gravity and scale of these crimes presuppose a state-like policy and that this element is fundamental to understanding the 'rationale underlying crimes against humanity' as it makes it possible to distinguish them from ordinary domestic crimes.[175] By contrast, Judge Eboe-Osuji's opinion in the Ruto & Sang acquittal adopted a victim-centred reading of the same element.[176] He found that the purpose of the organisational policy element lies in nothing more than 'the exclusion of unconnected crime waves' and he thereby constructed one of the broadest interpretations of Article 7(2)(a) at the Court.[177] Framing 'absurdity' as equivalent to 'injustice',[178] he argued that restricting jurisdiction to state-like organisations would exclude too many serious crimes and would amount to a miscarriage of justice. His approach drew extensively on the preamble and broadly construed the Statute's purpose as eliminating impunity.[179]

These two opinions demonstrate that a teleological approach can lead to both narrow and broad interpretations. However, the approach often skews

[173] Linderfalk (n 41) 203.

[174] *Situation in the Republic of Kenya* (Dissenting Opinion of Judge Hans-Peter Kaul to the Decision Pursuant to Article 15 of the Rome Statute on the Authorization of an Investigation into the Situation in the Republic of Kenya) ICC-01/09 (31 March 2010) para 56.

[175] *Situation in the Republic of Kenya* (Decision Pursuant to Article 15 of the Rome Statute on the Authorization of an Investigation into the Situation in the Republic of Kenya) ICC-01/09 (31 March 2010) para 92.

[176] *Ruto, Kosgey & Sang* (Acquittal Decision) (n 118) paras 403–415.

[177] ibid para 342.

[178] ibid paras 308, 309,353, 368,371, in particular para 309.

[179] *Ruto, Kosgey & Sang* (Acquittal Decision) (n 118) paras 320, 329,441.

toward expansive readings. Judges have drawn on open-ended purposes – such as victim protection or ending impunity – to broaden definitions of crimes.[180] This carries risks. In *Katanga*, the Trial Chamber explicitly cautioned that relying on a teleological approach to maximise impact could undermine legality, in particular the principles of strict construction and *in dubio pro reo*. It stressed that even laudable goals such as ending impunity must not generate interpretations that exceed the Statute's terms.[181]

Scholars have voiced similar concerns. Robinson warned against the importation of victim-oriented teleological reasoning from IHRL.[182] He described the recurring logic of ICL judges as: '(i) to adopt a purposive interpretive approach, (ii) to assume that the exclusive object and purpose of an ICL enactment is to maximize victim protection, and (iii) to allow this presumed object and purpose to dominate over other considerations – including, if necessary, the text itself'.[183] A striking example is Judge Odio Benito's separate opinion in *Lubanga*, and her focus on the protective aims of child soldier provisions: 'the statutory provisions *are meant to protect the life and personal integrity of children* under the age of 15', which makes it 'impermissible for a Chamber to decline to enter a comprehensive legal definition of a crime and leave it open to a case-by-case analysis or to the limited scope of the charges brought against the accused'. In doing so, she rejected limiting definitions and endorsed open-ended interpretations in the name of progressive legal development. This *reductive* way of approaching purpose is particularly problematic in crime interpretation, where the protection of victims is often used as a way to eclipse the rights of the accused.[184] Broad goals such as the protection of the lives of children should not be presented as the single purpose at work.

Finally, the ICC practice shows examples of both a subjective and an objective approach. In the context of the Rome Statute, a subjective reading – based on the drafters' intent – is complicated by the informal nature of many negotiations, for which no records exist. Access to the drafter's intent is therefore limited.[185] The best way to consult these preparatory discussions is through scholars who reported on them. As a result, it seems academic accounts have come to substitute for preparatory works, raising legitimacy concerns.[186] The debates over the inclusion of forced marriage, for example, reflect widely diverging intentions, making it difficult to identify a single coherent purpose. Depending on which party or coalition is taken as the reference point, the

[180] See, eg, Akande (n 83) 44; Grover (n 131) 557.
[181] ibid para 55.
[182] D Robinson, 'The Identity Crisis of International Criminal Law' (2008) 21 *LJIL* 925, 929.
[183] D Robinson, *Justice in Extreme Cases: Criminal Law Theory meets International Criminal Law* (CUP, 2020) 29.
[184] Robinson (n 183) 29; B McGonigle Leyh, 'Pragmatism over Principles: The International Criminal Court and a Human Rights-Based Approach to Judicial Interpretation' (2018) 41 *Fordham International Law Journal* 697.
[185] RS Lee, *The International Criminal Court: The Making of the Rome Statute: Issues, Negotiations and Results* (Kluwer Law International 1999) vii.
[186] E Wilmshurst, 'International Criminal Law' in M J Bowman and D Kritsiotis (eds), *Conceptual and Contextual Perspectives on the Modern Law of Treaties* (CUP, 2018) 635–36.

purpose underlying a provision may, therefore, appear fundamentally different.[187] Objective approaches draw instead on the Statute's text, especially its preamble.[188] However, the preamble's language – 'ending impunity', 'doing justice' – is so general that it can be used to justify nearly any interpretation.[189] While such references might reinforce decisions in procedural or institutional matters, they offer little constraint in crime interpretation. In practice, judges often invoke these aims selectively, favouring the goal of ending impunity over other purposes serving the reinforcement of, for example, complementarity or due process.[190] The uncertain outcome of this type of method makes it an inadequate guarantor for interpretations in line with the legality principle.

F. The VCLT and RS: a Blissful Union?

The analysis above confirms that the VCLT remains the dominant interpretative framework in ICL. Both the ICC and the ICTs regularly refer to Articles 31–33 VCLT, especially the general rule in Article 31(1), and jurisprudence and doctrine largely concur in treating the VCLT rules as the primary methods of interpretation in ICL.

However, this reliance has not been accompanied by a tailored adaptation to crime interpretation. Although Article 22 of the Rome Statute is occasionally acknowledged, no consistent effort has been made to align the VCLT's interpretative rules with the principle of legality. Early judgments discuss interpretative methods in general terms but do not address their application to crimes.[191] Later decisions do not specifically endorse this approach, but they have not rejected it either.[192] These two observations are regrettable given the remaining concerns and uncertainties – confirmed by several doctrinal accounts[193] – of how the VCLT methods should be made to fit the legality principle.

[187] See the point of view of the Women's Caucus for Gender Justice, 'Recommendations and Commentary for December 1997 Prep Com, Part III' (1997) recommendation 7 and compare it to Proposal submitted by Bahrain, Iraq, Kuwait, Lebanon, the Libyan Arab Jamahiriya, Oman, Qatar, Saudi Arabia, the Sudan, the Syrian Arab Republic and United Arab Emirates concerning the elements of crimes against humanity, submitted to the Preparatory Committee for the International Criminal Court. PCNICC/1999/WGEC/DP.39 (3 December 1999).

[188] *Situation in Congo* (AC Judgment) (n 119) para 31.

[189] *Prosecutor v Bemba* (Concurring Separate Opinion of Judge Eboe-Osuji) ICC-01/05-01/08 (14 June 2018) para 117.

[190] *Prosecutor v Bashir* (Decision on the Prosecution's Application for a Warrant of Arrest against Omar Hassan Ahmad Al Bashir) ICC-02/05-01/09-3 (4 March 2009) paras 41–42. For a much more restrictive view of the idea of ending impunity weighing in: *Prosecutor v Bemba* (Separate opinion Judge Christine Van den Wyngaert and Judge Howard Morrison) ICC-01/05-01/08 (8 June 2018) paras 5, 53. 'Ending impunity is only meaningful if it happens in full accordance with the values and principles that underpin the criminal justice process.'

[191] See, eg, *Bemba* (CoC Decision) (n 126) para 77.

[192] See, eg, *Prosecutor v Ntaganda* (Judgment) ICC-01/04-02/06 (8 July 2019), *Ongwen* (TC Judgment) (n 142).

[193] See Grover (n 94).

Specific rules have proven problematic. First, good faith, when tied to the principle of effectiveness, introduces a logic of maximisation that sits uneasily with strict construction, as seen in *Katanga*.[194] Yet this tension remains unaddressed in the ICC case law. Second, the teleological method frequently supports broad interpretations that are difficult to reconcile with Article 22. Although some judges and scholars recognise this risk – especially when object and purpose are framed broadly and one-sidedly around goals such as ending impunity or maximising victim protection – these concerns have not led to more restraint.

Despite some efforts to refine interpretative tools,[195] the application of the VCLT to crime interpretation remains largely uncontested. Only Jacobs questions whether the VCLT rules should apply at all, especially given the 'uneasy relationship between the Vienna Convention and the principle of legality'.[196] This raises a foundational issue: whether there exists any obligation to apply the VCLT to ICL – a question taken up in the next section.

V. SCRUTINIZING THE VCLT'S TRANSPLANT TO ICL

This section investigates whether a legal obligation exists for ICC judges to apply the VCLT rules of interpretation. The inquiry arises from the previous section's conclusion that, although the VCLT is frequently referenced, its compatibility with the criminal law character of the Rome Statute is not self-evident. This section deconstructs the legal grounds that have been put forward in support of such an obligation and shows that they are far less robust than typically assumed.

A. Applying the VCLT as Treaty Law: a Double Regime, a General Participation Clause or Neither?

ICC judges have frequently asserted that the Rome Statute, as a treaty, is governed by Articles 31 and 32 of the VCLT.[197] It implicitly assumes that every treaty falls under the VCLT's scope and that every treaty, whatever shape or form, is

[194] Robinson (n 183) 28: 'Maximal construction is, however, the diametric opposite of strict construction'.

[195] Grover (n 94); Grover (n 131) 557; LN Sadat and JM Jolly, 'Seven Canons of ICC treaty Interpretation, Making Sense of Article 25's Rorschach Blot' (2014) 27 *LJIL* 673; WA Schabas, 'Strict Construction and the Rome Statute' in S Dewulf (ed), *Liber Amicorum Chris Van den Wyngaert* (Maklu, 2017) 641; Akande (n 83) 44; GP Fletcher and JD Ohlin, 'Reclaiming Fundamental Principles of Criminal Law in the Darfur' (2005) 3 *JICJ* 539.

[196] Jacobs (n 18) rather surprisingly, this contribution of Dov Jacobs is cited in the *Katanga* (TC Judgment) (n 118) fn 97.

[197] See, eg, *Bemba* (CoC Decision) (n 126) para 75; *Ruto, Kosgey & Sang* (Acquittal Decision) (n 117) para 304; *Situation in Darfur, Prosecutor v Al Bashir* (The Hashemite Kingdom of Jordan's appeal against the "Decision under article 87(7) of the Rome Statute on the non-compliance by Jordan with the request by the Court for the arrest and surrender [of] Omar Al-Bashir") ICC-02 /05-01/0 (12 March 2018) fn 19.

subjected to the VCLT as treaty law. However, closer analysis of the VCLT's own scope (Articles 1–5) suggests that the matter is far from settled.[198]

While the Rome Statute as an interstate treaty fulfils the two criteria set in Article 1 – (1) it is a treaty, as defined in Articles 2(1)(a) VCLT and (2) it was concluded between states – and does not fall under one of the exceptions set out in Article 3 VCLT, this alone does not establish a binding obligation to apply the VCLT's interpretative rules. The VCLT was not simply meant to say that 'every treaty between States is *ipso facto* governed by the Convention'.[199] The *raison d'être* of Article 1 was, in the first place, to set limits to its scope. Contrary to the 1987 Convention on the Law of Treaties between States and International Organisations, which was meant to go further than the 1969 VCLT, the VCLT was meant to exclude treaties concluded by States and international organisations. The question remains which interstate treaties are excluded.

A first way of approaching this issue is through the general principle of *pacta tertiis nec nocent nec prosunt* enshrined in Article 34 VCLT. This rule holds that only parties can be bound by a treaty and prevents binding states that are not a party to the Convention. Given that 30 ICC state parties are not VCLT parties, including France and Venezuela, applying the VCLT would necessarily entail a double regime: VCLT rules would apply to some parties as treaty law, but only as custom to others.[200] If the customary rules of interpretation differ – even marginally – from those codified in the VCLT, non-party states could invoke the *pacta tertiis* rule to object to the application of the treaty regime. That said, maintaining a double regime is far from ideal from the perspective of legal certainty.

A second route towards better understanding the VCLT's scope is found in a closer examination of Article 4 VCLT on non-retroactivity. It states that the Convention applies only to treaties concluded after its entry into force '*with regard to such States*'. This raises the question of whether Article 4 functions as a general participation clause, namely a clause limiting the applicability of a treaty to cases involving states that are parties to that treaty.[201] When a non-state party 'becomes involved, then the instrument ceases to be applicable altogether, even among the states that are parties to it'.[202] The ICJ[203] and most scholars reject this reading

[198] See for discussion of the interpretative principles as customary law: see s V(B) below.

[199] P Gautier, 'Article 1. Convention of 1969. Article 1. Convention of 1986' in O Corten and P Klein (eds), *The Vienna Conventions on the Law of Treaties: A Commentary* (OUP, 2011) 24; Villiger (n 34); Sinclair (n 58) 6; EW Vierdag, 'Some Problems Regarding the Scope of International Instruments on the Law of Treaties' (1985) 23 *Archiv des Völkerrechts* 409, 422.

[200] The 30 states that are on 1/7/2025 party to the Rome Statute but not to the VCLT are: Antigua and Barbuda, Bangladesh, Belize, Botswana, Cabo Verde, Chad, Comoros, Cook Islands, Djibouti, Dominica, Fiji, France, Gambia, Grenada, Iceland, Jordan, Marshall Islands, Namibia, Norway, Romania, Saint Kitts and Nevis, Saint Lucia, Samoa, San Marino, Seychelles, Sierra Leone, South Africa, Uganda, Vanuatu and Venezuela.

[201] See Vierdag (n 199).

[202] EW Vierdag, 'The Law Governing Treaty Relations between Parties to the Vienna Convention on the Law of Treaties and States not Party to the Convention' (1982) 76 *American Journal of International Law* 779, 779.

[203] See, eg, *Kasikili/Sedudu Island (Botswana v Namibia)* (n 17) para 18.

because its consequences are so extreme and basically rendering the VCLT useless in cases concerning multilateral treaties.[204] Although a textual reading of Article 4 *can* support such an interpretation,[205] it was certainly not the intention of the drafters to insert a general participation clause into the VCLT,[206] nor was it anticipated that such a heavy meaning would potentially be given to the phrase *with regard to such States*. Moreover, such an interpretation undermines the principle of *effet utile*.[207] Conversely, construing Article 4 to mean that the VCLT applies to non-party states is equally problematic.[208] This dilemma is reflected in the intense debates at the Vienna Conference about whether the Convention amounted to a mere codification of customary international law or constituted progressive development.[209] To the extent that the VCLT simply reflects custom, the problem raised by Article 4 arguably becomes moot. Yet the very fact that the drafters included Article 4 suggests that equating the VCLT with customary law is an oversimplification.

The most balanced view is to accept a double regime: for VCLT parties, the interpretative rules apply as treaty law; for non-parties, their relevance depends on their status as customary law. This solution is unsatisfactory from the perspective of legal certainty, but it better respects the VCLT. This line of reasoning shifts the focus from treaty law to customary law, raising the more fundamental question of whether the VCLT's interpretative rules carry the same scope and content under both regimes – an issue explored in the next section.

B. Applying the VCLT as Custom

In the face of wide recognition of the VCLT canons as customary law, it might appear artificial or even nonsensical to analyse the scope of these interpretative rules under the VCLT's treaty regime and compare them with their customary scope.[210] On this view, any inquiry into the difference could be dismissed as purely theoretical. As this section shows, there are compelling reasons to examine whether the VCLT's interpretive methods operate identically under both regimes.

First, the VCLT was a hybrid project: the ILC intended not only to codify existing rules but also to develop new ones.[211] The Convention thus embodies elements of progressive development alongside codification. Second, Article 3(b)

[204] ibid 784.

[205] Only a minority of authors advocates for such a restricted reading of Article 4: H Thirlway, *International customary law and codification: An Examination of the Continuing Role of Custom in the Present Period of Codification of International Law* (Sijthoff, 1972) 108.

[206] In this sense, I agree with Rosenne on the issue of the drafter's intent.

[207] Vierdag (n 202) 783–87.

[208] PV McDade, 'The Effect of Article 4 of the Vienna Convention on the Law of Treaties 1969' (1986) 35 *International & Comparative Law Quarterly* 499, 506.

[209] Dörr and Schmalenbach (n 7) 81.

[210] S Rosenne, 'The Temporal Application of the Vienna Convention on the Law of Treaties' (1970) 4 *Cornell International Law Journal* 1, 23–24.

[211] As is reflected in the preamble of the convention; see also ibid 2–3.

clarifies that the VCLT does not affect the legal force of rules applicable to agreements beyond its formal scope – suggesting that some rules in the Convention were recognised as customary, while others were not. Third, Article 4 hints that the application of the rules under customary law is not hindered by the treaty regime.[212] The notion of progressive development, as well as the framework sketched in Articles 3 and 4 of the VCLT, illustrate that, at least at the time of the drafting, treaty and custom did not mirror each other. Yet the Convention offers no taxonomy identifying which interpretive rules fall into which category. While subsequent doctrine has sometimes addressed this question in relation to specific provisions, the broader status of Articles 31–33 has largely gone unexamined.[213] Some authors suggest these rules reflect progressive development;[214] others assume they mirror custom wholesale.[215] These assumptions warrant scrutiny.

A useful starting point is Article 15 of the ILC Statute, which defines progressive development as an evolving area not yet regulated or insufficiently developed in state practice, and codification as 'the more precise formulation and systematization of rules of international law in fields where there already has been extensive State practice, precedent and doctrine'.[216] Given the doctrinal diversity and competing schools of interpretation prior to the VCLT, it is difficult to claim that the interpretive rules were mere codifications. As Torres-Bernárdez observed, the rules of treaty interpretation in the VCLT could not be connected to one school. Their application required new techniques and reflected an effort to resolve pre-Vienna doctrinal divides.[217] This suggests that, in 1969, at least some of the VCLT's interpretive rules would have been classified as progressive development.[218] This, of course, does not bar the rules from having crystallized into custom since then. Today, the majority view is of the opinion that the VCLT rules are mirrored under customary law.[219] Only a minority of scholars departs from this idea, and it serves to examine the different arguments raised.

One objection against this majority view is based on the alleged lack of consistent state practice: The 'argument that the VCLT's rules on interpretation are customary rules with almost trans-historical validity' has been found 'deeply problematic',[220] since there 'is ample evidence that the interpretive approach set

[212] Sinclair (n 58) 7.

[213] Vierdag (n 202) 786–99: analyses how custom differs from the VCLT treaty provisions, but not of the rules of interpretation, which he says require a separate study. To the present author's knowledge, no such study has been conducted; McDade (n 208) 499–505.

[214] McDade (n 208) 499.

[215] Fitzmaurice (n 27) 176.

[216] Statute of the International Law Commission (adopted by the GA Res 174 (II) of 21 November 1947, as amended by resolutions 485 (V) of 12 December 1950, 984 (X) of 3 December 1955, 985 (X) of 3 December 1955 and 36/39 of 18 November 1981); See also S Torres-Bernárdez, 'Interpretation of treaties by the International Court of Justice following the adoption of the 1969 Vienna Convention on the law of treaties' in I Seidl-Hohenveldern (ed), *Liber Amicorum Professor Ignaz Seidl-HohenVeldern* (Springer, 1998) 731–35.

[217] Torres-Bernárdez (n 216) 735.

[218] Linderfalk (n 41) 3.

[219] See, eg, Dörr and Schmalenbach (n 7) 84.

[220] F Zarbiyev, 'A Genealogy of Textualism in Treaty Interpretation' in A Bianchi, D Peat and M Windsor (eds), *Interpretation in International Law* (OUP, 2015) 252–53.

forth in the VCLT has by no means prevailed throughout the history of international law'.[221]

Others argue that these interpretive methods are not legal rules in the strict sense, but rather methodological tools *suggesting* to judges [. . .] how relevant legal instruments may be read'.[222] Although they 'are immensely valuable; they do not fit the regular pattern of rules. One cannot, in any meaningful way, violate them.'[223] It follows that no practice can meaningfully be proven.[224] In ICL specifically, the VCLT's flexible framework has often resulted in interpretive incoherence across judgments, which makes this objection all the more relevant.[225] Further supporting this objection are the inconsistent referencing practices. As remarked by Nolte, 'adjudicatory bodies have rarely relied on subsequent agreements',[226] and seem equally absent from the ICC jurisprudence. Similarly, in *Katanga*, the Trial Chamber offered a detailed discussion of interpretation but omitted any reference to Article 31(2) without explanation.[227] In other decisions, Articles 32 or 33 are ignored altogether.[228] All of this suggests that, while the view that the VCLT's interpretive methods reflect customary law may be dominant, it should not be treated as beyond question. The following subsections consider arguments that limit the reach of the VCLT.

C. The Rome Statute as a Constitutive Treaty of an International Organisation

The third aspect examined is the nature of the Rome Statute and how it affects interpretation. The Rome Statute contains several indicators on how to understand its nature. Article 4(1) states that the Court 'shall have international legal personality' and 'such legal capacity as may be necessary for the exercise of its functions and the fulfilment of its purposes'.[229] The drafters explicitly opted not to place the ICC within the UN framework, but to create a distinct body with international legal personality.[230] The difference is important since treaties constitutive of international organisations trigger the application of different interpretative rules.[231]

[221] ibid 252–53.

[222] Klabbers (n 22) 31 (emphasis added).

[223] ibid 33.

[224] Sorel and Eveno (n 31) 811.

[225] Jain (n 96).

[226] See: G Nolte, Second report on subsequent agreements and subsequent practice in relation to the interpretation of treaties (Sixty-sixth session, 2014).

[227] *Katanga* (TC Judgment) (n 118) paras 43–45.

[228] *Katanga* (TC Judgment) (n 118) paras 43–45; see also A Papaux and R Samson, 'Article 33. Convention of 1969. Article 33 of the Convention of 1986' in O Corten and P Klein (eds), *The Vienna Conventions on the Law of Treaties: A Commentary*, vol 1 (OUP, 2011) 872–73.

[229] W Rückert, 'Art 4, Legal status and powers of the Court' in K Ambos and O Triffterer (eds), *The Rome Statute of the International Criminal Court, A Commentary*, 3rd edn (CH Beck - Hart – Nomos, 2016) 103.

[230] ibid 103–104.

[231] C Brölmann, *Specialized rules of treaty interpretation: international organizations* (Amsterdam Law School Legal Studies Research Paper, 2012) 2.

Article 5 VCLT recognises this by affirming that the Convention applies 'without prejudice to any relevant rules of the organisation'. This provision reflects that while the VCLT applies in principle, it defers to institutional law where appropriate – going beyond the usual *lex specialis* rule and requiring a more general conflict-solving rule.[232] This rule gives precedence 'to the institutional law of the organisation over general international law'.[233]

The ICJ has acknowledged the unique interpretive challenges posed by constitutive treaties.[234] In its WHO advisory opinion, for instance, it interpreted the WHO Constitution with reference to the organisation's object, context, and practice – recognising the hybrid nature of such treaties as both conventional and institutional.[235]

This opens the door to two interpretive frameworks.[236] The constitutional approach emphasises the independent existence of the organisation and views the constitutive instrument as a constitution functioning as an internal document. This approach prioritises solving interpretative issues by looking within the system. The contractual approach, by contrast, sees the Statute primarily as an agreement between states, governed by general rules of treaty law. A way to navigate these doctrines is to argue that the organisation has two faces: 'an open, inter-state treaty regime on the one hand, and an independent constitutional order on the other'.[237]

How should the Rome Statute be positioned on this spectrum? On the basis of theoretical frameworks of constitutionalism and constitutionalisation,[238] understood as analysing 'the process by which institutional arrangements in the non-constitutional global realm have taken on a constitutional quality',[239] and 'the autonomy of international law vis-à-vis State sovereignty and State consent',[240] there are several factors to consider. The ICC's limited executive

[232] Residual character is articulated in several VCLT provisions: see arts 12, 14, 15, 1,6, 22, 37, 77. See: H Anderson, 'Article 5 of the 1969 Vienna Convention' in O Corten and P Klein (eds), *The Vienna Convention on the Law of Treaties: A Commentary* (OUP, 2011) 24; Brölmann (n 231) 4.

[233] C Brölmann, *The Institutional Veil in Public International Law: International Organisations and the Law of Treaties* (Hart Publishing, 2007) 104; Sinclair (n 58) 6-ff.

[234] *Nuclear Weapons* Advisory Opinion (n 11) 66, 74–75.

[235] ibid.

[236] Brölmann (n 231) 6; see also in Brölmann (n 233) 77: 'International organisations [. . .] seem to be regarded as transparent legal constructs and their constitutive law as a special branch of [. . .] rather than as "internal" law [. . .]'. This has left room for a discussion that unwittingly moves between two poles – the will of the Member States (the organisation as an open structure) and the dictates of the legal system (the organisation as a closed structure).

[237] Brölmann (n 231) 113–14.

[238] A Peters, 'Constitutionalisation' in J D'Aspremont and S Singh (eds), *Concepts for International Law – Contributions to Disciplinary Thought* (Edward Edgar, 2019) 141–44 on the difference between constitutionalisation – used to label the positive law phenomenon – and constitutionalism – providing the more doctrinal underpinning.

[239] A Wiener and others, 'Global Constitutionalism: Human Rights, Democracy and the Rule of law' (2012) 1 *Journal of Global Constitutionalism* 1, 5.

[240] T Kleinlein, 'Alfred Verdross as a Founding Father of International Constitutionalism' (2012) 4 *Goettingen Journal of International Law* 385, 388.

reach – no independent police force, weak enforcement powers, no fiscal authority – and the marginal legislative authority of the Assembly of States Parties (ASP) favour a contractual reading.[241] But the Court's architecture also displays constitutional features. The separation of powers across the ASP, the Office of the Prosecutor, and the judiciary resembles a constitutional design.[242] Elderkin further argued that the ICC's ability to hold officials accountable indicates a quasi-constitutional function.[243] The ICC goes further than many orders considered constitutional in nature by articulating a sort of penal code, namely the *Elements of Crimes*, a feature not even found in the EU legal order.[244] This demonstrates that there are limitations to each international organisation, even those more easily labelled constitutional.[245]

The ICC Statute's dual nature justifies a functional approach,[246] considering 'the constitutional or the contractual face' of the rule at hand.[247] In areas of traditional inter-state cooperation – such as arrest procedures or information-sharing – the VCLT may appropriately govern interpretation. But for provisions defining individual criminal liability, the Statute operates more like internal law. In this context, the interpretative rules specific to international criminal law–and in particular the legality principle set out in Article 22 – should take precedence over the general methods of treaty interpretation.[248] The next section builds on this logic and considers from another angle how the relationship between a particular system and international law can be comprehended.

D. Beyond the Lex Specialis Principle: The ICC as a Self-contained Regime

As discussed above, Article 31(3)(c) VCLT introduces the principle of systemic integration, encouraging courts to interpret treaties in harmony with general

[241] D Bosco, *Rough Justice: The International Criminal Court in a World of Power Politics* (OUP, 2013) 4ff; JE Alvarez, *International Organizations as Law-Makers* (OUP, 2005) 15; R Bellelli, *International Criminal Justice: Law and Practice from the Rome Statute to Its Review* (Ashgate Publishing, 2010) 20.

[242] A Birdsall and AF Jr Lang, 'The International Criminal Court and global constitutionalism' in AF Jr Lang and A Wiener (eds), *Handbook on Global Constitutionalism* (Edward Elgar, 2017) 259.

[243] R Elderkin, 'The Impact of International Criminal Law and the ICC on National Constitutional Arrangements' (2015) 4 *Global Constitutionalism* 227.

[244] The UN, WTO and the EU have all been analysed in terms of their constitutional quality. See: T Broude, 'The Constitutional Function of Contemporary International Tribunals, or Kelsen's Visions Vindicated' (2012) 4 *Goettingen Journal of International Law* 519.

[245] The EU's competence in substantive criminal law is limited: see further P Csonka and O Landwehr, '10 Years after Lisbon – How "Lisbonised" is the Substantive Criminal Law in the EU?' (2019) 26 *New Journal of European Criminal Law* 261.

[246] Brölmann (n 233) 25: 'International organisations are functionally defined [and] exists for a particular purpose, or area of operation, that has been (initially) determined by its creators.'

[247] Dörr and Schmalenbach (n 7) 92.

[248] Jacobs (n 18) 469: there 'are both rules of international law, [. . .], and internal rules when applied in the vertical relationship between the organisation and its member states.'

international law.[249] It assumes that specialised regimes are part of a coherent legal system and installs a predisposition to resolve interpretative issues by turning to broader international norms. In contrast, the principle of *lex specialis* gives priority to more specific rules over general ones where a conflict arises.

An alternative idea is that of the self-contained regime.[250] Depending on the point of view, a treaty system is categorised as a 'separate, autonomous, and self-contained system',[251] a self-sustained system, or a closed system – even if the latter is difficult to perceive as possible.[252] In most understandings, the specialised regime is treated as functionally independent from general international law.[253] Rather than relying on *lex specialis* each time a conflict arises, or turning to external rules for interpretative guidance, the system is expected to resolve issues from within.[254] In this sense, self-containment has been described as a 'strong lex specialis', one that displaces the general framework altogether in favour of an autonomous regime.[255] Self-containment is described in different ways.[256] Some have argued that the notion of self-containment only favours looking at the particular branch of law instead of general international law. Given that the Rome Statute draws on PIL, IHL, IHRL and domestic criminal law, it would be excessive to portray the ICC as a fully closed legal system.[257] The Court does not operate in 'autistic isolation'.[258] Others argue that the ICC must solely look to ICL when confronted with certain interpretative problems not immediately solvable through internal sources.[259]

Most adequate to understand the relationship of the ICC System to PIL is to use the concept of functional differentiation developed in the previous section and combine it with the concept of self-containment. The ICC System should

[249] See s II above.

[250] G Hafner, 'Reservations' in O Trifferer and K Ambos (eds), *The Rome Statute of the International Criminal Court: A Commentary* (2016) 2284.

[251] AZ Borda, 'Decision-making Patterns at the First Trial of the ICC: A Perspective on the ICC' (2011) 2 *Creighton International and Comparative Law Journal* 30, 43.

[252] B Simma, 'Self-contained regimes' (1985) 16 *Netherlands Yearbook of International Law* 111, 111.

[253] ILC, 'Fragmentation of International Law: Difficulties arising from the Diversification and Expansion of International Law' (2006) UN Doc A/CN.4/L.702, paras 65–67.

[254] B Simma and D Pulkowski, 'Of planets and the universe: self-contained regimes in international law' (2006) 17 *EJIL* 483, 488.

[255] ibid 490.

[256] ILC, 'Fragmentation of International Law' (n 253) para 132: 'A self-contained regime [. . .] has effect predominantly through providing interpretative guidance and direction that in some way deviates from the rules of general law.'

[257] ibid 492: the notion of 'self-contained regimes' has been misconceived as an argument in favour of entirely autonomous legal subsystems'.

[258] *Situation in Kenya* (Dissenting Opinion of Judge Kaul) (n 174) para 30.

[259] J Nicholson, 'The Role Played by External Case Law in Promoting the Legitimacy of International Criminal Court Decisions' (2018) 87 *Nordic Journal of International Law* 189, 206: 'The ICC regime is self-contained, and the Court has a duty to apply and interpret the applicable law consistently and in line with its Statute. However, this should be done in the awareness that the ICC is part of a wider field of [ICL]'; See also Powderly (n 61) 453; C Davidson, 'How to Read International Criminal Law: Strict Construction and the Rome Statute of the International Criminal Court' (2017) 91 *St John's Law Review* 37, 100.

be understood as a system with a certain level of self-containment. It is neither a fully closed nor a fully open system. Given the Rome Statute's pluri-legal nature this functional method allows for differentiation depending on the interpretative issue. For crime interpretation, this means internal documents should function as the primary reference, much like a domestic penal code. The doctrine on self-contained systems is designed to have a specific subfield or subsystem function on its own accord and not under the tutelage of international law. As developed in the next chapter, this combination of self-containment and the functional approach diminishes the need to rely on the VCLT's interpretative framework.

E. Criminal Law: a Subject Matter too Different from International Law?

The final argument against the application of the VCLT is that a 'generic' or 'off the rack' interpretative approach is ill-suited to penal treaties.[260] It has been argued that ICL comprises 'at least three dimensions: the 'universalist' aspirations of public international law, the 'humanist' dimensions of human rights law and the 'legality and fairness-oriented foundations of criminal law.'[261] Of these, the last is essential. While PIL organises relations between states, ICL is concerned with individual criminal responsibility. The ICC's raison d'être is to hold individuals accountable for international crimes. Although ICL draws from PIL, IHL, and IHRL, its defining feature remains its criminal nature.

As noted, the VCLT rules were drafted by drawing on statutory rules of interpretation, but with the idea of a treaty as a contract between states in mind.[262] Furthermore, the VCLT became an interpretive tool to be used for all treaties, whatever their subject-matter. Jain rightly pointed out that this stands in sharp contrast with the domestic system that has different interpretative principles for particular subfields of law.[263] While contract and criminal law follow distinct principles domestically, the VCLT does not distinguish and would apply equally to all treaties.[264] However, given that criminal law and international law are 'two fundamentally different strains of law',[265] the penal treaties should be treated differently. Following the logic of the preceding sections, a distinction should be made between traditional treaty provisions that may be interpreted via the

[260] Van Schaack (n 90) 149.

[261] C Stahn and L van den Herik, '"Fragmentation", Diversification and "3D" Legal Pluralism: International Criminal Law as the Jack-in-The-Box?' (2012) in L van den Herik and C Stahn (eds), *The Diversification and Fragmentation of International Criminal Law* (Martinus Nijhoff Publishers, 2012) 23.

[262] Lauterpacht cited in Sinclair (n 58) 2.

[263] Jain (n 96) 46–47.

[264] ibid.

[265] Fletcher and Ohlin (n 195) 543.

VCLT, but criminal provisions requiring specific interpretative methods developed within criminal law. This distinction is reinforced by the Rome Statute, offering its own set of interpretative tools adequate for dealing with provisions establishing individual criminal liability. As the next chapter discusses, the legality principle and its three corollary rules offer a sufficient and more appropriate basis for interpreting crimes.[266]

VI. THE USEFULNESS OF RECONCILING THE VCLT AND THE ROME STATUTE

This section evaluates whether reconciling the VCLT's interpretative methods with ICL methods is *useful* and provides 'dispositive guidance',[267] and whether, in the face of the well-established practice of relying on the VCLT, the ICC can reasonably be expected to change its course.[268]

Several scholarly contributions have tried to reconcile the VCLT with ICL methods. They begin from the assumption that the VCLT applies, but seek to adapt its rules in light of ICL's features.[269] Most commentators adapt the VCLT in light of the specific features of ICL,[270] as it is considered that the VCLT canons 'allow enough latitude for all bodies to draw on their own method'.[271] Many commentators recognise that Articles 21 and 22 of the Rome Statute aimed to constrain judicial discretion. Consequently, authors often justify applying ICL-specific filters to general treaty interpretation.[272]

The first form of adaptation concerns the crucible approach. Some scholars seek to soften the idea that all interpretative methods operate at the same level by privileging one – usually textual – method while still professing loyalty to the unified interpretive process.[273] Yet the boundary between adhering to the crucible approach 'in which no single interpretive principle or element dominates' but one school is favoured, and the dismissal of the crucible approach in favour of a certain school is thin.[274]

A second, and more common, adaptation involves reconciling purposive reasoning with the principle of strict construction, as for example, reflected in Sadat and Jolly's proposed canons for ICC treaty interpretation. Their first

[266] See ch 5.

[267] WK Lietzau, 'Checks and Balances and Elements of Proof: Structural Pillars for the International Criminal Court' (1999) 32 *Cornell International Law Journal* 477, 484.

[268] Robinson (n 182) 935.

[269] J Pauwelyn and M Elsig, 'The politics of treaty interpretation: variations and explanations across international tribunals' in JL Dunoff and MA Pollack (eds), *Interdisciplinary Perspectives on International Law and International Relations* (CUP, 2011) 448.

[270] Grover (n 94) 29.

[271] Sorel and Eveno (n 31) 817.

[272] Powderly (n 61) 444.

[273] Sadat and Jolly (n 195) 762–63; Grover (n 131) 547; Jain (n 96) 53–54.

[274] Jain (n 96) 53.

canon calls for fidelity to the text, guided by ordinary meaning and good faith; the second canon demands that purpose-driven readings remain consistent with Article 22(2).[275] Regretfully, their account leaves out a clear understanding of good faith.[276] They rightfully point to the limits of a textual approach but lack an explanation of what it means to construe faithfully. As the concept of good faith is 'broad and fluid', it is questionable how it can be used for the purpose of crime interpretation and not impede the principle of strict construction. While the authors note the friction between the Rome Statute's object ('ending impunity') and Article 22(2), and find that some provision are 'susceptible to liberal overreach', judges should not 'craft extraordinarily rigid understandings of the Statute's more open-ended [. . .] provisions, but rather interpret these in a manner consistent with the object and purpose of the Statute'.[277] In a similar vein, Akande has cautioned against interpretations that 'construe ambiguous provisions more liberally' by recourse to a teleological approach, often with reference to the preparatory works.[278] He recalled that Article 31 VCLT allows for the recourse to preparatory works when the meaning is left 'ambiguous or obscure'. The *in dubio pro reo* principle, however, trumps the VCLT's solution on how to deal with ambiguity.[279] Also, Robinson has emphasised that the *in dubio pro reo* principle as well as the principle of strict construction are to be applied first. He dismissed, more resolutely, a purposive approach that is often victim-oriented.[280] Throughout this book, the argument is developed, further demonstrated by the discussion in the case studies, that the legality principle requires the exclusion of broad teleological interpretations, particularly when grounded in preambular goals like ending impunity, as it risks enabling overly expansive, victim-centred interpretations that stretch crime definitions to the detriment of the accused.

The third adaptation introduces textual primacy into the interpretative methodology. Grover explicitly argues that crime interpretation requires prioritising the plain meaning of the text and warns against using interpretative aids to 'broaden, modify, or override' it.[281] While Article 31(1) VCLT does not privilege textualism, the legality principle as *lex specialis*, according to Grover, mandates such primacy.[282] Furthermore, Grover rightly stresses that context, object and purpose, and supplementary tools like the Elements of Crimes should not override the text of the Statute. Building on this view, this book argues for excluding the VCLT altogether from crime interpretation.

[275] Sadat and Jolly (n 195) 764.
[276] ibid 765–66.
[277] ibid 766.
[278] Akande (n 83) 44.
[279] ibid 45.
[280] Robinson (n 182) 933–35.
[281] Grover (n 94) 557.
[282] Grover (n 94).

While various efforts have sought to adapt the VCLT to the ICC's interpretative framework, these reconciliations come at a cost. Each modification – whether prioritising textualism or limiting teleological reasonings – requires such significant departures from the VCLT's crucible approach, in which all methods operate on equal footing, that it is effectively dismantled. Rather than pursuing a strained and ultimately unproductive reconciliation, one cannot help but conclude that there might be more to gain from simply excluding the VCLT than stubbornly holding on to it. The next section explores that possibility.

VII. THE VCLT AND CRIME INTERPRETATION: A NECESSARY BREAK-UP?

The exclusion of the VCLT from crime interpretation has rarely been argued, yet Jacobs stands out in doing so. His proposal inspired this chapter's central inquiry: is the VCLT obligatory, useful, or constructive for crime interpretation? The answer is no. Its uneasy fit with the legality principle warrants exclusion, and ICC judges should rely only on interpretative rules that conform to legality.[283] This chapter supported Jacobs' two main arguments. First, *lex specialis* requires that the Rome Statute's specific interpretative rules in Articles 21 and 22 prevail over the VCLT's general framework.[284] Second, as a constituent treaty of an international organisation, the Statute has a dual nature: in criminal proceedings, it functions as internal law, rendering the VCLT inapplicable. VCLT rules may be relevant only in inter-State disputes over treaty interpretation, not in the interpretation of crimes.[285] Whereas it is true that old habits might die hard, this chapter offered several arguments to set the VCLT aside for crime interpretation. Applying the Rome Statute as internal law is supported by notions such a *lex specialis* and justified given that criminal law is a subject matter very different than what the VCLT was conceptualised for. Instead of looking *ailleurs*, crime interpretation should have an inward-looking focus on the criminal law nature of ICL. This proposition is further developed in chapter six.

To conclude, it is interesting to consider Koskenniemi's description of VCLT's rules of interpretation as 'constructive justifications'.[286] The ICC practice reveals an inconsistent and under-theorised reliance on the VCLT, resting more on habit than true constructive reliance.[287] To replace this reliance, the combination of self-containment and functional differentiation offers a legality-centred alternative to the 'slicing and dicing' of VCLT provisions.[288]

[283] Jacobs (n 18) 469.
[284] ibid 469.
[285] ibid 470.
[286] M Koskenniemi, *From Apology to Utopia, The Structure of International Legal Argument* (CUP, 2006) 531.
[287] Grover (n 131) 547–49.
[288] Grover (n 94) 31.

5

Evaluating the Interpretative Process and Result: The Principles of Legality

Lex non exacte definit, sed arbitrio boni viri permittit.[1]

I. INTRODUCTION

CHAPTER TWO EXPLAINED HOW a distinction can be made between the interpretative process and result and introduced the two-dimensional functional relationship between the applicable law and methods of interpretation. It showed how the legality principle affects both. Chapters three and four addressed, respectively, two aspects of the interpretative process: interpretative methods and applicable law. This chapter turns to how both process and result are, or should be, shaped by the principles of legality.

A. Applicable Law & Source Doctrine (Article 21 Rome Statute)

Multiple legality principles are mentioned here because Article 22 contains not only a general formulation of legality and non-retroactivity in the first paragraph, but also provides:

> The definition of a crime shall be strictly construed and shall not be extended by analogy. In case of ambiguity, the definition shall be interpreted in favour of the person being investigated, prosecuted or convicted.

Three sub-principles follow: (1) strict construction; (2) the prohibition against analogy; and (3) *in dubio pro reo*. This study evaluates the process through these three principles and the result through strict construction and fair labelling. While strict construction is firmly embedded in the Rome Statute, fair labelling lacks a statutory basis and can only be argued to be implicitly included in the ICC system. Both nonetheless offer adequate tools to evaluate

[1] The law does not define exactly but trusts in the judgment of a good man.

the interpretative result and to build a methodology that adheres to legality while remaining sensitive to fairness. The scheme above categorises interpretative results into four quadrants. The aim is not to treat outcomes as always neatly broad or strict, or clearly fair or unfair, but to identify those unacceptable in light of legality. Preferably, interpretations fall in the upper right area – strict and fair. The bottom left – broad and unfair – clearly violates legality. The remaining quadrants pose harder cases where the two principles may conflict. This framework provides the basis for examining how the sub-principle of legality affects or should affect the interpretative process and safeguard the interpretative result.

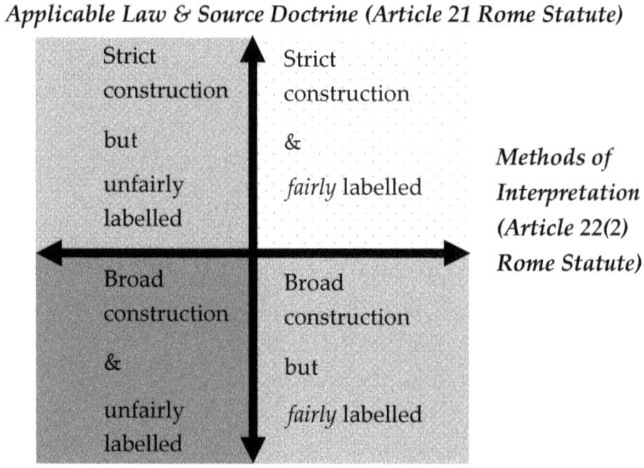

Table 1 A two-dimensional approach interpretative process with quadrantal categorisation of the interpretative outcomes

II. A LEGALITY-CENTRED EVALUATION OF THE INTERPRETATIVE PROCESS

This section discusses how the legality principle affects and should affect the interpretative process by examining the three novel legality principles in Article 22(2) Rome Statute. In terms of the structure of the preceding section, it is important to note that the principle of construction is discussed under both the process and the result as it understood to affect both aspects.

A. The Principle of Strict Construction

The Classical School first introduced strict construction, motivated by a profound distrust of judges and a conviction that only legislators should create law.[2] The

[2] C Beccaria, *On Crimes and Punishments and Other Writings* (Cambridge Texts in the History of Political Thought, CUP, 1764) 11–16.

aim was to strip the judge of *any* interpretative power and have the law applied automatically.[3] The principle can also be traced to civil law origins. The Classical School's influence on nineteenth-century codifications ensured its inclusion in most civil law systems, whether explicitly (eg, French Penal Code[4]), derived from the general legality clause (eg, Dutch Constitution and Penal Code[5]), or embedded in a broader principle (eg, Belgium's Constitutional *wettigheidsbeginsel*[6]). In relation to these civil law formulations, modern doctrine accepts that laws are general and imperfect, requiring judicial interpretation; strict construction prohibits excessively broad readings without excluding all interpretation.[7]

The idea of strict construction can also be found in common law, though the legality principle there does not require exclusive legislative competence to criminalise. As a result, the principle of strict construction had a meaning different from that in civil law systems. Blackstone in 1753, for example, noted that courts 'adhere more closely to the words' of penal statutes, but 'not so strictly as to defeat the obvious intention of the legislature.' The case must fall 'within the definition of the law' in its 'ordinary acceptation', avoiding giving the words a 'peculiar technical meaning'.[8] This reveals a long-standing tension between adhering to the text and looking to the drafter's intent. It also reveals that strict construction prohibits the judge from going too far from the text. This, however, does not mean that the judge is required to choose the strictest construction. Maxwell held that 'the language of a statute is generally extended to new things which were not known and could not have been contemplated by the Legislature when it was passed'.[9] As in civil law systems, strict construction in common law coexists with other methods.

In both systems, the theory's practical application is often 'so conflated with inconsistencies, that it is hard to discern widespread adherence to any general

[3] See further JGH Altena-Davidsen, *Het legaliteitsbeginsel en de doorwerking van Europees recht in het Nederlandse materiële strafrecht* (Wolters Kluwer, 2016) 31.

[4] Art 111-4 Code Pénal Français de 1e Mars 1994 (accessible www.legifrance.gouv.fr/codes/id/LEGITEXT000006070719/); See further X Pin, *Droit pénal général* (Les Cours Dalloz, 10 edn, Dalloz 2019) para 53ff.

[5] Art 1 Nederlandse Wetboek van Strafrecht, Wet van 3 maart 1881, (accessible on wetten.overheid.nl/BWBR0001854/2022-03-01): Art 16 Nederlandse Grondwet; see also MJ Borgers, 'De communicatieve strafrechter', *Controverses rondom legaliteit en legitimatie* (Handelingen Nederlandse Juristen-Vereniging, Kluwer 2011) 115.; Altena-Davidsen (n 3) 203ff.

[6] Art 12 Belgische gecoördineerde Grondwet van 17 februari 1994 (BS 17 February 1994) 4054; See also E Claes, *Legaliteit en rechtsvinding in het strafrecht: een grondslagentheoretische benadering* (Samenleving Criminaliteit & Strafrechtspleging Universitaire Pers Leuven, 2003); P-E Trousse, 'L'interprétation des lois pénales' (1952–53) *Revue de Droit Pénal et de Criminologie* 441; M van de Kerchove, 'La doctrine du sens claire des textes et la jurisprudence de la Cour de cassation de Belgique' in M van de Kerchove (ed), *L'interpretation en droit: approache pluridisciplinaire* (Publications des facultés universitaires Saint-Louis, 1978) 15ff.

[7] See, eg, R Legros, 'Considérations sur les lacunes et l'interprétation en droit pénal' (1966-67) *Revue de droit pénal et de criminologie* 3, 16–18.

[8] W Blackstone, *Commentaries on the Laws of England in Four Books* (Routledge–Cavendish, 1753) 672 (emphasis added).

[9] PB Maxwell and W Wyatt-Paine, *On the interpretation of statutes* (Sweet and Maxwell, 1920) 144–45.

policy of statutory construction'.[10] Despite the widespread acknowledgement of strict construction as a central part of legality, many authors have, over the years, attested to the limited adherence to the principle in practice,[11] underscored its limits,[12] or have documented the softening of the principle's application by other interpretative directives.[13] Moreover, multiple viewpoints exist on the degree of limitation imposed by strict construction.

Returning to the formulation of the principle in the Rome Statute, the first noticeable point is that it appeared late in the drafting process. A footnote to the applicable law provision proposed restating *nullum crimen sine lege* more explicitly: 'The provisions of article 5 shall be strictly construed and shall not be extended by analogy. . . .'[14] The Working Group on General Principles of Criminal Law later rephrased this to '[t]he definition of a crime shall be strictly construed'.[15] This articulation was retained and now features in Article 22(2). The drafting history and preparatory works are sparse, but the drafters agreed that the principle aimed to curb judicial creativity seen in earlier tribunals, creating a stricter constraint on judicial law-making.[16]

ICC judges have not defined strict construction in depth, making only 'perfunctory references' to it.[17] Either the decisions set out a general section with mention of the principle or the principle is said not to be violated in a particular case.[18] Decisions mostly either mention it in general terms or simply state that it is not violated.

The principle is indirectly raised in the *Lubanga case,* through a dissenting opinion of Judge Odio Benito. She found the majority erred in first not providing a legal definition of the concept of 'use to participate actively in the hostilities',[19] and second, not including sexual violence under the concept of use.[20] This triggered an academic debate on whether or not this approach violated the principle

[10] A Ashworth and J Horder, *Principles of Criminal Law*, 7th edn (OUP, 2013) 67–69.

[11] See, eg, Borgers (n 5) 114ff.

[12] See, eg, M Van Hoecke, 'De interpretatievrijheid van de rechter' (Rijksuniversiteit Gent, 1979) 72ff.

[13] See, eg, Claes (n 6) 26–35.

[14] Preparatory Committee, Report of the Preparatory Committee on the Establishment of an International Criminal Court, A/CONF.183/2/Add.1 (14 April 1998) fn 61.

[15] See also Report of the Working Group on General Principles of Criminal law to the Committee of the Whole, A/CONF.183/C.1/WGGP/L.4 (29 June 1998).

[16] J Powderly, 'The Rome Statute and the Attempted Corseting of the Interpretative Judicial Function: Reflections on Sources of Law and Interpretative Technique' in C Stahn (ed), *The Law and Practice of the International Criminal Court* (OUP, 2015); B Broomhall, 'Nullum crimen sine lege' in K Ambos and O Triffterer (eds), *The Rome Statute of the International Criminal Court, A Commentary* (Beck - Hart – Nomos, 2016) 950.

[17] WA Schabas, 'Strict Construction and the Rome Statute' in S Dewulf (ed), *Liber Amicorum Chris Van den Wyngaert* (Maklu, 2017) 425.

[18] See, eg, *Prosecutor v Bemba* (Decision on the Confirmation of Charges) ICC-01/05-01/08 (15 June 2009) para 423.

[19] *Prosecutor v Lubanga* (Separate and Dissenting Opinion of Judge Odio Benito to the Judgment) ICC-01/04-01/06 (12 March 2012) paras 15–22.

[20] ibid paras 16–17.

of strict construction.[21] IHL holds provisions on the direct participation in hostilities, a notion generally understood to be stricter than active participation, as the latter also can include indirect forms of support.[22] The question is whether being forcibly married or sexually enslaved constitutes some indirect way to support the combatants included in the formulation of the relevant child soldier provisions in the Rome Statute. Driven by a desire to protect children and the wish to address sexual violence, Judge Odio Benito advocated for a broad purposive approach, including sexual violence as an indirect form of support. This interpretation is, however, not supported by the text of the Statute. The ordinary meaning of the phrase 'use to participate in hostilities' is very difficult to understand as including sexual slavery. That the protection of the arsenal of weapons is considered to fall within these concepts is much more textually supported and does not need recourse to a purposive approach. Therefore, and as underscored by Ambos, this interpretation is an extension of the concept 'use' that violates Article 22(2).[23]

A second and rather peculiar decision mentioning the principle of strict construction was made in 2018. The charges against *Ruto and Sang* were vacated, and a judgment pronounced by Trial Chamber V(A) consisted of the majority opinion, divided into the reasons set out by Judge Fremr and reasons set out by Judge Eboe-Osuji, and a dissenting opinion of Judge Herrera Carbuccia.[24] This creates the strange impression of not having a majority opinion but rather having three separate opinions, which undermines its bearing.

Judge Eboe-Osuji's reasoning is notable. His teleological reading of Article 22(2)[25] equated strict construction with *in dubio pro reo*, triggered only where ambiguity remains after other methods fail.[26] This departs from Article 22(2) and is problematic for three reasons. The first is that the purpose of Article 22(2) was to curtail the interpretative freedom of the bench, which is not recognised by Judge Eboe-Osuji. The second reason is that the principle of strict construction is an interpretative principle separate from the *in dubio pro reo* principle,

[21] See, eg, T Rodenhäuser, 'Squaring the Circle? Prosecuting Sexual Violence against Child Soldiers by their "Own Forces"' (2016) 14 *Journal of International Criminal Justice* 171; R Grey, 'Sexual Violence against Child Soldiers: The Limits and Potential of International Criminal Law' (2014) 16 *International Feminist Journal of Politics* 601.

[22] S Vité, 'Between Consolidation and Innovation: The International Criminal Court's Trial Chamber Judgment in the Lubanga Case' in TD Gill and others (eds), *Yearbook of International Humanitarian Law*, vol 15 (TMV Asser Press, 2012) 77–78; see also S Bosch, 'The international humanitarian law notion of direct participation in hostilities – A review of the ICRC interpretive guide and subsequent debate' (2014) 17 *PER* 1.

[23] K Ambos, 'The first Judgment of the International Criminal Court (Prosecutor v Lubanga): A comprehensive Analysis of the Legal Issues' (2012) 12 *International Criminal Law Review* 115, 137–38.

[24] *Prosecutor v Ruto and Sang* (Dissenting Opinion of Judge Herrera Carbuccia) ICC-01/09-01/11 (5 April 2016).

[25] *Prosecutor v Ruto & Sang* (Decision on Defence Applications for Judgments of Acquittal) ICC-01/09-01/11 (5 April 2016) para 431.

[26] ibid paras 432–37.

and not conditioned on ambiguity. The third reason for rejecting Eboe-Osuji's reasoning is his view on the relation between strict construction and other interpretative principles. It omits to connect the principle of strict construction to the textual approach, which, although it is not to be equated with strict construction, is the best guarantee for a definition to be strictly construed. It positions strict construction at the end of the interpretative activity, when other principles have not succeeded in a coherent interpretative outcome, and there is still a need to resolve an ambiguity. The principle of strict construction should be at the forefront of an interpretative methodology in crime interpretation rather than at the back.

The ICC case law would benefit from a clarification such as that given in the ICTY's *Čelebići* judgment. The judges in this case explained 'that the language of a particular provision shall be construed such that no cases shall be held to fall within it which [. . .] do *not ordinarily fall within its express language.* [T]he legislature has not used words sufficiently comprehensive to include within its prohibition all the cases which should naturally fall within the mischief intended to be prevented, *the interpreter is not competent to extend them* [and] can only determine whether the case is within the intention of a criminal statute by *construction of the express language of the provision.*'[27] This passage explicitly links strict construction to the textual approach and, more specifically, to ordinary meaning – an association not developed in ICC jurisprudence.

As no evidence was found of a purposive approach supporting a narrow reading where the text does not make it possible to arrive at this reading independently and several instances exist of this method being used to broaden interpretations, its seems that the purposive approach is highly difficult to reconcile with strict construction and should be excluded from the first steps of crime interpretation as it used mostly in support of broad and victim-centred interpretations.[28] The principle of strict construction requires a textual over a teleological method.[29] Given the importance attached to the teleological and purposive approach in the VCLT, this very likely collision with the principle of strict construction offers a convincing argument to exclude the VCLT from the interpretative activity in relation to crimes. The crucible approach leaves too much room for uncertainty, which the legality principle in the context of crime interpretation seeks to avoid. The argument that the crucible approach allows for all sorts of adaptation and permits every imaginable interpretative activity

[27] *Prosecutor v Delalic et al (Čelebići case)* (Appeals Judgment) IT-96-21-A (20 February 2001) para 410 (emphasis added).

[28] See, eg, D Robinson, 'The Identity Crisis of International Criminal Law' (2008) 21 *LJIL* 925, 393ff.

[29] LN Sadat and JM Jolly, 'Seven Canons of ICC treaty Interpretation, Making Sense of Article 25's Rorschach Blot' (2014) 27 *LJIL*, 764; L Grover, *Interpreting Crimes in the Rome Statute of the International Criminal Court* (CUP, 2014), 398–99.

is problematic in crime interpretation. The principle of strict construction obligates a construction firmly established in the text, which brings certainty to the interpretation of crimes. This fixed idea of interpretation is completely at odds with the immense liberty granted by the crucible approach. Although some authors have also inserted textual primacy into their interpretative methodology, they have not rejected the crucible approach,[30] despite the fact that inserting textual primacy into the interpretative activity effectively replaces the crucible approach with a hierarchical idea of interpretation. That is why the next chapter seeks to provide an alternative approach.

B. The Prohibition on Analogy

In civil law, analogical reasoning is generally viewed as 'a tool to fill a gap in a code. In common law it is regarded as the technique for applying the *ratio decidendi* of a precedent to a new case'.[31] Whereas the principle of strict construction has a clear lineage in both civil and common law systems, the ban on analogy is a bit more difficult to trace in both legal families. MacCormick and Summers' comparative study nonetheless shows that many systems recognise it, though less strongly in Anglo-American law.[32] Legal argumentation is laced with reasoning by analogy, and some scholars even claim that analogy is 'what we mean when we talk of thinking like a lawyer.'[33] This makes it difficult to draw a firm line between permitted analogical interpretation and prohibited extension by analogy.[34] Judicial reasoning often involves deduction, and also the categorisation of certain conduct within a crime category, is not void of analogical logic. Analogy has long been a useful technique to capture conduct not expressly regulated.[35] The ban on analogy, however, prevents applying a statute to cases it was, strictly speaking, not designed for.[36] In those cases, it is argued that the drafter intended to exclude this conduct.[37] It is, in any event, a delicate

[30] Robinson (n 28) 393; Grover (n 29) 398–99.

[31] K Langenbucher, 'Argument by Analogy in European Law' (1998) 57 *The Cambridge Law Journal* 481, 481.

[32] N MacCormick and RS Summers, *Interpreting Statutes, A Comparative Study* (Darmouth Publishing Company Limited, 1991): See Argentina 47; Germany 81; France 200–201; Italy 219–20; for Poland, 277; Finland 161; Sweden 352; England, 388; United States, 471–72.

[33] BN Larson, 'Law's Enterprise: Argumentation Schemes & Legal Analogy' (2018) 87 *University of Cincinnati Law Review* 663, 663.

[34] W Naucke, 'Interpretation and analogy in criminal law' (1986) *Brigham Young University Law Review* 535.

[35] P Cugat, *Les crimes contre l'humanité dans le statut de la Cour internationale* (Schulthess 2006) 152–53; Broomhall (n 16) 961–62.

[36] See H Silving, 'Analogy and Extensive Interpretation' (1967) 36 *Rev Jur UPR* 311.

[37] KS Gallant, *The Principle of Legality in International and Comparative Criminal Law* (CUP, 2009) 36.

exercise to manoeuvre between this general reasoning technique and the specific prohibition in criminal law.

Analogical reasoning itself does not contradict the VCLT. Whether through contextual or teleological readings, the VCLT methodology embraces analogy. There are, however, two tensions between the prohibition on analogy in article 22(2) and the VCLT's invitation to use analogical reasoning. First, analogy results in the application of a statute to contexts outside its text. Such contextual reasoning is acceptable under the VCLT, but within the ICC system creates particular problems, most significantly when used outside of the confines of the two residual crime categories – 'other inhumane acts' and 'other forms of sexual violence' – in its statute. These *ejusdem generis* clauses necessitate analogical reasoning.[38] These categories offer flexibility while requiring comparable gravity to listed crimes.[39] Contextual readings entailing analogy must, therefore, be confined to these residual categories. Beyond them, stretching definitions violates legality. The Statute provides a framework for analogy, and extending it further is impermissible.[40] Second, analogy often entails that the intent of the drafter is invoked. The argument is made that the legislator wanted to include conduct not expressly covered by the Statute. To the extent that a teleological approach, combined with an analogue reasoning, requires the judge to set aside a text, it is problematic in light of the legality principle. This was, for instance, the case in the *Lubanga Confirmation of Charges Decision* in relation to the interpretation of 'national armed forces' in Article 8(2)(b)(xxvi).[41] The Pre-Trial Chamber held that '[t]he drafters of the Statute wanted to include under article 8 of the Statute a large array of criminal conduct committed in the context of an international armed conflict'.[42] Consequently, an analogy led the judges to include the UPC, a paramilitary-like group, under the label 'national armed forces'. This teleologically supported analogy was based on the VCLT and entirely ignored the limits set by Article 22(2).

This type of reasoning is not acceptable under the ban on analogy in the Rome Statute. Going beyond a text because it is ambiguous is one thing, but setting aside a text because it does not include certain conduct is quite another. Such teleological reasoning that sets aside the text is irreconcilable with the ban,

[38] FF Baetens, 'Ejusdem Generis and Noscitur a Sociis in Municipal and International Law: Interpretative Cross-Fertilisation?' in J Klinger, Y Parkhomenko and C Salonidis (eds), *Between the Lines of the Vienna Convention? Canons and Other Principles of Interpretation in Public International Law* (Wolters Kluwer, 2019) 133.

[39] I Haenen, 'Classifying Acts as Crimes Against Humanity in the Rome Statute of the International Criminal Court' (2013) 14 *German Law Journal* 796, 815.

[40] Grover (n 29) 214; L Grover, 'A Call for Arms: Fundamental Dilemmas Confronting the Interpretation of Crimes in the Rome Statute of the International Criminal Court' (2010) 21 *EJIL* 543. See Intro above and s IV(C).

[41] *Prosecutor v Lubanga* (Decision on Confirmation of Charges) ICC-01/04-01/06 (29 January 2007), paras 275–85.

[42] ibid para 284; see also Ambos (n 23).

which is why a teleological approach has to yield to a textual approach. This is again an argument to move away from applying the VCLT.

C. The *in Dubio Pro Reo* Principle

The notion of *in dubio pro reo* is firmly established in most legal traditions and requires that an ambiguity be resolved in favour of the accused. In many legal systems, it is understood as a procedural and evidentiary rule connected to the notion of presumption of innocence: in case of any doubt as to the guilt of the accused, acquittal must follow.[43] It is not understood as an interpretative principle. Judge Popović noted in his dissent in *Anchour* that the ECtHR has not even applied the principle in the context of legality.[44] Likewise, comparative insights suggest that in civil law traditions, the principle is not generally regarded as an interpretative principle.[45]

In the Anglo-American tradition, however, the principle also developed as an interpretative tool, often referred to as the rule of lenity.[46] In some approaches, the rule of lenity encompasses both the idea of strict construction and that an ambiguity needs to be solved in favour of the accused.[47] This conflation obscures the separate operation of the two principles and partly explains why lenity has been described as 'easy to define but difficult to apply'.[48] It is therefore important to stress that the Rome Statute explicitly splits up these two principles. The history of this rule of lenity also exposes different perspectives as to when the principle steps in. In some cases, it has been held that it only applies when all the tools of interpretation have been exhausted.[49] Other approaches suggest that the principle needs to operate much earlier in the interpretative process in order to successfully solve ambiguities.[50]

[43] F Quintard-Morénas, 'The presumption of innocence in the French and Anglo-American legal traditions' (2010) 58 *American Journal of Comparative Law* 107, 112; R Legros, 'Considérations sur les lacunes et l'interprétation en droit pénal' (1966–67) *Revue de droit pénal et de criminologie* 3, 17; European Union Agency for Fundamental Rights (FRA), *Presumption of Innocence and Related Rights, Professional Perspectives* (FRA 2021); GP Fletcher, 'Two Kinds of Legal Rules: A Comparative Study of Burden-of-Persuasion Practices in Criminal Cases' (1967) 77 *Yale LJ* 880, 880–81.

[44] *Achour v France* App no 67335/01, Dissenting Opinion of Judge Popovic (Grand Chamber) (29 March 2006) 45 EHRR 2.

[45] Fletcher (n 43).

[46] DS Romantz, 'Reconstructing the Rule of Lenity' (2018) 40 *Cardozo Law Review* 523.

[47] LM Solan, 'Law, Language, and Lenity' (1998) 40 *William and Mary Law Review* 57.Romantz (n 46) 523.

[48] Romantz (n 46) 523.

[49] Solan (n 47) 60.

[50] DD Ortner, 'The merciful corpus: The rule of lenity, ambiguity and corpus linguistics' (2016) 25 *BU Pub Int LJ* 101, 102–103.

The ICC case law leaves no doubt that this principle applies as an evidentiary principle linked to the presumption of innocence.[51] This contrasts with the lack of application of the principle in substantive matters. An exception is the *Katanga* Judgment, which clarified that the principle applies 'only after an unsuccessful attempt at interpretation effected in good faith and in accordance with the General Rule of the [VCLT] or in accordance with article 32 [VCLT]'.[52] The Trial Chamber continued that any residual doubt 'must be resolved in favour of the subject', 'and not in favour of the drafter, who was unclear'.[53] In the judges' view, Article 22(2) does not override the conventional methods of treaty interpretation.[54] Rather, the judges positioned *in dubio pro reo* within the VCLT framework.

The term 'ambiguity' deserves closer attention. Scholarship and case law often assume its meaning is self-evident, but it must be distinguished from related concepts such as vagueness, generality, or lacunae.[55] For example, generality requires specification of whether a case falls under a broad category.[56] Generality does, however, not necessarily create a multiplicity of meaning. Whereas ambiguity means 'capable of being understood in two or more possible senses or ways',[57] vagueness means that something is 'not clearly expressed; stated in indefinite terms; not clearly defined, grasped, or understood; not thinking or expressing one's thoughts clearly or precisely'.[58] Although these two terms are in ordinary language sometimes used interchangeably, legal theorists have stressed the technical difference. Solum described ambiguity as 'multiplicity of sense' and vagueness, referring to 'the existence of borderline cases: a term is vague if there are cases where the term might or might not apply.'[59] He further clarified that both are forms of indeterminacy.[60] Marmor argued that vagueness means 'we have no clear demarcation of where borderline cases begin and where they end' and as such, he saw no place for the rule of lenity to solve

[51] See, eg, *Prosecutor v Bemba* (Judgment on the appeal of Mr Jean-Pierre Bemba Gombo against Trial Chamber III's "Judgment pursuant to Article 74 of the Statute") ICC-01/05-01/08 (8 June 2018) paras 1368–72; *Prosecutor v Ntaganda* (Judgment) ICC-01/04-02/06 (8 July 2019) para 69.

[52] *Prosecutor v Katanga* (Judgment pursuant to article 74 of the Statute) ICC-01/04-01/07 (7 March 2014) para 54.

[53] ibid para 54.

[54] ibid para 54.

[55] To my knowledge, the most comprehensive studies on legality have not included an analysis of the difference between these concepts. Eg, Grover's study discusses different interpretative problems (8ff) but does not address the difference between vagueness and ambiguity.

[56] Q Zhang, 'Fuzziness-Vagueness-Generality-Ambiguity' (1998) 29 *Journal of Pragmatics* 13.

[57] Merriam-Webster Online Dictionary, www.merriam-webster.com/dictionary/ambiguous; see also Oxford English Dictionary's meaning of ambiguous: 'Doubtful, questionable; indistinct, obscure, not clearly defined'.

[58] Merriam-Webster Online Dictionary, www.merriam-webster.com/dictionary/vague; see also Oxford English Dictionary's meaning of vague: 'Of words, language, etc.: Not precise or exact in meaning'.

[59] LB Solum, 'The Interpretation-Construction Distinction' (2010) 27 *Constitutional Commentary* 95, 97–98.

[60] ibid 97.

vagueness.[61] Poscher furthermore stated that 'only vagueness is reflexive,'[62] and creates borderline cases, 'ambiguity is neither a borderline issue nor is it reflexive'.[63] Vagueness implies that there is a matter of scope that has to be solved through interpretation. It cannot be rendered entirely determinate up front and will always bring about borderline cases. An ambiguity is another matter and 'concerns those cases in which an expression has two possible, though unrelated, meanings.'[64] The *in dubio pro reo* principle can only *disambiguate* in favour of the defendant,[65] but does not affect rendering vagueness clearer. The lack of clarity between vagueness and ambiguity, as well as the confusion between the principles of strict construction and lenity in the Anglo-American tradition, creates a risk of overapplication of the *in dubio pro reo* principle.[66] When the principle is only applied in case of a genuine ambiguity, there is no need to fear its overapplication.

The second unresolved issue is the principle's position in the interpretative process. Some judges conclude that the rule of lenity is triggered only at the very end when other tools fail. Judge Eboe-Osuji, for example, stressed that it applies only in cases of 'real ambiguity' and is 'not the first port of call'.[67] Yet, as Robinson warns, deferring the principle to the end risks rendering it meaningless: ambiguities may already have been resolved against the accused through other methods, particularly victim-centred teleological reasoning.[68] As criticised by Jain, the principle is 'relegated to a secondary status *vis-a-vis* the VCLT' and 'it is difficult to see what place, if any, is left for the operation of the principle of legality'.[69] Davidson, by contrast, argued that if legality was 'prioritized above all else', Article 22(2) would demand resolution in favour of the accused at the very outset, which is why this principle cannot function at the very beginning of the process.[70] The question thus remains if not the beginning and not the end, where then should the principle feature in the interpretative exercise? The proposed way out of this conundrum is to set the VCLT aside. This exclusion facilitates the discussion on the position of this principle in the interpretative exercise. When the VCLT is excluded and an interpretative methodology is grafted upon Article 22, there is much less problem with *in dubio pro reo* being positioned at the end of the interpretative exercise. Within this legality-centred

[61] A Marmor, *The Language of Law* (OUP, 2014) 95.

[62] Ralf Poscher, 'Ambiguity And Vagueness In Legal Interpretation' in Peter Tiersma and Lawrence Solan (eds), *The Oxford Handbook of Language and Law* (OUP, 2012) 129.

[63] ibid 129.

[64] Marmor (n 61) 120.

[65] ibid 95.

[66] Grover (n 29) 206 (citation marks omitted).

[67] *Ruto & Sang* (Acquittal Decision) (n 25) 432–34.

[68] Robinson (n 28) 934.

[69] N Jain, 'Interpretive Divergence' (2017) 57 *Virginia Journal of International Law* 45, 62–63.

[70] C Davidson, 'How to Read International Criminal Law: Strict Construction and the Rome Statute of the International Criminal Court' (2017) 91 *St John's Law Review* 37, 75.

methodology, at least not all ambiguities will have been solved before this principle can be applied, not rendering it useless.

The *in dubio pro reo* principle should furthermore be judged on its own merits and function independently from the other two principles of Article 22(2). In line with the preceding analysis, the judge should first determine the type of indeterminacy. If there is an interpretative problem as a result of vagueness, the judge should take into consideration the principle of strict construction and consider that an interpretation, to abide by this principle, cannot stretch the concept to the detriment of the accused. If the interpretative problem is the result of an ambiguity, the *in dubio pro reo* principle forces the judge to take the meaning more favourable to the accused, when the context of the primary sources does not solve the ambiguity. It would be too strict to consider the principle to operate at each step of the interpretative exercise, but also too broad to consider it at the end. As Robinson demonstrates, the biggest danger lies in adopting a victim-oriented teleological approach that does away with any ambiguity before the *in dubio pro reo* steps in. Therefore, if a textual and contextual approach of the internal sources cannot solve the interpretative difficulties, this principle stands in the way of a teleological approach leading to a broad interpretation.

D. From the Process to the Result

By constraining interpretation, the principles of Article 22(2) already affect results: if the ban on analogy is breached or an ambiguity is not resolved in favour of the accused, the outcome is unlawful by virtue of the flawed process. No additional analysis of the result is therefore necessary for these principles. Strict construction is different. Even when the process is not defective – sources and methods are appropriately chosen, no analogy is misapplied, and no ambiguity is mishandled – the interpretative outcome may still be excessively broad. For that reason, legality requires a separate assessment of the interpretative outcome in light of strict construction. The following analysis, therefore, concentrates on strict construction as the principle that continues to operate at the result stage.

III. A LEGALITY-CENTRED EVALUATION OF THE INTERPRETATIVE RESULT

Substantive criminal law is built on a system of classification: offences are distinguished from defences, crimes are divided into categories, and objective (*actus reus*) and subjective (*mens rea*) elements are defined alongside theories of responsibility and causation.[71] Although this may seem obvious, these taxonomies

[71] *Encyclopedia Britannica*, 'The elements of crime' www.britannica.com/topic/criminal-law/The-elements-of-crime.

shape the judicial role. Judges must fit fact patterns into predetermined categories, interpreting and labelling conduct according to crime definitions. ICL functions according to the same principles and classification system.[72] While the ICTY and ICTR Statutes offered relatively rudimentary taxonomies, the Rome Statute and the Elements of Crimes provide a detailed classification system more developed than many domestic codes.[73] The ICC judge's core task is therefore to construe and label conduct within this framework.

This section evaluates whether such construction and labelling respect the principle of legality. Two principles are central: strict construction, codified in Article 22(2), and fair labelling, a principle that has shown increasing influence in the context of ICL and can be invoked as a general principle. Using the study's two-dimensional model, interpretative outcomes can be placed into four quadrants, indicating when a result is both strict and fair, neither, or one or the other. Some cases are straightforward, but others reveal tension between the two principles. However, given the unequal footing of the two principles, this is not a straightforward balancing exercise. This unequal footing has consequences in terms of the evaluation of the interpretative result, as this section will explain.

A. Strict Construction

This section examines how the principle of strict construction limits the breadth of interpretative outcomes. Although clear guidance is scarce, ICC jurisprudence shows that expansive interpretations may violate Article 22(2), often because they stem from flawed interpretative processes.

In some cases, the misapplication of the applicable law leads to overly broad interpretation. One example of this is when judges adopt a customary definition broader than the statutory crime. Strict construction requires that the narrower statutory text prevails, and opposes the broad customary definition that is used to enlarge a narrower statutory crime, as discussed in the case study on the organisational policy. Using the broader customary definition would both misapprehend the role of customary law and produce an impermissibly broad outcome.

In other cases, the flawed use of the interpretative methods results in such an impermissible outcome. In *Bemba*, the Trial Chamber underlined that it could not adopt interpretative methods that expanded the scope of crimes, but 'is bound to adhere to the letter of the provisions aimed at reprimanding only conduct the drafters expressly intended to criminalise'.[74] This articulation is

[72] WA Schabas, 'General Principles of Criminal Law in the International Criminal Court Statute (Part III)' (1998) 6 *European Journal of Crime, Criminal Law and Criminal Justice* 400.

[73] A Cassese, 'The Statute of the International Criminal Court: Some Preliminary Reflections' (1999) 10 *European Journal of International Law* 123 on how the Rome Statute introduced some essential changes in substantive ICL.

[74] *Prosecutor v Bemba* (Judgment pursuant to Article 74 of the Statute) ICC-01/05-01/08 (21 March 2016) para 73.

consistent with the principle of strict construction, which prioritises the textual method.

In some instances, however, an interpretation may follow from a sound process yet still exceed the limits of Article 22(2). The *Ongwen* judgment further clarified the boundary between permissible interpretation and impermissible extension concerning the category of 'other inhumane acts'. The Trial Chamber held that the interpretation 'must be *consistent with the essence of the offence* and in a manner which could have been *reasonably foreseen*'.[75] This two-step standard was imported from the case law of the ECtHR. The ECtHR has repeatedly held that 'the gradual clarification of the rules of criminal liability through judicial interpretation' is allowed, 'provided that the resultant development is consistent with the essence of the offence and could reasonably be foreseen'.[76] The key question, however, is whether this borrowed test provides a sufficiently rigorous legality standard for ICC judges, given the express codification of strict construction in Article 22(2).

In 2021, the Defence in the *Abd-Al-Rahman case* challenged the Court's jurisdiction and, as part of its argumentation, raised a violation of Article 22(1).[77] Leaving the jurisdictional matter aside, the case raised some interesting points in relation to the foreseeability test. The Appeals Chamber emhasised that the legality principle is a human right and held that prosecution must be reasonably foreseeable.[78] It considered factors 'such as the "flagrantly unlawful nature" of the crimes charged and the circumstances of the accused' relevant to this assessment.[79] Because the crimes occurred outside the territory of a State Party and the accused was not a national of a State Party, the Chamber found it insufficient to rely solely on the Rome Statute. Instead, 'a chamber must look beyond the Statute to the criminal laws applicable to the suspect or accused at the time the conduct took place and satisfy itself that a reasonable person could have expected, [. . .], to find him or herself faced with the crimes charged'.[80] Instead, the Chamber implemented this test in a peculiar way. Rather than analysing whether a legal basis existed in customary or Sudanese law, it turned to the accused's personal situation. By emphasising his leadership role in the Janjaweed militia, it concluded that 'he was reasonably capable of taking steps to comprehend and comply with his obligations under international law, and

[75] *Prosecutor v Ongwen* (Trial Judgment) ICC-02/04-01/15 (4 February 2021) para 2741 (emphasis added).

[76] See, eg, *Vasiliauskas v Lithuania*, App no 35343/05, Judgment (Grand Chamber) (20 October 2015) ECHR 923 paras 155-162; *Jorgic v Germany*, App no 74613/01, Judgment (12 July 2007) paras 100–116.

[77] *Prosecutor v Abd-Al-Rahman* (Judgment on the appeal of Mr Abd-Al-Rahman against the Pre-Trial Chamber II's "Decision on the Defence '*Exception d'incompétence*') ICC-02/05-01/20-302 (1 November 2021) para 83.

[78] ibid paras 83–85.

[79] ibid para 85.

[80] ibid para 85.

he was capable of appreciating the attendant penal consequences'.[81] As Galand observes, this effectively presumed foreseeability without verifying the underlying legal foundation, leaving it to the Trial Chamber to determine whether the charges were crimes under Sudanese or customary law.[82] The *Abd-Al-Rahman* Appeals Chamber, despite setting out a *foreseeability* test, did not really apply it, which leaves a lot uncertain.[83]

As several scholars have observed, the ECtHR's legality doctrine was designed to leave Member States discretion in shaping domestic criminal policy.[84] The ICC operates in a different context.[85] The Rome Statute reflects a clear policy choice for strict legality, while the standards of 'foreseeability' and 'essence of the offence' appear broad enough 'to permit just about anything'.[86] ICC judges should therefore resist borrowing the ECtHR's approach and instead articulate what strict construction means under Article 22(2). To date, however, no ICC decision has engaged seriously with the principle. Davidson proposes to remedy this by introducing a three-step test:

> First, judges should avoid usurpations of state authority. This inquiry looks at whether states have delegated lawmaking authority and reconceives the objects and purposes inquiry. Second, judges should avoid unfair surprise to defendants. This constraint looks at the strength of the support for a particular interpretation. Where the statute is ambiguous or vague, the absence of a preexisting international norm criminalising the conduct creates a rebuttable presumption of unfair surprise. Finally, judges should attempt to clarify ICL and international law generally.[87]

In relation to the first step of avoiding usurpation of state authority, Davidson proposed to examine whether states intended to exclude or include criminal conduct.[88] She made two specifications in relation to this step. First, she regarded the use of vagueness or constructive ambiguity to be a delegation of legislative authority. Second, she refused to qualify broad goals (e.g. ending impunity) as a blanket transfer of legislative authority. This distinction is useful in marking judicial boundaries, though weak in terms of the absence of substantive limits. Given the poor quality of the Rome Statute's preparatory works, it is doubtful that clear

[81] ibid para 88.

[82] AS Galand, 'The ICC Appeals Judgment on Abd-Al-Rahman Jurisdictional Challenge: A Foreseeable Turn to Substantive Justice?', *EJIL: Talk! Blog of the European Journal of International Law* (22 November 2021) www.ejiltalk.org/the-icc-appeals-judgment-on-abd-al-rahman-jurisdictional-challenge-a-foreseeable-turn-to-substantive-justice/.

[83] T de Souza Dias, 'The Principle of Legality in the ICC's Appeals Judgment on Abd-Al-Rahman's Jurisdictional Challenge: A Follow-up on Merits and Shortcomings', *EJIL: Talk! Blog of the European Journal of International Law* (1 December 2021) www.ejiltalk.org/the-principle-of-legality-in-the-iccs-appeals-judgment-on-abd-al-rahmans-jurisdictional-challenge-a-follow-up-on-merits-and-shortcomings/.

[84] Davidson (n 70) 83.

[85] Grover (n 29) 173; Davidson (n 70) 83–84.

[86] Davidson (n 70) 85.

[87] ibid 87.

[88] ibid 88–89.

intent can often be identified. For example, Davidson saw the definition of gender as a constructive ambiguity signalling delegation to judges by States.[89] It is highly unlikely, given the clear opposition to the inclusion of the concept in the Statute by some States, that many States support this so-called delegation.[90] In order to better recognise when judges should usurp legislative authority, an extra substantive limitation should be added to this first step. Inspired by the test of strict construction developed by the *Čelebići* Trial Chamber, which raised the bar and required that 'no case shall fall within a penal statute that does not comprise all the elements which, whether morally material or not, are in fact made to constitute the offence',[91] the proposition is to require *all* 'the essential ingredients' have to be present.[92] Such a standard is much more in conformity with the principle of strict construction. As will be demonstrated under the case study on forced marriage, recourse to a residual category is not permissible where there is an enumerated crime holding all the necessary ingredients to be applied to the fact pattern.[93] In such a case, an enumerated crime should be chosen over a broad, residual category.

In relation to the second step concerning the avoidance of unfair surprise, it is clear that Davidson shaped her own step of foreseeability. She rightly underscored the need to have an objective test conducted from the perspective of any reasonable accused and not a subjective test of notice. This study concurs: strict construction should not collapse into foreseeability, but foreseeability can serve as a valuable legality check.

The third step, obliging judges to clarify the law, is more problematic. Davidson suggested this usually requires interpretation consistent with IHL and IHRL,[94] diverging only in limited circumstances when a more 'narrower reading of ICL is warranted'.[95] Although this idea is not objectionable per se, it inserts a step which focuses more on external sources than on internal sources and introduces a similar obligation of coherence relation to IHL and IHRL that is not in line with Article 21. This study argues that it is unhelpful to introduce such requirements to the interpretative process, as these weigh down more than lighten the process towards a more sound construction of a crime. This study, therefore, does not include this step in its own proposition.

Building on Davidson, this study therefore proposes a two-step test. First, judges should verify whether a statutory provision exists containing all essential elements for application to the facts. If such a provision is available, it must be applied; resort to residual categories is not allowed, nor can external sources be used to create new crimes. Second, the interpretation must be foreseeable to a reasonable accused, assessed objectively.

[89] ibid 89–90.
[90] See further in Case Study 2, s II, for an understanding of gender.
[91] *Čelebići case* (Appeals Judgment) para 411.
[92] ibid para 411.
[93] Case Study II, Section 4.5, 456ff.
[94] Davidson (n 70) 99.
[95] ibid 88.

However, given the fact that a too strict regime of strict construction may lead to high 'expressive costs',[96] the next section introduces the concept of fair labelling as a principle impacting this exercise.

B. Fair Labelling

The principle of representative labelling, first coined in 1981 by Ashworth,[97] later renamed 'fair labelling' by Williams,[98] and also referred to as 'complete labelling',[99] is a principle generally understood to impose a duty on the legislator to make sure 'distinctions between kinds of offences and degrees of wrongdoing are respected and signalled by the law, and that offences are subdivided and labelled so as to represent the nature and magnitude of the law-breaking'.[100] Ashworth connected this principle to fair warning and legal certainty as well as proportionality.[101] The idea is that the label chosen by the legislators enables citizens to know the consequences of their actions. It holds that the label of an offence has to fairly, clearly and adequately express the wrongfulness of the act, reflect the gravity of the act and correspond to the degree of harm caused.[102] Labelling requires 'to mark out the differences in the moral gravity' of the conduct.[103]

i. *The Origin and Scope of the Principle*

Although Ashworth did not fully develop the normative underpinnings of the principle, later scholars traced it to criminological and expressivist theories.[104] Becker's labelling theory stressed that deviance arises from the social response to conduct, not the conduct itself.[105] While Ashworth did not adopt this

[96] ibid 69.

[97] A Ashworth, 'The Elasticity of Mens Rea' in C Tapper (ed), *Crime, Proof and Punishment: Essays in Memory of Sir Rupert Cross* (Butterworths, 1981): Ashworth first dubbed the principle 'representative labelling' but later, partly due to the intervention of Williams, renamed it 'fair labelling'. See also G Williams, 'Convictions and Fair Labelling' (1983) 42 *Cambridge Law Journal* 85.

[98] Williams (n 97) 85.

[99] JS Eskauriatza, '"Complete Labelling" and Domestic Prosecutions for Crimes Against Humanity' (2021) *Criminal Law Forum*.

[100] Ashworth and Horder (n 10) 77.

[101] V Tadros, 'Fair labelling and social solidarity' in L Zedner and JV Roberts (eds), *Principles and Values in Criminal Law and Criminal Justice: Essays in Honour of Andrew Ashworth* (OUP 2012) 67.

[102] See Ashworth and Horder (n 10) 77ff; B McGonigle Leyh, 'Pragmatism over Principles: The International Criminal Court and a Human Rights-Based Approach to Judicial Interpretation' (2018) 41 *Fordham International Law Journal* 697, 704; HM Zawati and TA Doherty, *Fair Labelling and the Dilemma of Prosecuting Gender-Based Crimes at the International Criminal Tribunals* (OUP, 2014).

[103] Tadros (n 101) 67–68.

[104] See, eg, ibid 28–30.

[105] H Becker, *Outsiders: Studies in the Sociology of Deviance*, 2008 edn (Free Press, 1963) 14; see also P Rock, 'Sociological Theories of Crime' in M Maguire, R Morgan and R Reiner (eds), *Oxford Handbook on Criminology* (OUP, 2002) 71ff.

sociological conception, his expressivist approach resonates with it:[106] criminal law should 'track the reasonable moral convictions of the community'.[107] Also, Feinberg articulated that punishment was a way of condemning and disavowing conduct.[108] He underscored the symbolic function of punishment.[109] In the same line, Simester and Sullivan argued that 'criminal law speaks to society as well as wrongdoers when it convicts them, and it should communicate its judgment with precision, by accurately naming the crime of which they are convicted'.[110] Other scholars named this the symbolic rather than the expressive function of criminal law and stress that 'the stigma of conviction corresponds to the wrongfulness of the act'.[111] One might argue that sentencing already sufficiently differentiates degrees of culpability. However, 'moral grasp is not important merely for sentencing. [. . .] When the definition of an offence gives us this grasp of what the defendant has done, it embodies the virtue of what we may call 'moral nominalism': the 'naming' of one's wrongdoing that is at the heart of the principle of representative labelling.'[112]

The fairness thus also has to be grasped by something other than the punishment or sentence. This is the prime reason that the fair labelling principle requires differentiations between crime labels both in terms of their objective and subjective elements. Several factors determine whether a label is sufficiently specific and fair: (a) the type of offence; (b) the degree of wrongdoing; (c) the nature of the law-breaking; (d) the magnitude of the law-breaking.[113] Apart from indicating *what* crime has been committed (a), the label also has to represent the severity (b & d) and nature of the wrongdoing (c). That means that the degree of guilt needs to find expression in the legal *mens rea* requirement, which is why different forms of *mens rea* (intention, recklessness and negligence) differentiate in blameworthiness.[114] It is quite logical that someone who recklessly carried out conduct is less guilty than someone who had the intention to harm. The same logic requires that there is also correspondence between the guilty mind and the

[106] Ashworth does not mention the theory of expressivism, but by stressing the importance of the label's expression to correspond to a social reality, nonetheless seems to import it. See also J Feinberg, *Doing and Deserving: Essays in the Theory of Responsibility* (Princeton University Press, 1970).

[107] Ashworth and Horder (n 10) 78.

[108] Feinberg (n 106) 101–102.

[109] ibid 102.

[110] J Chalmers and F Leverick, 'Fair Labelling in Criminal Law' (2008) 71 *Modern Law Review* 217, 226.

[111] T de Souza Dias, 'Recharacterisation of Crimes and the Principle of Fair Labelling in International Criminal Law' (2018) 18 *International Criminal Law Review* 788; M Aksenova, 'Symbolism as a Constraint on International Criminal Law' (2016) 30 *Leiden Journal of International Law* 475, 496; D Robinson, *Justice in Extreme Cases: Criminal Law Theory meets International Criminal Law* (CUP, 2020) 9.

[112] J Horder, 'Rethinking Non-Fatal Offences against the Person' (1994) 14 *Oxford Journal of Legal Studies* 335, 339.

[113] Ashworth (n 97) 77.

[114] Chalmers and Leverick (n 110) 243.

harmful act.[115] Furthermore, the different modes of liability in criminal law likewise contribute to a fair label. Evidently, the label of a direct perpetrator has to be set apart from the label of an instigator or contributor. It is also why criminal law differentiates between attempts and completed crimes.[116]

The operation of fair labelling is best illustrated through examples. Ashworth himself criticised robbery as overly broad, failing to distinguish between a minor push during theft and robbery involving serious violence.[117] Fair labelling has been associated not only with particular crimes but also with crime categories.[118] Sexual offences, for example, historically have an underdeveloped taxonomy, with rape often treated as the sole category, which made it impossible to express different degrees of sexual violence and assault.[119]

This study distils from the reviewed doctrine three concepts that are useful in capturing the different dimensions of fair labelling: the wrongfulness, harmfulness, and blameworthiness of the act. Each of these concepts adds a different perspective.[120]

The first perspective to consider is that of the offender. It is only *fair* to the offender that his wrongdoing is labelled proportionally.[121] As understood by Ashworth, the principle requires the label to fairly 'represent the offenders wrongdoing'.[122] The label must reflect no more wrongfulness than what the act entails, or it would be considered unfair to the accused. To measure this level of fairness, an objective or subjective standard can be used. An objective approach differentiates types of wrongfulness based on how much wrongfulness the deed of the accused carries. A subjective approach entails that the wrongfulness is primarily determined by the accused's motive or guilty mind. The articulation of labels such as murder and manslaughter reflects a differentiation based on the subjective wrongfulness.[123] The second relevant perspective is that of the victim, which raises the question of harm.[124] A label is only fair if it reflects how the victim was affected and the extent of the harm inflicted. This requires recognising the victim's experience in shaping how harmfulness is understood and ensuring the offence label captures

[115] DJJ Bright, 'Why the Criminal Law Principle of Correspondence Should Prevail over the Pragmatism of Constructed Liability' (2010) 2 *King's Student Law Review* 43, 43.

[116] J Edwards and A Simester, 'Crime, Blameworthiness, and Outcomes' (2019) 39 *Oxford Journal of Legal Studies* 50, 63–64.

[117] A Ashworth, 'Robbery re-assessed' (2002) *Criminal Law Review* 851, 856.

[118] DN Husak, 'The De Minimis "Defence" to Criminal Liability' in RA Duff and SP Green (eds), *Philosophical foundations of criminal law* (OUP, 2011) 349.

[119] See, eg, RA Fenton, 'Rape in Italian law: Towards the recognition of sexual autonomy' in C McGlynn and V Munro (eds), *Rethinking Rape Law: International and Comparative Perspectives* (Routledge, 2010) 188.

[120] Eskauriatza (n 99) 1; Tadros (n 101) 68.

[121] Chalmers and Leverick (n 110) 225–26.

[122] Ashworth (n 97) 53–54.

[123] See L Jordaan, 'The Principle of Fair Labelling and the Definition of the Crime of Murder' (2017) *Journal of South African Law* 569

[124] Chalmers and Leverick (n 110) 235.

that dimension.[125] Even more broadly, the community perspective is also of relevance. The label should reflect what a larger community finds blameworthy.[126]

The fair labelling idea was developed in common law doctrine. That does not mean that the normative idea underlying it is absent from continental tradition, where it has increasingly attracted scholarly attention.[127] Furthermore, the principle, as it was first developed, articulates an obligation resting on the legislator and not the judiciary.[128] The literature nonetheless shows that this principle also has implications for the judge and has developed into a principle that also has bearing for the judiciary.[129] Compared to doctrines of strict construction that have been with us for centuries, this principle has not had much doctrinal elaboration and has been very divergently approached. Some authors see it only as a principle functioning from the perspective of the offender, while others see the principle as requiring more broadly a label reflecting the harmfulness to the victim or blameworthiness towards the larger community. The issue now is to grasp how the principle of fair labelling operates at the ICC level.

ii. The Transplant of the Principle to International Criminal Law

Although not codified in the Rome Statute, scholars have argued that fair labelling deserves a role in ICL.[130] Cryer was among the first to introduce the concept, describing it in 2004 as a useful 'conceptual tool to evaluate criminal law', though without offering theoretical justification for its transplant into ICL.[131] Robinson likewise invoked fair labelling repeatedly when criticising the Joint Criminal Enterprise (JCE) doctrine for failing to distinguish adequately between different forms of participation. He described the principle as requiring that the offence label fairly reflect the wrongdoing so that the stigma of conviction corresponds to the accused's culpability. Yet, Robinson never explained why it should be part of ICL.[132] The only element clarified by both scholars is that the principle requires that different levels of culpability are made.[133]

It is only more recently that scholarship has directed its focus to accompanying this transplant with a more in-depth construction of the scope of this

[125] B Mitchel, 'Multiple Wrongdoing and Offence Structure: A Plea for Consistency and Fair Labelling' (2001) 64 *The Modern Law Review* 393, 399.

[126] Tadros (n 101) 74.

[127] See, eg, E van Sliedregt, 'Fair labelling (annotatie bij Gerechtshof 's-Gravenhage 7 juli 2011, LJN: BR0686; Rechtbank 's-Gravenhage 23 maart 2009, LJN: BI2444)' (December 2011) *Ars Aequi* 884.

[128] Ashworth (n 97); Ashworth (n 117); Ashworth and Horder (n 10) 77–79; Chalmers and Leverick (n 110); Edwards and Simester (n 116).

[129] Chalmers and Leverick (n 110) 225–26.

[130] See, eg, Eskauriatza (n 99).

[131] R Cryer, 'General Principles of Liability' in D McGoldrick, P Rowe and E Donnelly (eds), *The Permanent International Criminal Court: Legal and Policy Issues* (Studies in International Law, Hart Publishing, 2004) 259–62.

[132] Robinson (n 28) 927.

[133] R Cryer and others, *An Introduction to International Criminal Law and Procedure*, 2nd edn (CUP, 2010) 372; See also D Guilfoyle, 'Responsibility for Collective Atrocities: Fair Labelling and Approaches to Commission in International Criminal Law' (2011) 64 *Current Legal Problems* 255.

principle.[134] de Souza Dias was the first to thoroughly explain that labelling is inherent to the legislative exercise in ICL. The development of international crimes means that conduct that often already was an ordinary crime is afforded 'a more accurate descriptor' of international crimes.[135] She further framed fair labelling as part of the accused's fair trial rights, thereby constraining judicial recharacterisation at the ICC. She thereby understood the principle to have crossed over to the judicial realm.[136] Being connected to the principle of fair warning and the principle of legality, the principle has developed in a requirement for the judiciary to qualify conduct under the most adequate and foreseeable label and applies in any stage of the criminal proceedings.[137]

This notion of fair labelling protects defendants against an overrepresentation of their wrongdoing.[138] It is about fairness *to* the offender. However, also in ICL, more perspectives have been deemed relevant. Not only the offender's criminality but also the harm and injury need to be accurately described.[139] The international community is also increasingly important in the evaluation of the fairness of the label.[140] As the case study on forced marriage will clarify, the harm of victims can become so central to the labelling exercise that it results in a decrease in focus on the defendant's fair trial rights, which is problematic in light of strict construction.

In the ICC case law, it was Judge Van den Wyngaert who first named the principle and stated that it 'requires that the role played by the accused in bringing about the material elements of a crime must be adequately reflected in the form of criminal responsibility'.[141] In more recent case law, the judges have similarly connected the issue of criminal responsibility with the fair labelling principle. In the *Al Mahdi* judgment, it was, for example, held that the accused can only 'be convicted for 'one form of Article 25(3)(a) commission for each incident or discrete type of criminal conduct', as this otherwise would contribute 'little to the fair labelling of the responsibility of the accused'.[142] Also, Judge Eboe-Osuji referred to the principle in his opinions in a similar way.[143] In the *Ongwen* Judgment, the ICC judges connected the principle to the labelling of the *actus reus*.

[134] Grover (n 29) 403.

[135] de Souza Dias (n 111) 789; Eskauriatza (n 99) 6.

[136] de Souza Dias (n 111) 799–800.

[137] ibid 798.

[138] Eskauriatza (n 99) 4.

[139] de Souza Dias (n 111) 794; DL Nersessian, 'Comparative approaches to punishing hate: The intersection of genocide and crimes against humanity' (2007) 43 *Stanford Journal of International Law* 221, 255.

[140] Eskauriatza (n 99) 36.

[141] *Prosecutor v Ngudjolo Chui* (Concurring Opinion of Judge Christine Van den Wyngaert to the Judgment pursuant to Article 74 of the Statute) ICC-01/04-02/12 (18 December 2012) para 28; see also *Prosecutor v Katanga* (Dissenting Opinion of Judge Van den Wyngaert to the Decision on the Implementation of Regulation 55 of the Regulations of the Court and Severing the Charges against the Accused persons) ICC-01/04-01/07-3319 (21 November 2012).

[142] *Prosecutor v Al Mahdi* (Judgment and Sentence) ICC-01/12-01/15 (27 September 2016) para 60.

[143] *Prosecutor v Bemba* (Concurring Separate Opinion of Judge Eboe-Osuji) ICC-01/05-01/08 (14 June 2018) para 200; *Ruto & Sang* (Acquittal Decision) (n 25) reasons of judge Eboe-Osuji para 328.

The Trial Chamber held that forced pregnancy 'must be interpreted in a manner which gives this crime an *independent meaning* from the other sexual and gender-based violence crimes in the Statute'.[144] The latter was explained as requiring 'the *proper characterisation of the evil* committed, that is to say, *calling the crime by its true name*, is part of the *justice sought by the victims*'. The Trial Chamber held that it was 'not enough to punish it merely as a combination of other crimes' nor to let it be subsumed under the residual category of sexual violence.[145]

When the question of fair labelling is approached from the perspective of victims, the issues of intersectionality and concurrence of crimes are important to analyse.

In order to grasp the intersecting reasons that lie at the basis of discrimination, Crenshaw coined the term intersectionality and challenged both race theory and feminist theory for their inability to qualify the discrimination of Black women, because they were both women and black.[146] In the context of the US, she argued that discrimination against Black women was insufficiently understood: it is more than 'the sum of racisms and sexism' but rather the result of an intersectional experience that affects a particular group in a particular manner.[147] Although this theory was developed in this context specifically, it was soon more broadly used as a way of revealing how 'identity categories such as gender, race, class, sexuality' 'do not act independently of each other, but intersect as axes in systems of oppression'.[148] Her insights were welcomed by a range of fields and seen as a novel way of dissecting these systems of oppression.[149] Although many types of intersectional approaches exist,[150] intersectionality places 'power at the core of its analytical scope', and 'addresses fundamental concerns about oppression, privilege, and subordination'.[151] Collins illuminated that intersectionality should be understood as 'a matrix of domination'.[152]

These theoretical insights of intersectionality have travelled to international law and have been used as 'as a framework for understanding both individual

[144] *Ongwen* (TC Judgment) (n 75) para 2722.

[145] ibid para 2722.

[146] K Crenshaw, 'Demarginalizing the intersection of race and sex: A black feminist critique of antidiscrimination doctrine, feminist theory and antiracist politics' (1989) *University of Chicago Legal Forum* 139.

[147] ibid 140.

[148] SC Jennings, 'Women agents and double-agents: Theorizing feminine gaze in video games', *Feminism in Play* (Springer, 2018) 238.

[149] See S Cho, K W Crenshaw and L McCall, 'Toward a field of intersectionality studies: Theory, applications, and praxis' (2013) 38 *Signs: Journal of women in culture and society* 785; and in relation to international law: H Charlesworth, 'Feminist Methods in International Law' (1999) 93 *American Journal of International Law* 379, 384.

[150] See E Rooney, 'Intersectionality: Working in Conflict' in F Ní Aoláin and others (eds), *The Oxford Handbook of Gender and Conflict* (OUP, 2015) 338.

[151] R Agustín and E Lombardo, 'Intersectionality' in LJ Sheperd (ed), *Handbook on Gender and Violence* (Edward Elgar, 2019) 43.

[152] PH Collins, *Black Feminist Thought: Knowledge, Consciousness, and the Politics of Empowerment* (Unwin Hyman, 1990) 221ff.

and structural causes of wartime sexual offending, as well as the complex and diverse experiences of victimization'.[153] Also in ICL, it has been deemed necessary to respond to violence in an intersectional way,[154] with Office of the Prosecutor fully embracing an intersectional perspective in its policy papers on sexual and gender-based crimes.[155] Article 21(3) has been understood as a basis for interpreting and applying ICL 'in light of intersectionality'.[156] Most of these approaches have focused on how identities can be a reason why certain groups are discriminately targeted.[157] As a result, the relevance of intersectionality for ICL is particularly visible in the context of persecution, where it has been examined how to reflect intersecting grounds of persecution in the charging of the crime.[158] More broadly, however, the notion of intersectionality has also been seen as a lens through which intersecting or intersectional harms can be understood and addressed,[159] and therefore has been called a victim-centred framework.[160]

In relation to the labelling of sexual violence, ways were sought to best reflect the political, gendered, sexual or ethnic reasons for which these types of violence were perpetrated. For example, the forcible circumcision of Luo Men in the *Kenyatta case* was not qualified by the Pre-Trial Chamber as sexual because the acts were 'motivated by ethnic prejudice and intended to demonstrate cultural superiority of one tribe over the other'.[161] This particular *uni-sectional* approach was criticised because it is not because something is motivated by ethnicity that it is *not* motivated by sexual reasons as well.[162]

In order to translate these concerns for intersectional harms into crime labels, however, criminal law cannot always reflect all these grounds for harm, nor their

[153] N Henry, 'Theorizing wartime rape: Deconstructing gender, sexuality, and violence' (2016) 30 *Gender & Society* 44, 51.

[154] AM Beringola, 'Intersectionality: A Tool for the Gender Analysis of Sexual Violence at the ICC' (2017) 9 *Amsterdam Law Forum* 84.

[155] Office of the Prosecutor (ICC), 'Policy Paper on Sexual and Gender-Based Crimes' (June 2014) para 27; See also Office of the Prosecutor (ICC), 'Policy on Children' (November 2016) para 37.

[156] G Maučec, 'The International Criminal Court and the Issue of Intersectionality – A Conceptual and Legal Framework for Analysis' (2021) 21 *International Criminal Law Review* 1, 28.

[157] R Grey, 'Conflicting interpretations of 'sexual violence' in the International Criminal Court' (2014) 29 *Australian Feminist Studies* 273, 283; See also Rooney (n 150).

[158] Beringola (n 154) 103; see also R Grey and others, 'Gender-Based Persecution as a Crime against Humanity: The Road Ahead' (2019) 17 *Journal of International Criminal Justice* 957.

[159] See further: R Copelon, 'Surfacing Gender: Re-Engraving Crimes Against Women in Humanitarian Law' (1994) 5 *Hastings Women's Law Journal* 246, 246–47; DE Buss, 'The Curious Visibility of Wartime Rape: Gender and Ethnicity in International Criminal Law' (2007) 25 *Windsor YB Access Just* 9–10; DE Buss, 'Sexual violence, ethnicity, and intersectionality in international criminal law' in E Grabham and others (eds), *Intersectionality and Beyond: Law, power and the politics of location* (Routledge-Cavendish, 2009) 108; F O'Regan, 'Prosecutor vs. Jean-Pierre Bemba Gombo: The Cumulative Charging Principle, Gender-Based Violence, and Expressivism' (2012) 43 *Georgetown Journal of International Law* 1323.

[160] Beringola (n 154) 109.

[161] *Prosecutor v Muthaura, Kenyatta & Ali* (Decision on the Confirmation of Charges) ICC-01/09-02/11 (23 January 2012) paras 260–66.

[162] Grey (n 157) 280–83.

intersecting nature. The practice of labelling, inherent to criminal law, is intrinsically reductive. As a matter of fact, the process of trying to grasp conduct in legal terms reduces conduct and harm to a legal label, and comes with a structural loss, as something is always *lost in translation*. In other words, the question is whether a crime label can be genuinely intersectional, or whether intersectionality can only be grasped through the concurrent use of multiple labels or through the use of broad labels that allow for an intersectional narrative to be built in. In line with this, and coming back to the issue of fair labelling, the expressive function of the law is best fulfilled when intersectionality is addressed through the use of cumulative charging in order to encompass a breadth of harms. Although addressing *multiple* harms is not the same as addressing *intersecting* harms, it seems that, given the limits of criminal law and its categories, *more* labels seem to be better than *fewer* labels.[163] For example, intersecting reasons often lie at the basis of violence. If these reasons are sexual and ethnic, then labels should reflect this. The label, therefore, has to either represent that intersectional nature in all its dimensions or multiple labels should be used to qualify the same conduct. As a result, two elements are important in the context of fair labelling, and these are that when complex and intersecting harms are at stake, when do we (1) use multiple labels cumulatively, or (2) use broad and residual categories.

In relation to the first element, sometimes the same facts satisfy the legal definition of multiple crimes, and several crime labels can be used to qualify these facts.[164] This practice of cumulative charging and subsequent cumulative convicting is not strictly prohibited at the ICC nor in other ICL systems.[165] Furthermore, scholars have highlighted the potential of cumulative charging from the perspective of gender justice and expressivism.[166] Moreover, fair labelling from the perspective of the victim should reflect the harm as completely and widely as possible. Scholars have nonetheless also argued that cumulative charging can be detrimental to the rights of the accused, because the defence has to respond to each charge. It has therefore been limited, when unfair to the accused.[167] This can, for example, be the case when one crime is completely

[163] See the Office of the Prosecutor (ICC), *Policy Paper on Sexual and Gender-Based Crimes* (June 2014) para 72; see also KM Maloney, 'Ending impunity for forced marriage in conflict zones: The need for greater judicial emphasis on the human rights of girls' (2021) 19 *Journal of International Criminal Justice* 327.

[164] See further: C-F Stuckenberg, 'Cumulative charges and cumulative convictions' (2015) *The Law and Practice of the International Criminal Court* 840.

[165] The ICTY, ICTR, SCSL and STL allowed for cumulative convictions.

[166] See O'Regan (n 159) 1323; L Green, 'First-class crimes, second-class justice: Cumulative charges for gender-based crimes at the International Criminal Court' (2011) 11 *International Criminal Law Review* 529, 530.

[167] There is also discussion to what extent cumulative convictions are limited as a result of the *ne bis in idem* principle, which *sensu stricto* is intended to bar consecutive convictions for the same conduct and not for qualifying the same conduct under more than one label within one trial; See R Bartels, *The Interplay between International Human Rights Law and International Humanitarian Law during International Criminal Trials* (Amsterdam Law School Legal Studies Research Paper, 2018) 7–8.

subsumed under the other. When argued from the rights of the accused, both the principle of fair labelling – understood as reflecting no more wrongfulness than needed – and the principle of legality present arguments to provide the *most appropriate legal characterisation* and make a choice for the best fitting label.

In relation to the second element, broad categories allow much more for a narrative to be constructed around complex harms or intersecting harms. As a result, the utility of particularly the residual category of 'other inhumane acts' cannot be underestimated. There is, however, also a tension here as the residual category should be used *residually* and not every time harm is not *fully* captured by a listed label. This issue will be particularly important to analyse in the case study on forced marriage.[168]

While acknowledging the multi-dimensional nature of the principle of fair labelling and not opposing using it to incorporate the perspective of the victims as well as the international community in crime interpretation, the next chapter's proposition, however, will be to balance it against the principle of strict construction.

IV. CONCLUSION: STRADDLING THE DIVIDE BETWEEN STRICT CONSTRUCTION AND FAIR LABELLING

The law exists in general categories, and legal provisions are, by definition, a generalisation that needs to be able to fit more than one case. The open-textured nature of the law necessitates interpretation, and this interpretative exercise of squeezing a certain fact pattern into a legal label inevitably leads to a reduction of what actually occurred. At the beginning of this chapter, the quote referred to the law's indeterminacy and argued that the law should therefore trust in the judgment of good men. Without arguing from a distrust in the judiciary, this study finds that a blanket trust has not worked and is problematic in terms of legal certainty. While recognising that crime interpretation is a complex interpretative activity, difficult to regulate, and not an automated process in which absolute objectivity is possible and even desired[169] – some methodological tools might be beneficial in guiding the judge.

As the previous chapter has shown, the VCLT has been the dominant tool used for interpretation at the ICC, also in relation to crime interpretation. Given that Article 22(2)'s interpretative principles were introduced out of a desire to limit judicial discretion, however, the use of the VCLT is deemed problematic. In terms of the way the three legality principles in Article 22(2) impacted the interpretative exercise, this chapter reached three conclusions. First, the principle of strict construction requires textual primacy and restricts teleological interpretation. The principle particularly excludes broad teleological approaches,

[168] See Case Study 2, s IV(C) and (D).

[169] OM Fiss, 'Objectivity and Interpretation' (1981–1982) 34 *Stanford Law Review* 739.

including victim-centred readings or reliance on broad goals such as those set out in the preamble. Second, while analogical reasoning is not *per se* prohibited, the ban on analogy confines it to the residual categories of 'other inhumane acts' and 'other forms of sexual violence'. Third, *in dubio pro reo* should be understood as an interpretative principle as well as an evidentiary one, but its role must be limited: it applies only in cases of genuine ambiguity, not vagueness, and should operate at the end of the interpretative process.

In terms of the result, this chapter concluded that a construction of a crime needs to aim at being strict while attempting to be fair. This is the delicate task resting on a judge, and it is by no means an easy one. This study nonetheless finds that it is possible that two principles – the principle of strict construction and the principle of fair labelling – can aid the judge in completing this task successfully. However, the most crucial element in executing this task is that the judge does not fall victim to the *balancing consciousness* on the basis of which both legal and non-legal thinkers misleadingly think that 'all conflicts can, and should, be resolved by balancing conflicting considerations'.[170] While recognising the importance of balancing considerations, reasons (first-order considerations) can exist for excluding considerations (second-order considerations), as a result of which a balancing exercise is no longer necessary. Strict construction is a principle protecting the accused. Fair labelling goes beyond this perspective and also has victims and the international community as beneficiaries. Given the fundamentally different positions of the accused and victims in a criminal trial, it would be problematic to consider that their interests simply have to be balanced in order to arrive at a just conclusion.[171]

The principle of strict construction does not require the strictest construction but necessitates a crime interpretation that uses labels that hold *all the essential ingredients* of the conduct portrayed. This approach does not allow for residual categories to be used when enumerated crimes incorporate all these essential ingredients. This label should moreover be *foreseeable* for any reasonable accused. This approach to strict construction allows for some flexibility through fair labelling.

Fair labelling necessitates the judge to afford a label that, as best as possible, *reflects the totality of the criminal conduct*. In that regard, it should, in all its elements – *actus reus*, *mens rea*, mode of liability – represent the *wrongfulness, harmfulness* and *blameworthiness* of what occurred. This principle engages multiple perspectives. Providing the correct expression of that norm requires that the accused is not held responsible for more wrongfulness than the label expresses and, in that regard, fair labelling protects the accused against overinclusion. Fair labelling demands a certain openness for the harm done to

[170] I Porat, 'The Dual Model of Balancing: A Model for the Proper Scope of Balancing in Constitutional Law' (2006) 27 *Cardozo Law Review* 1393.

[171] See also B McGonigle Leyh, *Procedural justice? Victim Participation in International Criminal Proceedings* (Intersentia, 2011) 360–62.

the victims. An adequate norm expression entails the inclusion of that harm. And lastly, within the limits of the principle of strict construction, adequate norm expression can also lead to the blameworthiness towards the international community to be taken into account. To the extent that different interpretative outcomes are possible, the judge can take the label most reflective of the wrongfulness, harmfulness and blameworthiness of the conduct. In that way, the principle of fair labelling moderates and softens the edges of strict construction while still keeping the rights of the accused central to crime interpretation.[172]

[172] ibid 361.

6

Proposing an Alternative Legality-Centred Approach to Crime Interpretation

'Justice carries all the promise of a passionate love affair; the rule of law offers the stability of a good marriage.'[1]

I. INTRODUCING A LEGALITY-CENTRED INTERPRETATIVE METHODOLOGY

THIS CHAPTER DEVELOPS AN interpretative methodology based on the principle of legality. The previous chapters revealed the shortcomings of the ICC's current interpretative paradigm. Chapter three demonstrated how a confused source doctrine leaves judges too much discretion in choosing between statutory law, treaties, and custom, whereas a legality-centred reading of Article 21 Rome Statute would not allow this. Chapter four exposed the risks of importing the VCLT's crucible approach and its teleological leanings, which sit uneasily with the demands of Article 22's emphasis on textual primacy. Chapter five confirmed that the legality principles of Article 22(2) have often been sidelined or misunderstood in ICC practice, where expansive or victim-centred readings retain too prominent a place.

This chapter, therefore, presents an alternative. The main proposition is to view the legality principle as a type of Hartian secondary rule. This study takes Hart's definition and qualifies the legality principle as a secondary rule: it is a rule 'concerned with the primary rules themselves' specifying how 'the primary rules may be conclusively ascertained, introduced, eliminated, varied, and the fact of their violation conclusively determined'.[2] In line with the argumentation of scholars such as Franck, secondary rules are seen as normative standards that define how rules are to be 'made, *interpreted*, and applied'.[3] In a similar regard, Leiter defined secondary rules as rules that 'instruct officials how to create, change, *identify*, and resolve disputes about rules, both primary and – with

[1] GP Fletcher, *Basic Concepts of Criminal Law* (OUP, 1998).
[2] HLA Hart, *The Concept of Law*, 2nd edn (Clarendon Press, 1994) 94.
[3] TM Franck, *The power of legitimacy among nations* (OUP, 1990) 184.

one exception – secondary.'[4] The principle of legality meets these criteria, as it functions as a rule governing the judicial ascertainment and interpretation of criminal provisions.

The central objective of this chapter is thus to provide a stand-alone, step-by-step interpretative methodology that can be used as a roadmap in the interpretation of crimes. To the researcher, it offers a framework that can be tested in relation to other case studies beyond those included in the second half of the book. To the practitioners, it offers a tool that can be used to build arguments. And finally, to the judge, it offers a guide to be used for the interpretation of crime provisions.

This chapter is conceived as a self-standing instrument. The methodology is articulated in a step-by-step format, with each step stated as an operational rule followed by a concise justificatory note. The design is intentionally built to enable readers who have not engaged with previous chapters to use and implement it without the need to consult preceding chapters. In this way, the chapter functions both as a practical guide for immediate application in concrete interpretative problems in relation to crime provisions as well as a blueprint that can be scrutinised on its own terms in relation to other case studies.

The chapter's interpretative methodology is based on Article 22(2)'s principles. Given that paragraph 2's addition to the legality principle stems from the desire to limit judicial discretion, the proposition here is to take this article seriously as a genuine constraint on the judge's interpretative role. This roadmap consists of six steps, each divided into multiple rules to apply in that interpretative step. The first three steps pertain to the interpretative process, and the last three steps are related to the interpretative result.

II. A LEGALITY-CENTRED ROADMAP

STEP 1: a Textual Interpretation of the ICC's Internal Sources

The **principle of strict construction** demands that an interpretation of crimes conducted in good faith starts with **the textual interpretation of the internal sources** (the Rome Statute and the Elements of Crimes). This is required under the hierarchy of Article 21, which gives primacy to these internal sources and allows only for reliance on external sources in the second order. The principle of strict construction forces the interpreter to solve vagueness and provide precision. This, however, does not necessitate that the strictest definition is adopted. This first step, therefore, breaks down into five rules:

RULE 1.1 | Use textual primacy as the primary interpretative method

A good faith interpretation can only adhere to the principle of strict construction

[4] B Leiter, 'Explaining Theoretical Disagreement' (2009) 76 *University of Chicago Law Review* 1215, 1221: the exception is the Rule of Recognition.

when it remains faithful to the text. That means that textual primacy is required in the context of crime interpretation.

RULE 1.2 | Exclude the principle of effectiveness
A good faith interpretation cannot rely on the principle of effectiveness. For an interpretation in this context to be reasonable, it has to refrain from notions of maximalisation or effectiveness.

RULE 1.3 | Exclude broad and reductionist purposive approaches
A good faith interpretation cannot rely exclusively on the general object and purpose of the Rome Statute, nor reduce interpretation to a single overarching object. This reductionist purposive approach should be firmly excluded at this stage of the interpretative process.

RULE 1.4 | Adopt a broad textual approach
A textual approach is not so limited as to only accept the 'ordinary meaning' but also includes the internal context of the text (eg, a subsection of the law) or assesses similar concepts throughout the statute, as well as understands the technical/legal conception given to terms.

RULE 1.5 | Use the internal sources first
Respecting the hierarchy of Article 21, a good faith interpretation requires that interpretative problems be first addressed by relying on the internal sources. Only if these prove inadequate may the interpreter turn to external sources, and then only in conformity with the Article 21 hierarchy, which is clarified in the next step.

When Step 1 proves inadequate – it results in multiple potential interpretations and not one interpretative solution is clearly preferable –, then the interpreter should turn to Step 2. If the interpretation is clear on the basis of Step 1, then the interpreter should turn to Step 4.

STEP 2: A Contextual or Purposive Approach Limited by the Ban on Analogy

A restricted contextual or purposive approach to crime interpretation can be conducted, which may entail looking to the preparatory works as well as external sources. This step is **limited by the ban on analogy,** requiring that no extension is made of the criminal conduct beyond the text of the internal sources. This step consists of the following rules:

RULE 2.1 | Conducting a restricted contextual interpretation
A contextual approach should first focus on the internal context. Where a broader contextual approach is chosen – taking into account systemic features of the ICC – the interpreter must prioritise the logic and constraints of criminal law over any other systemic considerations. A contextual approach generally needs to rely on the textual context and not include conduct not strictly speaking covered by the text.

RULE 2.2 | relying on external sources in conformity with Article 21's hierarchy of applicable law
External sources may be consulted only if the hierarchy of Article 21 is respected. Reliance on such sources must not extend criminal conduct beyond what is contained in the internal sources.

RULE 2.3 | Limit analogical reasoning to ejusdem generis categories
Analogy is only permissible in relation to the residual categories of 'other inhumane acts' and 'other forms of sexual violence'. Even here, flexibility is permitted only when:

- the 'similar gravity' test is applied rigorously, and
- existing labels that adequately encompass the conduct are considered before resorting to residual categories.

RULE 2.5 | restricting the purposive approach
A purposive method cannot be based on a single or general purpose (eg, ending impunity), nor on open-ended goals such as victim justice. Only where there is an overwhelming and clearly evidenced drafter's intent in the preparatory works may purpose play a role.

STEP 3: Resolving Ambiguity through in dubio pro reo

When, after applying Step 1 and Step 2, an ambiguity remains, the principle of *in dubio pro reo* requires that the ambiguity be resolved in favour of the accused. This principle applies only to genuine ambiguity and not to other interpretative difficulties such as vagueness or generality.

RULE 3.1 | Distinguish ambiguity from vagueness and generality
Ambiguity exists when a term or provision has two or more distinct possible meanings (multiplicity of sense). This differs from vagueness, which concerns borderline cases where the scope of a concept is unclear, and from generality, which requires specification but does not necessarily produce multiple meanings. *In dubio pro reo* applies only where genuine ambiguity remains unresolved, not where the text is vague or general.

RULE 3.2 | Resolve genuine ambiguity in favour of the accused
If, after good faith interpretation in accordance with Step 1 (textual approach) and Step 2 (restricted contextual or purposive approach), a genuine ambiguity persists, the interpretation most favourable to the accused must be adopted. This ensures that no residual uncertainty is resolved to the detriment of the accused.

After having conducted an interpretation of a crime taking into account the preceding steps, the result needs to be tested against the principle of strict construction and the principle of fair labelling. This breaks down into three steps.

STEP 4 Ensuring Interpretations Remain within the Boundaries of the Law

The **principle of strict construction** entails that the judge assesses whether the interpretation remains within the boundaries of the law. To conduct this evaluation, parameters are articulated that help distinguish when the law is *interpreted* and when it is instead *created*. Although most problematic instances should already have been excluded through the earlier steps, the following rules identify situations that clearly fall outside the boundaries of the law:

> **RULE 4.1 | Exclude reliance on general treaty purpose**
> The judge should exclude all crime interpretation on the basis of the general treaty purpose (eg, the fight against impunity).
>
> **RULE 4.2 | Apply provisions that contain all essential elements**
> Where the applicable law contains a provision with all the essential ingredients for application to the case at hand, that provision must be applied. The judge cannot bypass such provisions in order to resort to residual categories or to formulate new crimes using external sources.
>
> **RULE 4.3 | Follow clear legislative intent; interpret constructive ambiguities narrowly**
> The judge should examine whether there is a clear, specific and broadly carried legislative intent to include or exclude criminal conduct within the scope of an existing crime definition, in which case this intent has to be followed. In the absence of such a clear intent, the judge assesses whether there is a constructive ambiguity allowing for more flexibility in interpretation. Constructive ambiguities are interpreted narrowly and will not comprise instances where there was dissension amongst the drafters that was solved by means of a compromise concept in relation to which parties heavily disagreed. Only where a concept was deliberately left open will be included.

STEP 5 Assessing the Foreseeability of the Interpretative Result

The final stage in the judge's evaluation of the interpretative result is an assessment of foreseeability. Once an interpretation – or multiple potential interpretations – has been identified, the judge must determine whether the outcome is foreseeable. If Step 4 has been conducted diligently, this assessment should not be difficult: applying a provision that contains all the essential ingredients of the fact pattern will usually be more foreseeable than resorting to residual categories or external sources.

> **RULE 5.1 | Apply foreseeability as an objective standard**
> The test is whether the interpretation would have been foreseeable to a reasonable accused. It is not a subjective notice standard assessing whether the particular accused could have anticipated liability.

RULE 5.2 | Do not reduce foreseeability to fair notice

Although foreseeability overlaps with the doctrine of fair notice, the legality principle functions as an interpretative principle and cannot be collapsed into a mere question of notice.

STEP 6 Ensuring Fair Labelling of the Interpretative Result

As a final safeguard, this study proposes adding the principle of fair labelling to the evaluation of the interpretative result. The principle requires that the chosen crime label fairly represents three essential elements: the **wrongfulness** of the conduct, its **harmfulness**, and the **blameworthiness** of the offender. Each element highlights a different perspective that must be reflected in the label.

Importantly, the judge should not fall into a *balancing consciousness*—the mistaken belief that a just interpretation is achieved by merely weighing competing considerations. Certain **first-order considerations** (such as the protection of the accused through strict construction) override **second-order considerations** (such as broader justice to victims). Moreover, the position of the accused in a criminal trial is fundamentally different from that of victims: their perspectives cannot be equated or offset against one another in a balancing exercise. This distinction must guide the application of fair labelling when determining crime labels.

RULE 6.1 | Reflect the wrongfulness

The label should accurately express the wrongfulness of the conduct, thereby recognizing the perspective of the accused.

RULE 6.2 | Reflect the harmfulness

The label should adequately capture the harm caused, incorporating the perspective of the victims.

RULE 6.3 | Reflect the blameworthiness

The label should correspond to the blameworthiness of the act in light of its gravity, thereby reflecting the perspective of the international community.

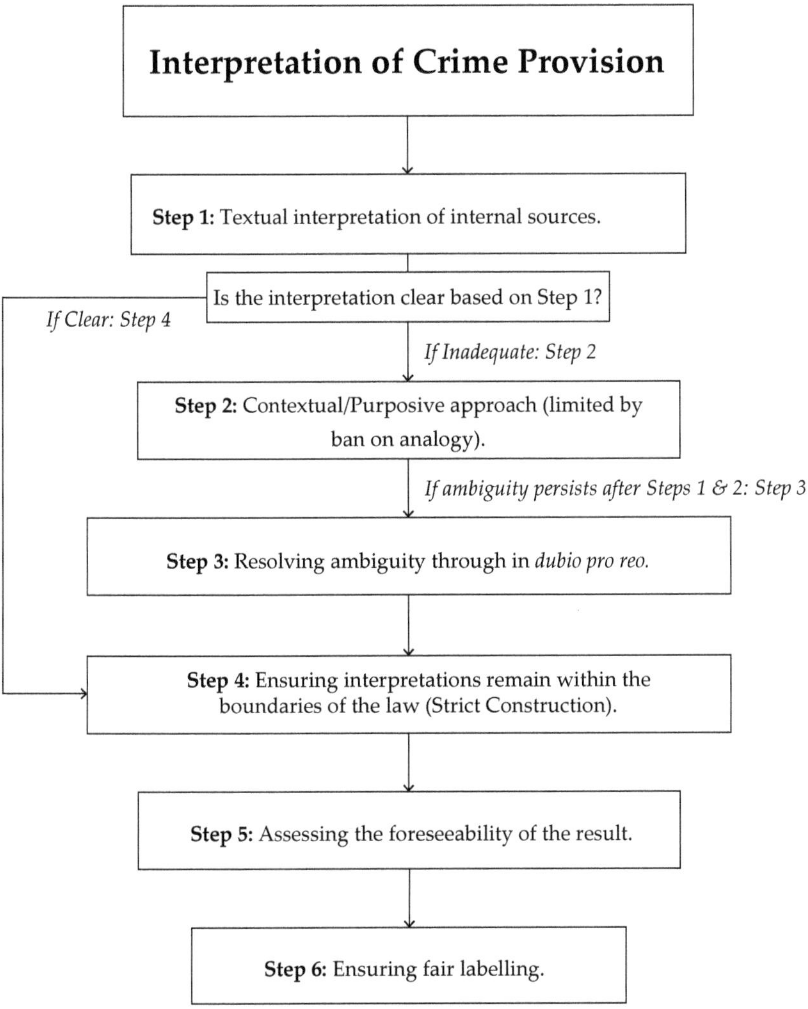

Figure: The Legality-Centred Roadmap for Crime Interpretation. A six-step methodology based on the principle of legality, articulating an interpretative process (Steps 1–3) and a testing phase for the interpretative result (Steps 4–6).

Case Study 1

Interpreting Organisational Policy as a Contextual Element of Crimes Against Humanity

> [T]he atrocities and humiliations that count as crimes against humanity are, in effect, the ones that turn our stomachs, and no principle exists to explain what turns our stomachs.[1]

I. INTRODUCTION

ARTICLE 7 DEFINES CRIMES against Humanity (CaH) as acts committed as part of a widespread or systematic attack against civilians, carried out 'pursuant to or in furtherance of a State or organisational policy'. The contextual elements of CaH[2] – existence of an attack of a widespread or systematic nature,[3] targeting a civilian population,[4] and a State or organisational policy[5] – draw a line between ordinary crimes and international wrongdoing, ensuring that only a certain type of criminality reaches the threshold for international accountability. CaH have long been described as 'notoriously elusive'[6] and 'tantalizingly ambiguous'.[7] Each

[1] D Luban, 'A theory of crimes against humanity' (2004) 29 *Yale Journal of International Law* 85, 101.

[2] For the purpose of this case study, there is no need to discuss the subjective contextual elements (knowledge of the attack).

[3] See further C Roberts, 'On the Definition of Crimes against Humanity and Other Widespread or Systematic Human Rights Violations' (2017) 20 *University of Pennsylvania Journal of Law and Social Change* 1.

[4] See further LN Sadat, 'Putting Peacetime First: Crimes against Humanity and the Civilian Population Requirement' (2016) 31 *Emory International Law Review* 197; RAA Fernández and JS Estapà, 'Towards a Single and Comprehensive Notion of "Civilian Population" in Crimes against Humanity' (2017) 17 *International Criminal Law Review* 47.

[5] Rome Statute of the International Criminal Court (adopted 17 July 1998, entered into force 1 July 2002) Art 7(2)(a).

[6] MM deGuzman, 'The Road from Rome: The Developing Law of Crimes against Humanity' (2000) 22 *Human Rights Quarterly* 335, 336; see further MM deGuzman, 'Crimes against Humanity' in WA Schabas and N Bernaz (eds), *Routledge Handbook of International Criminal Law* (Routledge, 2010); CC Russell, 'The Chapeau of Crimes against Humanity: The Impact of the Rome Statute of the International Criminal Court' (2011) 8 *Eyes on the ICC* 25, 27.

[7] H Arendt, *Eichmann in Jerusalem, a Report on the Banality of Evil* (Revised and Enlarged Edition edn, The Viking Press, 1964) 255.

part of the definition has been the subject of disagreement.[8] While some debates focus on the severity and scale required for CaH,[9] the focus of this chapter is on the organisational element, which is one of the key elements in distinguishing international, collective and politically-enabled crimes from ordinary offences.[10]

Based on charges examined against 18 defendants, this case study examines the type of entity that can fulfil the organisational policy element of CaH.[11] The growing influence of non-state actors in global affairs makes it increasingly urgent to clarify their accountability under international criminal law (ICL). While ICL has traditionally targeted individuals operating within state structures, developments in the last decades have increasingly required it to be extended to non-state entities.[12] The central question is whether individuals acting within or alongside such entities can be held responsible for CaH.[13]

Controversy arises in cases involving organised criminal groups – such as the Japanese Yakuza,[14] the Chinese Triads,[15] the Sicilian Cosa Nostra,[16] Mexican drug cartels[17] – where it is debated whether these groups qualify as

[8] N Geras, *Crimes Against Humanity: Birth of a Concept* (Manchester University Press 2011), vi; D Robinson, 'Defining "crimes against humanity" at the Rome conference' (1999) 93 *American Journal of International Law* 43; E Zoller, 'La définition des crimes contre l'humanité' (1993) 120 *Journal du droit international* 549; B Van Schaack, 'The Definition of Crimes Against Humanity: Resolving the Incoherence' (1998) 37 *Columbia Journal of Transnational Law* 787; Y Dinstein, 'Crimes against Humanity' in Jerzy Makarczyk and Krzysztof Skubiszewski (eds), *Theory of International Law at the Threshold of the 21st Century, Essays in honour of Krzysztof Skubiszewski* (Kluwers Law International, 1996).

[9] M Halling, 'Push the Envelope Watch It Bend: Removing the Policy Requirement and Extending Crimes against Humanity' (2010) 23 *Leiden Journal of International Law* 821

[10] See further Luban (n 1) 87.

[11] Having passed the confirmation of charges stage and therefore included in this analysis are the following accused in chronological order of the confirmation of charges decision: Lubanga, Katanga, Ngudjolo, Bemba, Muthaura, Kenyatta, Ali, Ruto, Kosgey, Sang, Ntaganda, Gbagbo, Blé Goudé, Ongwen, Al Mahdi, Ngaïssona, Yekatom, Al Hassan. The selection of cases was closed as of 1 December 2021.

[12] See further J Summers and A Gough (eds), *Non-State Actors and International Obligations: Creation, Evolution and Enforcement* (Brill | Nijhoff, 2018).

[13] See further A Clapham, 'Extending International Criminal Law Beyond the Individual to Corporations and Armed Opposition Groups' (2008) 6 *Journal of International Criminal Justice* 899; LN Sadat, 'Crimes against humanity in the modern age' (2013) 107 *American Journal of International Law* 334; WA Schabas, 'State Policy as an Element of International Crimes' (2008) 98 *Journal of Criminal Law and Criminology* 953, 965.

[14] See further JM Smith, 'An International Hit Job: Prosecuting Organized Crime Acts as Crimes against Humanity' (2009) 97 *Georgetown Law Journal* 1111, 1116–18.

[15] See further D Silverstone, A Chung and J Whittle, 'China: the "red-black nexus", organised crime and politics' in F Allum and S Gilmour (eds), *Handbook of Organised Crime and Politics* (Edward Elgar, 2019).

[16] See further M Vittorio, 'Italy: politics, local government and mafias' in F Allum and S Gilmour (eds), *Handbook of Organized Crime and Politics* (Edward Elgar, 2019).

[17] See further: R Le Cour Grandmaison, 'Mexico: politics, cartels and violence' in F Allum and S Gilmour (eds), *Handbook of Organised Crime and Politics* (Edward Elgar, 2019); JS Eskauriatza, '"Complete Labelling" and Domestic Prosecutions for Crimes Against Humanity' (2021) *Criminal Law Forum*.

'organisations' under the Rome Statute.[18] Because organised crime today often operates through fluid and networked structures rather than rigid hierarchies, defining what constitutes an 'organisation' has become increasingly complex. To adapt to this reality, the field of organised crime has been confronted with a very similar definitional uncertainty to that in relation to CaH, which is reflected in adding the denomination 'serious' to the category of organised crime.[19] Because the boundaries of organised crime remain unclear, it is often difficult to distinguish crimes against humanity committed by organisations from serious crimes committed by organised criminal groups.

Similar debates on whether ICL should directly address terrorist groups or rely on interstate cooperation to combat terrorism. Traditionally, terrorism has been treated outside ICL,[20] yet the rise of hybrid phenomena such as narco-terrorism[21] blurs this boundary. The once-clear divide – terrorist groups driven by politics and organised crime groups by profit – has eroded: terrorist networks increasingly pursue financial gain,[22] while organised crime groups often infiltrate political structures,[23] as seen with the Italian Mafia and Pablo Escobar's cartel.[24] The ICC also deals with non-state armed groups, whose organisational capacity determines whether they meet Article 7(2)(a)'s threshold. Unlike the vague notion of organisation, however, organised armed groups are better defined in international law.[25] Beyond these, political organisations without profit or extremist aims, as well as cults or similarly structured groups, challenge the conceptual limits of CaH.[26] Some even argue that no organisational proof is required, suggesting individual actors alone could suffice.[27] These organisational divergences

[18] See further E Bookbinder, 'Crimes committed against civilian population by transnational criminal organizations should be considered crimes against humanity and leaders prosecuted by ICC' (2016) 23 *Willamette Journal of International Law and Dispute Resolution* 255; Smith (n 14); H van der Wilt, 'Legal responses to transnational and international crimes: towards an integrative approach?' in H Van der Wilt and C Paulussen (eds), *Legal Responses to Transnational and International Crimes* (Edward Elgar, 2017).

[19] L Paoli and TV Beken, 'Organized Crime, A Contest Concept' in L Paoli (ed), *The Oxford Handbook of Organized Crime* (The Oxford Handbooks in Criminology and Criminal Justice, 2014).

[20] See further B Weißer, 'Transnational Organised Crime and Terrorism' in P Hauck and S Peterke (eds), *International Law and Transnational Organised Crime* (OUP, 2016).

[21] van der Wilt (n 18).

[22] Weißer (n 20); A Schloenhardt, 'Transnational Organised Crime and the International Criminal Court Developments and Debates' (2005) 24 *University of Queensland Law Journal* 93.

[23] See further AP Schmid, *Revisiting the Relationship between International Terrorism and Transnational Organised Crime 22 Years Later* (ICCT Research paper, 2018); C Dishman, 'Terrorism, crime and transformation' (2001) 24 *Studies in Conflict and Terrorism* 43.

[24] G Borrelli, 'Foreword: organised crime and its relationship with politics as seen from Italy' in F Allum and S Gilmour (eds), *Handbook of Organised Crime and Politics* (Edward Elgar, 2019).

[25] See further C Ryngaert, *Non-State Actors and International Humanitarian Law* (Institute for International Law, 2008); T Rödenhauser, *Organizing Rebellion: Non-State Armed Groups under International Humanitarian Law, Human Rights Law, and International Criminal Law* (Oxford Monographs in International Humanitarian & Criminal Law, OUP, 2018).

[26] T Obokata, *Organised Crime in International Law* (Hart Publishing, 2010) 7.

[27] See further Russell (n 6) 63–65.

and the connected uncertainty, as when they reach the organisational quality required under Article 7(2)(a), are visualised in this scheme:

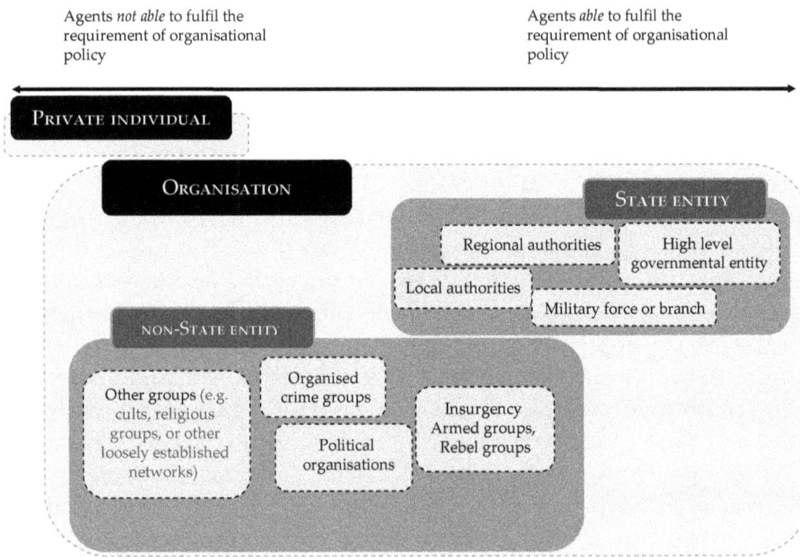

This definitional uncertainty regarding the required organisational level is why this study proposes a legality-centred solution,[28] defining the constitutive properties of an organisation while using inferences only as a supplementary tool. Doing so clarifies which collective entities fall within the Rome Statute's reach and prevents over-inclusion.[29]

There are multiple elements that lead to interpretative confusion surrounding the organisational policy element. The first primarily stems from the Statute's and Elements' internal inconsistencies. Neither defines organisation, and their formulations diverge syntactically and across language versions. The Elements merely state that a policy requires a State or organisation to 'actively promote or encourage' an attack and that it must be 'implemented by State or organisational action' as explained in a footnote.[30] Beyond this, only Article 7(1)(h) on

[28] See Introduction to the Elements of Crimes against Humanity: 'Since article 7 pertains to [ICL], its provisions, consistent with article 22, must be strictly construed, taking into account that [CaH] are among the most serious crimes of concern to the international community as a whole, warrant and entail individual criminal responsibility, and require conduct which is impermissible under generally applicable international law, as recognized by the principal legal systems of the world'; see also: G Werle and B Burghardt, 'Do Crimes against Humanity Require the Participation of a State or a State-Like Organization' (2012) 10 *JICJ* 1151, 1158–59.

[29] JPP-L Acevedo, 'The Close Relationship Between Serious Human Rights Violations and Crimes Against Humanity: International Criminalization of Serious Abuses' (2017) 17 *Anuario Mexicano de Derecho Internacional*, 145; DF Orentlicher, 'Settling Accounts: The Duty to Prosecute Human Rights Violations of a Prior Regime' (1991) 100 *Yale Law Journal* 2537, 2585.

[30] Footnote 6 to the Introduction of Article 7, Crimes against humanity in the ICC Elements of Crimes.

enforced disappearances mentions an 'organisation', referring vaguely to a 'political organisation'. It is not clear what the prefix political entails.[31] Preparatory works offer little guidance, as the notion was inserted late at Rome without clear boundaries of inclusion or exclusion.[32] Compounding the ambiguity, the Elements and Statute use differing syntax – 'State or organisational policy' versus 'State or organisation' – leading to disagreement over whether the provision presupposes an entity at all.[33] Finally, discrepancies among the six authentic UN language versions deepen uncertainty.[34] Although all authentic languages of the Statute are presumed identical in meaning (the principle of linguistic equality in treaty interpretation), translation issues often make it difficult for judges to adopt an interpretation that works across all versions.[35] One of the issues taken up later in this chapter is how to ensure definitional coherence when, for example, the English 'organisational policy' contrasts with the French' *politique d'une organisation*.[36]

A second interpretative challenge is connected to the external sources, more specifically, how customary law, generally found to be broader in scope and lacking a policy requirement,[37] interacts with the narrower statutory definition under Article 7.[38] This difficulty stems from disagreements over how customary law is formed, as the seemingly simple formula of state practice and *opinio juris* fails to capture its complexity, particularly regarding the role of external jurisprudence in its formation. Since the ICTY and ICTR Statutes omitted an organisational policy element, it is crucial to assess how such jurisprudence has shaped ICC interpretation, also in light of Article 21, which does not recognise external jurisprudence as a source of law.[39] Broadening the statutory

[31] The reference to a 'political organization' does not appear in Art 3 of the UN Declaration on the Protection of All Persons from Enforced Disappearance (adopted 18 December 1992 by UNGA Res 47/133); in the Inter-American Convention on the Forced Disappearance of Persons (adopted 9 June 1994, entered into force 28 March 1996); nor in the UN International Convention on the Protection of All Persons from Enforced Disappearance (adopted 12 January 2007 by UNGA Res 61/177, entered into force 23 December 2010).

[32] Bureau of the Preparatory Committee, Discussion Paper Part 2: Jurisdiction, Admissibility and Applicable Law – Article 5 'Crimes Within the Jurisdiction of the Court' A/CONF.183/C.1/L.59 (10 July 1998); see also: RS Clark, 'History of Efforts to Codify Crimes Against Humanity From the Charter of Nuremberg to the Statute of Rome' in LN Sadat (ed), *Forging a Convention for Crimes Against Humanity* (CUP, 2011) 20–21; Robinson (n 8).

[33] Preparatory Commission for the International Criminal Court, Annex III, Elements of Crimes, PCNICC/1999/L.5/Rev.1/Add.2 (22 December 1999).

[34] Art 50(1) and Art 128 RS.

[35] Vienna Convention on the Law of Treaties (adopted 23 May 1969, entered into force 27 January 1980) 1155 UNTS 331, Art 33(3).

[36] As discussed in sections II(A)(i) and II(D)(ii) and most importantly III(B).

[37] G Sluiter, '"Chapeau Elements" of Crimes Against Humanity in the Jurisprudence of the UN Ad Hoc Tribunals' in L N Sadat (ed), *Forging a Convention for Crimes against Humanity* (CUP, 2011).

[38] Sadat (n 13) 77–78.

[39] N Arajärvi, *The changing nature of customary international law: methods of interpreting the concept of custom in international criminal tribunals* (Routledge, 2014) 16–30; N Arajärvi, 'The Role of the International Criminal Judge in the Formation of Customary International Law' (2007) 1 *European Journal of Legal Studies* 1.

definition by way of customary inspiration further risks violating the legality principles. Ongoing efforts to draft a Convention on Crimes against Humanity require further understanding of how evolving external norms can reshape interpretation.[40]

A third interpretative challenge is that many judges invoke the VCLT framework and its teleological and effectiveness-based reasoning, which risks undermining legality by stretching the statutory text to serve victim-centred aims. The following pathways illustrate how these interpretative challenges unfold and how the legality-centred approach responds.

II. INTERPRETATIVE PATHWAYS

This section surveys ICC case law on the different interpretations of 'organisation'. Before addressing which organisations qualify under Article 7(2)(a), a distinction must be made between those *committing* and those *condoning* CaH. The threshold for both categories is not the same. Condoning organisations must involve a state or quasi-governmental entity,[41] which is a threshold largely undisputed. This section, therefore, focuses only on which entities can commit CaH. It proceeds from the broadest to the narrowest interpretations, as this visualisation shows:

The first interpretative pathway requires no organisation at all. It suffices that an individual, acting independently of any entity, sets a policy to attack a civilian population. The following pathways recognise that entities – particularly non-state actors – can fulfil the organisational policy requirement, progressing from broader to narrower understandings.[42]

A. No Organisation Required (Pathway I)

This pathway does not require an organisation to break down into two variants, an explicit and implicit sub-pathway.

[40] This project, which originated in the lap of the Crimes Against Humanity Initiative publishing a Proposed Convention on the Prevention and Punishment of Crimes Against Humanity in 2010, has, as of 2014, been taken over by the ILC. The ILC Special Rapporteur Murphy produced several reports (See, eg, SD Murphy, *Fourth report on crimes against humanity* (A/CN4/725, International Law Commission 2019). The ILC submitted this to the General Assembly in 2019 (see ILC, Report of the International Law Commission on its Seventy-first session (29 April–7 June and 8 July–9 August 2019) A/74/10; led to the *2024 adoption of GA Resolution 79/122* to convene a UN Diplomatic Conference. See further LN Sadat, *The Long Arc of Justice: Forging a Convention for Crimes Against Humanity* (Legal Studies Research Paper Series, Paper No 25-08-03).

[41] Rödenhauser (n 25) 265–67.

[42] ibid 214.

Organisation | overview of the different pathways & sub-pathways

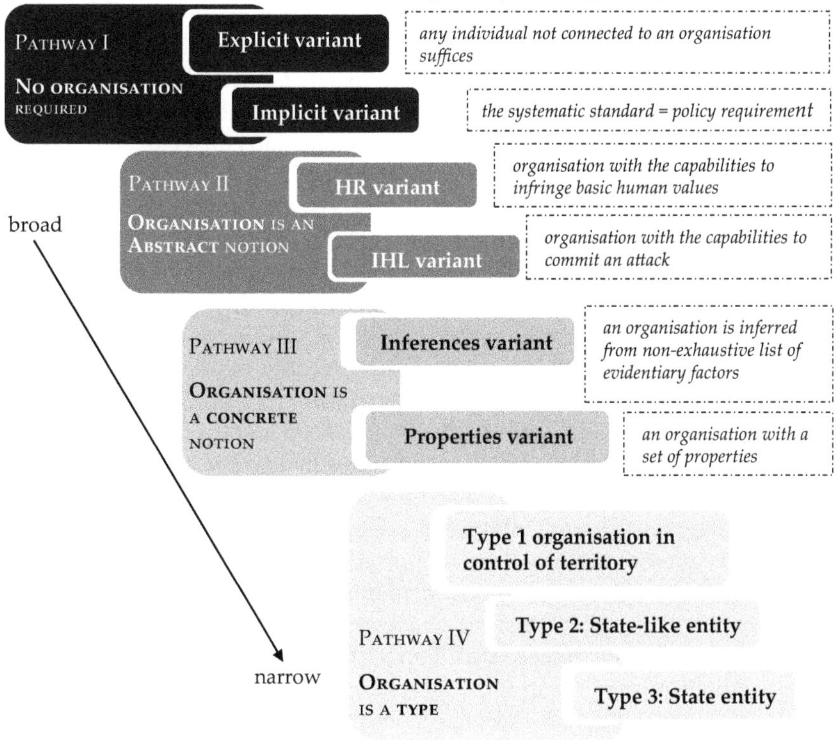

i. The Explicit Variant: the Lone Wolf Suffices

The broadest view, advanced by Judge Eboe-Osuji in the *Ruto & Sang Judgment*, interprets the organisational policy requirement as excluding only sporadic or random acts of violence.[43] He argued that organisational policy should 'mean no more than a coordinated course of action',[44] encompassing both multiple systematic attacks by one individual and a single large-scale attack with widespread civilian harm.[45] In his view, there is no need to prove the existence of a 'corporeal organisation'[46] or 'aggregate entity,[47] or 'aggregate complicity'.[48]

[43] *Prosecutor v Ruto & Sang* (Decision on Defence Applications for Judgments of Acquittal) ICC-01/09-01/11 (5 April 2016) – reasons of Judge Eboe-Osuji para 343.
[44] ibid paras 302 and 462 (quotation marks in citation omitted).
[45] ibid para 302.
[46] ibid para 302.
[47] ibid para 307.
[48] ibid para 311.

The *Ruto & Sang* case, arising from Kenya's 2007–2008 post-election violence, centred on whether the attacks were orchestrated by an organised Network.[49] At the Confirmation of Charges, the Prosecutor alleged that it had five branches: a media, political, military, financial and tribal branch.[50] At trial, the Prosecution described the Network as three-tiered: Ruto at the top, followed by political allies, prominent Kalenjin businessmen, and tribal elders who oversaw the third-tier youth leaders, who implemented the policy through Kalenjin youth.[51] Following the defence's move to proceed with a 'no case to answer', the charges were vacated for insufficient evidence of such a structure.[52] The Majority, consisting of Judges Fremr and Eboe-Osuji, reached this conclusion in separate reasons. Judge Herrera Carbuccia dissented.[53] Judge Eboe-Osuji used the opportunity to reconceptualise the organisational element itself. Rejecting a literal reading that demands proof of a collective entity, he adopted a purposive and victim-oriented interpretation pursuant to Article 31 VCLT.[54]

He first of all warned against 'the siren call of literal reading',[55] arguing that a strict grammatical approach could absurdly exclude even mass atrocities committed by a lone actor.[56] The only acceptable grammatical approach is the one that construes organisational policy 'to mean nothing more than a coordinated course of actions'.[57] He supported this with extensive authoritative sources on international, statutory, and common law interpretation, which he regarded as unproblematic.[58] Instead, he viewed the element's purpose as ensuring that only systematic or large-scale attacks fall within the ICC's jurisdiction. To illustrate, he posited the example of a single individual dropping a nuclear bomb – an act that, though executed alone, would clearly meet the Statute's jurisdictional thresholds.[59]

He furthermore set out his purposive approach, grounding his reasoning in the Preamble and highlighting the Statute's aims of ending impunity for crimes that 'shock the conscience of humanity' and 'threaten the peace, security and

[49] See *Prosecutor v Ruto & Sang* (Decision on the Confirmation of Charges) ICC-01/09-01/11 (23 January 2012) paras 31–32, 181; See also: TO Hansen, 'The Policy Requirement in Crimes against Humanity: Lessons from and for the Case of Kenya' (2011) 43 *Washington International Law Review* 21–22; see also: FM Sosteness, *The Post-Election Violence in Kenya: Domestic and International Legal Responses*, vol 2 (International Criminal Justice Series, Asser Press, 2015) 202–203.

[50] *Ruto & Sang* (CoC Decision) (n 49) + ICC-01/09-01/ll-261-AnxA paras 25 and 43.

[51] *Ruto & Sang* (Acquittal Judgment) (n 43) – reasons of Judge Fremr paras 28–29.

[52] See further A Niv, 'The Schizophrenia of the 'No Case to Answer 'Test in International Criminal Tribunals' (2016) 14 *Journal of International Criminal Justice* 1121.

[53] *Prosecutor v Ruto and Sang* (Dissenting Opinion of Judge Herrera Carbuccia) ICC-01/09-01/11 (5 April 2016).

[54] *Ruto & Sang* (Acquittal Judgment) (n 43) – reasons of Judge Eboe-Osuji para 303.

[55] ibid paras 307–308.

[56] ibid para 323.

[57] ibid para 415.

[58] ibid paras 308: citing Grotius (Dutch) and Vatel (French); paras 309–315; 319: citing common law scholars Maxwel, Bennion, Lord Reid and Holmes etc.

[59] ibid footnote 502 and para 415.

well-being of the world'.[60] His reasoning favours a teleological approach based on the Statute's overarching purpose, without examining its multiple or conflicting purposes or the aims of specific subsections. In his mind, there is only one single overarching goal: the exclusion of 'singular, random or sporadic instances of criminal conducts', or 'fleeting episodes of social unrest'.[61] Requiring proof of collective complicity, he maintained, would frustrate this. Accordingly, he construed the organisational policy element as only requiring a coordinated course of action capable of producing widespread or systematic attacks, whether executed by a group or an individual.

Judge Eboe-Osuji further extended his teleological reasoning to the principle of legality, narrowing it to mean the same as the rule of lenity and thus minimising the constraining effect.[62] He thereby failed to distinguish between the principle of strict construction and the *in dubio pro reo* rule.[63] Echoing some of the ICTs case law, he held that the rule of lenity only solves remaining ambiguity after all interpretive methods have been used to resolve it.[64] Because he saw ambiguity so narrowly, Article 22(2)'s constraining effect is effectively nullified.[65]

Some aspects of Judge Eboe-Osuji's reasoning are problematic, yet his straightforward interpretation provides clarity amid the prosecution's convoluted presentation of the 'Network', improving foreseeability. Explicitly explaining interpretative methods is a welcome improvement over typical ICC judgments, which rarely detail their approach to Articles 21 or 22. Nonetheless, several substantive flaws remain.

First, the grammatical method is misrepresented. While rejecting a purely literal approach is justified, Judge Eboe-Osuji unduly downplays the complexity of textual interpretation, which also requires considering semantic context, syntax, and language versions of the internal sources. His dismissal of the grammatical method oversimplifies it before rejecting it altogether.[66]

Second, his argument that requiring proof of an entity is absurd reflects an implicit use of the VCLT's principle of effectiveness, contrasting the absurd restrictive view with a supposedly effective no-entity approach. This reasoning equates undesirability with absurdity and disregards the fact that most decision-making is about degrees of effectiveness.[67] The nuclear bomb hypothetical exemplifies this: though such an attack would be catastrophic, it is improbable that a lone individual could execute it without state or organisational backing. Including such scenarios risks overextending CaH, potentially encompassing

[60] ibid para 439, see also para 323.

[61] ibid paras 320, 341,343, 344–346.

[62] ibid para 430–437.

[63] ibid para 436.

[64] ibid para 433 and see *Prosecutor v Stakic* (Trial Chamber Judgment) IT-97-24-T (31 July 2003) para 416.

[65] *Ruto & Sang* (Acquittal Judgment) (n 43) – reasons of Judge Eboe-Osuji para 430.

[66] ibid paras 366ff.

[67] H Lauterpacht, 'Restrictive interpretation and the Principle of effectiveness in the Interpretation of Treaties' (1949) 26 *British Yearbook International Law* 48, 70.

acts like a large-scale cyberattack by one hacker. The organisational requirement exists precisely to prevent this and to preserve complementarity. The principle of effectiveness invites the question of whose interests it advances. Expansive readings serve the victims, restrictive ones protect the accused. Yet, strict construction mandates restraint, giving little scope to effectiveness in interpreting crimes.[68]

Third, his purposive and victim-centred approach is overly broad.[69] By grounding interpretation almost entirely in the Statute's preamble and the fight against impunity, he treats justice for victims as the overriding *telos*. This reasoning lacks limits: if followed consistently, even widespread domestic or partner violence might fall within ICC jurisdiction.[70] The argument ignores that the organisational policy element was included to delineate CaH from ordinary crime. His notion of fair labelling, furthermore, treats victims and accused as equal beneficiaries of broad interpretation,[71] a 'balancing consciousness' that misconstrues their fundamentally different positions.[72] As the domestic violence example shows, this victim-oriented interpretation sweeps away important considerations connected to the rights of the accused. CaH are merely seen as the 'correlative to human rights'.[73] It is important to remember that ICL is hybrid in nature, and the emphasis on justice for victims runs the risk of disregarding the criminal law tenets of the system.[74]

Fourth, despite extensive discussion of interpretative methods, the decision neglects source hierarchy under Article 21. Judge Eboe-Osuji denies that internal sources must be applied first and relies implicitly on ICT jurisprudence without clarifying how to understand the widespread standard, for example, in terms of how many victims would be required. He effectively sidelines the policy element without providing an alternative standard.

Finally, the resulting interpretation is excessively broad and insufficiently strict. It presents a false dichotomy between a restrictive yet ineffective interpretation and a broad yet effective one. Effectiveness, however, depends on perspective, and legality requires textual primacy and primacy of internal-sources hierarchy, which both are missing here. While strict construction does not demand the narrowest possible reading, it does demand restraint. On these grounds, Judge Eboe-Osuji's interpretation cannot be accepted.

[68] See s III(B) of ch 4.

[69] *Ruto & Sang* (Acquittal Judgment) (n 43) – reasons of Judge Eboe-Osuji para 449.

[70] ibid para 342.

[71] ibid para 328.

[72] BM Leyh, 'Pragmatism over Principles: The International Criminal Court and a Human Rights-Based Approach to Judicial Interpretation' (2018) 41 *Fordham International Law Journal* 697, 712: 'The impartiality deficit has to do with an [. . .] compulsion to convict and downplay the rights of the accused so as to fulfil its mandate of ending impunity and providing justice to victims'.

[73] SL Goldenberg, 'Crimes Against Humanity – 1945–1970' (1971) 10 *Western Ontario Law Review* 1, 3-ff; see also: M Renzo, 'Crimes Against Humanity and the Limits of International Criminal Law' (2012) 31 *Law and Philosophy* 443; Roberts (n 3); Geras (n 8) 49ff.

[74] L Grover, 'A Call for Arms: Fundamental Dilemmas Confronting the Interpretation of Crimes in the Rome Statute of the International Criminal Court' (2010) 21 *European Journal of International Law* 543, 550.

ii. The Implicit Variant: Systematic Attack as Entailing Policy

This interpretation, like the previous one, denies the need for an organisation, but does so implicitly by equating the systematic requirement with the existence of a policy. It explains the policy element requiring the attack to be organised, follow a regular pattern and involve public or private resources.[75] Drawing on ad hoc tribunal jurisprudence,[76] it treats policy as an evidentiary matter showing the organised nature of an attack rather than a separate constitutive element. Because those tribunals relied on customary law, where no policy element existed, no organisational proof was required.[77] It remains a matter of contention how the customary definition affects the interpretation of the statutory definition. This study supports the current line of jurisprudence that understands Article 21(1)(b)'s 'rules and principles' as a reference to customary law but rejects ICC judges' circumvention of the rules of custom ascertainment not conducting an independent examination of state practice and *opinio juris*. External jurisprudence can only be used as a supplementary means and not enter independently at this level of the hierarchy of sources.

iii. Intermediate Conclusion: The Denial of a Policy Element is a Blunt Violation of the Legality Principle

Both sub-pathways deny a distinct organisational policy requirement and a separate entity threshold. Their reasoning conflicts with the Rome Statute's textual primacy and legality principle, favouring a broad, victim-centred teleological approach over strict construction. Such interpretations are overly expansive and unfair. They misuse fair labelling to serve victims alone while neglecting protection for the accused. In the four-quadrantal model, this approach therefore occupies the quadrant representing the broadest and least fair interpretation, illustrating its incompatibility with both the principle of legality and fair labelling.

Judge Herrera Carbuccia's dissent in *Ruto and Sang* stresses that CaH protect civilians from severe human rights violations, regardless of state or organisational backing. Her interpretation held that an organisation should have the capability to infringe basic human values. Given that she stresses 'the distinctive perversion of politics' underlying CaH, her reasoning leans toward requiring an entity behind the individual, which is the perfect bridge to the following interpretation.[78]

[75] *Prosecutor v Katanga & Ngudjolo Chui* (Decision on the Confirmation of Charges) ICC-01/04-01/07 (30 September 2008) para 396.

[76] See, eg, *Prosecutor v Kunarac et al* (Appeal Judgment) IT-96-23 & IT-96-23/1-A (12 June 2002) para 98.

[77] See further: L van den Herik, 'Using Custom to Reconceptualize Crimes Against Humanity' in S Darcy and J Powderly (eds), *Judicial Creativity: The International Criminal Tribunals* (OUP, 2010).

[78] *Ruto and Sang* (Dissenting Opinion of Judge Herrera Carbuccia) (n 53) para 44.

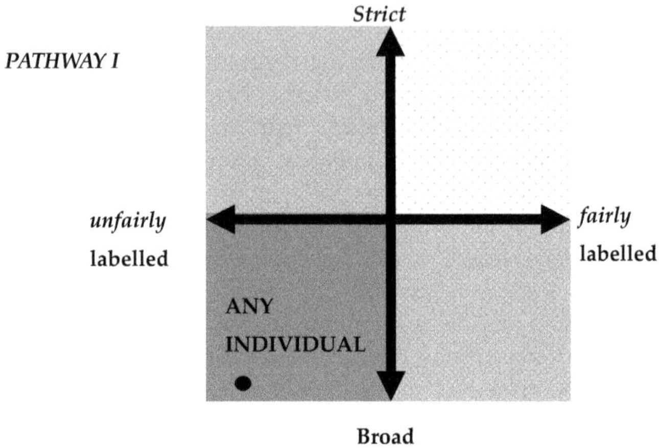

B. Abstract Definition of an Organisation: The Capability Understanding (Pathway II)

ICC judges have repeatedly held that determining whether a group qualifies as an organisation under the Statute must be made *on a case-by-case basis*.[79] Building on this approach, ICC jurisprudence often formulates an *abstract* definition that describes an organisation in terms of capacity, rather than through fixed structural criteria. The focus lies not on formal attributes (such as hierarchy, size, or institutional design) but on whether the group can act collectively.[80] This section examines two variants of this abstract approach.

i. The Human Rights Variant: Organisations Capable of Infringing Basic Human Values

The *Kenya Investigation Decision* pioneered this abstract understanding. The Pre-Trial Chamber rejected rigid structural tests, reasoning that the 'formal nature of a group and its level of organisation' are not decisive.[81] Instead, any private group 'capable of performing acts which infringe on basic human values' could satisfy Article 7(2)(a).[82] While acknowledging that the different language versions of the Statute support the existence of an organisation behind

[79] *Situation in the Republic of Kenya* (Decision Pursuant to Article 15 of the Rome Statute on the Authorization of an Investigation Into the Situation in the Republic of Kenya) ICC-01/09 (31 March 2010) para 93; *Ruto & Sang* (CoC Decision) (n 49) para 185.

[80] See further T Rodenhäuser, 'Beyond State Crimes: Non-State Entities and Crimes Against Humanity' (2014) 27 *Leiden Journal of International Law* 913, 953.

[81] *Situation in Kenya* (Decision Pursuant to Article 15 of the Rome Statute on the Authorization of an Investigation into the Situation in the Republic of Kenya) ICC-01/09-19-Corr (31 March 2010) para 90.

[82] ibid para 90.

the policy, the Chamber declined to set formal criteria.[83] This formulation was subsequently echoed in later Kenya-related cases,[84] some of which supplemented the abstract definition with a series of non-exhaustive factors.[85]

A notable feature of the *Kenya Investigation Decision* is its heavy reliance on academic commentary, rather than on the sources in Article 21 of the Statute.[86] The Chamber primarily drew from Di Fillipo, who – writing about terrorism – advocated a broad notion of organisation to allow terrorist groups to fall within crimes against humanity. Di Fillipo explicitly framed this as a *normative proposal* for the future development of ICL, not an interpretation of existing law.[87] The Chamber also cited Robinson's 1999 article on CaH, which does not argue for such breadth and implicitly assumes the need for an organisational actor.[88] Robinson's later work emphasised the importance of scale, associativity and the group nature of these crimes. He warned against over-inclusiveness, which is inconsistent with the Chamber's abstraction.[89] Likewise, Burns, another cited author, merely considered whether certain non-state groups (eg, narco-terrorists or mafia-like networks) might theoretically fall under Article 7 if they intentionally targeted civilians. None of these sources, therefore, articulated the standard the Chamber adopted.[90]

The second major reference point was the 1991 ILC Draft Code of Crimes, which mentioned that 'private individuals with *de facto* power or organized in criminal gangs or groups' might also commit systematic or mass *violations of human rights*.[91] The Chamber's reliance on this text imported human-rights language into the ICL context, even though the 1991 Draft Code neither used the term crimes against humanity nor required a perpetrator to act on behalf of an organisation.[92] This human-rights framing is historically anomalous.[93]

[83] ibid fn 82.

[84] *Prosecutor v Ruto & Sang* (Decision on the Prosecutor's Application for Summons to Appear for WS Ruto, HK Kosgey and JA Sang) ICC-01/09-01/11 (15 March 2011) para 28; *Prosecutor v Muthaura, Kenyatta & Ali* (Decision on the Prosecutor's Application for Summonses to Appear for Francis Kirimi Muthaura, Uhuru Muigai Kenyatta and Mohammed Hussein Ali) ICC-01/09-02/11-1 (8 March 2011) para 21; *Ruto & Sang* (CoC Decision) (n 49) para 186; *Prosecutor v Muthaura, Kenyatta & Ali* (Decision on the Confirmation of Charges) ICC-01/09-02/11 (23 January 2012) para 112.

[85] *Prosecutor v Muthuara, Kenyatta & Ali* (Decision on the Prosecutor's Application for Summonses to Appear) (n 84) para 21.

[86] *Situation in Kenya* (Investigation Decision) (n 81) para 90 and fn 84.

[87] M Di Filippo, 'Terrorist Crimes and International Co-operation: Critical Remarks on the Definition and Inclusion of Terrorism in the Category of International Crimes' (2008) 19 *European Journal of International Law* 533, 567.

[88] *Situation in Kenya* (Investigation Decision) (n 81) para 90 and fn 84 citing Robinson (n 8).

[89] D Robinson, 'Crimes Against Humanity: A Better Policy on "Policy"' in Carsten Stahn (ed), *The Law and Practice of the International Criminal Court* (OUP, 2014) 122ff.

[90] P Burns, 'Aspect of Crimes Against Humanity and the International Criminal Court' (Symposium on the International Criminal Court, Beijing, 2007) 11.

[91] *Situation in Kenya* (Investigation Decision) (n 81) para 91.

[92] Draft Code of Crimes against the Peace and Security of Mankind (YBILC 1991, Vol II, Part 1); see further Clark (n 32) 16–17.

[93] Y Dinstein, 'Case Analysis: Crimes Against Humanity After Tadic' (2000) 13 *Leiden Journal of International Law* 372, 379.

It emerged during debates on detaching crimes against humanity from a war nexus, but was later abandoned. The 1994 Draft Statute[94] and 1996 Draft Code,[95] reverted to a criminal-law framing, defining crimes against humanity as acts instigated or directed by a government or by any organisation or group and finding 'the factors of scale and deliberate policy'[96] to be crucial for definitional purposes. By citing only the 1991 Draft while omitting the subsequent, more relevant drafts, the Chamber effectively cherry-picked from preparatory materials, privileging expansive language over strict construction.

This human right framing together with the bypassing of Article 21's sources is the most striking elements that make this interpretative process problematic.[97] The Chamber's reasoning relied almost exclusively on academic writings and the 1991 Draft Code, neither of which qualify as primary or secondary sources under Article 21. Even under Article 38 of the ICJ Statute, Di Fillipo's work would not count among 'highly qualified publicists' in ICL. No justification was provided for treating such materials as authoritative, which makes this approach flawed at the level of source doctrine. The Pre-Trial Chamber thereby demonstrated a substandard reliance on the Statute and EoC, for example, by ignoring the EoC's reference to a 'State or organisation', which suggests that governmental or organisational action is the rule.[98]

Furthermore, the Chamber's selective use of preparatory works is also problematic. In relation to methods of interpretation, it is flawed that the judges invoked the drafters' intent only to support the inclusion of what seems to be all non-state actors, ignoring the unresolved debate on which *types* of non-state actors were envisaged. The Chamber made minimal use of the Statute and the EoC, which clarify that a policy requires active promotion or encouragement by a State or organisation, with inaction being exceptional. These safeguards against circular reasoning–inferring organisational action from the mere existence of an attack–were not addressed. The simplification of what the drafters intended creates the impression that no discussion existed, while the opposite is true.

In terms of interpretative result, the 'capability to infringe basic human values' test is excessively broad. It risks encompassing virtually any group capable of coordinated violence, from local militias to criminal gangs. In the *Kenya Situation,* the judges found that 'various groups including local leaders, businessmen and politicians associated with the two leading parties, as well as with members of the police force acting at the material time constituted organisations

[94] ILC, Report of the International Law Commission on the Work of Its Forty-Third Session (29 April–19 July 1991) UN Doc A/46/10, 265.265.

[95] Draft Code of Crimes against the Peace and Security of Mankind with commentaries (YBILC 1996, vol II, Part 2).

[96] ILC, Report of the Forty-Third Session (n 94) 265.

[97] See also for criticism on this decision: Hansen (n 49) 34–35; CC Jalloh, 'Situation in the Republic of Kenya' (2012) 106 *American Journal of International Law* 118, 544–545; Rodenhäuser (n 80) 914; Sadat (n 13) fn 246.

[98] EoC Introduction para 3 and fn 6 EoC.

within the meaning of Article 7(2)(a) of the Statute'.[99] Hypothetically, a wide range of groups would qualify under this definition, if not any group.[100] Recalling the quote of Judge Herrera, that CaH are the 'perversion of politics', it is this study's position that these non-state actors, at a minimum, have to be implicated at some sort of political level. Otherwise, loosely structured entities such as the Hells Angels – for example, if terrorising a community and forcing residents to flee – could theoretically fall within the definition. A purely human-rights-capability test risks conflating transnational crime with crimes against humanity. Such an interpretative outcome conflicts with the principle of legality and stretches CaH beyond their intended political and systemic character.

Some scholars adopt this human-rights–inspired, normative approach, equating CaH humanity with particularly grave violations of human rights.[101] These approaches often focus on the gravity or seriousness of the act and find that the differentiating criteria between ordinary and international crimes lie precisely in their extremely inhumane nature.[102] Geras argued that the normative groundwork of CaH lies in two fundamental conditions: (1) these acts are particularly grave or 'inhumane' acts, and (2) they are acts against the human status or condition.[103] While such reasoning highlights the gravity of the acts, it may permit international intervention in cases lacking sufficient severity. May's minimalistic approach underscores the need for caution: only state inaction in grave circumstances should justify ICC involvement, preserving the system from overextension.[104]

The *Kenya Investigation Decision* similarly makes clear why caution is needed. Its human-rights-based definition is methodologically flawed and overly inclusive, disregarding the Rome Statute's textual limits. The policy element should distinguish ordinary crimes from CaH by marking the contextual threshold that internationalises conduct. Yet, by leaving the 'group behind the policy' undefined, the decision risks overinclusion, diluting the category's severity and undermining legality and fair labelling. The following section examines whether a more precise formulation of this 'capability' concept can produce a more defensible interpretation.

ii. The Humanitarian Variant: Organisations Capable of Committing an Attack

Before the *Kenya Investigation Decision*, ICC Pre-Trial Chambers approached the organisational policy element through a humanitarian lens, defining it as a

[99] *Situation in Kenya* (Investigation Decision) (n 81) para 117.

[100] deGuzman (n 6) 131; see also E Schmid, *Taking Economic, Social and Cultural Rights Seriously in International Criminal Law* (CUP, 2015) 87.

[101] Renzo (n 73) 453.

[102] Roberts (n 3).

[103] Geras (n 8) 38ff.

[104] L May, *Normative account of Crimes against Humanity* (Cambridge Studies in Philosophy and Law, CUP, 2004) 7.

group capable of committing a widespread or systematic attack. This variant, reflected in the *Katanga & Ngudjolo* and *Bemba* cases,[105] contrasts with the human rights-inspired approach by emphasising the military or armed nature of the group, aligning closely with the concept of 'organized armed groups' under Article 8(2)(f).[106] A 'policy may be made either by groups of persons who govern a specific territory or by any organisation with the capability to commit a widespread or systematic attack against a civilian population'.[107]

In both cases, the presence of structured armed groups, such as the Union of Congolese Patriots (UPC) in *Katanga* and the Armée de Libération du Congo (ALC) in *Bemba*, made it relatively straightforward to establish the organisation requirement. The Pre-Trial Chambers relied heavily on the 1991 Draft Code and on ICTY and ICTR jurisprudence, even though these external precedents differ from the Rome Statute and fall outside Article 21's hierarchy of sources.[108] The ICTY required a war nexus,[109] while the ICTR included discriminatory intent.[110] These tribunals did not consistently treat the policy element as a separate legal requirement, which makes reliance by ICC judges, without a detailed analysis of its relevance, tricky.[111]

The *Katanga CoC* Decision referenced several ad hoc tribunal judgments to support its interpretation of the organisational policy element. The ICTR *Akayesu Trial* Judgment[112] and the ICTY *Kordic and Cerkez* case[113] building on *Blaskic*,[114] which held that evidence of a policy could demonstrate a systematic attack, but the policy element itself was not treated as a separate legal requirement.[115] The Katanga Pre-Trial Chamber, however, also used the *Kayishema and Ruzindana* judgments,[116] which relied on the broader 1991 ILC Draft Code, including 'private individuals with *de facto* power or organised in criminal

[105] Considering that the charges were not confirmed against Mathieu Ngudjolo Chui, the present analysis focuses on Katanga.

[106] Art 8(2)(f) differentiates between NIAC's and 'merely internal disturbances and tensions, such as riots, isolated and sporadic acts of violence or other acts of a similar nature'.

[107] *Katanga & Ngudjolo Chui* (CoC Decision) (n 75) para 396; *Prosecutor v Bemba* (Decision on the Confirmation of Charges) ICC-01/05-01/08 (15 June 2009) para 81.

[108] *Bemba* (CoC Decision) (n 107) para 84.

[109] Statute of the International Criminal Tribunal for the former Yugoslavia (adopted by UNSC Res 827, 25 May 1993) Art 5.

[110] Statute of the International Criminal Tribunal for Rwanda (adopted by UNSC Res 955, 8 November 1994) Art 3.

[111] See, eg, *Prosecutor v Tadić* (Opinion and Judgment) IT-94-1-T (7 May 1997) para 644: 'there must be some form of a governmental, organizational or group policy to commit these acts'; see also: *Prosecutor v Kupreškić et al* (Trial Judgment) IT 95-16 (14 January 2000) paras 551ff.

[112] *Prosecutor v Akayesu* (Trial Chamber Judgment) ICTR-96-4-T (2 September 1998) para 580.

[113] *Prosecutor v Kordić & Čerkez* (Trial Chamber Judgment) IT-95-14/2-T (27 February 2001) para 182.

[114] *Prosecutor v Blaškić* (Judgment) IT-95-14-T (3 March 2000) paras 203–204.

[115] See also Sluiter (n 37).

[116] *Prosecutor v Kayishema and Ruzindana* (Trial Judgment) ICTR-95-l-T (21 May 1999) paras 123–125.

gangs',[117] rather than the narrower 1996 Draft Code that recognised only governments or organisations.[118]

The main flaw in the PTC's reasoning was its heavy reliance on external precedent without justification or methodological explanation. Article 21 of the Rome Statute does not list such precedents in its hierarchy of sources,[119] and while they may play a subsidiary role, their use must be warranted and explicitly motivated.[120] Here, it was not: the tribunal statutes did not include a policy element, and their case law on policy was inconsistent, so reliance on them should have been explained.

The *Katanga* Trial Chamber clarified what constitutes an organisation, confirming that the UPC/FPLC was a well-organised military group with formal political and military structures, resources, and trained soldiers.[121] The Chamber followed a similar reasoning to that of the PTC and concluded that the organisation had 'sufficient means to promote or encourage the attack,[122] retaining the capability-based notion while distinguishing the contours of the actors included under the organisation from the issues of policy or the systematic nature of the attack.[123]

Several interpretative methods can be distilled from its reasoning. It began with the dictionary meaning of organisation, but since this failed to establish clear boundaries, the judges turned to a more contextual interpretation of the text. The juxtaposition of organisation and State in the Statute made clear that this concept goes further than only including state organs.[124] The Chamber reasoned that, considering 'modern asymmetric warfare', private entities not possessing a formal structure could still qualify,[125] provided they had the capacity to commit an attack. It defined essential features as the 'capacities for action, mutual agreement and coordination'.[126] This line of reasoning was followed in the *Bemba* case in relation to the ALC.[127]

Methodologically, the Chamber improved on the CoC Decisions by grounding its analysis more clearly in internal sources and adopting a textual approach. However, problems remain. Despite following Article 21 at first, the Chamber later justified reliance on external precedent by invoking Article 38

[117] Article 18 of the Draft Code of Crimes against the Peace and Security of Mankind with commentaries (YBILC 1996, vol II, Part 2).

[118] Art 21 Draft Code of Crimes against the Peace and Security of Mankind (YBILC 1991, Vol II, Part 1) as referenced by *Katanga & Ngudjolo Chui* (CoC Decision) (n 75) fn 507.

[119] See ch 3, ss IV(B) and V(B), 136ff.

[120] AZ Borda, 'Appraisal-Based and Flexible Approaches to External Precedent in International Criminal Law' (2015) *Leiden Journal of International Law* 643.

[121] *Prosecutor v Katanga* (Judgment Pursuant to Article 74 of the Statute) ICC-01/04-01/07 (7 March 2014) para 677.

[122] ibid para 1119.

[123] ibid paras 1117–23.

[124] ibid para 1119.

[125] ibid para 1119.

[126] ibid para 1120.

[127] *Prosecutor v Bemba* (Judgment Pursuant to Article 74 of the Statute) ICC-01/05-01/08 (21 March 2016) paras 131–36.

of the ICJ Statute. This and the continued use of *ad hoc* tribunal jurisprudence constitute an unwarranted deviation from the Statute's source doctrine. A further shortcoming lies in the failure to distinguish sufficiently between the standards of Articles 7(2)(a) and 8(2). Although the factual context, namely armed groups with clear military hierarchies, did not require testing the lower threshold of organisation, the Chamber missed the opportunity to clarify the distinct criteria separating organisations under Article 7(2)(a) from organised armed groups under Article 8(2).[128] This issue was later criticised by Judge Ozaki in her Separate Opinion in *Bemba*, who noted that the Court had concentrated too heavily on defining *policy* rather than *organisation*.[129] Judges Van den Wyngaert and Morrison echoed this concern, stressing that the interpretation of the organisational policy element remained unconvincing and underdeveloped.[130] Finally, this interpretative outcome also lacks precision. The Chamber's reliance on the abstract notion of a 'capability to perform an attack' remains insufficiently defined. Even in its stricter humanitarian form, this standard leaves ambiguity as to whether loosely structured political movements could qualify.

In the same year as the *Katanga Judgment*, the *Ntaganda* case entered the confirmation of charges phase. Yet, by 2014, most confirmation of charges procedures had shifted toward evidentiary assessment rather than legal interpretation.[131] Unlike the 2008 *Katanga* and 2009 *Bemba* decisions, the *Ntaganda* CoC Decision did not analyse the constituent legal elements. It simply found that the Union des Patriotes Congolais/Forces Patriotiques pour la Libération du Congo (UPC/FPLC) had an organisational policy to attack non-Hema civilians and that its formal hierarchy, disciplinary system, and communication networks sufficed to qualify it as an organisation.[132] It explained that the FPLC is the military wing with Commander in Chief and Chief of Staff, Floribert Kisembo, and as Deputy Chief of Staff, Bosco Ntaganda.[133] Considering that this decision

[128] This issue is further complicated by the manifest lack of agreement among judges over what constitutes an attack under Article 8 as seen in the *Ntaganda* case (*Prosecutor v Ntaganda* (Public redacted version of Judgment on the appeals of Mr Bosco Ntaganda and the Prosecutor against the decision of Trial Chamber VI of 8 July 2019 entitled 'Judgment') ICC-01/04-02/06 (30 March 2021); *Prosecutor v Ntaganda* (Partly Concurring Opinion of Judge Eboe-Osuji to the Appeal Judgment) ICC-01/04-02/06-2666-Anx5 (30 March 2021), paras 112–13.

[129] *Prosecutor v Bemba* (Separate opinion of Kuniko Ozaki to the Judgment pursuant to Article 74 of the Statute) ICC-01/05 -01/08 (21 March 2016) para 25.

[130] *Prosecutor v Bemba* (Separate opinion Judge Christine Van den Wyngaert and Judge Howard Morrison) ICC-01/05-01/08 (8 June 2018) paras 69-ff.

[131] This is not the place to go into the matter, but the role of the PTC in setting out the law has been subject to ongoing debate. For further discussion on their role: C Kreß, 'The Procedural Law of the International Criminal Court in Outline: Anatomy of a Unique Compromise' (2003) 1 *Journal of International Criminal Justice* 603.

[132] *Prosecutor v Ntaganda* (Decision Pursuant to Article 61(7)(a) and (b) of the Rome Statute) ICC-01/04-02/06 (9 June 2014) paras 16–17.

[133] ibid para 15.

lacked a legal debate, little is to be gained from further analysis, which is equally the case for the *Ongwen* CoC Decision, which similarly focused on evidence rather than setting out the law.

In its 2019 Judgment, the *Ntaganda* Trial Chamber acknowledged divergent interpretations of 'organisation' but declined to adopt any.[134] Because the UPC/FPLC was a clearly structured armed group, the Chamber found elaboration unnecessary. It treated the notion of 'organised armed group' under Article 8(2)(f) as satisfying Article 7(2)(a),[135] implicitly adhering to the *Katanga* and *Bemba* logic that capability suffices.[136] While beneficial in terms of judicial expediency, this approach is unsatisfactory given the persistent uncertainty surrounding which non-state actors are encompassed. The Chamber left the organisational policy element largely unexplored, seemingly maintaining the humanitarian variant of the capability test.[137]

If any consistent line of ICC jurisprudence exists, this humanitarian capability standard currently prevails. The *Ongwen* Judgment of 2021 confirmed that it is enough for an organisation to possess 'a set of structures or mechanisms, whatever those may be, that are sufficiently efficient to ensure the coordination necessary to carry out an attack'[138]

The *Al Hassan* Trial Judgment of 2024 further consolidates this humanitarian trajectory. Unlike the *Ntaganda* Judgment, which avoided taking a clear stance on the organisational element, the *Al Hassan* Chamber explicitly endorsed the definition articulated in *Katanga*.[139] In doing so, it alleviated some of the concerns surrounding judicial expedience that arise when Chambers simply assume the organisational element without explanation. However, the *Al Hassan* case, which involved several interconnected entities operating under the broader umbrella of *Ansar Dine*, including the *Islamic Police* and the *Islamic Court* established in Timbuktu, remained unclear as to which of these entities the judges considered to fulfil the capability requirement of Article 7(2)(a). In her dissenting opinion, Judge Akane, discussing issues of responsibility under Article 25, emphasised that authority and lines of command were not uniform across the *Islamic Police* and the *Hesbah*, a point that complicates the assessment of how these organs met the capability standard. Accordingly, *Al Hassan* improves methodological clarity but leaves unresolved which entity, on the facts, satisfies the capability requirement.

[134] *Prosecutor v Ntaganda* (TC Judgment) ICC-01/04-02/06 (08 July 2019) para 675.

[135] ibid paras 675, 704–15.

[136] ibid para 680.

[137] The Ntaganda appeal readdressed the issue of organisational policy, but mainly in relation to the policy prong, which is not further assessed in the context of this book.

[138] *Prosecutor v Ongwen* (Trial Judgment) ICC-02/04-01/15 (4 February 2021) para 2677.

[139] *Prosecutor v Al Hassan* (n 124).

iii. Intermediate Conclusion: Insufficient Construction in the Internal Sources

The two abstract approaches to defining an organisation are problematic in their interpretative methodology. Most notably, the source doctrine invoked to justify them reflects a weak adherence to Article 21, both in terms of hierarchy and substance. The examined decisions reveal a general neglect of internal sources: the *Katanga* and *Bemba* Confirmation of Charges Decisions barely engaged with them. The *Katanga* Judgment is the exception, beginning with a detailed discussion of the Statute and Elements of Crimes. Yet it remains doubtful whether the capability understanding of the organisation prong can truly be derived from those instruments. The internal sources appear to have carried limited interpretative weight.

Implicitly, the abstract definition seems to have drawn more from the broader notion found in customary law. None of the ICC's decisions, however, deconstructs the customary definition of the organisational policy element. Instead, they rely on external jurisprudence or the ILC Draft Codes as indirect evidence of custom. While these materials may assist in identifying custom, the decisions offer no transparent methodology of customary ascertainment, which requires a reasoned analysis of state practice and *opinio juris*. The reliance on external precedent is especially problematic in this context, since the organisational policy element is absent from the statutes of the ad hoc tribunals. Their jurisprudence is moreover inconsistent on the element's existence and function. By selectively invoking decisions that support particular positions, the ICC Chambers have risked misrepresenting the customary development of crimes against humanity. Given that ICC judges are under no obligation to interpret in conformity with customary law, the rationale for invoking such divergent precedent remains unclear.[140]

The interpretative outcomes, in both variants, are insufficiently constructed and broad. Both abstract definitions of organisation tend to be circular. As Judge Ozaki rightly pointed out, they do 'nothing to guard against the risk of simply reasoning backwards, using the fact that such an attack occurred to infer the existence of an organisation'.[141] The argument assumes that any attack presupposes an organisation capable of carrying it out. No clear criteria are given for the entity; its capability is inferred from the attack rather than defined on its own. As a result, neither versions specify sufficiently which non-state actors are encompassed and thus lacks foreseeability. Furthermore, it is unclear how the two versions should be viewed vis-à-vis each other. The evolution of the human rights version in the *Kenya Investigation Decision* towards the humanitarian law version is not motivated.

The human rights version certainly presents the broadest interpretation of the two and is tied more to concerns of fairness than the humanitarian variant.

[140] See ch 3, s IV(B).
[141] *Bemba* (Separate opinion of Ozaki) (n 129) para 25.

These considerations of fairness, nevertheless, are not sufficient to justify such a broad take. On the contrary, fairness is inadequately addressed, as these interpretations risk overinclusion of crimes not grave enough to merit the label of crimes against humanity. Since the label would then misrepresent the wrongfulness and neglect the accused's perspective, such constructions should be rejected. The interpretation is categorised in the model as follows:

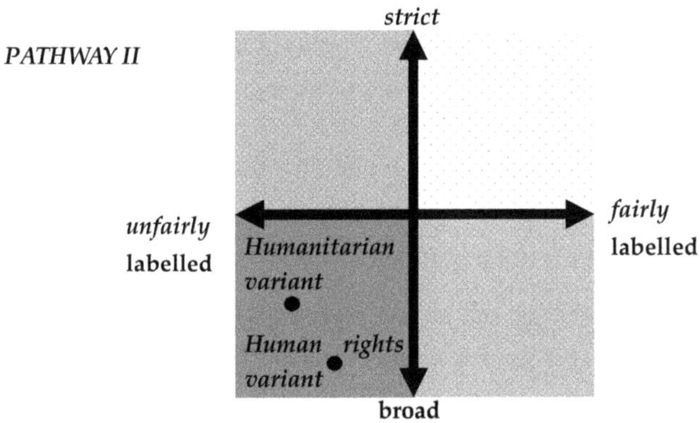

Concerns about the lack of clarity on which entity can be included under Article 7(2)(a) led to the development of the subsequent approach to the organisation prong that concretises the organisation's characteristics.

C. Organisation with a Set of Concrete Characteristics (Pathway III)

In *Ruto and Sang*, some judges expressed concern that the involvement of a determinate entity in the CaH had not been sufficiently proven. As explained in the previous section, the Prosecution in the *Kenya Investigation* was adamant in building a case around a very complex idea of a Network. Judge Fremr doubted whether the evidence presented was able to show the existence of such an entity and how it 'functioned in practice, including how command and control was ensured within it'.[142] Judge Fremr opposed the Prosecution advancing a 'network existed by virtue of a common plan'.[143]

Two main approaches concretise the notion of an organisation: one infers its existence from a non-exhaustive set of indicative factors, while the other seeks to define its essential characteristics.

[142] *Ruto & Sang* (Acquittal Judgment) (n 43) – reasons of Judge Fremr para 32.
[143] ibid paras 26–30.

i. The Inference-Based Variant: a Non-exhaustive List of Evidentiary Factors

In the *Kenya Investigation Decision*, the Pre-Trial Chamber supplemented the abstract definition with a list of factors that may be considered when deciding on the existence of an organisation:

- whether the group is under a *responsible command*, or has an *established hierarchy*;
- whether the group possesses, in fact, *the means* to carry out a widespread or systematic attack against a civilian population;
- whether the group has *criminal activities against the civilian population* as a primary purpose;
- whether the group articulates, explicitly or implicitly, *an intention to attack* a civilian population.[144]

In other decisions, the following factors emerged:

- whether the group exercises *control over part of the territory* of a State;
- whether the group is *part of a larger group*.[145]

These factors operate as evidentiary inferences through which an organisation may be established, rather than as essential legal properties whose absence would negate organisational policy. The *Muthaura, Kenyatta, and Ali* case illustrates how this list of factors has been applied.[146] In that case, attacks were largely carried out by PNU supporters, particularly the PNU Youth and Mungiki members.[147] The PTC's focus was on the Mungiki.[148] This group has been termed an 'ethnicity-based militia'[149]; a 'civil militia',[150] a gang active in the slums of Nairobi,[151] a devil-worshipping sect, and a religious movement.[152] The PTC held

[144] *Situation in Kenya* (Investigation Decision) (n 81) para 93; *Muthuara, Kenyatta & Ali* (Decision on the Prosecutor's Application for Summonses to Appear) (n 84) para 20 (emphasis added).

[145] *Situation in Republic of Côte d'Ivoire* (Decision Pursuant to Article 15 of the Rome Statute on the Authorisation of an Investigation) ICC-02/11-14 (15 November 2011) para 57; *Ruto & Sang* (CoC Decision) (n 49) para 185.

[146] *Muthuara, Kenyatta & Ali* (Decision on the Prosecutor's Application for Summonses to Appear) (n 84) para 14.

[147] See, eg, Justice Truth, and Reconciliation Commission, *Commissions of Inquiry – CIPEV Report (Waki Report)*, 2008) and Kenya National Commission on Human Rights, *The Cry of Blood Report on Extra-Judicial Killings and Disappearances'* (September 2008).

[148] *Muthuara, Kenyatta & Ali* (Decision on the Prosecutor's Application for Summonses to Appear) (n 84).

[149] CC Jalloh, 'What makes a Crime against Humanity a Crime against Humanity' (2012) 28 *American University International Law Review* 381, 434.

[150] N Nyabolao, 'The legal challenge of civil militia groups in Kenya' (2009) 18 *African Security Review* 90.

[151] P Hauck and S Peterke (eds), *International Law and Transnational Organized Crime* (OUP, 2016) 425.

[152] See further Canada: Immigration and Refugee Board of Canada, *Kenya: The Mungiki sect, including organizational structure, leadership, membership, recruitment and activities; the relationship between the government and sects, including protection offered to victims of devil worshippers and sects, such as the Mungiki (2010-October 2013) (KEN104594.E)*, 2013) 26–27.

there to be reasonable grounds to believe that the Mungiki was a criminal organisation that carried out an attack against the non-Kikuyu population.[153] It was held that several features fitted the list above: 'a large and complex hierarchical structure featuring various levels of command and a clear division of duties in the command'; breaches of internal rules which were subjected to strict disciplinary measures; a trained military wing; and control over core societal activities (eg, control over services such as electricity and water; over the transport sector and the ability to appoint people in key position such as judges).[154] In the *CoC Decision*, the PTC similarly concluded that the Mungiki was 'a hierarchically structured organization', with a disciplinary system, 'a trained quasi-military wing', and control over essential social services, fulfilling the requirements of article 7(2)(a).[155]

Despite its flaws, the list of factors has two benefits. First, it clarifies what type of organisation can carry out attacks, linking capacity to hierarchy, structure, control, and resources. Second, it encourages an active process of checking criteria. Unfortunately, it is primarily effective for armed groups, and less so for more unconventional organisational forms or other types of groups, as the scheme on different non-state actors indicated.[156] The Mungiki's involvement in the post-election violence and the choice of the Prosecutor to build a case around its involvement created the opportunity for the PTC to settle this and clarify better how to apply Article 7(2)(a) to other groups than armed groups. Although the *Kenyatta* and *Muthaura* cases were discontinued and the Mungiki issue never reached trial, some observations on these decisions can still be made.

First, there seems to be a disconnect between the generic factors listed and their application to the Mungiki, and this is specifically in relation to the intent. In the *Summons to Appear Decision,* the fourth listed factor is the existence of an *intention* to attack a civilian population.[157] Many questions arise in relation to this formulation. Unlike co-perpetrators, whose shared intent defines a common plan, it is unclear why an organisation itself should have intent. Were the judges aiming to describe the policy's characteristics rather than the organisation's intent? The decision does not clarify this point, nor was it addressed at the confirmation of charges stage. This list of indicators can only function effectively if each factor is properly tested and clarified.

[153] *Muthuara, Kenyatta & Ali* (Decision on the Prosecutor's Application for Summonses to Appear) (n 84) para 17.

[154] ibid paras 21–22; see further: SD Mueller, 'Kenya and the International Criminal Court: Politics, the Election, and the Law' (2013) Working Paper, Boston University African Studies Center and Hansen (n 49) 25.

[155] Professor H Maupue, an expert on the political and social Kenyan structures and the Mungiki, testified on its organisational structure: see: *Prosecutor v Muthaura and Kenyatta* (Prosecution's second report on joint instruction of experts) ICC-01/09-02/11 (30 November 2012).

[156] See fig 1 above.

[157] *Muthuara, Kenyatta & Ali* (Decision on the Prosecutor's Application for Summonses to Appear) (n 84) para 21.

Second, beyond the list's shortcomings, its factors themselves are questionable, as they reflect a specific view of organisational policy shaped by the notion of capacity. Textual analysis shows that organisation does not necessarily imply weapons, hierarchy, or a disciplinary system. The list does not provide guidance as to how an organisation would be different from a mere individual or a mere *ad hoc* collaboration, or any other type of more loosely defined network or group. Questions like whether an organisation can consist of just two people or must exist for a certain duration remain unanswered, and group characteristics are unspecified.

By leaving these aspects unaddressed and focusing on this notion of capacity to attack, the list fits the circular type of reasoning Judge Osaki warned about.[158] Once an attack occurs, care must be taken not to infer organisational factors from the attack itself and then use them to prove the entity's existence. If no factor is truly tested, the existence of an organisation can hardly be considered proven.[159]

Another issue with the factor-listing approach is its resemblance to the judicially developed standard on proving the existence of organised armed groups in non-international armed conflicts.[160] In the *Katanga Judgment,* it was held that the following non-exhaustive list of factors should be considered:

> the force or group's internal hierarchy; its command structure and the rules applied within it; the extent to which military equipment, including firearms, are available; the force or group's ability to plan military operations and put them into effect; and the extent, seriousness, and intensity of any military involvement. None of these factors are individually determinative. Accordingly, since article 8(2)(f) of the Statute requires only that the armed group be "organized", the Chamber holds that some degree of organisation suffices to establish the existence of an armed conflict be assessed case-by-case. It underscores that exertion of control over a part of the territory by the groups concerned is not required.[161]

When the group qualifies as an armed group in this regard, it is almost automatic that the organisation requirement in Article 7(2)(a) is considered fulfilled.[162] As said, this reasoning leaves open whether organisations outside the armed group model fall under Article 7(2)(a), failing to test the limits of CaH. If proof of an entity is required, the threshold question of which groups qualify must be addressed, and the contours of the entity, however small or fluid, should be examined. To do so, some inferences need closer examination. This section focuses on two: (i) structure, hierarchy, and command as understood in the context of Article 8(2)(f, and (ii) the group's purpose.

[158] *Bemba* (Separate opinion of Ozaki) (n 129) para 25.
[159] *Katanga* (TC Judgment) (n 121) para 1109.
[160] See as discussed in the next section.
[161] *Katanga* (TC Judgment) (n 121) para 1186.
[162] See the following section for further discussion of 'organised armed group'.

a. 'Organised Armed Group': Inferences on Structure, Hierarchy and Responsible Command

Inspired by Common Article 3 of the Geneva Conventions (GC)[163] and imported from Article 1(1) of the Second Additional Protocol (APII),[164] Article 8(2)(f) of the Rome Statute puts forward a standard for organised armed groups in relation to the finding of non-international armed conflict (NIAC). Since the APII formulates an extra requirement that the group has to be under 'responsible command', which was not included in GVs, there is an ongoing debate whether the ICC regime holds such a requirement.[165] The organisational requirements of armed groups have been extensively elaborated by the ICRC. The core idea is that upholding IHL presupposes a sufficient level of organisation in non-state armed groups.[166] These groups 'have to be under a certain command structure and have the capacity to sustain military operations'.[167] Furthermore, the group must have 'the level of organisation of state armed forces, it must possess a certain level of hierarchy and discipline and the ability to implement the basic obligations of IHL'.[168] The logic of imposing certain obligations is that it can only be deemed possible to adhere to IHL obligations with a minimum level of organisation.

In line with this standard, several factors have been further developed in the tribunals' case law.[169] In *Boškoski and Tarčulovski*, the ICTY held that an armed group requires 'some hierarchical structure' and outlined five elements to gauge its level of organisation:

[163] Common Art 3 to the Geneva Conventions: *Geneva Convention I for the Amelioration of the Condition of the Wounded and Sick in Armed Forces in the Field* (adopted 12 August 1949, entered into force 21 October 1950) 75 UNTS 31 (First Geneva Convention); *Geneva Convention II for the Amelioration of the Condition of Wounded, Sick and Shipwrecked Members of Armed Forces at Sea* (adopted 12 August 1949, entered into force 21 October 1950) 75 UNTS 85 (Second Geneva Convention); *Geneva Convention III Relative to the Treatment of Prisoners of War* (adopted 12 August 1949, entered into force 21 October 1950) 75 UNTS 135 (Third Geneva Convention); *Geneva Convention IV Relative to the Protection of Civilian Persons in Time of War* (adopted 12 August 1949, entered into force 21 October 1950) 75 UNTS 287 (Fourth Geneva Convention).

[164] Article 1.1 of the Additional Protocol II of 8 June 1977 to the Geneva Conventions of 12 August 1949 and relating to the Protection of Victims of Non-International Armed Conflicts.

[165] See further MM Bradley, '"Protracted Armed Conflict": A Conundrum. Does Article 8(2)(f) of the Rome Statute Require an Organised Armed Group to Meet the Organisational Criteria of Additional Protocol II?' (2019) 32 *South African Journal of Criminal Justice* 291.

[166] D Schindler, 'The Different Types of Armed Conflicts According to the Geneva Conventions and Protocols' (1979) 2 *Recueil des Cours* 117, 147.

[167] ICRC, *'How is the Term 'Armed Conflict' Defined in International Humanitarian Law?'* (2008) Opinion Paper 3.

[168] International Committee of the Red Cross, *Convention (I) for the Amelioration of the Condition of the Wounded and Sick in Armed Forces in the Field. Geneva, 12 August 1949 Article 3: Conflicts not of an international character*, 2016).

[169] See, eg, *Tadić* (Opinion and Judgment) (n 111) para 592; *Prosecutor v Limaj et al* (Trial Judgment) IT-03-66-T (30 november 2005) paras 94–134; *Prosecutor v Haradinaj et al*. (Trial Judgment) IT-04-84 (3 April 2008) para 60; *Prosecutor v Boškoski and Tarčulovski* (Trial Chamber Judgment) IT-04-82-T (10 July 2008) paras 194–207.

- the existence of a command structure;
- the fact that the group could carry out operations in an organised manner;
- elements indicating a level of sophistication with respect to logistics;
- the existence of internal discipline; and
- the ability to speak with 'one voice'.[170]

As with organisational policy, there is disagreement on how to set limits to the required notion of organisation and on the usefulness of listing non-exhaustive factors.[171] The following analysis turns to the *Katanga,*[172] *Ntaganda*[173] and *Ongwen Judgments*.[174] Each is assessed on its concept of organised armed groups, with a view to drawing conclusions for the organisational policy element.

In *Katanga*, the organisational requirements under Article 7(2)(a) were discussed alongside the organised nature of the armed group under Article 8(2)(f).[175] It was examined whether the 'group of commanders and Ngiti commanders of Walendu-Bindi collectivité was of an organised nature'.[176] The Chamber, in assessing the structure under Article 8(2)(f), was confronted with the difficulty of multiple armed groups and units, but nevertheless, found that they were 'organised within a single militia',[177] an approach criticised in the dissenting opinion of Judge Van den Wyngaert.[178] In relation to Article 8(f), the Chamber discussed several of the traditional hierarchical and structural trademarks of an organised armed group: military structure of camps, division of duties, and centralisation of weapons.[179] Under the assessment of Article 7(2), these findings were recalled.[180] The Trial Chamber reasoned that 'most of the *collectivité's* camps had put in place a military-type structure, and the Ngiti militia was headed by a president'.[181] The structural and hierarchical criteria for Article 7(2)(a) were borrowed from Article 8(f) findings, overlooking that the two articles have distinct standards and resulting in an underdeveloped assessment of organisational requirements under Article 7(2)(a).

In the *Bemba Trial Judgment*, the analysis of organised armed groups was also more detailed than that of the organisation requirement for crimes

[170] *Boškoski and Tarčulovski* (TC Judgment) (n 169) para 199; See also: Rödenhauser (n 25) 62ff.
[171] Rödenhauser (n 25)
[172] *Katanga* (TC Judgment) (n 121) para 136.
[173] *Prosecutor v Ntaganda* (Judgment on the appeal of Mr Ntaganda against the "Second decision on the Defence's challenge to the jurisdiction of the Court in respect of Counts 6 and 9") ICC-01/04-02/06 (15 June 2017) para 704.
[174] *Ongwen* (TC Judgment) (n 138) para 2685.
[175] *Prosecutor v Tadić* (Decision on the Defence Motion for Interlocutory Appeal on Jurisdiction) IT-94-1 (2 October 1995) para 70.
[176] *Katanga* (TC Judgment) (n 121) para 671.
[177] ibid.
[178] *Prosecutor v Katanga* (Minority Opinion of Judge Christine Van den Wyngaert to the Judgment pursuant to article 74 of the Statute) ICC-01/04-01/07 (7 March 2014) para 269.
[179] *Katanga* (TC Judgment) (n 121) para 674ff.
[180] ibid para 1139.
[181] ibid para 1139.

against humanity. The *Bemba* Trial Chamber first adopted the approaches of the *Lubanga* and *Katanga* Trial Chambers,[182] but added the additional indicator of responsible command, which includes the possibility to impose discipline.[183] In this way, it chose to follow the description of an organised armed group given in APII, which the Commentary to the AP II interprets as follows:

> The existence of a responsible command implies some degree of organization of the insurgent armed group or dissident armed forces, but this does not necessarily mean that there is a hierarchical system of military organization similar to that of regular armed forces. It means an organization capable, on the one hand, of planning and carrying out sustained and concerted military operations, and on the other, of imposing discipline in the name of a *de facto* authority.[184]

The *Bemba* Trial Chamber held that 'some degree of organization' includes 'the possibility to impose discipline and the ability to plan and carry out military operations'.[185]

Following in the footsteps of foregoing chambers, the *Ntaganda Judgment* dealt with the UPC/FPLC and considered this organisation to be both an 'organised armed group' as well as an organisation in the sense of Article 7(2)(a). In relation to an organised armed group it considered the following factors and indicators:

> (i) the existence of a command structure, the existence of headquarters, the issuing of political statements, and the use of official spokespersons; (ii) the military (operational) capacity of the armed group, which may be shown by, for example, the ability to define a unified military strategy, the use of military tactics, the ability to carry out (large scale or coordinated) operations, the control of territory, and having a territorial division into zones of responsibility; (iii) the logistical capacity of the armed group, indicated, among others, by the existence of a supply chain for military equipment, as well as by the group's ability to move troops around and to recruit and train personnel; (iv) the existence of an internal disciplinary system and the ability to implement IHL; and (v) the group's ability to speak with one voice, indicated, for example, by the capacity of the leadership to act on behalf of its members in political negotiations and to conclude agreements, such as cease-fire or peace agreements.[186]

Given the well-organised structure of the UPC/FPLC, the *Ntaganda* Trial Chamber deemed further discussion of Article 7(2)(a) unnecessary, emphasising the command structure in line with the Bemba Chamber. The *Ongwen* Judgment took a similar approach: the Sinia Brigade's hierarchy and structure

[182] *Prosecutor v Lubanga* (Judgment pursuant to Article 74 of the Statute) ICC-01/04-01/06 (14 March 2012) para 537; *Katanga* (TC Judgment) (n 121) para 1186.
[183] *Bemba* (TC Judgment) (n 127) para 136.
[184] ICRC Commentary on the AP I and II, para 4463.
[185] *Bemba* para (TC Judgment) (n 127) 135.
[186] ibid para 704.

sufficed to qualify it as an 'organised armed group', allowing the Chamber to follow the Katanga precedent without further analysis.[187]

Future cases are likely to follow this line of reasoning when armed groups are concerned. This was already suggested by the *Yekatom and Ngaïssona* case, where the Defence in the Pre-Trial phase questioned whether the Anti-Balaka militia had sufficient structure and hierarchy to qualify as an organisation. The PTC nonetheless found reasonable grounds to believe such an organisation existed.[188] However, rather than simply reproducing earlier jurisprudence, the Trial Chamber acknowledged that prior case law had not clearly defined the contours of an 'organisation'. It reiterated the statement of the *Katanga* Trial Chamber that it 'suffices that the organisation has a set of structures or mechanisms, whatever those may be, that are sufficiently efficient to ensure the coordination necessary to carry out an attack'. It nonetheless specified further that the organisation need not be a 'homogenous, or otherwise a strictly hierarchical, top-down organisation' and may include 'a variety of groups' so long as it has the mechanisms to coordinate an attack. This clarification moves in the right direction towards establishing a standard independent from the armed-group test under Article 8.[189]

While borrowing elements from the standard developed in Article 8 can help, there are strong reasons to develop independent criteria for the organisational policy element in CaH. The first reason is that, in relation to the concept of 'organised armed group', the hierarchy of sources in Article 21 functions differently. This is noticeable in particular with regard to Article 21(1)(b). This study understands Article 21(1)(b) to hold a reference to customary law and does not oppose customary law being considered at this level of the hierarchy.[190] The concept of an 'organised armed group' has a distinct customary law history from the organisational policy element, making its direct transplant from Article 8(f) to Article 7(2) an improper application of Article 21's hierarchy. There are too many differences in their customary history. First, the organisational policy element has no real international legislative precedent. Contrary thereto, the concept of organised armed group has legislative precedent in Common Article 3 GC's and in Article 1(1) APII. Second, tribunal jurisprudence developed

[187] *Ongwen* (TC Judgment) (n 138) para 2677, 2685.

[188] *Prosecutor v Yekatom & Ngaïssona* (Corrected version of Public Redacted Version of 'Decision on the Confirmation of Charges against Alfred Yekatom and Patrice-Edouard Ngaïssona) ICC-01/14-01/18-403-Red-Corr (14 May 2020) paras 67–70.

[189] *Prosecutor v Yekatom and Ngaïssona* (Trial Judgment) ICC-01/14-01/18 (24 July 2025) paras 3925–26.

[190] See also F Pocar, 'Symposium on the Rome Statute at Twenty: Transformation of Customary Law Through ICC Practice' (2018) doi.org/10.1017/aju.2018.55; J Powderly, 'The Rome Statute and the Attempted Corseting of the Interpretative Judicial Function: Reflections on Sources of Law and Interpretative Technique' in C Stahn (ed), *The Law and Practice of the International Criminal Court* (OUP, 2015) 478–79; A Pellet, 'Applicable Law' in A Cassese, P Gaeta and J Jones (eds), *The Rome Statute of the International Criminal Court: A Commentary*, vol 2 (OUP, 2002); GP Fletcher and JD Ohlin, 'Reclaiming Fundamental Principles of Criminal Law in the Darfur' (2005) 3 *Journal of International Criminal Justice* 539.

differently, as their statutes lack an organisational policy element, and case law on 'minimum organisation' for armed groups is broader and more consistent than for organisational policy. Tribunal case law on organisational policy is inconsistent; unlike armed group criteria, which are more grounded in customary law and treaties, organisational policy is recent and less settled. Uncritically transplanting factors from one concept to another without considering the organisation's specific characteristics is thus problematic in terms of the interpretative process. Note that, for instance, in the *Kenya Investigation Decision*, the 'under responsible command' requirement is also mentioned in the list of organisational policy. This is an example of ill-considered copying, as this does not fit groups such as the Mungiki.

Apart from the process showing flaws, there are also some problematic aspects in terms of the result. By reading into the term 'organisation', characteristics such as 'responsible command', the judges risk transgressing their interpretative role and entering the realm of law-making. This infusion of command-related criteria into Article 7 is particularly problematic given that the Court, at the same time, leaves entirely open what the textual meaning of 'organisation' itself entails. The result is a contradictory construction: judges overstep by introducing standards not grounded in the text, yet fail to clarify those that are. Even if such factors are framed as mere evidentiary indicators, this approach undermines legal certainty and runs counter to the legality principle, as it leaves parties without a stable understanding of what organisational features are required under Article 7(2)(a). For example, how many individuals can form an organisation? How long does a cooperation have to exist before being qualified as an organisation? Subsequent interpretations meet these considerations to a much larger extent.

b. The Purpose of the Group: Criminal Activities (Against the Civilian Population)

Discussed under this section are two factors:

- whether the group has criminal activities against the civilian population as a primary purpose;
- whether the group articulates, explicitly or implicitly, an intention to attack a civilian population.[191]

The scope of both factors differs. The first factor, in some regards, is broader than the second, since it refers to criminal activities and thereby departs from the more IHL-inspired and narrow approach referring to an attack. Nonetheless, some aspects of the first factor are narrower ('primary purpose') than the formulation of the second factor ('an intention'). Both factors remind of similar

[191] *Situation in Kenya* (Investigation Decision) (n 81) para 93.

formulations in the domain of organised crime. These indicators raise the question of their relevance and overlap, and whether they meaningfully apply to CaH.

In relation to the first factor, it can be observed that having criminal activities is not a factor which excludes many groups from the scope of crimes against humanity. Returning to the discussion on non-state actors, it is immediately clear that the examples provided of organised crime groups would fall under this scope, as they too have a criminal purpose. Olasolo notes that ICL and transnational criminal law have distinct purposes, requiring separate analysis, though some overlap exists. Applying his approach to these groups would not automatically exclude organised crime groups from CaH.[192] He concluded that the application of international criminal justice might be justified when:

(1) states are too weak to shield large groups of their own population against the collective crimes committed by such organisations; and
(2) the resulting destruction of the political system of the states concerned will have an evident impact on the international community.[193]

Also helpful to consider is May's perspective he calls 'an in-principle, morally minimalist, account of the justification of international prosecutions'.[194] He attached great weight to sovereignty and argued that it remains within the power of the State to organise state affairs in which other States cannot intervene.[195] May even contended that States have done 'a reasonable job of protecting the well-being and freedom of their subjects'.[196] In his view, sovereignty can only legitimately be pierced when the State fails to ensure the security of its citizens (the security principle).[197] International prosecution is justified when a State either harms its citizens or fails and is unable or unwilling to protect them.[198] This largely jurisdictionally influenced principle[199] is further supplemented by a second principle, ie, the international harm principle requiring 'a non-individualized feature of the victim'.[200] Only group-based harms offer an argument for international involvement, namely harm to humanity.[201] May's two-tier test justifies piercing state sovereignty and triggering international criminal proceedings.[202] The test aims to keep international intervention minimal, placing the

[192] H Olásolo, 'Is international criminal law an appropriate mechanism to deal with organised crime in a global society?' in H Van der Wilt and C Paulussen (eds), *Legal Responses to Transnational and International Crimes* (Edward Elgar, 2017) 50ff.
[193] ibid 66.
[194] May (n 104) 7.
[195] ibid 10–11.
[196] ibid 11.
[197] ibid 10–11.
[198] ibid 64ff, in particular 68.
[199] ibid 76–77.
[200] ibid 80ff, in particular
[201] ibid 83.
[202] He argued in favour of a discriminatory intent requirement but agrees with the abolishment of the war nexus. See: May (n 104) 124ff.

primary responsibility on the State. May interprets CaH narrowly, holding that international involvement is justified only when the actions of States or State-like actors make a domestic matter internationally relevant.[203] Ideally, both the victims and perpetrators are group-based – victims targeted for shared characteristics, and perpetrators acting on behalf of a State or State-like entity –and the harm is widespread and systematic.[204]

Luban is less minimalistic in his understanding of the normative footing of CaH. His legitimisation of this crime category being part of the traditional taxonomy of international crimes lies in the value it protects: the defining feature of these offences is the value they injure, namely, humanness.[205] He drew on Arendt to stress that humanity refers to humankind, not individual human qualities, framing CaH as the outcome of 'politics gone cancerous' in socially organised human communities.[206] In that regard, he focused on the collective character of CaH, which is reflected in the policy element.[207] One of its characteristic features, according to Luban, is that they are committed by politically organised groups acting under the colour of policy.[208] He noted that while the ICTY relaxed the state policy requirement compared to Nuremberg, a war nexus still implied army or government involvement. Under the Rome Statute's 'state or organizational policy' requirement, however, he concluded that crimes must be 'committed through political organization.'[209] Luban was more sceptical than May, rejecting the view that States generally protect their citizens effectively. The starting point is not a presumption in favour of the State but rather formulating a set of criteria on the basis of which a breach of sovereignty is legitimised. He critiques May for leaving little to no room for the list of crimes to expand progressively over time.[210] He sees the main purpose of ICL as criminalising state involvement, since national systems often cannot address it, though he does not require state involvement in every case.

These three authors share their view that CaH are crimes engaged at a political level, which is precisely the element absent from *mere* organised crime groups. The group's political involvement, which prevents national authorities from addressing the crimes, justifies international intervention. While not the sole factor for crimes against humanity, it helps narrow the scope of 'groups engaged in criminal activities.'[211] The number of groups drawn in by this type of indicator is huge. Judges should consider whether the criminal activities aim to undermine the political system, enabling groups to act with impunity; if not,

[203] ibid 88.
[204] ibid 89.
[205] Luban (n 1) 87.
[206] ibid 90.
[207] R Cryer and others, *An Introduction to International Criminal Law and Procedure,* 2nd edn (CUP, 2010) 239–40.
[208] Luban (n 1) 95–98.
[209] ibid 97.
[210] D Luban, 'Beyond Moral Minimalism' (2006) 20 *Ethics & International Affairs* 353–54.
[211] Olásolo (n 192) 58ff.

what justifies international intervention? This is why the next section explores further insights from organised crime studies.

ii. The Properties-Based Variant: Ozaki's UNTOC-inspired Definition

Appended to the *Bemba* Trial Judgment is Judge Ozaki's Separate Opinion, which advances a novel interpretation in ICL and critiques the majority's circular reasoning. This majority approach understood the term 'organisation' to be connected to 'the existence of the attack and not to its systematic or widespread nature', which 'presupposes that the organisation has sufficient resources, means and capacity to bring about the course of conduct or the operation involving the multiple commission of acts'.[212] The problem with this reasoning is that the attack itself seems to prove the organisation. Judge Ozaki instead proposed reading 'organisation' through the lens of the UNTOC Convention.[213] She rejected reliance on *ad hoc* tribunal case law and insisted that interpretation must begin with the Rome Statute itself.[214]

Her analysis began with the ordinary meaning of organisation, citing the Oxford English Dictionary – defining it as an organised body of people with a particular purpose–and Black's Law Dictionary – defining it as a body of persons, such as a union or corporation, formed for a common purpose – similar to the majority's approach.[215] The novel aspect of her examination lies in the second half of her reasoning and her reliance on UNTOC, which defines an organised criminal group as:

> a structured group of three or more persons, existing for a period of time and acting in concert with the aim of committing one or more serious crimes or offences established in accordance with this Convention, in order to obtain, directly or indirectly, a financial or other material benefit.[216]

Judge Ozaki acknowledged that the Court cannot directly rely on the UNTOC Convention. Still, she noted that the dictionary definitions endorsed by the majority overlap with UNTOC, since both require 'a collective, or plurality,

[212] *Bemba* (TC Judgment) (n 127) para 155; see also *Katanga* (TC Judgment) (n 121) para 1119.

[213] United Nations Convention against Transnational Organized Crime (adopted 15 November 2000 entered into force 29 September 2003) 2225 UNTS 209; see also: Protocol to Prevent, Suppress, Punish Trafficking in Persons, Especially Women and Children, Supplementing the United Nations Convention Against Transnational Organized Crime (adopted 15 November 2000, entered into force 25 December 2003) 2237 UNTS 319; Protocol Against the Smuggling of Migrants by Land, Sea and Air, Supplementing the United Nations Convention Against Transnational Organized Crime (adopted on 15 November 2000, entered into force 28 January 2004) 2241 UNTS 507; Protocol Against the Illicit Manufacturing of and Trafficking in Firearms, Their Parts and Components and Ammunition, Supplementing the United Nations Convention Against Transnational Organized Crime (adopted on 31 May 2001, entered into force 3 June 2005) 2326 UNTS 208.

[214] *Bemba* (TC Judgment) (n 127) para 26.

[215] ibid para 27.

[216] Art 2(a) UNTOC.

of persons' and 'a particular purpose or aim'.[217] Ozaki added that a 'certain degree of temporal duration or continuity' is required as this delineates 'an organization from, for example, a mere mob or otherwise randomly formed and dissolved group of people engaging in spontaneous criminal conduct'.[218] A requirement of some continuity of existence aligns with Article 2(c) UNTOC, which excludes groups 'randomly formed for the immediate commission of an offence' or 'in the course of a riot'.[219] Ozaki nonetheless rejected the UNTOC's requirement of a financial aim as this does not fit the definition of crimes against humanity in the Rome Statute. Her proposed definition was:

> i) a collectivity of three or more persons; (ii) existing for a certain period of time, which, at least, transcends the period during which the policy was formed and implemented; (iii) with a particular aim or purpose, whether it is criminal or not, and (iv) with a certain structure.[220]

Judge Ozaki's approach, unlike earlier liberal views, sharply distinguished issues of definition from issues of proof and evidence, offering the clearest interpretation yet. It sets out clear properties instead of a loose, non-exhaustive list from which proof of the *existence* of an organisation might only be inferred. In that regard, the requirements in Article 22(2) concerning strict construction are given greater consideration. Case law built on these four requirements would ensure far greater foreseeability than the *ad hoc*, case-by-case assessments prevalent in the ICC case law so far.

Another reason to consider this approach is that the conceptual refinement of the term 'organisation' in the field of organised crime is more advanced than in ICL. This field has a better empirical understanding of phenomena such as criminal organisations and how they operate.[221] Extensive research has been conducted on defining an organisation.[222] Interesting in this context is that the UNTOC's three-member requirement is stricter than the two-person threshold for conspiracy.[223] Furthermore, multiple models of organised criminal groups have been identified: hierarchical organisations, local-cultural organisations, enterprise-like structures and network structures.[224] Each of these models, in

[217] *Bemba* (TC Judgment) (n 127) para 28.

[218] ibid para 28.

[219] See *Travaux Préparatoires of the Negotiations of the United Nations Convention Against Transnational Organized Crime and the Protocols Thereto* (UNODC, Official Records, 2006) 15.

[220] *Bemba* (TC Judgment) (n 127) para 29.

[221] See further F Allum and S Gilmour (eds), *Handbook of Organised Crime and Politics* (Elgar Handbooks in Political Science, Edward Elgar, 2019).

[222] AV Orlova and JW Moore, 'Umbrellas or Building Blocks: Defining International Terrorism and Transnational Organized Crime in International Law' (2004) 27 *Houston Journal of International Law* 267, 282–84.

[223] Schloenhardt (n 22) 414.

[224] UNODC, *New Forms of Organised Crime: Network Structure* www.unodc.org/e4j/en/organized-crime/module-7/key-issues/networked-structure.html.

turn, comes with its own set of definitions or unique characteristics. That is also why Judge Ozaki's approach, with its technical-legal precision, merits attention.

The first problem with Ozaki's approach is that it is insufficiently grounded in the hierarchy of Article 21. Although Ozaki rightly criticises overreliance on tribunal jurisprudence, her use of UNTOC is also hard to justify under the Rome Statute's source hierarchy. She acknowledges that UNTOC cannot directly guide interpretation, yet immediately treats it as a central reference – a questionable choice, even if organised crime terminology is useful for shaping the concept of 'organisation'. Judge Ozaki could have framed UNTOC as reflective of customary law under Article 21(b), given its 189 parties. Yet this rationale is limited, as UNTOC addresses transnational crime, not international crimes. As UNTOC's legislative guide specifies, it only addresses 'groups that through their activities seek to obtain, directly or indirectly, a "financial or other material benefit"'.[225] This definition likely excludes groups with purely non-material goals, but it risks encompassing more organisations than intended by the Rome Statute. This is also why any judicial reliance on it should explicitly justify its status as a customary standard.[226] Despite its more developed nature, the UNTOC definition has also been blamed for being both over- and under-inclusive, and as such, this transplant is not without consequence.[227] The discussion on the scope of the concept is directed at two aspects: what type of crime falls under its scope ('what') and what type of organisation is needed to speak of organised crime ('who').[228]. To narrow its scope, this aspect is increasingly considered under the rubric of *serious* and organised crime.[229] For present purposes, only the second aspect matters: while organised crime was once seen as hierarchical with a strict division of labour, it now also includes looser networks without a clear structure.[230]

The analysis of Judge Ozaki halts at the UNTOC definition and does not consider the vast amount of academic, legal and institutional definitions. Although many notions of organised crime exist, Judge Ozaki does not reference European or American practice, which could offer a more accurate and relevant perspective. Whereas the UNTOC definition, and also the European definition

[225] *Legislative Guide for the Implementation of the United Nations Convention Against Transnational Organized Crime* (UNODC, 2004) 1031.

[226] K von Lampe, *Definitions of Organized Crime* www.organized-crime.de/organizedcrimedefinitions.htm.

[227] Orlova and Moore (n 222) 284; Paoli and Beken (n 19) 13.

[228] Paoli and Beken (n 19) 21-23.

[229] See EU example: Europol, *EU Serious and Organised Crime Threat Assessment (EU-SOCTA): Identifying the Priorities in the Fight Against Major Crime* www.europol.europa.eu/publications-events/main-reports/eu-serious-and-organised-crime-threat-assessment-eu-socta.

[230] Y Zabyelina, 'Unpacking Pandora's box: Defining transnational crime and outlining emerging criminal trends.' (2010) 4 *Central European Journal of International & Security Studies* 124, 128–29.

in the EU's Framework Decision on the fight against organised crime,[231] have a more conceptually broad legal definition, there is one particular definition that has been heavily relied on because it offers a different framework to analyse the concept. In 1997, the Council of the European Union connected the following characteristics to organised crime:

1) Collaboration of more than two people;
2) Each with his/her own appointed tasks;
3) For a prolonged or indefinite period of time;
4) Using some form of discipline or control;
5) Suspected of committing serious criminal offences;
6) Operating at an international level;
7) Using violence or other means suitable for intimidation;
8) Using commercial or business-like structures;
9) Engaged in money laundering;
10) Exerting influence on politics, the media, public administration, judicial authorities or the economy;
11) Determined by the pursuit of profit and/or power.[232]

The notable feature of this definition is that not all characteristics must be met: criteria 1, 3, 5, and 11 are mandatory, plus any two additional traits.[233] This flexible, widely used framework accommodates the evolving nature of criminal groups. While designed for law enforcement, it can also inform judicial interpretation, in a similar way to the factor-based list for 'organised armed groups,' but with the added benefit of specifying traits truly constitutive of an organisation. Even so, Ozaki's opinion shows reliance on selective sources. Although her use of UNTOC is valuable, it is questionable whether a purely linguistic approach could not have led to the same result. other interpretative paths might yield an even sharper understanding. Whereas the interpretative result is much more constructed than the abstract capacity formulation, and this interpretation is closer to the text, other interpretative pathways might offer an even more refined construction.

[231] Art 2 of the Council Framework Decision (EU) 2008/841/JHA of 24 October 2008 on the fight against organised crime [2008] OJ L300/42: 1. 'criminal organisation' means a structured association, established over a period of time, of more than two persons acting in concert with a view to committing offences [. . .] to obtain, directly or indirectly, a financial or other material benefit; 2. 'structured association' means an association that is not randomly formed for the immediate commission of an offence, nor does it need to have formally defined roles for its members, continuity of its membership, or a developed structure'.

[232] In 1997, this list of criteria was developed (see: Council of the European Union (1997) 6204/2/97. ENFOPOL 35, Brussels, 21 April 1997) which was subsequently used as the leading methodology in the EU (see: PC Duyne and TV Beken, 'The incantations of the EU organised crime policy making' (2009) 51 *Crime, Law and Social Change* 261, 270).

[233] See, eg, Europol, OCTA 2006, 7: 'OC groups are also becoming increasingly heterogeneous and dynamically organised in structural terms, moving towards loose networks rather than pyramidal monoliths'.

iii. Intermediate Conclusion: Slowly Arriving at the Constitutive Properties of an Organisation

This section highlights both challenges and opportunities. A key issue is that ICC case law rarely examines the characteristics truly constitutive of an organisation. Because most cases involve organised armed groups, Article 7(2)(a) is often treated as secondary to Article 8(2)(f), typically assessed via a backwards-looking list of inferences. While sufficient for armed groups, this approach leaves unclear which other types of groups fall under Article 7(2)(a), posing risks for future cases outside the archetype of an organised armed group. In terms of source doctrine, the decisions discussed were insufficiently motivated by using Article 21. Although the body of law on organised crime might offer opportunities, its use was insufficiently justified. In order to go beyond the traditional organised armed groups, it would be interesting to see how UNTOC could be a legitimate source of inspiration while adhering to the requirements set by Article 22.

Both pathways outperform previous approaches. The properties-based variant is especially strong, clearly defining which entities meet the standard. While fair labelling was less emphasised, both constructions are fairer to the accused than ad hoc, case-by-case assessments. Consequently, these two interpretative outcomes achieve a higher standard of clarity and fairness.

PATHWAY III

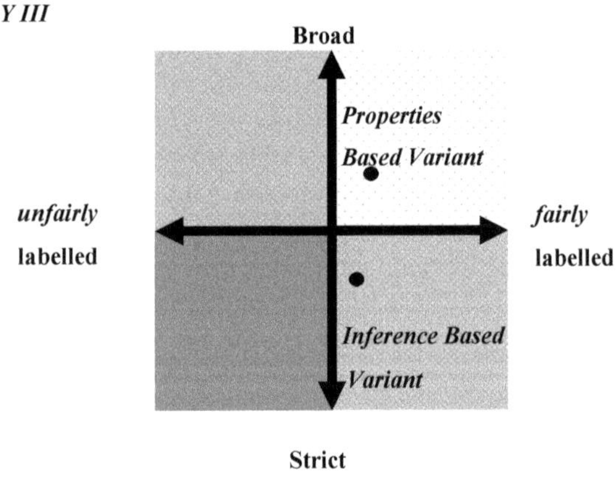

D. Typologies of an Organisation (Pathway IV)

A final approach to the organisation requirement considers specific types of entities. First are organisations that control territory, the broadest category, and clearly recognised under Article 7(2) in ICC case law. Second are state-like entities, a limitation proposed by only one ICC judge. Third are state entities, a strict reading no longer followed at the ICC, though some scholars continue to support it.

i. An Organisation in Control of a Territory

Judges repeatedly formulate the policy requirement as tied either to groups governing a specific territory or to groups capable of launching a widespread or systematic attack against civilians.[234] The second part of this standard formulation was already tackled under the second interpretative pathway addressing abstract formulations. The first part of this formulation is the focus of this section. Although it already came to light as a factor in the non-exhaustive list, it has not yet been discussed in detail. This is because the origin of the characteristic stems from viewing the organisation as something resembling a state entity very closely. While sometimes treated as an inference, much of the case law frames it as a distinct type of organisation, standing alongside groups capable of committing attacks. It is therefore addressed here as a separate typology, comparable to the sub-pathways of state-like and state entities and closely linked to the earlier discussion on organised armed groups.

In many ICC cases, the accused are members of non-state armed groups, so the organisation requirement is examined in that context. In Côte d'Ivoire, investigations focused on pro-Gbagbo and pro-Ouattara forces, which in 2011 controlled parts of the territory and engaged in hostilities.[235] The Pre-Trial Chamber held that a policy can be implemented either by groups governing a territory or by organisations capable of committing widespread or systematic attacks against civilians, framing these as alternatives. Thus, territorial control alone could suffice to trigger Article 7.[236]

Later, the Chamber listed non-exhaustive factors similar to those in the Kenya decision, again including territorial control. It thereby applied the same element to both the organisation and policy prongs. It is unclear how territorial control evidences a policy, or why such double use is justified. More broadly, the jurisprudence has not clarified how such lists should be constructed. The territorial component itself remains ambiguous, though its origin can be traced to the ICTY *Tadić* case, which recognised forces exercising de facto control over territory.[237] According to Robinson, one of the delegates of the Canadian government at the negotiation table in Rome, this case is particularly important since it had a paramount effect on the inclusion of the organisational policy element into the Rome Statute.[238] He accounted for the fact that the Canadian Proposal of 1 July 1998, introducing the policy element,[239] was particularly influenced by this *Tadic*

[234] *Katanga & Ngudjolo Chui* (CoC Decision) (n 75) para 396; *Bemba* (CoC Decision) (n 107) para 81.

[235] *Situation in Republic of Côte d'Ivoire* (Investigation Decision) (n 145) para 26.

[236] ibid.

[237] *Tadić* (Opinion and Judgment) (n 111) para 654: this decision was in turn influenced by the ILC Draft Code of 1991.

[238] See also recognising this influence: C Kreß, 'On the Outer Limits of Crimes Against Humanity: The Concept of Organization Within the Policy Requirement: Some Reflections on the March 2010 ICC Kenya Decision' (2010) 23 *Leiden Journal of International Law* 855; Van Schaack (n 8).

[239] Canadian Delegation, *Background Paper on Some Jurisprudence on Crimes Against Humanity* (1 July 1998); see also: R Dubler SC and M Kalyk, *Crimes against Humanity in the 21st Century, Law, Practice and Threats to International Peace and Security* (Brill | Nijhoff, 2018)

passage.[240] This was a remarkable turn in the development of the law on CaH. Up to that point in the negotiations, there were still a considerable number of delegates in favour of upholding a war nexus.[241] For those States, it was difficult to live with a low threshold of the disjunctive test of widespread or systematic attack. According to Bassiouni, the organisational policy element was inserted to keep at bay NGOs that wanted to expand CaH to massive human rights violations.[242] The fact that the origin story of the organisation policy element lies in the *Tadic* precedent is, in any event, an argument for a more restrictive consideration in its interpretation.

ii. A State-like Organisation

One of the most restrictive approaches to interpret the policy element in the ICC case law is that it can only be fulfilled by an organisation that partakes in at least some characteristics of a State. The prime example of such a strict position is that of Judge Kaul, who, in several dissenting opinions, sets out his arguments.[243] In the context of the *Kenya Investigation Decision*, Judge Kaul criticised that the organisation should *merely* 'have the capabilities to infringe basic human values.'[244] In his view, this low threshold resulted in the Court tackling potentially any infringement of human rights[245] Judge Kaul rejected the idea that CaH are defined by mass victimisation or extreme cruelty.[246] For him, their distinctiveness lies in being enabled by a State policy, planned and executed through public power, targeting civilians deprived of fundamental rights.[247]

Judge Kaul's interpretation held that the Statute's way of framing State and organisation next to each other is 'an indication that even though the constitutive

[240] Robinson (n 8) 50–51; see also H Von Hebel and D Robinson, 'Crimes within the jurisdiction of the Court' in RS Lee (ed), *The International Criminal Court, The Making of the Rome Statute, Issues, Negotiations, Results* (Kluwer Law International, 2009).

[241] P Hwang, 'Defining Crimes Against Humanity in the Rome Statute of the International Criminal Court' (1998) 22 *Fordham International Law Journal* 457, 498.

[242] CM Bassiouni, 'Negotiating the Treaty of Rome on the Establishment of an International Criminal Court' (1999) 32 *Cornell International Law Journal* 443, 462: Bassiouni chaired the drafting committee at the Rome Conference that finalised the text of Article 7.

[243] These three dissenting opinions: *Situation in the Republic of Kenya* (Dissenting Opinion of Judge Hans-Peter Kaul to the Decision Pursuant to Article 15 of the Rome Statute on the Authorization of an Investigation Into the Situation in the Republic of Kenya) ICC-01/09 (31 March 2010); *Prosecutor v Muthaura, Kenyatta & Ali* (Dissenting Opinion by Judge Hans-Peter Kaul to Pre-Trial Chamber II's 'Decision on the Prosecutor's Application for Summonses to Appear for Francis Kirimi Muthaura, Uhuru Muigai Kenyatta and Mohammed Hussein Ali') ICC-01/09-02/11 (15 March 2011); *Prosecutor v Ruto & Sang* (Dissenting Opinion by Judge Hans-Peter Kaul to Pre-Trial Chamber II's 'Decision on the Prosecutor's Application for Summons to Appear for WS Ruto, HK Kosgey and JA Sang)' ICC-01/09-01/11 (15 March 2011).

[244] *Situation in Kenya* (Investigation Decision) (n 81) para 90.

[245] *Situation in Kenya* (Dissenting Opinion of Judge Hans-Peter Kaul to the Decision Pursuant to Article 15 of the Rome Statute on the Authorisation of an Investigation Into the Situation in the Republic of Kenya) ICC-01/09 (31 March 2010) para 53.

[246] ibid para 52.

[247] ibid para 60.

elements of statehood need not be established those "organizations" should partake of some characteristics of a State'.[248] The entity should have quasi-state abilities, and its characteristics could involve the following:

a) a collectivity of persons;
b) which was established and acts for a common purpose;
c) over a prolonged period of time;
d) which is under responsible command or adopted a certain degree of hierarchical structure, including, as a minimum, some kind of policy level;
e) with the capacity to impose the policy on its members and to sanction them; and
f) which has the capacity and means available to attack any civilian population on a large scale.[249]

Although he refrained from excluding regional actors from falling under this definition, he heightened the standard by stating that it envisaged, in some shape or form, the involvement of higher echelons.[250] Deconstructing Judge Kaul's arguments reveals several interpretative methods and doctrinal influences.

By referring to Article 7(2)(a) as a 'jurisdiction-endowing provision elevating ordinary crimes to the level of international crimes', he revealed that his normative understanding of the crime is very much influenced by a jurisdictional logic.[251] There is no necessity for international prosecutions of mere violence-prone groups, mobs, groups of organised crime, groups of armed civilians or criminal gangs because the State will not fail to go after these private entities.[252] This position is very close to that of Bassiouni and Schabas,[253] and reflects much of the theory of May in 'that international prosecution is appropriate when the perpetrator is an agent of a State or State-like entity, or is attempting to advance a plan of the State'.[254]

Second, Judge Kaul analysed the different language versions of the policy element. He stated that the English formulation of organisational policy might lead some to conclude that it refers to 'the nature of such policy as being (only) of an organised, planned or systematic manner' and since the broader formulation in the English text does not address 'the question of attribution to a specific authorship', an entity is not required.[255] He cited the French text ('la politique d'un Etat ou d'une organisation') and the Spanish text of the Statute ('de conformidad con la politica de un Estado o de una organización'), and argued that the

[248] ibid para 51.
[249] ibid para 51.
[250] ibid para 43.
[251] ibid para 26.
[252] ibid para 52.
[253] C Bassiouni and WA Schabas, *The legislative history of the international criminal court*, vol 2 (International Criminal Law Series, Brill, 2016) 170.
[254] May (n 104) 88.
[255] *Situation in Kenya* (Dissenting Opinion of Judge Hans-Peter Kaul) (n 245) para 37.

Arabic, Chinese and Russian texts mirror the linguistic structure of the Spanish and French versions.[256] Having examined the different language versions, he cautioned that the English text is the odd one out and in contrast, the French, Spanish, Arabic, Chinese, and Russian versions all more clearly frame it as the policy of a State or organisation. He therefore concluded that the Statute opted that 'organizational' shall be construed as meaning to pertain to an organisation.[257] As the proposed interpretative solution at the end of this chapter demonstrates, this conclusion of Judge Kaul is correct, yet he makes the wrong linguistic assumptions.[258]

The third point is that Judge Kaul grounded his view in Nuremberg's legacy, contrasting with the Majority's reliance on the ad hoc tribunals.[259] He rightly questioned their neglect of the ad hoc tribunals' abandonment of the policy requirement but fell into a similar trap. While some precedents suggest the IMT included a policy element and the ICTY did not, others show the opposite.

Judge Kaul is very concerned with the strict construction of the term organisation. The rights of the accused necessitate, in his view, that this term is strictly construed. He rejected openly interpretations that are overly concerned with bringing justice to victims. This study affirms the primacy of strict construction in crime interpretation but rejects Kaul's excessively narrow application of it.

iii. A State Organisation

Unlike the examples above, this final interpretation is not reflected in ICC jurisprudence but has been explicitly rejected by the Chambers.[260] It is included here since it represents one of the most restrictive interpretations on the spectrum. It is held by Bassiouni, whose version of the policy element required the involvement of a state entity.[261] His argumentation was largely built around the need to differentiate between ordinary and international crime,[262] and puts forward an interpretation in line with the historical development of the crime.[263] He relies greatly on IMT and NMT jurisprudence in support of this vision[264] and emphasises an interpretation that does not include terrorist like organisations such as

[256] ibid para 37.

[257] ibid para 38.

[258] See Section 2.4.2, 349.

[259] *Situation in Kenya* (Investigation Decision) (n 81) paras 61–65, 86.

[260] A Chouliaras, 'A Strategic Choice: The State Policy Requirement in Core International Crimes' (2015) 28 *Leiden Journal of International Law* 953, 957.

[261] CM Bassiouni, *The Legislative History of the International Criminal Court: Introduction, Analysis and Integrated Texts*, 1st edn (Transnational Publishers, 2003) 152.

[262] CM Bassiouni, *Crimes Against Humanity: historical evolution and contemporary application*, 2nd edn (CUP, 2013) 8ff.

[263] ibid, 10–12.

[264] See, eg, *United States v Alstötter et al (the Justice Case)* Trials of War Criminals before the Nuremberg Military Tribunal under Control Council Law No 10, Vol III, 984; *United States v Ohlendorf et al (Einsatzgruppen case)* Trials of War Criminals before the Nuremberg Military Tribunal under Control Council Law No 10, Vol IV, 498.

al-Qaeda.[265] Based on a survey of 267 multilateral instruments, he distilled 25 categories of international crimes and found that CaH owe their international character to a state policy. This state policy justified international intervention, as the state was unlikely to act. Bassiouni warned that relying on mass victimisation could cause selective targeting.[266] It is the abuse of State power that turns a domestic crime into an international crime.[267]

What this point of view misses is what Bassiouni himself touched upon, and that is that it remains 'a matter of international legislative policy' how wide the net is cast.[268] The Rome Statute makes a choice to include an organisational policy element which cannot simply be ignored. It is therefore no surprise that his view changed,[269] and he later included 'groups or organisations of nonstate actors who have characteristics and capabilities similar to state actors, and who engage in large-scale atrocities against civilian populations'.[270] It is therefore also logical that Bassiouni's early point of view has largely lost support[271] and most reflections on the topic are now geared towards determining which non-state actors can fulfil the policy element.[272]

The systematic review of the ICC's case law reveals there are no decisions in which the judges support the narrow reading of only allowing a state policy to fulfil the policy element. The Court clearly held that 'the drafters of the Statute intended to exclude non-State actors from the term "organization", they would not have included this term in article 7(2)(a) of the Statute'.[273]

iv. Intermediate Conclusion: the Overstrictness of these Typologies

These last interpretative pathways are too narrow to be textually supported. Strict construction does not justify adding organisational properties not required by the text. This is exactly what is done here. It is not quite clear how textual primacy leads to the finding that a state entity is necessary or that an organisation requires state-like features. These interpretations also do not consider fairness. The extra thresholds created are unnecessary and are not justifiable in terms of the wrongfulness, harmfulness and blameworthiness of the label. These interpretations are qualified as follows:

Much of the reasoning under these typologies carries traces of IHL and seems to be inspired by the history of war crimes. Since Nuremberg, the crimes against humanity category has legally existed separately from the war crime category.

[265] C Davidson, *Crimes Against Humanity: Historical Evolution and Contemporary Application* (JSTOR, 2012).
[266] Bassiouni (n 262) 8–9.
[267] ibid 10.
[268] ibid 12.
[269] ibid 12.
[270] ibid 17 (footnotes omitted).
[271] Kreß (n 238) 859: Kress confirms that Bassiouni stands alone in his point of view.
[272] See, eg, Rodenhäuser (n 80).
[273] *Situation in Kenya* (Investigation Decision) (n 81) para 92.

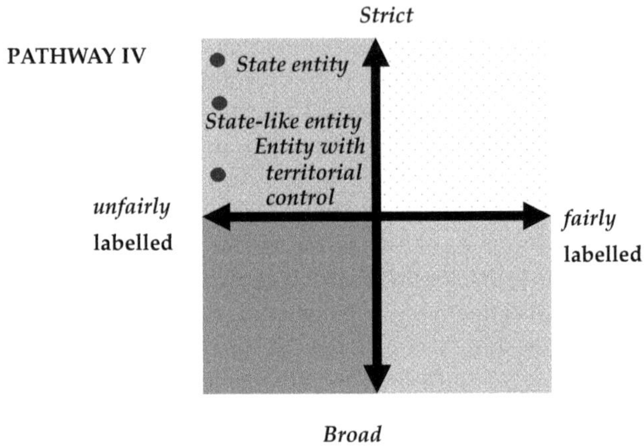

Nonetheless, traces of the war nexus existed until the ICTY judges decided that this was no longer a requirement for crimes against humanity. The Rome Statute, inspired by the *Tadić* precedent, further consolidated the separation of these two crime categories by introducing an alternative formulation of CaH that no longer required a war nexus.[274] Although the separation of these distinct crime categories has largely succeeded, traces of IHL logic still seem to be carried over to the interpretation of crimes against humanity. Requiring that an organisation has territorial control or the means to carry out an attack seems to be constructed with organised armed groups in mind. As previously shown, other non-state actors are increasingly important in ICL. This begs the question whether it would not be wise for ICC Judges to construct a separate standard of organisation, fitting of the crimes against humanity category. The concluding section formulates how such a construction could be articulated.

III. A PROPOSED INTERPRETATIVE SOLUTION

This book adopts a textual approach informed by a linguistic perspective to identify the entity envisaged by the Statute. Before explaining its two-step approach, it describes how this approach is grounded in the normative and historic logic underpinning the organisational policy element. This first step of this approach formulates the constitutive properties of an organisation. The second step follows in the footsteps of internal precedent and develops a list of additional inferences from which the existence of an organisation can be inferred.

[274] T Meron, 'War Crimes Law Comes of Age' (1998) 92 *American Journal of International Law* 462, 468.

A. The Normative and Historical Grounding of the Two-Step Approach

Rödenhauser attested to the fact that a wide variety of accounts exist on how to define CaH, ranging from characterising them as particularly inhumane human rights violations that 'deny their victims the status of human being', over crimes that 'harm the interests of humankind as a collective entity', to 'group crimes that are committed both against groups and by groups'.[275] Jalloh argued that underlying these divergent interpretations are contrasting views on the role of ICL.[276] Kress similarly observed that interpretations of CaH should be guided by the deeper rationales to establish the ICC in the first place.[277] Recalling the works of Luban, May and Olasolo, stressing the intrinsically political nature of CaH, it is precisely this element that necessitates the existence of the ICC. Atrocities are performed by collective endeavours that remain unpunished at the level of the State precisely because their political power gives them the tools to escape accountability. The ICC's reason for existence is to tackle those perpetrators within those entities and cast the net sufficiently wide while also not going beyond so as to diminish its effectiveness and catch too many little fish. The ICC exists to target groups with sufficient influence to shield crimes, aligning with Haque's observation that politically organised groups can co-opt or neutralise the State.[278] That is why this study supports the interpretation that the prime reason for ICL is to target those groups with considerable power, defusing the State's reaction to these crimes.

The organisational policy element emerged as a compromise between broad (disjunctive) and narrow (conjunctive or war-nexus) thresholds for CaH. This is why a solid interpretation should balance these extremes and be situated between Judge Eboe-Osuji's wide reading and Judge Kaul's restrictive approach.[279] The opinion of Judge Ozaki can be placed exactly in the middle, and although methodologically flawed, it offers a valuable bridge to the solution proposed. Its organised crime inspiration, which is informed by ample research into the increasing hybridisation (ie, criminal organisations have economic and political goals that are deeply intertwined)[280] and diversification (ie, mafia-structures but also network-like organisations exist)[281] of organised crime groups, is ideal to better understand these groups in the context of ICL. Drawing from

[275] Rodenhäuser (n 80) 915ff.
[276] Jalloh (n 149) 410.
[277] Kreß (n 238) 855.
[278] AA Haque, 'Group violence and group vengeance: Toward a retributivist theory of international criminal law' (2005) 9 *Buffalo Criminal Law Review* 273, 302.
[279] Jalloh (n 149) 411.
[280] A Sinn, 'Transnational Organised Crime: Concepts and Critics' in P Hauck and S Peterke (eds), *International Law and Transnational Organised Crime* (OUP, 2016) 31ff; see also T Makarenko, 'The Crime-Terror Continuum: Tracing the Interplay between Transnational Organised Crime and Terrorism' (2004) 6 *Global Crime* 129.
[281] P Williams, 'Transnational Criminal Networks' in J Arquila and D Ronfeldt (eds), *Networks and Netwars: The Future of Terror, Crime and Militancy* (RAND, 2001) 61ff.

the field of organised crime helps develop certain properties which ICL has failed to set out. However, a simple transplant of organised crime to ICL would include too many groups. Therefore, the next section not only develops a set of properties primarily inspired by insights on organised crime, but also adds the inferences precisely to limit the groups falling under Article 7(2) to groups with considerable political power. The two-step approach developed next is informed by the normative and historical perspective on CaH.

B. A Textual, Linguistic Analysis

Werle and Burghardt argued that although the term organisation can have three meanings – 'the act of putting things in order'; 'the order or structure itself' or 'an association of persons' – the fact that five authoritative texts hold the 'of construction' means that also the English text refers to the policy of an organisation and not an organised policy.[282] Based on a grammatical approach, Werle and Burghardt opted for the third interpretation and find that a 'single person or very small group cannot, terminologically, form an organisation, any more than a group of persons existing only for a specific situation or an assemblage of people without a common purpose can do so.'[283] Based on the different language formulations, Judge Kaul also argued that the English version is broader than the other language versions and concluded that organisational shall be construed as meaning to pertain to an organisation.[284] Wherle, Burghardt and Kaul argue that the phrase "of construction" implies an entity and that the English text must align with the other language versions. None of the pathways fully addresses the term or its variations across the Statute's six languages, a semantic issue interpreted divergently by scholars and judges.[285]

These opinions raise some interesting points. Is the 'of construction' less broad than the formulation of organisational policy? Are these formulations different in their requirement of involving an entity? Is the English version necessarily broader because it does not entail the 'of construction' and therefore potentially can be interpreted as *not* requiring proof of an organisation? Purely based on texts in the different language versions, is there a requirement for an entity behind the policy?[286]

[282] Werle and Burghardt (n 28) 1155.
[283] ibid 1156.
[284] *Situation in Kenya* (Dissenting Opinion of Judge Hans-Peter Kaul) (n 245) para 38.
[285] As also came to light when discussing the dissenting decision of Judge Kaul.
[286] Several specialists within the language and philosophy department of Ghent University were contacted and asked how, from a linguistic point of view, they would interpret the phrase in their respective languages. They were asked how they would interpret the phrase as requiring the organisational policy element on the basis of an extract from Article 7 of the Rome Statute and the Elements of Crimes, as well as part of Judge Kaul's Dissenting decision (paras 37–38).

The first step was to deepen the understanding of the language least familiar to the author. An interview with an Arabic language specialist confirmed that the 'of construction' implies an existing entity to which the policy is linked.[287] Unfortunately, no similar insights were provided by French or Spanish experts.[288] Given the English version's divergence from other language versions, a detailed analysis was conducted with Miriam Taverniers, Associate Professor of English Linguistics at Ghent University and an expert in grammatical metaphors and comparative linguistics. She developed the following analytical scheme:[289]

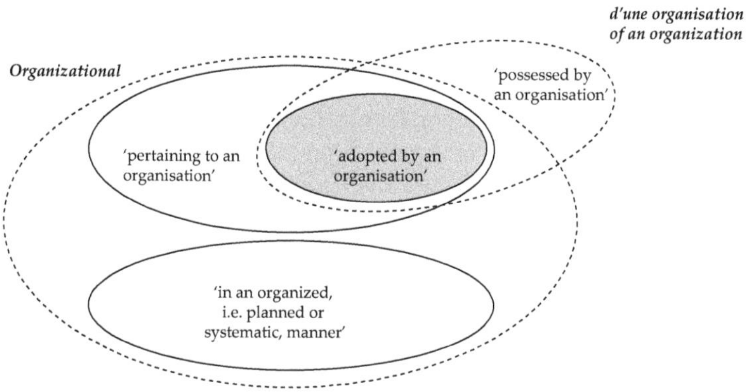

Engl.	**"in furtherance of**	*Fr.*	**"en application ou dans la poursuite de**
	a		la
	State or organizational policy		**politique d'un État ou d'une organisation**
	to commit such an attack"		**ayant pour but une telle attaque"**
		Sp.	**la** politica de un Estado o de una organización
		Ara.	=
		Rus.	=
		Chin.	=

On the basis of her insights, it was found that the English version uses a grammatical metaphor, which is a concept that 'has to do with the lack of a one-to-one relationship between meaning and form'.[290] It is a form often used to leave different options open to interpretation by way of *packing* different meanings

[287] M Termonia is a lecturer in Arabic and Islamic Studies at the UGhent. The interview took place on 24 October 2019.

[288] B Chen is a Chinese philosopher. Correspondence via email on this issue took place in October 2019 (on file with the author).

[289] This scheme was presented by Taverniers to this author on 23 October 2019 (on file with the author). She agreed that this scheme would be used for this study.

[290] M Taverniers, 'Semantics' in Geoff Thompson and others (eds), *Cambridge Handbook of Systemic Functional Linguistics* (CUP, 2019) 61.

into one phrase. Opposite stands a more congruent form.[291] Considering the context as described above, there are two reasons for choosing this type of textual ordering in the English text, and opting for the more metaphorical instead of the congruent form. The first is fluency. The 'of construction' in the English language is not the best option considering the established formulation of 'state policy'. One would never say 'policy of a state'; similarly, 'policy of an organisation', while more consistent, sounds awkward alongside the formulation of state policy. The second reason is that the grammatical metaphor gives an opportunity to interpret in coherence with the best meaning in light of the context. As the above scheme demonstrates, three potential meanings can be afforded to the term: 'pertaining to an organisation'; 'adopted by an organisation'; and 'in an organized, ie planned or systematic, manner'.[292] On the basis of the context, Taverniers argued that the organisation policy element, in her non-legal opinion, needs to be adopted by an organisation and, as a result, requires an entity. This linguistic argument is a more than convincing reason to decide that the interpretation of organisational policy needs an organisation.

C. A Two-step Approach of Properties and Optional Inferences

Now that the linguistic insights have led to the conclusion that an organisation is needed, it must be made clear what kind of entity qualifies. Most pathways skip defining an organisation's core properties, relying on inferences instead. The proposed approach remedies this and first sets essential properties and second, adds supporting inferences.

i. First Step: Properties of an Organisation

Drawing inspiration from case law, this study formulates a set of essential properties against which each case can be assessed.[293] The Katanga Judgment defines an organisation as an association . . . that sets itself specific objectives." While noting that this does not fully circumscribe its contours, the Chamber emphasised that an organisation must have a specific objective, considering also its means and resources.[294]

The second instance in which a judge revealed some of the properties of an organisation is in the dissenting opinion of Judge Ozaki. She departs from UNTOC to propose this definition of an organisation:

1) a collectivity of three or more persons;
2) existing for a certain period of time, which, at least, transcends the period during which the policy was formed and implemented;

[291] MAK Halliday, 'Language and knowledge: The "Unpacking" of Text' (1998) *Text in Education and Society* 157, 160.
[292] Interview with Taverniers in October 2019.
[293] See also Rodenhäuser (n 80) 928.
[294] *Katanga* (TC Judgment) (n 121) para 1119.

3) with a particular aim or purpose, whether it is criminal or not, and
4) with a certain structure.[295]

The third instance in which insights were given on the properties of an organisation is the dissenting opinion of Judge Kaul, articulating three criteria of the entity:

1) a collectivity of persons;
2) which was established and acts for a common purpose;
3) over a prolonged period of time[296]

From these formulations, four constitutive properties of an organisation emerge. Any assessment of CaH must establish that these four elements are present.

Collectivity of at least three persons

A textual reading, consistent with the *Katanga* Trial Chamber, shows that an organisation is an association requiring more than one person. Just as the notion of an attack on a civilian population implies a collective of victims, the perpetrators' side must likewise have a collective character. Organised crime instruments and studies confirm that such groups may consist of as few as two individuals acting in concert. This study proposes to raise the bar and require a collectivity of at least three persons.[297] This raises the UNTOC's threshold and, in that way, ensures stricter construction and fairer labelling for the gravest crimes.

A common and identifiable purpose

All three of the presented interpretations in this conclusion tie the existence of an organisation to a specific purpose. Similarly, the linguistic analysis revealed that for something to be organised in nature, a purpose is needed. Evidence must show a clear common purpose, though not necessarily a criminal one. This does not add liability but recalls concepts of collective criminality, particularly Joint Criminal Enterprise (JCE).[298] The ICC has not taken over the JCE doctrine but rather developed 'a doctrine of co-perpetration based on the control over crime theory'.[299] The only reference to a common purpose is found in Article 25(d) of the Rome Statute, which holds a person liable who '[i]n any other way contributes to the commission or attempted commission of such a crime by *a group of persons acting with a common purpose*'. The common purpose serves

[295] *Bemba* (Separate opinion of Ozaki) (n 129) para 29.
[296] *Situation in Kenya* (Dissenting Opinion of Judge Hans-Peter Kaul) (n 245) para 51.
[297] Rodenhäuser (n 80) 915ff.
[298] See *Prosecutor v Tadic* (Appeals Chamber Judgment) IT-94-1-A (15 July 1999).
[299] See further JD Ohlin, 'Joint Intentions to Commit International Crimes' (2011) 11 *Chicago Journal of International Law* 693; JD Ohlin, E Van Sliedregt and T Weigend, 'Assessing the Control Theory' (2013) 26 *Leiden Journal of International Law* 725; S Kafedžić, 'Determining Modes of Liability in International Criminal Law: Why the Common Purpose Doctrine is the Strongest Legal Response to Mass Atrocity Crimes' in C Riffel and R Burke (ed), *New Zealand Yearbook of International Law* (Brill | Nijhoff, 2018).

to show how a group organises itself, not to link individuals to specific acts. The threshold is low–meant only to distinguish organised groups from random associations–a notion reinforced by UNTOC's definition of a criminal organisation as a structured group.[300]

A prolonged period of time

In a similar fashion to the previous property, this property quite logically follows from the fact that something has to exist for a certain amount of time before being referred to as an organisation. All three of the judicial decisions underscore this requirement. Again, this standard is comparable to that of UNTOC, which mentions that the organisation has to exist for 'a period of time.'[301]

A certain durability is required, but this does not mean that a quantitative standard should be imposed. In this regard, the formulation in the 1995 working definition of the Council of the European Union helpfully explains this factor as an 'indication of stability and potential permanence'.[302] The obligation for the judge is thus to assess whether the association existed for a time that suggests such stability and permanence.

Structure: more than a loose collaboration

In the three cited judicial decisions, only the opinion of Judge Ozaki recalls that there has to be a certain structure to qualify as an organisation. This judge thereby used the UNTOC standard of structured group, which is a group 'not randomly formed for the immediate commission of an offence'. It does not need to have 'formally defined roles for its members, continuity of its membership or a developed structure'. A similar definition can be found in the Framework Decision 2008/ 841/ JHA of the Council of the European Union of 24 October 2008 on Combatting Organized Crime that refers to a 'structured association, established over a period of time, of more than two persons acting in concert with a view to committing offences'.[303]

Critics note that existing definitions of organised crime fail to capture less hierarchical, flexible networks, as such groups increasingly operate as loose, dynamic associations rather than rigid hierarchies. It would be counterintuitive for organised crime to require stricter structural thresholds than ICL, which addresses more serious offences; judges should therefore assess whether an association's form evidences some degree of organisation rather than demand a formal structure.[304]

[300] Art 2(a) UNTOC see also: Schloenhardt (n 22) 414.
[301] ibid.
[302] Sinn (n 280).
[303] See F Calderoni, Organized Crime Legislation in the European Union, Berlin, Heidelberg, Springer, 2010, 27.
[304] Europol, OCTA 2006, 7.

ii. Second Step: Additional Inferences

As shown, the system of inferences need not be dismissed but should be refined to align with the textual approach. Its main flaw is the absence of a minimum set of required indicators. Drawing on Judge Ozaki's reasoning, UNTOC, and the 1997 EU framework, this study proposes a structured list of inferences, with at least one indicator proven per category, thereby ensuring greater legal certainty than a case-by-case approach.

The **first category of inferences** concerns the **reach and power of an organisation** and adds to the constituent properties as formulated above. Judges should be able to infer whether the organisation has at least one of these three characteristics. Either the organisation has a:

- criminal purpose, ie criminal activities against the civilian population;
- political power;
- or territorial control.

The **second set of inferences** concerns **the capability to develop a policy** suitable to direct an attack against a particular victim population. This set of inferences is particularly formulated around the notion of *capability* denoting 'a unique fitness for achieving a defined end' and is chosen instead of ability, as capability is a better 'choice in contexts requiring a greater degree of precision'.[305] It is also a notion consistently used in ICC case law, which means it can be easily implemented. In order to have this capability, it needs to be proven that the entity can be

- hierarchical in nature;
- represents a complex structure;
- or has a complex decision-making process.

The first inference on hierarchy is, in large part, a continuation of the ICC jurisprudence, as it has been mentioned several times.[306] The second inference is precisely to allow for inclusion under the organisation requirement of organisations going beyond this notion of a hierarchical organisation. The field of organised crime has already acknowledged that the mafia-type structures have been traded in for more network-type structures. The network-type structure entails horizontally connected offender groups operating across regional and transnational levels. These range from small, loosely associated groups without hierarchy, to medium-sized core groups with distinct planning and operational tiers, and larger formations of twenty to fifty members with multilayered hierarchies and chains of command. Such groups cooperate intermittently and

[305] Ability, capacity, capability. Merriam-Webster's Dictionary of Synonyms. Springfield, MA; Merriam-Webster Inc; 1984:4.

[306] See, eg, *Ntaganda*, Judgment (n 134), para 769.

sustain informal links.[307] Non-state actors committing international crimes have increasingly diversified, which raises the issue whether it is necessary to infuse the organisation provision with the obligation of being hierarchical. This study does not see how a textual approach would necessitate such a reading, and when other considerations - teleological and contextual – underscore other organisations being included as well.

The **third set of inferences concerns the capability to attack** a victim population and is more directed at making clear how, at a practical level, the organisation was capable of executing this attack. Whether the organisation has the capability is inferred from whether they have:

- certain logistics such as an advanced communication system;
- certain infrastructure, such as advanced military camps;
- certain resources such as access to certain raw materials (oil, coal, etc.);
- access to weapons;
- or territorial control.

These more specific inferences are found throughout the case law and do not represent a novelty.

IV. CONCLUSION

This case study underscores that the policy element is first and foremost directed at excluding crimes of individuals which might fit a pattern of widespread crime waves but are not tied together by a collective entity behind it. This crime category should be understood as a *collective* crime with an 'associative dimension'.[308] Attaching the CaH label has an expressive function: it is reserved for a particular type of crime and represents a particular type of wrongdoing, harmfulness and blameworthiness. Crimes against humanity must remain a distinct category reserved for atrocities that are collective and politically driven. Overextension dilutes its meaning; strict construction and fair labelling guard against that risk. The organisational policy element ensures that isolated or opportunistic crimes are excluded by requiring a link to an organised entity.

This chapter advanced a balanced interpretation: grounding the definition in textual primacy, it identifies the *organisation* as a collectivity of at least three persons, united by a common purpose, existing with stability and minimal structure. This approach preserves the expressive and moral gravity of crimes against humanity – crimes born of politics turned *cancerous* – by ensuring that only those truly collective wrongs receive this most serious label. This approach could function as a roadmap to judges in setting out the necessary qualities of

[307] Sinn (n 280) 30.
[308] ibid.

the concept of organisational policy. It would allow for a better respect of the principle of legality, as this principle requires a differentiation between the legal elements and how something is proven. Foreseeability would be enhanced considerably through defining properties rather than merely having a non-exhaustive list of inferences determine decision-making in this respect. This approach has attempted to fill the gap in terms of the constitution of the concept of organisational policy and provides understanding by setting out its necessary properties.

The solution offered furthermore stems from the belief that it is not sufficient to think that judges *will know a crime against humanity when they see it*. The ontological haziness, interpretative divergence and general historical confusion on this element have proven that more tools are needed to arrive at a more consistent and legality-proof reading of organisational policy. To accommodate both the principle of legality as well as the principle of fair labelling, this interpretative solution is found to adequately protect against overinclusive and general devaluation of the crime category, while at the same time allowing for a particular set of crimes of a particular set of non-state actors to be labelled as crimes against humanity.

Case Study 2

Labelling and Interpreting Forced Marriage

I could not refuse because I was not free. I was under his authority.[1]

I. INTRODUCTION

SINCE NUREMBERG, EVERY STATUTE of an international tribunal with jurisdiction over crimes against humanity has concluded its enumeration of criminal acts with the residual category of 'other inhumane acts'.[2] To the extent that some of the conduct that arose in international proceedings could not be qualified under the listed crimes, this category has been used to address a wide range of crimes not specifically listed in the Statutes, and as such, allowed to respond to new conduct.[3] Article 7(1)(k) of the Rome Statute (RS or Statute) follows this lineage and specifies that 'other inhumane acts of a similar character intentionally causing great suffering, or serious injury to body or to mental or physical health' are included as crimes against humanity. As a result of the growing call to tackle sexual violence, the Statute included a broad list of sexual crimes, with, at the end, a second residual category that resembles the 'other

[1] *Prosecutor v Ongwen (*Testimony of Witness P-0236) ICC-02/04-01/15-T-16-Red-ENG (transcript 16 November 2015) 22.

[2] Category of other inhumane acts in instruments adopted prior to the Rome Statute in chronological order: Nuremberg Charter (annex to the Agreement for the Prosecution and Punishment of the Major War Criminals of the European Axis, signed 8 August 1945) Art 6(c); Charter of the International Military Tribunal for the Far East (annexed to the Special Proclamation by the Supreme Commander for the Allied Powers, 19 January 1946) Art 5(c); Statute of the International Criminal Tribunal for the former Yugoslavia (adopted by UNSC Res 827, 25 May 1993) Art 5(i); Statute of the International Criminal Tribunal for Rwanda (adopted by UNSC Res 955, 8 November 1994) Art 3(i); Instruments adopted after the Rome Statute in chronological order: Regulation No 2000/15 on the Establishment of Panels with Exclusive Jurisdiction Over Serious Criminal Offenses (adopted 6 June 2000) Art 5.1(k); Statute of the Special Court for Sierra Leone (annexed to the Agreement between the UN and the Government of Sierra Leone, signed 14 August 2000) Art 2(i); Statute of the Extraordinary Chambers in the Courts of Cambodia (annexed to the Agreement between the UN and the Royal Government of Cambodia, signed 6 June 2003) Art 5; Law No 05/L-053 on the Specialist Chambers and Specialist Prosecutor's Office (3 August 2015) Art 13(j).

[3] See further ST Jyrkkiö, 'Other Inhumane Acts as Crimes against Humanity' (2011) *Helsinki Law Review* 183.

inhumane acts' category. Article 7(1)(g) stipulates a crime of 'any other form of sexual violence of comparable gravity'.[4]

The use of these residual categories presents a particularly interesting case study in terms of the potential collisions with the legality principle. First, these categories have been qualified as *ejusdem generis* provisions. *Ejusdem generis* means 'of the same genus'[5] or more generally, 'things of the same kind'.[6] The principle instructs judges to extend the residual clause only to conduct of the same kind, applying a form of analogical reasoning.[7] Given the ban on analogy in Article 22(2), it is a delicate assessment to include something under this category because it is of a similar or analogical gravity, while at the same time not conducting a forbidden extension by analogy. Second, these two residual categories, because of their open-ended nature and despite their built-in limitation of similar gravity, present a risk for broad interpretations violating the principle of strict construction. Third, the logic of these residual categories is that they should be used only when other labels fail. This consequently entails an examination of more than only the residual label but involves the listed labels as well.

This is also why the labelling practice is examined in relation to fact patterns labelled as forced marriage, a phenomenon that has triggered the application of both residual and listed labels. Forced marriage has raised international concern, and several international criminal courts and tribunals have been tasked with the legal qualification of this phenomenon. Many labels circulate, and the phenomenon has been denominated by a variety of concepts 'including, but not limited to, marriage by capture, servile marriage, forced conjugal associations, war brides, and marriage in absentia'.[8] Also, labels used in other fields have become important to International Criminal Law (ICL). For example, the discussion in International Human Rights Law (IHRL) on the differences and similarities of forced and arranged marriage has relevance for the discussion in ICL.[9] At the

[4] The SCSL Statute, as well as the Law on the Kosovo Specialist Chambers, hold a category of 'other sexual violence'. The ECCC, ICTY and ICTR Statutes hold no other sexual crimes apart from rape.

[5] D MacKay, 'The Ejusdem Generis Principle of Interpretation' (1920) 90 *Central Law Journal* 285.

[6] KS Gallant, *The Principle of Legality in International and Comparative Criminal Law* (CUP, 2009) 124; see also F Baetens, 'Ejusdem Generis and Noscitur a Sociis in Municipal and International Law: Interpretative Cross-Fertilisation?' in J Klinger, Y Parkhomenko and C Salonidis (eds), *Between the Lines of the Vienna Convention? Canons and Other Principles of Interpretation in Public International Law* (Wolters Kluwer, 2019) 133.

[7] See ch 5, Intro and s II(B).

[8] A Bunting, BN Lawrance and RL Robert, 'Introduction: Something Old, Something New? Conceptualizing Forced Marriage in Africa' in A Bunting, BN Lawrance and RL Robert (eds), *Marriage by Force? Contestation over Consent and Coercion in Africa* (Ohio University Press, 2016) 1.

[9] See NA Goodfellow, 'The Miscategorization of Forced Marriage as a Crime against Humanity by the Special Court for Sierra Leone' (2011) 11 *International Criminal Law Review* 831; M Enright, 'Choice, Culture and the Politics of Bel ongoing: The Emerging Law of Forced and Arranged Marriage' (2009) 72 *The Modern Law Review* 331; S Anitha and A Gill, 'Introduction: Framing forced marriage as a form of violence against women' in S Anitha and A Gill (eds), *Forced Marriage: Introducing a Social Justice and Human Rights Perspective* (Zed Books, 2011) 3–5.

national[10] and regional level,[11] the term of forced marriage has been used as an 'umbrella term' to connote a range of issues.[12] Sometimes the label emphasises the sexual aspect of this phenomenon and qualifies it primarily as a type of sexual violence.[13] Other labels find the sexual nature to be of lesser importance and qualify it as another inhumane act in the hopes of also capturing the non-sexual harm of the crime.[14] In other instances, the servile nature of the crime resulted in the categorisation as slavery or sexual slavery.[15] Several experts have named the phenomenon a gender-based crime as well,[16] more precisely, a form of gender-based persecution.[17]

Because this chapter's focus is on the legal characterisation by the ICC judges of forced marriage, it primarily assesses whether, when and how fact patterns are brought under one of the following qualifications:

1. Enslavement, a listed non-sexual crime (Art 7(1)(c) Rome Statute)
2. Sexual slavery, a listed sexual crime (Art 7(1)(g) Rome Statute)
3. The residual category of other inhumane acts (Art 7(1)(k) Rome Statute)

[10] See, eg, H Askola, 'Responding to Vulnerability – Forced Marriage and the Law' (2018) 41 *UNSWLJ* 977; I Haenen, *Force & Marriage: The criminalisation of forced marriage in Dutch, English and international criminal law* (Intersentia, 2014).

[11] The right to marry freely is protected under the Universal Declaration of Human Rights (adopted 10 December 1948) UNGA Res 217 A(III) Art 16(2) and International Covenant on Civil and Political Rights (adopted 16 December 1966, entered into force 23 March 1976) 999 UNTS 171 Art 23(2); Convention on the Elimination of All Forms of Discrimination against Women (adopted 18 December 1979, entered into force 3 September 1981) 1249 UNTS 13 Art 16 qualifies forced marriage as a form of discrimination against women. At the African level, Protocol to the African Charter on Human and Peoples' Rights on the Rights of Women in Africa (adopted 1 July 2003, entered into force 25 November 2005) Art 6 requires marriage to take place with the free and full consent of both parties; in Europe, action has been taken at the level of the European Union (eg Fundamental Rights Agency, *Addressing forced marriage in the EU: legal provisions and promising practices*, 2014). The Inter-American Convention on the Prevention, Punishment, and Eradication of Violence against Women, Convention of Belém do Pará (adopted 9 June 1994, entered into force 5 March 1995) does not specify anything on marriage but it has been reported on by this Convention's monitoring mechanism: Mecanismo De Seguimiento Convención Belém Do Pará (Mesecvi), *Informe Hemisférico Sobre Matrimonios Y Uniones Infantiles, Tempranas Y Forzadas En Los Estados Parte De La Convención De Belém Do Pará (MESECVI/CEVI/doc.265/21)*, 29 November 2021).

[12] E Rude-Antoine, *Forced marriages in Council of Europe member states: a comparative study of legislation and political initiatives* (Council of Europe Publishing, 2005) 7.

[13] JE Burnet, 'Situating Sexual Violence in Rwanda (1990-2001): Sexual Agency, Sexual Consent, and the Political Economy of War' (2012) 55 *African Studies Review* 97.

[14] ASJ Park, '"Other inhumane acts": Forced marriage, girl soldiers and the Special Court for Sierra Leone' (2006) 15 *Social & Legal Studies* 315.

[15] I Haenen, 'The Parameters of Enslavement and the Act of Forced Marriage' (2013) 13 *International Criminal Law Review* 895; PV Sellers, 'Wartime Female Slavery: Enslavement' (2011) 44 *Cornell International Law Journal* 115–43.

[16] M Frulli, 'Advancing International Criminal Law: The Special Court for Sierra Leone recognizes forced marriage as a "New" Crime against Humanity' (2008) 6 *Journal of International Criminal Justice* 1033, 1039 and in particular fn 26; V Oosterveld, 'The special court for Sierra Leone's consideration of gender-based violence: Contributing to transitional justice?' (2009) 10 *Human Rights Review* 73.

[17] L Davis, 'Reimagining Justice for Gender-Based Crimes at the Margins: New Legal Strategies for Prosecuting ISIS Crimes Against Women and LGBTIQ Persons' (2018) 24 *William & Mary Journal Of Women and The Law* 521; Haenen (n 10) 335.

4. The residual category of other forms of sexual violence (Art 7(1)(g) Rome Statute)
5. Gender-based persecution (Art 7(1)(h) Rome Statute)

Apart from assessing interpretations in terms of their coherence with Article 22, this chapter also evaluates labels in terms of their conformity with the principle of fair labelling. A crucial issue in this regard is the question of how this label is informed and whether the perspective of the accused, victim or the international community weighs in on the label chosen. This case study reveals that the perspective of the victim in labelling forced marriage has become increasingly important, which creates tensions with the principle of strict construction.[18]

Applying these labels also involves a problem of the concurrence of crimes. When the same facts satisfy the legal definition of multiple crimes, several crime labels can be used to qualify these facts.[19] This practice of cumulative charging and convicting is not strictly prohibited under the ICC's system nor other ICL systems,[20] but judges have limited it when it is unfair to the accused.[21] Accordingly, the Appeals Chamber in the *Čelebići case* held it was only possible to charge cumulatively when the conduct involves at least one *distinct* material element (*Čelebići* test).[22] The *Ongwen* Pre-Trial Chamber and Trial Chamber endorsed the *Čelebići* test,[23] but the *Bemba* Pre-trial Chamber had a more restrictive test and found that multiple charges cannot be brought on the basis of the same evidence.[24] In any event, cumulative conviction is generally not accepted where one crime is completely subsumed under the other. As discussed in relation to the principle of fair labelling,[25] drawing from 'the utility of cumulative charging from the point of view of expressivism', some scholars have argued that limiting it impedes achieving

[18] JS Eskauriatza, '"Complete Labelling" and Domestic Prosecutions for Crimes Against Humanity' (2021) *Criminal Law Forum* 36.

[19] See C-F Stuckenberg, 'Cumulative charges and cumulative convictions' (2015) *The Law and Practice of the International Criminal Court* 840.

[20] The ICTY, ICTR, SCSL and STL allowed for cumulative convictions; see BC Majola, 'Cumulative Charges under International Criminal Law: Issues and Perspectives', *Promoting Accountability under International Law for Gross Human Rights Violations in Africa* (Brill Nijhoff, 2015).

[21] See R Bartels, *The Interplay between International Human Rights Law and International Humanitarian Law during International Criminal Trials* (Amsterdam Law School Legal Studies Research Paper, 2018) 7–8.

[22] *Prosecutor v Delalic et al (Čelebići case)* (Appeals Judgment) IT-96-21-A (20 February 2001) paras 411–13; as endorsed by *Prosecutor v Bemba* (Judgment on the Appeal of Mr Jean-Pierre Bemba Gombo against Trial Chamber III's 'Judgment pursuant to Article 74 of the Statute') ICC-01/05-01/08 (8 June 2018).

[23] *Prosecutor v Ongwen* (Decision on the Confirmation of Charges) ICC-02/04-01/15 (26 March 2016) paras 29–33; *Prosecutor v Ongwen* (Trial Judgment) ICC-02/04-01/15 (4 February 2021) para 3037.

[24] *Prosecutor v Bemba* (Decision on the Confirmation of Charges) ICC-01/05-01/08 (15 June 2009) para 202.

[25] See ch 5, s III(B).

gender justice.[26] However, given the strain this method puts on the defence that has limited resources to respond to every charge, extensive ways of applying cumulative charging should be restricted.[27] Cumulative charging is also problematic when applying a residual and listed label to the same facts. Given that residual categories such as the other inhumane category should only be used when other labels fail, this type of cumulative conviction for the same facts is unacceptable.

This chapter argues that the most appropriate interpretative response to cases of forced marriage is to first determine whether an existing listed crime applies – primarily slavery or sexual slavery, depending on the sexual dimension of the conduct. In making this distinction, judges should consider the victims' perspective and the nature of the harm suffered. Only when no listed label fits should the residual categories be invoked. It is proposed that ICC judges refine and apply the *Čelebići* test, using residual categories solely where a distinct element renders a listed crime inapplicable, not merely where additional elements exist. The chapter also examines how gender-based persecution may serve to cumulatively address forced marriage practices.

II. SEXUAL AND GENDER-BASED CRIMES

Before turning to the ICC's current approach, it is instructive to recall how earlier tribunals addressed sexual violence and how gender-based violence gradually came to be integrated into the framework of international criminal justice. The ICTY and ICTR, whose Statutes only listed rape,[28] often charged sexual violence as 'outrages upon personal dignity' or 'humiliating and degrading treatment'. Experts stated that this framing obscured the nature of sexual violence as a violation of bodily integrity and sexual autonomy.[29] In *Furundžija*, for example, rape was described as a 'most humiliating and degrading attack upon human dignity', with the Chamber concluding that dignity outweighed legality concerns in broadening the definition.[30] Despite the critique that this language did not grasp the core of sexual violence, violating bodily security and autonomy rather than their honour,[31] it was used to qualify not only rape,[32] but

[26] L Green, 'First-class crimes, second-class justice: Cumulative charges for gender-based crimes at the International Criminal Court' (2011) 11 *International Criminal Law Review* 529, 530; F O'Regan, 'Prosecutor vs. Jean-Pierre Bemba Gombo: The Cumulative Charging Principle, Gender-Based Violence, and Expressivism' (2012) 43 *Geo J Int'l L* 1323.

[27] Majola (n 20); see also C Stahn, *A Critical Introduction to International Criminal Law* (CUP, 2019) 360–65.

[28] ICTY Statute Art 5(g); ICTR Statute Art 3(g).

[29] See KD Askin, 'Sexual violence in decisions and indictments of the Yugoslav and Rwandan tribunals: Current status' (1999) 93 *American Journal of International Law* 97, fn 31.

[30] *Prosecutor v Furundžija* (Trial Judgment) IT-95-17/1 (10 December 1998) paras 174–84.

[31] K Boon, 'Rape and forced pregnancy under the ICC statute: Human dignity, autonomy, and consent' (2000) 32 *Columbia Human Rights Law Review* 625, 627.

[32] *Prosecutor v Kunarac et al* (Trial Judgment) IT-96-23-T& IT-96-23/1-T (22 February 2001) para 159.

also forced undressing,[33] forcing prisoners to perform oral sex on each other,[34] or forcing victims to dance naked.[35] Critics argued this reinforced stereotypes of women as passive victims,[36] and undermined the accused's rights, since humiliation depended merely on the victim's subjective sensitivity.[37] The *Kunarac* Trial Chamber therefore held that outrages upon personal dignity should be evaluated on an objective rather than a subjective basis. The conduct must be such that a reasonable person would be outraged.[38]

Although the statutes only list rape as a sexual crime, the ICTs' case law elucidates more broadly when violence is considered *sexual*. In the *Kvočka* case, sexual mutilation not amounting to enforced sterilisation was qualified as sexual violence.[39] In the *Todorovic case*, the ICTY Trial Chamber qualified biting a penis and kicking in the genital area as sexual assault.[40] Furthermore, the sexual nature of an act not only depends on physical contact.[41] However, defining what counts as 'sexual' is obscured by the frequent classification of sexual violence as an 'other inhumane act'.[42] At the SCSL, for instance, the AFRC Trial Chamber held that since the Court's Statute contained an exhaustive list of sexual crimes, the residual offence of 'other inhumane acts' had to be interpreted narrowly and limited to non-sexual conduct amounting to an affront to human dignity.[43]

In the Rome Statute negotiations, women's groups, particularly the Women's Caucus for Gender Justice (WCGJ), from 1997 onwards became increasingly influential.[44] Their advocacy, first and foremost, focused on shifting sexual crimes away from the 'dignity' paradigm.[45] There was a general consensus that sexual crimes should be disconnected from outrages against personal dignity.[46] Another aspect advocated for was the expansion of the SGBC list. The final

[33] *Prosecutor v Akayesu* (Trial Judgment) ICTR-96-4-T (2 September 1998) para 688.

[34] *Furundžija* (Trial Judgment) (n 30) para 272.

[35] *Kunarac et al* (Trial Judgment) (n 32) paras 16, 162–66.

[36] V Oosterveld, 'Feminist Debates on Civilian Women and International Humanitarian Law' (2009) 27 *Windsor YB Access Just* 385, 392–93.

[37] *Prosecutor v Aleksovski* (Trial Judgment) IT-95-14/1-T (25 June 1999) para 54.

[38] *Kunarac et al* (Trial Judgment) (n 32) paras 16, 162–66.

[39] *Prosecutor v Kvocka et al* (Trial Judgment) IT-98-30/1-T (2 November 2001) fn 343.

[40] *Prosecutor v Todorović* (Sentencing Judgment) IT-95-9/1-S (31 Jul 2001) para 38.

[41] *Akayesu (TC Judgment) (n 33)* para 688.

[42] ibid para 688.

[43] *Prosecutor v Brima et al (AFRC Case)* (Trial Judgment) SCSL-04-16-T (20 June 2007) para 697.

[44] KK Grewal, 'International criminal law as a site for enhancing women's rights? Challenges, possibilities, strategies' (2015) 23 *Feminist Legal Studies* 149; F Benedetti, K Bonneau and JL Washburn, *Negotiating the International Criminal Court, New York to Rome, 1994-1998* (Brill, 2014) 69–71, 148–49.

[45] H Durham, 'The Role of Civil Society in Creating the International Criminal Court Statute: Ten Years On and Looking Back' (2012) 3 *Journal of International Humanitarian Legal Studies* 3, 18-19; Benedetti, Bonneau and Washburn (n 44) 149-ff; Z Pearson, 'Non-governmental organizations and the International Criminal Court: Changing Landscapes of International Law' (2006) 39 *Cornell Int'l LJ* 243, fn 40; R Lehr-Lehnardt, 'One Small Step for Women: Female-Friendly Provisions in the Rome Statute of the International Criminal Court' (2002) 16 *BYU J Pub L* 317, 338.

[46] Lehr-Lehnardt (n 45) 338; See further J Halley, 'Rape at Rome: Feminist interventions in the criminalization of sex-related violence in positive international criminal law' (2008) 30 *Mich J Int'l L* 156–58; K Ambos and O Trifferer, *The Rome Statute of the International Criminal Court A Commentary* (CH Beck-Hart-Nomos, 2016) 478, para 654.

Rome Statute text delivered a mixed result: Article 7(1)(g) lists a notably expansive set of sexual crimes – rape, sexual slavery, enforced prostitution, forced pregnancy, enforced sterilisation, and 'any other form of sexual violence of comparable gravity' – which marked a major gain for gender justice.

Yet every item was contested during negotiations – for instance, the Vatican sought to replace 'forced pregnancy' with 'forced impregnation' to avoid implications for domestic abortion laws.[47] The WCGJ, however, succeeded in having the forced pregnancy included, with Article 7(2)(f) as a disclaimer saying that the provision will not affect 'national laws relating to pregnancy'. Another WCGJ's victory is the inclusion of both sexual slavery and enforced prostitution.[48] However, the WCGJ failed in having the residual category of 'other forms of sexual violence' without a gravity threshold.[49] The WCGJ also pushed for the inclusion of gender violence and succeeded in including gender as a discriminatory ground for persecution.[50] Article 7(3) of the Rome Statute defines gender as 'two sexes, male and female, within the context of society'. This compromise definition has been widely criticised for conflating sex and gender.[51] As Gilleri explains, contemporary understanding distinguishes between biological sex (derivative) and socially constructed gender roles, recognising that gender is fluid and independent of biology (oppositional).[52] More recent scholarship even questions the stability of the sex binary itself, arguing that both sex and gender are culturally produced rather than fixed categories.[53] This debate shines through

[47] M Markovic, 'Vessels of Reproduction: Forced Pregnancy and the ICC' (2007) 16 *Michigan State Journal of International Law* 439, 445–46.

[48] B Bedont and K Hall-Martinez, 'Ending Impunity for Gender Crimes under the International Criminal Court' (1999) 6 *Brown Journal of World Affairs* 65, 65–73.

[49] Women's Caucus for Gender Justice, 'Gender Justice and the ICC. Paper presented at the Rome Conference' (Rome, Italy, 15 June to 17 July 1998); R Grey, 'Conflicting interpretations of 'sexual violence' in the International Criminal Court' (2014) 29 *Australian Feminist Studies* 273, 276; LN Sadat and RS Carden, 'The New International Criminal Court: An Uneasy Revolution' (2000) 88 *Georgetown Law Journal* fn 316.

[50] Working Group on Definition of Crimes, Preparatory Committee on the Establishment of an International Criminal Court, Draft Consolidated Text, A/AC.249/ 1997/WG.1/CPR.5 (1997); see also BS Moshan, 'Women, War, and Words: The Gender Component in the Permanent International Criminal Court's Definition of Crimes against Humanity' (1998) 22 *Fordham International Law Journal* 154, 173ff; NE Erb, 'Gender-based crimes under the draft statute for the permanent International Criminal Court' (1998) 29 *Columbia Human Rights Law Review* 401, 433–34.

[51] V Oosterveld, 'The definition of gender in the Rome Statute of the International Criminal Court: A step forward or back for international criminal justice' (2005) 18 *Harv Hum Rts J* 55, 62–66.

[52] G Gilleri, 'Gender as a hyperconstruct in (rare) regional human rights case-law' (2020) 12 *European Journal of Legal Studies* 25, 26–34.

[53] M Zalewski, 'Gender/s' in Laura J Sheperd (ed), *Handbook on Gender and Violence* (Edward Elgar, 2019) 15; HL Moore, 'Understanding sex and gender', *Companion encyclopedia of anthropology* (Routledge, 2002) 814–15; H Charlesworth, 'Feminist Methods in International Law' (1999) 93 *American Journal of International Law* 379, 394; T Ingold, 'Introduction to social life' in Tim Ingold (ed), *Companion encyclopedia of anthropology* (Routledge 1994); G-P Dotto, 'Gender and Sex – Time to bridge the gap' (2019) 11 *EMBO Molecular Medicine*; See also A Fausto-Sterling, *Sex/Gender, Biology in a Social World* (Routledge, 2012); K Karkazis, 'The Misuses of "Biological Sex"' (2019) 394 *The Lancet* 1898, 1899; B Cossman, 'Gender Performance, Sexual Subjects and International Law' (2002) 15 *Canadian Journal of Law & Jurisprudence* 281.

in the gender definition in the Rome Statute.[54] Both derivative and oppositional understandings of gender were represented among the drafters.[55] On one side, certain Arab and Catholic States and pro-family NGOs defended a strict equation of gender with sex. Limiting gender to men and women would exclude, for instance, the persecution of transgender persons as gender-based persecution.[56] On the other side, several delegations, including the WCGJ, advocated for a broad conception of gender as a social construct, encompassing aspects such as sexual orientation.[57] Unfortunately, this resulted in Article 7(3) being 'oddly worded and circular'.[58] It first equates sex and gender, then tentatively opens the concept 'within the context of society', only to close it again by insisting that no other meaning may be given than that 'set out in this definition'.

As a result, a great variety of interpretations exist. Oosterveld presents Article 7(3) as a constructive ambiguity, which is 'a term used in diplomacy to refer to the use of ambiguous words that give comfort to those on different sides of a debate, thereby promoting agreement.'[59] She understands it as 'indefinite language'[60] that provides the judge with 'normative flexibility' and quasi-legislative discretion.[61] The question is whether each hard-fought diplomatic compromise qualifies as a constructive ambiguity even if not deliberately inserted.[62] The definition of gender was the only one to which all parties would agree,[63] but it was questionably left *intentionally ambiguous*.[64] This is contrary to some issues that were clearly deliberately left to the judges to decide.[65] The compromise on gender rather allows each side being able to claim its interpretation

[54] Oosterveld (n 51) 55.

[55] V Oosterveld, 'Gender-Based Crimes Against Humanity' in LN Sadat (ed), *Forging a Convention for Crimes Against Humanity* (CUP, 2011) 80; See further: Moshan (n 50) 178; V Oosterveld, 'Constructive Ambiguity and the Meaning of "Gender" for the International Criminal Court' (2014) 16 *International Feminist Journal of Politics* 563; JH Joseph, 'Gender and International Law: How the International Criminal Court Can Bring Justice to Victims of Sexual Violence' (2008) 18 *Texas Journal of Women and the Law* 61, 68–70.

[56] Summary records of the plenary meetings and of the meetings of the Committee of the Whole (Rome 15 June-17 July 1998) A/CONF. 183/13 (United Nations Diplomatic Conference of Plenipotentiaries on the Establishment of an International Criminal Court) (Vol II); Summary Record of the 25th Meeting, 272 para 61.

[57] Oosterveld (n 55) (2014) 569; CB Moore, 'Embracing Ambiguity and Adopting Propriety: Using Comparative Law to Explore Avenues for Protecting the LGBT Population under Article 7 of the Rome Statute of the International Criminal Court' (2016) 101 *Minnesota Law Review* 1287.

[58] Oosterveld (n 51) 56.

[59] Oosterveld (n 51) fn 14.

[60] Oosterveld (n 55) (2014) 563.

[61] ibid 568, 574.

[62] D Hunt, 'The International Criminal Court: High Hopes, "Creative Ambiguity" and an Unfortunate Mistrust in International Judges' (2004) 2 *Journal of International Criminal Justice* 56, 61.

[63] C Steains, 'Gender Issues in the Statute of the International Criminal Court' in RS Lee (ed), *The International Criminal Court: The making of the Rome Statute* (Kluwer Law International, 1999) 374–75; See also Oosterveld (n 55) (2014) 569–70.

[64] C Davidson, 'How to Read International Criminal Law: Strict Construction and the Rome Statute of the International Criminal Court' (2017) 91 *St John's Law Review* 37, 64.

[65] C Kreß, 'The Procedural Law of the International Criminal Court in Outline: Anatomy of a Unique Compromise' (2003) 1 *Journal of International Criminal Justice* 603, 605.

prevailed.[66] That is why some commentators have argued that the definition of gender is 'stunningly narrow',[67] and dismisses the qualification as a constructive ambiguity.[68] Copelon argued that the word gender does not support the exclusion of sexual orientation as it necessarily includes prescribed gender roles.[69] The ordinary meaning has nonetheless also been used to support the opposing view that understands gender as a 'synonym for women and/or male and female'.[70] But since the dictionary meaning of the term gender confirms it as a social construct,[71] and the text of the Rome Statute would not have encompassed both sex and gender if there was no difference between the two, this approach is not acceptable.[72]

Oosterveld indicated that 'gender is usually understood as a socially constructed concept of '*maleness*' and '*femaleness*' that can vary across cultures and over time'.[73] Charlesworth similarly stated: 'gender is a constructed and contingent set of assumptions *about* female and male roles'.[74] Given the centrality of textual primacy in order to adhere to the legality principle, this study supports the conclusions made by Suhr stating that 'the distinction between gender and sex cannot be abandoned altogether, as the Rome Statute's definition clearly acts on the assumption of a binary system of two sexes and, based on this, on two socially constructed gender roles'.[75] The legality principle requires adherence to the clear wording, and any broader reading extending the behaviour by analogy would violate it.[76] Because it is nearly impossible to abide by the wording of the statute,[77] it is no surprise that the most recent drafts for the Convention on Crimes against Humanity have dropped the definition of gender altogether.[78] Given that none of the other grounds, such as race or

[66] Davidson (n 64) 64.

[67] Cossman (n 53) 283–84; Steains (n 63) 367ff; Bedont and Hall-Martinez (n 48) 69; See also M Glasius, *Who is the real civil society?: Women's groups versus pro-family groups at the International Criminal Court negotiations* (Routledge, 2004).

[68] M Bohlander, 'Criminalising LGBT persons under National Criminal Law and article 7 (1)(h) and (3) of the ICC Statute' (2014) 5 *Global Policy* 401, 409; see also R Copelon, 'Gender crimes as war crimes: Integrating crimes against women into international criminal law' (2000) 46 *McGill Law Journal* 217.

[69] Copelon (n 68) 137.

[70] J Adolphe, 'Gender Wars at the United Nations' (2012) 11 *Ave Maria L Rev* 1, 4.

[71] 'Gender' in *Oxford English Dictionary* (online edn, Oxford University Press) www.oed.com/dictionary/gender_n.

[72] VV Suhr, *Rainbow Jurisdiction at the International Criminal Court, Protection of Sexual and Gender Minorities Under the Rome Statute*, vol 30 (International Criminal Justice Series, Asser Press – Springer, 2021) 225.

[73] V Oosterveld, 'The ICC Policy Paper on Sexual and Gender-Based Crimes: A Crucial Step for International Criminal Law' (2017) 24 *William & Mary Journal of Women & Law* 443, 448.

[74] Charlesworth (n 53) 394.

[75] Suhr (n 72) 231.

[76] ibid.

[77] H-P Kaul, 'Preface' in Bergsmo and S Tianying (eds), *On the Proposed Crimes Against Humanity Convention* (Torkel Opsahl Academic EPublisher, 2014)

[78] See for the latest on the status of this Convention: L Sadat, 'Crimes Against Humanity and Customary International Law' *Washington University in St. Louis Legal Studies Research Paper* 25-03 (2025) 06.

ethnicity, are defined, this is an argument in support of deleting the definition of gender.

In contrast to gender, the term 'sex' remains undefined. Now, how should we then understand *gender* violence vis-à-vis *sexual* violence? Gender violence has been defined as violence targeting or affecting women, because they are women.[79] Gender violence has also been understood as the broader category of sexual violence.[80] Gender crimes allow tackling violence towards 'men or women because of their gender roles, which may or may not have a sexual element'.[81] The 2014 OTP Policy Paper specifies that an act of a sexual nature is not limited to physical violence, and may involve no physical contact at all.[82] Hall argued that sexual violence is carried out through *sexual means*, with a *sexual motive* or by *targeting sexuality*'.[83] These three modalities – means, motive, and target – provide a functional tool to identify when conduct should fall under a sexual crime label and ensure that a broad range of behaviour can be captured. Drumond, however, proposed a more critical approach: the sexual label depends on contextual factors and on how both perpetrators and victims ascribe meaning to the violence. That is why even rape has been said to have little to do with sexuality itself.[84] The term 'sexual' is 'indefinite and elusive',[85] but understanding the 'grammar of interaction between victim, perpetrator, and audience' may help to grasp the complexity and meaning.[86]

A central question is whether the Rome Statute, which includes a residual category of 'other forms of sexual violence', can still rely on the category of 'other inhumane acts' to qualify conduct of a sexual nature.[87] The preparatory works show that several delegations introduced this second residual category precisely to prosecute acts of a sexual nature, such as 'forced nudity and sexual mutilation'.[88] According to the Trial Chamber, sexual acts can be carried out

[79] Moshan (n 50) 157; PV Sellers, *The prosecution of sexual violence in conflict: the importance of human rights as means of interpretation* (WRGU, 2007) 4.

[80] Moshan (n 50) fn 15.

[81] 'Women's Caucus for Gender Justice (WCGJ), 'Recommendations and Commentary to the Elements, Annex and the Rules of Procedure and Evidence Submitted to the Preparatory Commission (12 June 2000)' iccwomen.org/wigjdraft1/Archives/oldWCGJ/icc/iccpc/062000pc/elements annex.html.

[82] Office of the Prosecutor (ICC), 'Policy Paper on Sexual and Gender-Based Crimes' (June 2014).

[83] CK Hall, J Powderly and N Hayes, 'Art 7(3)' in K Ambos and O Triffterer (eds), *The Rome Statute of the International Criminal Court*, 3rd edn (CH Beck, 2016) 216.

[84] P Drumond, 'What about men? Towards a critical interrogation of sexual violence against men in global politics.' (2019) 95 *International Affairs* 1271, 1277–80; R Siefert, 'War and rape: A preliminary analysis' in A Stiglmayer (ed), *Mass rape: The War against Women in Bosnia Herzegovina* (University of Nebraska Press, 1994) 54–55.

[85] SJ Usprich, 'A New Crime in Old Battles: Definitional Problems with Sexual Assault' (1987) 29 *Criminal Law Quarterly* 202.

[86] Drumond (n 84) 1281.

[87] See below s IV(C) and (D).

[88] V Oosterveld, 'Gender-sensitive justice and the international criminal tribunal for Rwanda: lessons learned for the international criminal court' (2005) 12 *New England Journal of International & Comparative Law* 119, 124.

through sexual means or by targeting sexuality,[89] which means it embraced two out of three of Hall's modalities. The omission of a sexual motive does not come as a surprise since deriving the sexual nature from a sexual motive might have the downside of requiring a specific intent, which is not a requirement of all CaH.[90] The discussion of the labels will show that it is not always clear how to choose between the two residual labels since the sexual nature of acts is not always easily determinable.

In 2020, the WIGJ developed the Hague Principles on Sexual Violence,[91] enumerating a very instructive list of indicia in qualifying violence as sexual:

- The act involved exposing a "sexual body part" or physical contact with such a body part, including over clothing;
- The act was intended to be sexual by the perpetrator or was perceived as such by the affected person or their community as being sexual in nature;
- The act, while not necessarily sexual in itself, was intended to impact:

  a. the affected person's sexual autonomy or sexual integrity, including their capacity to engage in sexual activity, feel sexual desire, or have intimate relationships;
  b. the affected person's sexual orientation or gender identity; or
  c. the affected person's reproductive capacity or reproductive autonomy;

- The act involved sexual innuendos or language with implicit or explicit sexual connotations for the affected person, the community, or the perpetrator;
- The act involved the use, interference, control, or degradation of fluids or tissue associated with sexual and reproductive capacity, including semen, vaginal fluids, menstrual blood, breast milk, or placenta.[92]

This list allows judges to encompass a broad range of acts while at the same time providing clarity and foreseeability as to when acts will be considered sexual. It also incorporates the perspective of the perpetrator as well as the victim.

III. THE LABELLING HISTORY OF FORCED MARRIAGE IN INTERNATIONAL CRIMINAL LAW

At the ICTs, the issue of forced marriage was not central to the prosecution's cases, and references to this phenomenon are only marginal despite sources reporting that forced marriage was 'a common form of sexual slavery during the

[89] ibid.
[90] See Usprich (n 85).
[91] Women's Initiatives for Gender Justice, 'The Hague Principles of Sexual Violence' (2020).
[92] ibid 45-15.

Rwandan conflict'.[93] The *Akayesu case* mentions the practice of forced marriage only in passing.[94] Scholars mostly criticised this missed opportunity, paying little attention to a discussion about the preferred qualification of the crime.[95] At the ICTY, a fact pattern of forced marriage did not arise. The *Kvočka* Trial Chamber, nonetheless, stated that sexual violence includes forced marriage.[96]

However, forced marriage was already on the Rome Statute's drafting agenda.[97] As early as 1997, the WCGJ treated it as gender violence and enslavement, emphasising its non-sexual aspects, and cited international instruments and UN reports confirming its status as a slavery-like practice.[98] No participant advocated a separate crime label, likely because phenomena such as bush wives were considered covered under slavery or sexual slavery.[99]

Later, the SCSL and ECCC served as testing grounds for applying various labels to forced marriage.

A. The SCSL and the Bush Wife Phenomenon

The SCSL was considerably modelled after the ICC, and the SCSL Statute's subject-matter jurisdiction largely mirrored the Rome Statute's CaH provisions, with an identical set of sexual crimes.[100] In other aspects, the SCSL departed from the Rome Statute. It, for instance, held no crime of gender-based persecution, nor did it have a definition of gender. During the Sierra Leone Civil War (1991–2002), sexual violence was pervasive. One practice drew international attention: the so-called *bush wives* phenomenon, in which young girls were abducted and forced to live as the wives of rebel commanders.[101] Scholars

[93] B Nowrojee, *Report Human Rights Watch – Shattered Lives: Sexual Violence during the Rwandan Genocide and its Aftermath* (1996) 32.

[94] See, eg, *Akayesu (TC Judgment) (n 33)* para 389; See also: Askin (n 29) 107.

[95] See MS Kalra, 'Forced Marriage: Rwanda's Secret Revealed' (2001) 7 *UC Davis Journal of International Law & Policy* 197.

[96] *Kvocka et al* (Trial Judgment) (n 39) para 180 and fn 434.

[97] WCGJ Recommendations and Commentary for the Elements (Annex) submitted to the Preparatory Commission for the International Criminal Court; Women's Caucus for Gender Justice, 'Recommendations and Commentary for December 1997 Prep Com, Part III' (1997) see also: Halley (n 46) 80.

[98] Supplementary Convention on the Abolition of Slavery, the Slave Trade, and Institutions and Practices Similar to Slavery (adopted 7 September 1956, entered into force 30 April 1957) 266 UNTS 3 Art 1(c) Any institution or practice whereby: (i) A woman, without the right to refuse, is promised or given in marriage on payment of a consideration in money or in kind to her parents, guardian, family or any other person or group; GJ McDougall, 'UU Rapporteur's Final Report on Systematic rape, sexual slavery and slaverylike practices during armed conflict' (22 June 1998) E/CN4/Sub2/1998/13, para 30.

[99] WCGJ (n 81).

[100] UNSC Res 1315 (2000) on the Establishment of a Special Court for Sierra Leone, Art 2(g).

[101] See for a detailed study of the topic: C Coulter, *Bush Wives and Girl Soldiers: Women's Lives through War and Peace in Sierra Leone* (Cornell University Press, 2009).

have analysed its legal,[102] as well as its sociological and anthropological dimensions.[103] This section examines how the SCSL addressed the phenomenon in the *AFRC*, *RUF*, and *Taylor* cases. The Trial Chamber in the *AFRC* case was the first to label the bush wives phenomenon. The case suffered procedural difficulties, notably a late amendment adding the charge of 'other inhumane acts', which partly explains why the practice was ultimately classified as sexual slavery,[104] despite the Prosecution's narrative, shaped by experts Bangura and Scharf, framing it as an inhumane act.[105] Bangura offered a socio-cultural account of forced marriage, tracing its long-term social, cultural, physical, and psychological consequences.[106] She distinguished peacetime arranged marriages – family-negotiated and ceremonial –from wartime forced marriages lacking consent or ritual.[107] The term *wife*, she explained, was deliberate, signalling the rebel's control and the expectation of conjugal obedience.[108] Victims endured deep stigma for their prolonged captivity and perceived collaboration, often facing harsher community rejection than women who had been raped but not forced into marriage.[109]

The Trial Chamber nonetheless classified forced marriage as sexual slavery, reasoning that the prosecution's evidence for forced marriage in fact substantiated sexual slavery. Except for one witness, none described a marriage ceremony or perceived themselves as married.[110] The perpetrators exercised control over the victims' sexuality, movements, and labour, which established a relationship of ownership, not one of a marital or quasi-marital nature based on mutual obligations.[111]

[102] See, eg, K Belair, 'Unearthing the Customary Law Foundations of "Forced Marriages" during Sierra Leone's Civil War: the Possible Impact of International Criminal Law on Customary Marriage and Women's Rights in Post-Conflict Sierra Leone' (2006) 15 *Columbia Journal of Gender and Law* 551, 551–58; Coulter (n 101) 74ff; MC Ferme, *The Underneath of Things Violence, History, and the Everyday in Sierra Leone* (University of California Press, 2001); see also: T Kelsall, *Culture under cross-examination: International justice and the Special Court for Sierra Leone* (CUP, 2009) 243–55.

[103] Frulli (n 16): arguing in favour of qualification as another inhumane act; MP Scharf and S Mattler, *Forced Marriage: Exploring the Viability of the Special Court for Sierra Leone's New Crime Against Humanity* (Case Research Paper Series in Legal Studies, 2005); R Slater, 'Gender Violence or Violence against Women – The Treatment of Forced Marriage in the Special Court for Sierra Leone' (2012) 13 *Melbourn Journal of International Law* 732.

[104] *Prosecutor v Brima et al (AFRC Case)* (Trial Chamber Decision on Prosecution Request for Leave to Amend the Indictment) SCSL-04-16-PT (6 May 2004) para 58.

[105] K Grewal, 'Using War to Shift Peacetime Norms: The Example of Forced Marriage in Sierra Leone' in R Shackel and L Fiske (eds), *Rethinking Transitional Gender Justice, Gender, Development and Social Change* (Gender, Development and Social Change, Palgrave Macmillan, 2019) 82.

[106] C Davidson, 'Explaining Inhumanity: The Use of Crime-Definition Experts at International Criminal Courts' (2015) 48 *Vanderbilt Journal of Transnational Law* 359, 383–86.

[107] *Prosecutor v Brima et al (AFRC case) – Annex A Expert Report on the phenomenon of 'forced marriage' in the Context of the Armed Conflict in Sierra Leone* (Prosecution filing of expert report pursuant to rule 94(bis) and decision on prosecution leave to call an additional expert witness) SCSL-2004-16-T (8 August 2005) 13.

[108] ibid 14–15.

[109] ibid 19–20.

[110] *Brima et al (AFRC case)* (Trial Judgment) (n 43) para 712.

[111] ibid para 711.

The rule of duplicity barred conviction under both the crime of forced marriage and sexual slavery. Two separate opinions addressed this issue. Judge Sebutinde reversed her earlier view that classified forced marriage as another inhumane act, arguing – based on the Bangura report – that the bush wife phenomenon was fully encompassed by sexual slavery.[112] Judge Doherty, in dissent, reached the opposite conclusion, also citing Bangura. She held that the use of the term *wife* signified a forced marital status with lasting psychological harm, stigma, and obstacles to reintegration. In her view, the crucial element of 'forced marriage' is the imposition, by threat or physical force 'of a forced conjugal association'.[113]

This Trial judgment was overturned on appeal. The Appeal judges found no reason to support the restrictive interpretation that crimes with a gender or sexual component cannot qualify as another inhumane act.[114] The judgment held that the imposition of a forced conjugal association is not the same as the exercise of the rights of ownership.[115] While sexual slavery and forced marriage share elements, 'such as non-consensual sex and deprivation of liberty', 'forced marriage involves a perpetrator compelling a person by force or threat of force, through the words or conduct of the perpetrator or those associated with him, into a forced conjugal association with another person resulting in great suffering, or serious physical or mental injury on the part of the victim'. Forced marriage 'implies a relationship of exclusivity' which is not necessarily present in sexual slavery.[116] The Appeals Chamber finally, on the basis of the physical injury (eg, 'repeated acts of rape and sexual violence, forced labour, corporal punishment'), psychological trauma (eg, 'being forced to watch the killing or mutilation of close family members') and stigmatisation (eg, the label wives resulted in them being ostracised from their communities and carried over to children as well[117]), concluded that the different elements of the other inhumane acts category were met.

Shortly after this *Appeal Judgment*, the RUF Trial Chamber, with great ease, stated that, given the widespread nature of the phenomenon, women being taken as wives was well-known and understood.[118] The absence of any formal or legal ceremony did not prevent the SCSL from qualifying the conduct as an inhumane act. While noting duplicity between the charges of sexual slavery and

[112] *Prosecutor v Brima et al (AFRC case)* (Separate Concurring Opinion of the Justice Julia Sebutinde appended to judgment pursuant to rule 88 (c)) SCSL-2004-16-T (20 June 2007) paras 1–16.

[113] *Prosecutor v Brima et al (AFRC case)* (Partly Dissenting Opinion of Justice Doherty on Count 7 (Sexual Slavery) and Count 8 ('Forced Marriages') appended to judgment pursuant to rule 88 (c)) SCSL-2004-16-T (20 June 2007) paras 47–53.

[114] *Prosecutor v Brima et al (AFRC case)* (Appeals Judgment) SCSL-04-16-A (22 February 2008) paras 181–86.

[115] ibid paras 189–90.

[116] ibid para 195.

[117] ibid para 199.

[118] *Prosecutor v Sesay et al (RUF Case)* (Trial Judgment) SCSL-04-15-T (2 March 2009) para 1295.

other sexual violence, the Chamber accepted cumulative charging of sexual slavery and another inhumane act.[119] Its language largely mirrored that of the Bangura report and Judge Doherty's opinion, later echoed in ICC jurisprudence, where judges adopted several of the same defining characteristics.[120]

As a final chapter in the SCSL's jurisprudence, the Taylor Trial Judgment concluded that forced marriage was a form of sexual slavery.[121] Witnesses testified that there was no marriage ceremony, but that 'the only ceremony is to go and sleep'.[122] The Chamber described the bush wife phenomenon as a 'forced conjugal association'.[123] This judgment thus closed a line of conflicting case law, illustrating how the SCSL's case law was characterised by shifting labels and rationales.

B. The ECCC and Collectivised, Communist Weddings and Marriages

The ECCC with its much more limited subject-matter jurisdiction – the only sexual crime is that of rape – took a more conservative approach.[124]

In Cambodia, the Communist Party of Kampuchea (CPK or *Angkar*) sought to dissolve family bonds that conflicted with its revolutionary vision.[125] It replaced traditional, family-arranged marriages with state-imposed unions, often between strangers, formalised in mass ceremonies pledging loyalty to both spouse and party. Parents were typically barred from attending.[126] Focused on reproduction, couples mainly cohabited during fertile periods.[127] Unlike Sierra Leone, where only women were victimised by coerced unions, in Cambodia, both men and women were victims of the regime's marriage policy.[128]

In Case 002, forced marriage was not initially included in the indictments.[129] It was added only after the Civil Parties' Lawyers requested further investigation

[119] ibid para 458.

[120] See specifically in relation to the use of other inhumane acts below, s IV(C).

[121] *Prosecutor v Taylor* (Trial Judgment) SCSL-03-01-T (18 May 2012) paras 422–30.

[122] ibid para 916.

[123] ibid para 916.

[124] S Williams and E Palmer, 'The Extraordinary Chambers in the Courts of Cambodia: Developing the Law on Sexual Violence?' (2015) 15 *International Criminal Law Review* 452.

[125] See T De Langis and others, *'Like Ghost Changes body' A Study on the Impact of Forced Marriage under the Khmer Rouge Regime* (2014).

[126] BA Toy-Cronin, 'What is forced marriage? Towards a definition of forced marriage as a crime against humanity' (2010) 19 *Columbia Journal of Gender and Law* 539, 544–46.

[127] ibid 547–50.

[128] ibid 552–54.

[129] *Prosecutors v Nuon Chea & Kieu Samphan (Case 002)* (Civil Parties' Co-Lawyers' Request for Supplementary Preliminary Investigations) 001/18-07-2007-ECCC/TC (9 February 2009); *Prosecutors v Nuon Chea & Kieu Samphan (Case 002)* (Civil Parties' Co-Lawyers' Second Request for Investigative Actions Concerning Forced Marriages and Forced Sexual Relations) 002/19-09-2007-ECCC/OCIJ (15 July 2009).

by the co-investigating judges.[130] The 2018 judgment against Nuon Chea and Khieu Samphan devoted extensive attention to the issue, including a detailed reconstruction of pre-revolutionary marriage practices and over a hundred pages analysing the CPK's marriage policy. Viewing traditional marriage as a 'backward tradition discriminating against women',[131] the CPK developed a policy to abolish and control such marriages and reshape them to serve communist ideology and population growth objectives.[132] Family involvement was eliminated, and consent, though formally required, was found to be coerced.[133] Mass ceremonies replaced individual rites,[134] emphasising ideological loyalty and excluding religious elements.[135] Marriages were primarily reproductive: couples were expected to consummate the union and, when necessary, were forced to have sexual intercourse under supervision.[136]

On the legal side, the Chamber held that '[i]ndividuals were married in a widespread climate of fear and the consent purportedly given either before or during wedding ceremonies did not amount in most cases to genuine consent.'[137] The *Angkar* instructions were given under the threat of being killed if they refused to marry.[138] The Chamber further set out that individuals were 'neither consulted nor informed in advance' and in many cases they did 'not even know their spouse until the moment they arrived at the wedding venue'. After the marriage was concluded, individuals were monitored to make sure the marriage was consummated. This pressure 'led victims to feel that they were obliged to have sexual intercourse which caused serious mental or physical suffering or injury or constituted a serious attack on the human dignity of the victims'.[139]

[130] *Prosecutors v Nuon Chea & Kieu Samphan (case 002)* (Office of the Co-Investigating Judges, Statement from the Co-Investigating Judges on Judicial Investigation) 19-09-2007-ECCC/OCIJ (5 November 2009). See also N Jain, 'Going Beyond Prosecutorial Discretion: Institutional Factors Influencing Thematic Prosecution' in M Bergsmo and CW Ling (eds), *Thematic Prosecutions of International Sex Crimes* (Torkel Opsahl Academic Epublisher, 2012); Williams and Palmer (n 124) 471–72; M Elander, 'Prosecuting the Khmer Rouge Marriages', in L Kent and M Demian (eds), *Transitional Justice in Law, History and Anthropology* (Routledge, 2020) 160–72; R Grey, 'Symposium on the ECCC: Beyond Forced Marriage – Sexual, Gender-Based and Reproductive Crimes in the ECCC', 3 November 2022, available online at opiniojuris.org/2022/11/03/symposium-on-the-eccc-beyond-forced-marriage-sexual-gender-based-and-reproductive-crimes-in-the-eccc/; M O'Brien, 'Symposium on the ECCC: Forced Marriage in the ECCC', 3 November 2022, available online at: opiniojuris.org/2022/11/02/symposium-on-the-eccc-forced-marriage-in-the-eccc/.

[131] *Prosecutors v Nuon Chea & Kieu Samphan (case 002)* (Trial Chamber Judgment) 002/19-09-2007/ECCC/TC (16 November 2018) paras 265–73.

[132] ibid paras 3549–63.

[133] ibid paras 3592–625.

[134] ibid paras 3630–32.

[135] ibid paras 3630–32.

[136] ibid paras 3564–91.

[137] ibid para 3690.

[138] ibid para 3690.

[139] ibid para 3691.

Unfortunately, the Chamber did not set out the rationale behind the use of the other inhumane acts category. The reliance on this residual category partly reflects the absence of adequate labels for sexual violence, though it would have been valuable to situate these findings in relation to the SCSL's jurisprudence. Another element explaining the use of other inhumane acts instead of slavery labels is the absence of slavery-like facts in the Cambodian fact pattern. Both men and women were victims of the policy, and unlike the bush wife phenomenon, there was no domination of the perpetrator over the victim. In the ECCC situation, the recourse to the other inhumane acts category seemed inevitable, as another crime category for this practice could not be used to label this practice. In 2022, the ECCC confirmed this approach in the *Samphân Khieu Judgment* by referring to the *Ongwen Judgment*.[140]

IV. LABELLING FORCED MARRIAGE

This section examines how the ICC has labelled fact patterns referred to as forced marriage. A mapping exercise was conducted across all situations and cases before the Court to identify charges involving sexual and gender-based crimes and, more specifically, instances in which conduct akin to forced marriage was prosecuted.[141]

The *Katanga* and *Ngudjolo cases* were the first in which sexual violence charges were brought. Regretfully, even before the confirmation of charges stage, evidentiary issues arose, which resulted in the charges of rape and sexual slavery only being added later.[142] Evidentiary issues persisted at the trial level, with witnesses giving contradictory evidence and judges disagreeing on how to deal with this.[143] In the end, the charges against *Ngudjolo* were severed, and *Katanga* was acquitted for both rape and sexual slavery, which was, at least partly, the result of these evidentiary issues. This chapter nevertheless includes an analysis of how the decisions have set out the law on sexual slavery.

In 2014, the charges were confirmed against *Ntaganda* for both rape and sexual slavery, both qualified under war crimes and CaH.[144] Much of the qualification debate in this case revolved around the issue of sexual violence against

[140] Case 002/02 (Appeal Judgment of the Supreme Court Chamber) 002/19-09-2007-ECCC/SC (23 December 2022) paras 1175ff.

[141] The mapping exercise is on file with the author.

[142] *Prosecutor v Katanga & Ngudjolo Chui* (Decision on the Confirmation of Charges) ICC-01/04-01/07 (30 September 2008) para 212; see also Women's Initiatives for Gender Justice, *Gender Report Card on the International Criminal Court*, 2014) 162–63.

[143] *Prosecutor v Katanga* (Minority Opinion of Judge Christine Van den Wyngaert to the Judgment pursuant to article 74 of the Statute) ICC-01/04-01/07 (7 March 2014) fn 189; para 152.

[144] *Prosecutor v Ntaganda* (Decision Pursuant to Article 61(7)(a) and (b) of the Rome Statute) ICC-01/04-02/06 (9 June 2014) para 53ff.

one's own forces, which is of limited relevance to the present discussion.[145] The case is only included for its elaboration on the legal elements of sexual slavery.

Absolutely central to this chapter is the *Ongwen case*. In this case, the labels of enslavement, sexual slavery and other inhumane acts are used in relation to the forced marriage phenomenon. Dominic Ongwen, born around 1978 in Northern Uganda, was abducted by the LRA at about ten years old and forced into service as a child soldier.[146] The SGBC charges in the *Ongwen case* can be divided under crimes deemed directly perpetrated (charges 50-60)[147] and those not directly perpetrated (Count 61-68) by the accused.[148] As for those directly perpetrated, the case is built around evidence of these crimes against seven of his wives.[149] In order to see how the different labels are used, this analysis focuses on the charges of crimes directly perpetrated and Ongwen's conduct in relation to these seven wives.

A final case that is essential to the present chapter's analysis is the *Al Hassan case*. This case concerns crimes that occurred during the 2012-2013 occupation of Timbuktu by the armed group Ansar Dine, also referred to as Al Qaeda in the Islamic Maghreb (AQIM). Al Hassan, a member of Ansar Dine and de facto chief of the Islamic Police, stood trial for his involvement in, inter alia, a policy of sexual and gender-based crimes.[150] Ansar Dine encouraged men to marry – often regardless of existing marriages[151] – and many such unions lasted only for the duration of their stay in Timbuktu.[152] The group maintained a fund to finance these marriages,[153] including dowries, which members of the Islamic Police frequently used. Married women were housed in government buildings, divided into separate chambers.[154] Marriage thus became a means to legitimise sexual and gendered violence.[155] Of particular interest is the Pre-Trial Chamber's classification of forced marriage as sexual slavery, other inhumane acts, and gender-based persecution. While this section focuses on that decision, it will also address the Trial Judgment's subsequent acquittal of Al Hassan on these charges.[156]

[145] See *Prosecutor v Ntaganda* (Judgment on the Appeal of Mr Ntaganda Against the 'Second decision on the Defence's Challenge to the Jurisdiction of the Court in Respect of Counts 6 and 9') ICC-01/04-02/06 (15 June 2017).

[146] *Ongwen* (TC Judgment) (n 23) paras 26–31.

[147] *Ongwen* paras (CoC Decision) (n 23) 66–117.

[148] ibid paras 118–24.

[149] *Ongwen* para (TC Judgment) (n 23) 209.

[150] *Procureur c Al Hassan* (Version publique expurgée Rectificatif à la Décision relative à la confirmation des charges portées contre Al Hassan Ag Abdoul Aziz Ag Mohamed Ag Mahmoud) ICC-01/12-01/18 (13 November 2019) para 571. See also *Procureur c Al Hassan* (Version publique expurgée du Rectificatif de la Décision portant modification des charges confirmées le 30 septembre 2019 à l'encontre d'Al Hassan Ag Abdoul Aziz Ag Mohamed Ag Mahmoud) ICC-01/12-01/18 (23 Avril 2020).

[151] ibid para 576.

[152] ibid para 573.

[153] ibid para 577.

[154] ibid para 574.

[155] ibid para 571.

[156] *Prosecutor v Al Hassan* (n 124).

A. Slavery/enslavement[157]

The label of slavery or enslavement[158] has a rich history and has existed as a crime against humanity since 1945.[159] At the NMT, the judges in the *Pohl case* approached 'compulsory uncompensated labour' as slavery and held that 'involuntary servitude, even if tempered by humane treatment, is still slavery'.[160] Also at the IMTFE, forced labour of male prisoners of war was qualified as a CaH of enslavement.[161] Regretfully, the widespread slavery policy of Comfort Women was not prosecuted under this crime label.[162] After Nuremberg, several human rights treaties elaborated on the prohibition of slavery. Not only have there been several specialised treaties on the topic,[163] but also several international and regional human rights treaties contain a slavery prohibition.[164] The crime is additionally included in all the ICTs' Statutes.[165] The prohibition on slavery has a firm basis in customary international law and, since 1970, is considered an obligation *erga omnes*.[166]

[157] The terms slavery – more commonly used in IHRL – and enslavement – more commonly used in criminal law – are used interchangeably. See S Scarpa, 'The Nebulous Definition of Slavery: Legal Versus Sociological Definitions of Slavery' in J Winterdyk and J Jones (eds), *The Palgrave International Handbook of Human Trafficking* (Springer International Publishing, 2020) 3; N Siller, '"Modern Slavery" Does International Law Distinguish between Slavery, Enslavement and Trafficking?' (2016) 14 *Journal of International Criminal Justice* 405.

[158] As early as 1863, national instruments held prohibitions on slavery, see eg Article 58 of the Instructions for the Government of Armies of the United States in the Field (Lieber Code) (24 April 1863); Hague Convention (IV) respecting the Laws and Customs of War on Land: Regulations concerning the Laws and Customs of War on Land (18 October 1907); thereafter two specialised conventions were adopted: Slavery Convention (adopted 25 September 1926, entered into force 9 March 1927) 60 LNTS 253; Convention concerning Forced or Compulsory Labour (ILO Convention No 29) (adopted 28 June 1930, entered into force 1 May 1932) 39 UNTS 55.

[159] J Allain, *Slavery in International Law: Of Human Exploitation and Trafficking* (Martinus Nijhoff, 2012) 105–42; CK Hall and K Ambos, 'Article 7: Crimes against Humanity' in K Ambos and O Trifferer (eds), *The Rome Statute of the International Criminal Court* (CH Beck - Hart – Nomos, 2016) 188–90.

[160] *United States v Pohl et al (Pohl case)* Trials of War Criminals before the Nuremberg Military Tribunal under Control Council Law No 10, Vol V970; see also: *United States v Milch et al (Milch Case)* Trials of War Criminals before the Nuremberg Military Tribunal under Control Council Law No 10, Vol II371.

[161] *Judgment of the International Military Tribunal for the Far East* (November 1948) 445–63.

[162] CM Argibay, 'Sexual slavery and the comfort women of World War II' (2003) 21 *Berkeley J Int'l L* 375; KD Askin, *War crimes against women: Prosecution in international war crimes tribunals* (Martinus Nijhoff, 1997) 73.

[163] Supplementary Slavery Convention (n 98); Convention concerning the Abolition of Forced Labour (ILO Convention No 105) (adopted 25 June 1957, entered into force 17 January 1959); See also on the different international instruments touching upon slavery: C Bassiouni, 'Enslavement as an international crime' (1990) 23 *New York University Journal of International Law and Politics* 445, 454ff.

[164] UDHR (n 11) Art 4; ICCPR (n 11) Art 8.; European Convention on Human Rights (adopted 4 November 1950, entered into force 3 September 1953) ETS 5 Art 4; ACHPR (n 11) Art 5; American Convention on Human Rights (Adopted 22 November 1969, entered into force 18 July 1978) Art 6; Arab Charter on Human Rights (adopted 22 May 2004, entered into force 15 March 2008) 12 *Int'l Hum Rts Rep* 893 Art 10.

[165] Art 5(c) ICTY Statute; Art 3(c) ICTR Statute; Art 2(c) SCSL Statute; Art 9 ECCC Statute.

[166] *Barcelona Traction, Light and Power Company, Limited (Belgium v Spain, second phase)* (Judgment) [1970] ICJ Rep 3, paras 32–34.

Over the years, the crime has increasingly widened to include slavery-like practices.[167] While there is a growing consensus to include so-called contemporary or modern forms of slavery,[168] some scholars have warned against the gradual dilution of the concept,[169] and rendering it 'effectively meaningless'.[170]

The *actus reus* of the crime of enslavement in the Rome Statute (Article 7(1)(c)) is defined in the Elements of Crimes (EoC) as involving 'a perpetrator exercising any or all of the powers attaching to the rights of ownership over the person'.[171] This can involve 'purchasing, selling, lending or bartering' the victim, 'or by imposing on them a similar deprivation of liberty'. The terminology on the rights of ownership has been taken over from the 1926 Slavery Convention's definition.[172] The Elements of Crimes in footnote 11 also refers to 'lesser servitudes', because of which it has been debated whether some forms of servitude are included.[173]

i. *The Label in the Ongwen Case*

This section departs from the *Ongwen case,* given that it is the only case using the label 'enslavement'. Ongwen was convicted of enslaving three of the seven wives. He was convicted cumulatively for both the forced marriage and other inhumane acts, as well as the enslavement of P-0099. He was only convicted for the enslavement of P-0235 and P-0236, who, despite also being his wives, were not considered the victims of other inhumane acts.[174]

The Ongwen Trial Chamber commences its interpretation correctly by using a textual focus on the internal sources. The Chamber recalled the definition of the crime in Article 7(2)(c) as 'the exercise of any or all of the powers attaching to the *right of ownership* over a person'.[175] It further referenced the EoC's non-exhaustive list of forms of ownership.[176] A remarkable aspect is that footnote 11 of the EoC is referenced, which mentions the 1956 Supplementary Convention. Although the Elements indeed explicitly include this antecedent instrument,

[167] See further Bassiouni (n 163) 455.

[168] See further J Allain, *The Law and Slavery: Prohibiting Human Exploitation* (Brill | Nijhoff, 2015) 478–79; The specification in the EoC of trafficking is an indication of it being considered as a contemporary form of slavery; see on this issue: C Corliss, 'Human Trafficking as "Modern Slavery": The Trouble with Trafficking as Enslavement in International Law' (2019) 71 *SCL Rev* 603.

[169] Siller (n 157) 408; S Miers, *Slavery in the Twentieth Century: The Evolution of a Global Problem* (Altamira Press, 2003) 453; J Quirk, 'Defining slavery in all its forms: Historical inquiry as contemporary instruction' (2012) *The Legal Understanding of Slavery* 253, 254.

[170] J Allain and R Hickey, 'Property and the Definition of Slavery' (2012) 61 *International & Comparative Law Quarterly* 915, 916.

[171] See further Corliss (n 168); Siller (n 157) 415–18.

[172] Art 1(1); see further K Bales and PT Robbins, '"No one shall be held in slavery or servitude": A critical analysis of international slavery agreements and concepts of slavery' (2001) 2 *Human Rights Review* 18.

[173] See further Allain (n 168) 188–92.

[174] It will be assessed under the label of 'other inhumane acts', why these wives were not the victim of this crime. See below s IV(C).

[175] *Ongwen* (TC Judgment) (n 23) para 2711 (emphasis added).

[176] ibid.

the Rome Statute's definition is based on the 1926 Slavery Convention. As such, confusion is created on whether the more restrictive 1926 Convention's definition of slavery or the potentially more expansive definition in the 1956 Supplementary Convention is preferred.[177] The first fundamental problem with the interpretation of enslavement in this case lies in the misrepresentation and incomplete articulation of the crime's definition. This issue was clearly identified in an *Amicus Curiae* submission by Allain during the Appeals proceedings in *Ongwen*, which observed that although the 1956 Supplementary Convention indeed enumerates certain practices that may constitute slavery, the 1926 definition remains operative and establishes the minimum threshold for slavery as the exercise of powers attaching to the right of ownership.[178] The *Amicus* rightly emphasised that, while the 1956 Convention extends the scope to include practices such as debt bondage and serfdom, it explicitly retains the 1926 definition. Accordingly, these slavery-like practices only fall within the definition of slavery where they amount to the exercise of the right of ownership. The Trial Chamber, by omitting to set out this history, failed to illuminate that the slavery definition in the Rome Statute is still the slavery definition of the 1926 Convention and wrongfully created the impression that the definition of slavery is broader. Allain analysed the genesis of particular lines of interpretation and explained that the 1926 Slavery Convention's definition is to be understood as presenting the legal definition on which consensus exists.[179] Since the Rome Statute adopts the 1926 definition, slavery entails exercising ownership rights over a person.[180] The notion of ownership is best understood in terms of property and should consist of '[c]ontrol tantamount to possession'.[181] To better delineate the legal definition, the Bellagio-Harvard Guidelines on the Legal Parameters of Slavery were developed, reinforcing the view that slavery centres on control and possession over a person and drawing clear parallels with property relations.[182] Article 21(1)(b) allows drawing from treaties *where appropriate*.[183] Given the explicit borrowing by the Rome Statute of the terminology in the 1926 Convention, the appropriateness standard is certainly met.

The Trial Chamber heavily relied on a list of indicia of powers being exercised that are attached to this right of ownership:

(i) control or restrictions of someone's movement and, more generally, measures taken to prevent or deter escape;

[177] Supplementary Slavery Convention (n 98), Art 7(a).

[178] *Prosecutor v Ongwen* (Amicus Curiae Observations on the issue of Sexual and Gender-based Crimes: Sexual Slavery & Forced Marriage) ICC-02/04-01/15 (19 December 2021) paras 33–36.

[179] Allain and Hickey (n 170) 915–19.

[180] Slavery Convention Article 1(1) (n 158).

[181] Allain and Hickey (n 170) 936.

[182] Research Group on the Legal Parameters of Slavery, 'Bellagio-Harvard Guidelines on the Legal Parameters of Slavery of 2012' in J Allain (ed), *Slavery in International Law: Of Human Exploitation and Trafficking* (Brill | Nijhoff, 2013).

[183] See ch 3, s IV(C).

(ii) control of physical environment;
(iii) psychological control or pressure;
(iv) force, threat of force or coercion;
(v) duration of the exercise of powers attaching to the right of ownership;
(vi) assertion of exclusivity;
(vii) subjection to cruel treatment and abuse;
(viii) control of sexuality;
(ix) forced labour or subjecting the person to servile status; and
(x) the person's vulnerability and the socio-economic conditions in which the power is exerted.[184]

The list of indicia was drawn from both internal and external case law, notably *Ntaganda*[185] and *Katanga*,[186] which dealt with sexual slavery. A comparison of these lists shows that the *Ongwen* Chamber copied them without sufficient distinction. It retained factors such as 'control of sexuality', which are relevant to sexual slavery but misplaced in defining enslavement. Similarly, including 'assertion of exclusivity' as an indicator of enslavement is inconsistent, as this factor later serves to distinguish forced marriage from sexual slavery.[187] The Chamber should have tailored separate lists for each crime, clarifying their conceptual differences.

The external precedent cited consists of four ICT judgments and one human rights judgment from the Inter-American Court of Human Rights (IACtHR). The *Kunarac* case was the first to address a pattern of sexual slavery.[188] The Trial Chamber, upheld on appeal, adopted the Prosecutor's list of factors for enslavement: control of movement, environment, and sexuality; psychological control; prevention of escape; coercion; duration; exclusivity; abuse; and forced labour. Subsequent judgments (*Taylor*, *RUF*, and *Duch*) replicated this list verbatim, even when dealing with non-sexual forms of slavery.[189]

The IACtHR's judgment in the *case of Hacienda Brasil Verde v Brasil* is an interesting reference for several reasons. First, the IACtHR relied on the ICT's case law and formulated a similar approach with a list of factors. Yet, this list differs from the *Kunarac* list:

(i) the restriction or control of an individual's autonomy;
(ii) the loss or restriction of freedom of movement;
(iii) the accruing of some gain to the perpetrator;

[184] *Ongwen* (TC Judgment) (n 23) para 2712.
[185] *Prosecutor v Ntaganda* (Judgment) ICC-01/04-02/06 (8 July 2019) para 952.
[186] *Prosecutor v Katanga* (Judgment Pursuant to Article 74 of the Statute) ICC-01/04-01/07 (7 March 2014) para 976.
[187] See further in s B.
[188] *Kunarac et al* (Trial Judgment) (n 32) para 543.
[189] *Sesay et al (RUF case) (Trial Judgment) (n 118)* para 199; *Prosecutors v Kaing Guek alias Duch* (Trial Chamber Judgment) 001/18-07-200/ECCC/TC (26 July 2010) para 342; *Taylor (Trial Judgment) (n 121)* para 447.

(iv) the absence of the victim's consent or free will, or it is rendered impossible or irrelevant by the threat or use of force or other forms of coercion, the fear of violence, deception or false promises;
(v) the use of physical force or psychological oppression;
(vi) the victim's position of vulnerability;
(vii) detention or captivity;
(viii) exploitation.[190]

The IACtHR's judges also provided a detailed historical assessment of slavery, and underscored that the right of ownership could be explained through the notion of possession,[191] which is expressed by such a level of control that it results in 'the loss of a person's own will', or a 'considerable decrease in personal autonomy'.[192] Why the Ongwen Chamber used the indicia but not the precedent to define the crime remains unclear. The variable composition of this list undermines legality and cannot substitute for a definition. Adams usefully distinguished indicators of control from those of exploitation,[193] and argued that legal certainty requires an abstract understanding of the powers attaching to ownership.[194] This study concurs, finding that the *Ongwen* Chamber, though identifying negative criteria (no need for ill-treatment, transaction, or minimum duration),[195] failed to develop positive properties rooted in control and exploitation.

The Chamber's interpretation of enslavement versus sexual slavery reveals three views: (1) sexual slavery as a subcategory of slavery (lex specialis),[196] risking dilution of the latter;[197] (2) sexual slavery as redundant, since enslavement already encompasses it - Adams attributing this duplication to political motives;[198] and (3) sexual slavery as a distinct offence with separate elements and protected interests.[199]

[190] *Case of Hacienda Brasil Verde v Brazil* (Judgment) Inter-American Court of Human Rights Series C No 318 (20 October 2016) paras 271–72.

[191] ibid.

[192] ibid para 271.

[193] A Adams, 'Sexual Slavery: Do We Need This Crime in Addition to Enslavement?' (2018) 29 *Criminal Law Forum* 279, 292.

[194] ibid.

[195] *Ongwen* (TC Judgment) (n 23) para 2713.

[196] V Oosterveld, 'Sexual slavery and the International Criminal Court: advancing international law' (2003) 25 *Mich J Int'l L* 605, 608: Sexual slavery is 'a specific kind of slavery'.

[197] PV Sellers and JG Kestenbaum, 'The International Crimes of Slavery and the Slave Trade: A Feminist Critique' (2020) Cardozo Legal Studies Research Paper 54.

[198] Adams (n 193) 299–300. see also: McDougall (n 98) para 30.

[199] *Prosecutor v Ongwen* (Amici Curiae Observations on Sexual- and Gender-Based Crimes, Particularly Sexual Slavery, and on Cumulative Convictions Pursuant to Rule 103 of the Rules of Procedure and Evidence) ICC-02/04-01/15 A A2 (23 December 2021), para 2; Argibay (n 162) 386; see also: F Mahmood, 'Prosecuting Human Trafficking for the Purpose of Sexual Exploitation under Article 7 of the Rome Statute: Enslavement or Sexual Slavery' (2019) 35 *Journal of Trafficking and Human Exploitation* 35, 47.

The *Ongwen* Trial Chamber did not enter cumulative convictions for slavery and sexual slavery, suggesting that it followed a *lex specialis* approach in which sexual slavery was treated as a subcategory of enslavement. If this reasoning was intended, the Chamber should have clarified the boundary between the two offences and when conduct is sexual or non-sexual in nature. Precedents existed that could have guided such differentiation.[200] The Chamber appeared to assume that the *ting tings* were enslaved but not sexually enslaved,[201] whereas the wives were both sexually enslaved and subjected to other inhumane acts.[202] When addressing concurrence,[203] the judges made a distinction between convicting Ongwen for slavery in relation to some of the wives and convicting him for sexual slavery in relation to other wives, again implying that sexual slavery was the *lex specialis* and therefore precluded cumulative conviction. Although the Chamber did not state this explicitly, it invoked the *Bemba* Appeals Chamber standard that multiple convictions are barred 'where the same conduct fulfils the elements of two offences even if these offences have different legal elements, for instance if one offence is fully consumed by the other offence or is [. . .] subsidiary to it'.[204]

The judges found no problem of concurrence in relation to other inhumane acts.[205] The absence of an explanation in the judgment on why P-0099 is a victim of both enslavement and other inhumane acts, and the complete lack of cited evidence in the passage in which this concurrence issue is tackled, is striking. The judges only explained what enslavement entailed and how the deprivation of personal liberty, the restriction in their movements, the forced labour, the physical as well as psychological abuse, were an expression of Ongwen exercising 'powers attaching to the right of ownership over these women'.[206] Implicitly, there nonetheless lies a certain logic behind this application of the labels by the *Ongwen Trial Chamber*. The label slavery is applied to women used as *ting tings* during the time of the charges, but who only became wives after the time of the ICC's temporal jurisdiction. The Chamber held in relation to these girls that although their status as *ting tings* (the household servants) did not protect them from being sexually exploited, they generally 'were not sexually enslaved, but enslaved'.[207] This is the case for P-0235 and P-0236. This reasoning, however, remains unstated in the legal analysis.

By focusing only on the wives, the Chamber failed to clarify the distinction between the enslavement of the *ting tings* and the forced marriage of the

[200] See, eg, *Prosecutor v Krajisnik* (Trial Chamber Judgment) IT-00-39-T (27 September 2006) para 815.
[201] *Ongwen* (TC Judgment) (n 23) para 3086.
[202] See ss B and C below.
[203] *Ongwen* (TC Judgment) (n 23) para 3050.
[204] ibid para 3051.
[205] ibid para 2797.
[206] ibid para 3053.
[207] ibid para 3086.

wives.[208] It likely followed the view that the *ting specialist* phase was a preliminary stage before becoming a wife, which was evidenced by Ongwen monitoring the menstruation of the girls.[209] If so, it would not have been logical to search for testimony of household servants who were only enslaved and explain the practice as contrasting with the practice of forced marriage.[210] Yet this reasoning sits uneasily with the cumulative conviction of slavery and forced marriage as another inhumane act. If the *ting ting* stage formed part of the process of becoming a wife, it is inconsistent to criminalise that phase separately under a distinct label. Given the Chamber's own finding that cumulative conviction is impermissible without a distinct element, the enslavement phase should have been subsumed under the category of other inhumane acts.

In conclusion, too much of the reasoning in the *Ongwen judgment* is left implicit, as a result of which the interpretative process was seriously flawed. The several absentee sources in the judgment are remarkable. Notably, the Chamber neither elaborated on the treaty basis of the crime of enslavement nor did it discuss its basis in customary law. This misuse of Article 21 is in violation of the principle of legality. Given that the crime is firmly established in ICL, the immediate jump to precedent was unnecessary and regrettable. It creates the unwanted impression that Article 21's structure was not even considered. In terms of the result, this study finds that there is no reason why the bush wives phenomenon should not be qualified as slavery and agrees with the historical arguments that this label has always been designed to encompass also acts of a sexual nature.

ii. An Alternative Interpretation of Enslavement

Considering the specific case of the LRA's bush wives, there is a set of arguments that favour it being labelled as slavery. As explained by Allain, 'the extent of the control over these girls and women was so overwhelming that if it was exercised over a thing owned, we would recognise it as 'possession' in property law'.[211] He argued that possession and control – established here through sexual violence – fall squarely within the traditional notion of enslavement under the 1926 Slavery Convention.[212] The 1956 Supplementary Convention merely clarified that practices such as forced marriage, where women are transferred or given without consent, constitute slavery.[213] Thus, a forced marriage in which

[208] See: *Prosecutor v Ongwen* (Separate Opinion of Judge Marc Perrin de Brichambaut) ICC-02/04-01/15 (6 June 2016) paras 143–61.

[209] *Ongwen* (TC Judgment) (n 23) paras 2248–55.

[210] *Ongwen* (Amici Curiae Observations on Sexual- and Gender-Based Crimes, Particularly Sexual Slavery, and on Cumulative Convictions) (n 199) para 18, see also: E Baines, 'Forced marriage as a political project: Sexual rules and relations in the Lord's Resistance Army' (2014) 51 *Journal of Peace Research* 405, 414.

[211] *Ongwen* (Amicus Curiae on Sexual Slavery & Forced Marriage) (n 178) para 29.

[212] Allain (n 168) 403.

[213] Supplementary Slavery Convention (n 98) Art 1(c).

ownership is exercised amounts to enslavement.[214] Contemporary scholars likewise affirm that slavery includes sexual dimensions; Sellers, for instance, noted that judges have often failed to recognise forced marriage as enslavement.[215] – a view echoed by the SCSL *Taylor* Trial Chamber.[216]

In line with these conclusions, this study argues that the label of enslavement is perfectly capable of being applied to this bush wife scenario and grasps the nature of this phenomenon adequately.[217] A textual approach to the internal sources clarifies that the core of enslavement is the exercise of the rights of ownership. Derived from the notions of property, it is understood as 'control over a person like a thing', allowing to exclude 'lesser forms of exploitation from slavery',[218] and including only those that, by exercising the rights of ownership, remove 'the victim's autonomy and agency'.[219] It has to be established whether there is evidence of such control and ownership.

As Quirk observes, when someone is forced into marriage and their partner exercises powers of ownership over their productive and reproductive capacities, and they cannot leave due to threats or violence, their situation meets the 1926 definition of slavery.[220] Ongwen exercised full control over his wives. The indicia identified by the Trial Chamber clearly demonstrated this control – restrictions on movement, confinement, and the ever-present fear of punishment. Several women testified that refusal to become a wife could cost them their lives, and many described being transferred and distributed to commanders, a hallmark of possession.[221] It is therefore puzzling that the Chamber failed to recognise this system of distribution as one of enslavement.[222]

The slavery label is capable of encompassing both sexual and non-sexual conduct. The ICC's reluctance to use it – echoing the SCSL's reasoning – appears to stem from the perception that the bush wives phenomenon included too many non-sexual aspects, making other inhumane acts a better fit.[223] Yet the non-sexual harm, such as stigma and difficulty reintegrating, could just as well fall under enslavement. A second argument holds that the bush wives phenomenon fits better under other inhumane acts, as the harm extends beyond the sexual and differs from that of other LRA victims. Whether they faced greater social exclusion than rape survivors, child soldiers, or *ting tings* is ultimately

[214] McDougall (n 98) para 30.
[215] ibid para 29.
[216] *Taylor (Trial Judgment) (n 121)* para 427.
[217] See, eg, Adams (n 193).
[218] ibid 293.
[219] Haenen (n 15) 903.
[220] Quirk (n 169) 271.
[221] *Ongwen* (TC Judgment) (n 23) para 2204: testimony of P-0351; para 2212: testimony of P-0396; see also paras 2219, 2220,2222, 2225,2226.
[222] ibid paras 2143-2182.
[223] In the *Taylor Judgment,* the Trial Chamber argued that also enslavement could be a gendered crime and can include much more than sexual violence: *Taylor (Trial Judgment) (n 121)* paras 1697–1699.

an evidentiary question – one that the judgment fails to substantiate or clearly reference. Moreover, given the confidential nature of expert reports on the issue of forced marriage, a matter that can be criticised independently of the entire labelling debate, and the highly redacted nature of the testimonies of the wives, it is difficult to understand for outsiders how this issue is grounded in evidence. A review of the Ongwen transcripts, however, suggests the opposite: all returnees faced severe reintegration challenges. If lasting stigma was not unique to the wives, the argument against applying the slavery label loses its force.

The conclusion is that there is some kind of reluctance to classify wives as victims of enslavement and that this stems from a perceived need to distinguish their status from that of *ting tings*. It seems that judges wanted both types of crimes distinguished and that it was considered unfair that *ting tings* and wives were both qualified as victims of enslavement. While this concern for differentiation is understandable, it prioritises fairness in labelling over legal precision. The way the arguments in favour of fair labelling fall were presented falls into the trap of what has been called the *balancing consciousness* – the judicial impulse to reconcile conflicting considerations through compromise and balancing.[224] Since strict construction is a first-order principle and fair labelling only a second-order one from the victim's perspective, the former must prevail over the latter.[225] As a result, fair labelling cannot result in a label perfectly capable of encompassing the phenomenon of bush wives being disregarded. Since the harm is captured by enslavement, this study proposes labelling both the wives' forced marriages and the ting tings' slavery as enslavement.

B. Sexual Slavery

Compared to the crime of enslavement, the crime of sexual slavery has a much more recent pedigree. The first traces of it being considered to feature as a crime in the Rome Statute date back to 1997.[226] Because many delegates found it needed to be specifically named,[227] the WCGJ proposed to have a list of SGBC that featured sexual slavery.[228] The Holy See argued that its inclusion was unnecessary as it could be perfectly captured by enslavement and wanted to erase the reference to it in favour of 'enslavement or any other kind of involuntary servitude that emerges from the theatre of war or armed conflict'.[229] There seemed to

[224] I Porat, 'The Dual Model of Balancing: A Model for the Proper Scope of Balancing in Constitutional Law' (2006) 27 *Cardozo Law Review* 1393, 1399.

[225] See ch 5, s III(A) for Strict Construction and s III(B) for Fair Labelling.

[226] CK Hall, 'The third and fourth sessions of the UN Preparatory Committee on the Establishment of an International Criminal Court' (1998) 92 *American Journal of International Law* 124, 127; Oosterveld (n 196) 611f; Bedont and Hall-Martinez (n 48) 72.

[227] Oosterveld (n 196) 623; Halley (n 46) 94-96.

[228] 'Recommendations and Commentary for December 1997 Prep Com, Part III', Recommendation 7 (n 97); See also Halley (n 46) 90.

[229] Holy See, 'Proposal Submitted by the Holy See' (9 December 1997) A/AC.249/1997/WG.1/DP.12.

be little enthusiasm to follow the Holy See in this proposal, and the inclusion of sexual slavery 'was adopted without debate'.[230] Interestingly, the crime of sexual slavery is included as both a war crime and a crime against humanity, whereas enslavement is only a crime against humanity.

The Elements define sexual slavery by the same core element as enslavement – 'the exercise of any or all of the powers attaching to the right of ownership' – with the added requirement that the victim was forced to engage in acts of a sexual nature.[231] During negotiations, concerns arose about distinguishing the two crimes. The WCGJ justified listing both by noting that women might be forced into maternity or temporary marriages involving sexual and non-sexual aspects, allowing prosecutors to charge both enslavement and sexual slavery. This shows that, even during the Rome Statute's drafting, marriage-like practices were already understood as forms of slavery.[232]

i. The Label in the Katanga, Ntaganda and Ongwen Cases

As indicated, the label of sexual slavery was first tested in the *Katanga & Ngudjolo* case, involving two commanders accused of the 2003 attacks against the non-Hema population of Bogoro. Both were charged with rape and sexual slavery as CaH.[233] The WIGJ,[234] which collected field evidence in the DRC, testified that a broader range of SGBC had occurred and criticised the limited scope of the charges.[235] They reported on the *bush wives* phenomenon and that commanding officers were assigned wives.[236] The Prosecutor likewise stated that women were 'forced into marriage as combatant wives or detained as sexual slaves by Katanga's or Ngudjolo's soldiers'.[237]

During the confirmation proceedings, women testified they were forced to become men's wives.[238] The Pre-Trial Chamber found sufficient evidence to unequivocally classify these acts as sexual slavery[239] It reaffirmed that sexual slavery is a separate offence and a particular form of enslavement, citing footnotes 11 and 18 of the *Elements of Crimes* referencing the 1956 Supplementary Convention on Slavery.[240] It cited practices such as rape camps and forced temporary marriages as examples of treating women as chattel, stressing

[230] Oosterveld (n 196) 614.
[231] Article 7(1)(g)-2 Crime against humanity of sexual slavery, Elements of Crimes, Element 1 and 2.
[232] Justice, 'Recommendations and Commentary for December 1997 Prep Com, Part III'WC (n 97) 4.4; Oosterveld (n 196) 624.
[233] *Katanga & Ngudjolo Chui (CoC Decision) (n 142)* paras 428ff.
[234] Recalling that the Women's Caucus for Gender Justice (WCGJ) was renamed the Women's Initiative for Gender Justice (WIGJ) in 2003.
[235] WIGJ, *Gender Report Card 2010* (2010) 160, available at www.iccwomen.org/documents/GRC10-WEB-11-10-v4_Final-version-Dec-.pdf.
[236] ibid 161.
[237] *Prosecutor v Ongwen* (Transcript) ICC-01/04-01/07-T-80-ENG (24 November 2009) 25.
[238] *Katanga (CoC Decision) (n 142)* fn 453.
[239] *ibid paras* 347–49.
[240] ibid para 430.

that sexual slavery entails both sexual acts and control over a victim's sexual autonomy.[241]

The *Katanga* Trial Chamber offered a fuller analysis, grounding the crime in the exercise of ownership: the 'use, enjoyment and disposal of a person regarded as property', resulting in total dependence and loss of autonomy.[242] After the example of enslavement and drawn from both ICTY and SCSL decisions, the judges developed a non-exhaustive list of indicia:

> detention or captivity and their respective duration; restrictions on freedom to come and go or on any freedom of choice or movement; and, more generally, any measure taken to prevent or deter any attempt at escape. The use of threats, force or other forms of physical or mental coercion, the exaction of forced labour, the exertion of psychological pressure, the victim's vulnerability and the socioeconomic conditions in which the power is exerted.[243]

The second constituent material element of 'acts of a sexual nature' was explained similarly to the *CoC Decision*. The Trial Chamber added 'that women and girls are forced to share the existence of a person with whom they have to engage in acts of a sexual nature'.[244] The judgment offered little discussion of marriage itself, apart from a passage in which the judges considered that P132's husband indeed exercised powers attaching to the right of ownership, and she had no consent in the marriage.[245] Another witness referred to the men who held her captive as 'husbands' but specified nothing about a so-called marriage.[246] The Chamber therefore concluded that the status of wife was imposed merely so that sexual favours and sexual intercourse could be obtained.[247]

Interestingly, the *Katanga Judgment* mentioned the fact that these women 'were rejected by their community'.[248] As discussed further on, this element of societal ostracism, social stigma, and the difficulty of reintegration and rehabilitation has been mentioned as an additional harm that requires qualification as another inhumane act.[249]

In the *Ntaganda* case, the Deputy Chief of Staff of the FPLC faced charges for crimes committed in Eastern DRC. Although much of the litigation focused on whether child soldiers were protected against SGBC, the case also revealed evidence of girls taken as wives. According to the Prosecutor, commanders 'took young girls as so-called wives', forcing them to perform domestic labour and submit to sexual exploitation.[250]

[241] ibid para 431.
[242] *Katanga* (TC Judgment) (n 186) para 975.
[243] *Katanga* (TC Judgment) (n 186) para 986.
[244] ibid para 978.
[245] ibid paras 1007-1008.
[246] ibid para 1016-1018.
[247] ibid para 1016.
[248] ibid para 950.
[249] *Sesay et al (RUF case) (Trial Judgment) (n 118)* para 1296.
[250] *Prosecutor v Ntaganda* (Opening Statement of the Prosecutor) ICC-01/04-02/06-T-23 (25 September 2015) 61.

The *CoC Decision* did not engage in a thorough discussion of the substantive elements of sexual slavery,[251] but only clarifies that mere imprisonment is not sufficient to satisfy the element of ownership over the victim.[252] The *Ntaganda* Trial Chamber reiterated the non-exhaustive list of factors set out by the *Katanga* Trial Chamber, and found two girls to be enslaved on the basis of this list.[253]

Interestingly, the Chamber observed that the term wife was commonly used for coerced sexual relationships – an observation that arguably weakens the position that the bush wives phenomenon has to be labelled another inhumane act.[254] If this is a correct assertion, then it possibly can be an argument debunking the use of the residual category of 'other inhumane acts' to the bush wives phenomenon.

In the Ongwen case, the accused was convicted of sexually enslaving four of his seven wives (P-0101, P-0214, P-0226, P-0227).[255] The Chamber defined sexual slavery as enslavement involving control over a victim's sexual autonomy.[256] Because these girls were subjected to sexual acts, including rape, the conduct was classified as sexual slavery; where no sexual violence occurred, it was labelled as enslavement.[257] The following section argues for a stricter distinction between the two crimes.

ii. An Alternative Interpretation of the Category of Sexual Slavery

The fact that sexual slavery is labelled separately and is 'treated as a separate category' in the Rome Statute reveals a particular problem, namely, it 'reflects an unduly narrow conception of the parameters of 'slavery in all its forms', because it fails to adequately consider the many different roles that slaves have historically performed.[258] Because of this, this study sides with Adams that the crime of sexual slavery should be erased from the Rome Statute. The label of enslavement has always included acts of a sexual nature, and for coherence and to avoid overlap, the most desirable outcome would be that the enslavement label is more appreciated.

Since abolishing the offence of sexual slavery is unlikely, this study seeks to preserve its distinct function without making it redundant. It proposes that the label be reserved for cases where the violence and resulting harm are primarily, if not exclusively, sexual in nature. This shifts away from viewing sexual slavery as merely *enslavement plus sexual acts* and avoids implying that enslavement is a lesser offence. The label would thus better apply to contexts such as 'rape

[251] *Ntaganda* (CoC Decision) (n 144) paras 53–57 and endnotes 208 and 209.
[252] ibid 53.
[253] *Ntaganda* (TC Judgment) (n 185) paras 951–52.
[254] ibid footnotes 458 and 1156.
[255] *Ongwen* (TC Judgment) (n 23) paras 3044–55.
[256] ibid para 2716.
[257] ibid para 2715.
[258] Quirk (n 169) 275.

camps', where the harm is chiefly sexual, while broader practices like *bush wives* are more appropriately captured under the wider concept of enslavement, which encompasses both sexual and non-sexual harm.

C. Other Inhumane Acts

This residual category of CaH is as old as the international prosecution of crimes against humanity itself. As the introduction has explained, this category has been included in every ICT statute since Nuremberg.[259] Its meaning has nonetheless evolved. The first formulations after WWII were formulated without a similar gravity requirement.[260] The 1954 ILC Draft Code introduced an understanding of the category that required a nexus to other crimes.[261] Article 18 of the 1996 ILC Draft articulated that other inhumane acts are those acts 'which severely damage physical or mental integrity, health or human dignity, such as mutilation and severe bodily harm'.[262] The ILC furthermore instituted the requirement that the acts need to be 'similar in gravity to those listed in the preceding subparagraphs.[263]

The ICTY and ICTR Statutes referred simply to other inhumane acts, leaving their scope to judicial interpretation. In *Čelebići*, the Trial Chamber drew on the 1996 ILC Draft and human rights law on torture and ill-treatment, finding the concept to be relative.[264] It held that inhumane treatment is conduct causing serious mental or physical suffering, though less severe than torture,[265] and thus encompasses acts seriously harming physical or mental integrity or constituting a grave affront to human dignity.[266] In the *Kordic & Cerkez* Appeal Judgment, the judges refined this reasoning, holding that the acts must have caused 'serious bodily or mental harm', with the degree of severity assessed case by case, having regard to individual circumstances[267], adding that the act must be of 'a similar seriousness to the other enumerated acts'.[268] CTR chambers echoed this formula, requiring that such acts be 'similar in nature, character, gravity and seriousness'.[269] Jurisprudence has applied it to a wide spectrum of

[259] See footnote 2 for the relevant provisions.

[260] London Charter (n 2) Article 6(c) and Tokyo Charter (n 2) Art 5(c) refer to 'other inhumane acts, before or during the war'.

[261] Draft Code of Offences against the Peace and Security of Mankind with commentaries (YBILC 1954, vol II) 136.

[262] ibid vol II, Part 2, 47.

[263] ibid 103.

[264] *Prosecutor v Delalic et al (Čelebići Case)* (Trial Chamber Judgment) IT-96-21-T (16 November 1998) paras 533–41.

[265] ibid para 542.

[266] ibid para 543.

[267] *Prosecutor v Kordic and Cerkez* (Appeals Judgment) IT-95-14/2-A (17 December 2004) para 117.

[268] *Prosecutor v Karadžić* (Trial Judgment) T-95-5/18-T (24 March 2016) para 494.

[269] *Prosecutor v Musema* (Judgment and Sentence) ICTR-96-13-T (27 January 2000) para 232.

conduct: forced nudity,[270] the desecration of corpses.[271] Some of the acts previously considered other inhumane acts now feature as listed crimes in the Rome Statute: enforced disappearance,[272] forcible transfer or displacement,[273] and enforced prostitution.[274]

At the ICTY, concerns arose as to the compatibility of some of these inclusions with the principle of legality.[275] The extent to which it can be used to subsume a broad range of behaviour makes the category susceptible to unforeseeable inclusion.[276] This necessitated limitations to this category,[277] which is why the Elements of Crimes of Article 7(1)(k) are formulated as follows:

1. The perpetrator inflicted great suffering, or serious injury to body or to mental or physical health [. . .]
2. Such act was of a character similar to any other act referred to in article [7(1)]

This wording preserves flexibility while anchoring the clause in legality through three cumulative constraints: a threshold of harm, an *ejusdem generis* requirement, and a specification of the residual character.

First, the other inhumane act needs to create great suffering or serious injury.[278] This necessarily entails a 'value judgment' which means a case-by-case assessment is preferable.[279] The ICTY Trial Chamber in the *Krstic case* stated that the harm must not be permanent or irremediable. It nonetheless must go beyond 'temporary unhappiness, embarrassment or humiliation'.[280] This means that 'a grave and long-term disadvantage to a person's ability to lead a normal and constructive life', qualifies as an inhumane act.[281] The Pre-Trial Chamber in the *Muthuara, Kenyatta* and *Ali case* found that the victims had suffered greatly by witnessing the killing and mutilation of their family members.[282]

[270] *Akayesu (TC Judgment) (n 33)* para 598.

[271] *Prosecutor v Bagosora* (Judgment and Sentence) ICTR-98-41-T (18 December 2008) paras 2219–20.

[272] *Prosecutor v Kupreškić et al* (Trial Judgment) IT 95-16 (14 January 2000) para 566.

[273] *Prosecutor v Stakic* (Appeal Chamber Judgment) IT-97-24-A (22 March 2006) paras 315ff; *Prosecutor v Krstic* (Judgment) IT-98-33-T (2 Augustus 2001) para 523.

[274] *Kupreškić* (Trial Judgment) (n 272) para 566.

[275] para 565; see further J Lincoln, '*Nullum Crimen Sine Lege* in International Criminal Jurisprudence, The Problem of a Residual Category of Crime' (2010–2011) 7 *Eyes on the ICC* 137, 148ff.

[276] Hall and Ambos (n 159) 235.

[277] H Von Hebel and D Robinson, 'Crimes within the Jurisdiction of the Court' in RS Lee (ed), *The International Criminal Court, The Making of the Rome Statute, Issues, Negotiations, Results* (Kluwer Law International, 2009) 102; G Witschel and Wi Rückert, 'Article 7(1)(k) – Crime Against Humanity of Other Inhumane Acts' in RS Lee (ed), *The International Criminal Court: Elements of Crimes and Rules of Procedure and Evidence* (Transnational Publishers, 2001) 107.

[278] I Haenen, 'Classifying Acts as Crimes Against Humanity in the Rome Statute of the International Criminal Court' (2013) 14 *German Law Journal* 796, 816.

[279] ibid 817.

[280] *Krstic* (n 273) para 513.

[281] ibid para 513.

[282] *Prosecutor v Muthaura, Kenyatta & Ali* (Decision on the Prosecutor's Application for Summonses to Appear for Francis Kirimi Muthaura, Uhuru Muigai Kenyatta and Mohammed Hussein Ali) ICC-01/09-02/11-1 (8 March 2011) para 277.

Second, this category is a category of *ejusdem generis* requiring an assessment of the similarity of the listed acts with those considered under the residual clause. The acts must be similar *in character*. The Trial Chamber has specified that this should be assessed in terms of 'nature, harm suffered and protected interests involved'.[283]

Third, the introduction of the word 'other' means that an act considered under the listed acts cannot be simultaneously considered as an inhumane act.[284] The ICC judges have stressed the subsidiary relationship to the listed acts,[285] but held that it is also not required that the conduct in question, 'in its entirety, falls completely outside any act under Article 7(1)(a)–(j)'.[286] Haenen argued that the standard is similar to the one used in relation to cumulative convictions and requires a materially distinct element.[287] To not 'expand uncritically the scope' of CaH,[288] the interpretation given to Article 7(1)(k) 'must be consistent with the essence of the offence' and reasonably foreseeable.[289] This is why the ICC case law supports an additional requirement of the materially distinct element requirement.

One of the difficulties surrounding this category is the doubt as to whether it can tackle sexual violence not captured under Article 7(1)(g)'s enumeration of sexual crimes. This raises how the residual category in paragraph (g) relates to other inhumane acts. The former should address sexual crimes, leaving the latter for non-sexual violence.

i. The Label of Other Inhumane Acts in the Ongwen and Al Hassan Cases

Forced marriage has been understood as a multi-layered or compound crime that can include rape, enslavement, sexual slavery, forced domestic labour, forced pregnancy, and several acts of sexual violence and forms of inhumane treatment.[290] Some of these acts individually amount to crimes against humanity; others might not, taken separately, rise up to the needed level. There is no doubt that forced marriage can share characteristics with sexual slavery and enslavement, but these crimes can also be fundamentally different.[291] The practice of forced marriage has also been understood as not fully described by any of the

[283] *Ongwen* (TC Judgment) (n 23) para 2746.
[284] *Katanga (CoC Decision) (n 142)* para 452.
[285] *Ongwen* (TC Judgment) (n 23) para 2873, para 2891, para 2944, para 2990.
[286] ibid para 2747.
[287] Haenen (n 278) 810–12.
[288] *Muthuara, Kenyatta & Ali* para 269.
[289] *Ongwen* (TC Judgment) (n 23) para 2741.
[290] N Jain, 'Forced Marriage as a Crime against Humanity Notes and Comments' (2008) 6 *JICJ* 1013, 1021; Slater (n 103) 742; Haenen (n 10) 4; V Oosterveld, 'Forced Marriage during Conflict and Mass Atrocity' in F Ní Aoláin and others (eds), *The Oxford Handbook of Gender and Conflict* (OUP, 2015) 250; VM Kerr, 'Should Forced Marriages Be Categorized as "Sexual Slavery" Or "Other Inhumane Acts" in International Criminal Law?' (2020) 35 *Utrecht Journal of International and European* Law 1, 16.
[291] Jain (n 290) 1029.

single crimes enumerated.[292] Furthermore, several authors have warned against describing it as merely sexual in nature.[293] These reasons make most authors advocate for the crime being qualified as another inhumane act.[294]

Two ICC cases addressed forced marriage under other inhumane acts. In *Ongwen*, the LRA abducted girls as bush wives, some served as household workers, others were given as wives to commanders. In *Al Hassan*, AQIM leaders in Mali arranged forced marriages through families, sometimes paying dowries and holding ceremonies to legitimise them. Unlike the LRA's strategic motives, AQIM's were religious and ideological, aiming to reshape Timbuktu's society under an Islamic regime.

This section examines whether, in these two cases, the three material elements required for 'other inhumane acts' are effectively fulfilled. These are discussed in the following order: (1) the similar gravity/equal harm requirement, (2) the similar character requirement; and (3) the requirement of a materially distinct element. The materially distinct element is argued to be reflected by several distinctive characteristics: the imposition of marriage; the exclusivity created by the forced conjugal association, an additional and different harm that is not necessarily sexual in nature but has been framed in terms of a violation of the basic rights to consensually marry and establish a family, a long-lasting social stigma or a difficulty of reintegration into society as a result of the label wife and rejection by their families and the community as a result of the marriage. All these elements are interconnected and usually offered simultaneously in support of the residual category.

a. The Similar Gravity Requirement:[295] Equally Severe, but Different Harm

Both the *Ongwen* and *Al Hassan* cases examined the harm caused by forced marriage, finding it equally severe yet distinct, thereby using it to substantiate two of the three material elements of other inhumane acts.

The *Ongwen* Pre-Trial Chamber relied on both SCSL[296] and ECCC judgments[297] to find that forcing the victims 'to serve as conjugal partner' can cause great suffering.[298] The Trial Chamber held that the harm consists 'of being ostracized from the community, mental trauma, the serious attack on the victim's dignity, and the deprivation of the victim's fundamental rights to choose his or

[292] Frulli (n 16) 1036.

[293] A Bunting and IK Ikhimiukor, 'The Expressive Nature of Law: What We Learn from Conjugal Slavery to Forced Marriage in International Criminal Law' (2018) 18 *International Criminal Law Review* 331, 340–41; V Oosterveld, 'Force Marriage: Terminological Coherence and Dissonance in International Criminal Law' (2019) 27 *William & Mary Bill of Rights Journal* 1263, 1266–67.

[294] Park (n 14); Scharf and Mattler (n 103); Toy-Cronin (n 126); Bunting, Lawrance and Robert (n 8).

[295] G Boas, JL Bischoff and NL Reid, *International Criminal Law Practitioner Library, vol 2, Elements of Crimes Under International Law* (CUP, 2009) 101.

[296] *Ongwen (CoC Decision) (n 23)* para 89 relying on both the RUF and AFRC Appeal Judgment.

[297] ibid para 90 relying on ECCC, Case 002.

[298] ibid para 91.

her spouse'.[299] The *Al Hassan* Pre-Trial Chamber produced a similar reasoning.[300] The judge found that the absence of choice in a spouse, as well as the stigmatisation, were elements that created great suffering.[301] Additionally, the judge held that not being able to choose when to procreate, as well as the miscarriages the women suffered, were additional elements causing great suffering. The PTC also held that suffering depends on the vulnerability of the victims.[302] While *Al Hassan* was acquitted on this charge, the trial judgment, which refers to the Ongwen Appeal Judgment, further defines this suffering in terms of gendered harm. The marital state creates gendered expectations and 'involves social, ethical and religious effects which can seriously impact the victim's physical and psychological well-being'.[303] With these two decisions, we see an evolution to further define forced marriage's non-sexual nature in gender terminology.

Up to this point, this study finds there is nothing problematic in terms of the principle of legality. The practices of marriage certainly generated great and equal suffering to the other listed acts. The judges' use of analogy aligns with Article 22(2) and does not breach the ban on analogy. However, this study contests whether the harm identified is truly distinct or already covered by other crimes.[304]

The first element is that the harm is primarily non-sexual and thus falls outside the scope of sexual slavery. Both in the *Ongwen* and *Al Hassan* cases, the judges stressed the non-sexual nature of the phenomenon.[305] It remains unclear why enslavement could not capture the phenomenon's non-sexual aspects. The *Ongwen* Trial Chamber explained that 'while crime of sexual enslavement penalises the perpetrator's restriction or control of the victim's sexual autonomy while held in a state of enslavement', 'forced marriage penalises the perpetrator's imposition of 'conjugal association' and 'does not necessarily require the exercise of ownership over a person, an essential element for the existence of the crime of enslavement'.[306]

The second reason to resort to the residual category is that forced marriage is found to create an additional harm because it violates the basic right to consensually marry and establish a family.[307] In the *Ongwen case*, the Trial Chamber found that the community might even see the victim as a 'legitimate spouse', and even the victim themselves can see themselves as bound.[308] This harm is distinct from the harm that comes from violating the physical or sexual integrity

[299] *Ongwen* (TC Judgment) (n 23) para 2749.
[300] Al *Hassan* (CoC Decision) (n 150) paras 560–61.
[301] ibid para 560.
[302] ibid para 561.
[303] *Prosecutor v Al Hassan* (TC Judgment) (n 156) para 1187.
[304] See ch 5, Intro and s II(B).
[305] *Ongwen* (TC Judgment) (n 23) para 2750; *Hassan* (CoC Decision) (n 150) para 553; Al Hassan (TC Judgment) (n 156) para 1188.
[306] *Ongwen* (TC Judgment) (n 23) para 2750.
[307] ibid para 2748; *Al Hassan* (TC Judgment) (n 156) para 1187.
[308] *Ongwen* (TC Judgment) (n 23) para 2748.

or personal liberty, a value that is traditionally protected by the laws against sexual crimes such as sexual slavery.[309] This was said in similar wording in the *Al Hassan case*.[310]

A third element is that the stigmatisation and trauma of the victims go beyond that caused by being a rape victim alone.[311] It is not clear how the evidence supports that claim, as the Chamber only refers to the *Al Hassan CoC Decision*. In the referenced paragraph of that decision, the Pre-trial Chamber indeed finds the stigmatisation of victims of forced marriage '*bien particulièr*' and touches upon the social dimension.[312] The label of wife results in the victim being seen in a specific way by the community.[313]

Based on the transcripts in the *Ongwen case* and the questioning of the wives in the Pre-Trial Article 56 Proceedings, as well as the expert testimony given on the issue of forced marriage, this analysis accommodates the lack of clarity in the Trial Judgment. The Judgment does not show how their suffering differed from other LRA victims.[314] Experts noted that all returnees experienced trauma,[315] with women and victims of sexual violence particularly affected. Reicheter added that nearly all survivors of sexual violence suffer lasting harm.[316] This indicates that although the individual effects of SGBC varied, all are affected, and there is no sensible way to make distinctions of the degree of harm. One of Ongwen's wives confirmed that her harm stemmed from injury and lack of education rather than marriage. The main source of stigma was whether returning girls had children.[317] Experts noted that women who returned with children faced greater shame, stigma, and social isolation.[318] In conclusion, the public evidence examined does not substantiate this differentiation in harm between wives and other SGBC victims. It is still possible that the answer is in confidential evidence. It nonetheless consists of a significant methodological problem: the passage in the judgment is not supported by evidence but rather is substantiated by external precedent. The claim that the harm and trauma of victims of forced marriage is different from victims of other SGBC is proven by referring to the *Al*

[309] *Ongwen* (CoC Decision) (n 23) para 94.

[310] *Hassan* CoC decision para 554; *Al Hassan (*TC Judgment) (n 156) para 1188.

[311] *Ongwen* (TC Judgment) (n 23) para 2750.

[312] *Hassan (*CoC Decision) (n 150) para 555.

[313] ibid para 555.

[314] *Prosecutor v Ongwen* (Testimony of Prof Allen) ICC-02/04-01/15-T-28-ENG (Transcript of 16 January 2017) 73.

[315] *Prosecutor v Ongwen (*Testimony of Prof Wessels) ICC-02/04-01/15-T-28-ENG (Transcript of 15 May 2018) 17; *Testimony of Allen (n 314)* 73.

[316] *Prosecutor v Ongwen,* (Testimony of Prof Reicheter) Transcript of 14 May 2018 (ICC-02/04-01/15-T-175-Red-ENG).

[317] *Testimony of Wessels (n 315)* 8; *Prosecutor v Ongwen,* (Testimony of Prof Musisi) ICC-02/04-01/15-T-177-ENG (Transcript of 23 May 2018) 23; *Prosecutor v Ongwen* (Testimony of Prof Allen) ICC-02/04-01/15-T-28-ENG (Transcript of 16 January 2017) 105; *Prosecutor v Ongwen,* (Testimony of Teddy Atim) ICC-02/04-01/15-T-174-ENG (Transcript of 4 May 2018) 21–22.

[318] *Prosecutor v Ongwen,* (Article 56 proceedings P-0236) ICC-02/04-01/15-T-174-ENG (transcript of 16 November 2015*)* 36

Hassan Confirmation of Charges Decision, which in turn relied on the *Ongwen* Confirmation of Charges Decision. This is extremely problematic as the finding on trauma of victims is an evidentiary and case-specific matter entirely.

b. The Similar Character Requirement

The gravity assessment was part of the previous section's analysis. The core of this section's assessment is the determination of a similar character. Footnote 30 in the Elements stipulates that the character 'refers to the nature and gravity of the act'. A similar character has also been articulated 'in terms of harm and protected interest involved'.[319] This restriction to the open-endedness of the category was motivated by a desire to adhere to the principle of legality.[320] Because this category requires analogical reasoning, foreseeability must guide its application to avoid violating the ban on analogy.

In proving the similarity in nature of the conduct, there are two aspects noticeable. First, judges often link this assessment to human rights, finding that serious infringements of fundamental rights may qualify as conduct 'similar in nature'.[321] Some even say the residual clause provides 'flexibility to cover serious violations of human rights not specifically enumerated'.[322] Second, the inquiry into whether the acts are inhumane in a comparable way has been tied to the concept of human dignity.[323] The category has thus been described as one encompassing 'certain serious transgressions against human dignity'.[324]

Traces of human rights and human dignity reasoning can be found in the Ongwen case. The *Ongwen* Pre-Trial Chamber stated that the wives' 'basic right to consensually marry and establish a family' was violated.[325] The judges found that by forcing the victims into conjugal relationships, they endured 'serious physical or mental suffering or injury or a serious attack on *human dignity* of a degree of gravity comparable to that of other crimes against humanity'.[326] Luckily, the reference to human dignity was not taken over by the Trial Chamber. The reintroduction of this terminology via the other inhumane acts category would go against the intention of the WCGJ to disconnect the language of honour and dignity from SGBC.[327]

[319] *Ongwen* (TC Judgment) (n 23) para 2837.

[320] Hall and Ambos (n 159) 237; CM Bassiouni, *Crimes Against Humanity: historical evolution and contemporary application*, 2nd edn (CUP, 2013) 409.

[321] *Katanga (CoC Decision)* (n 142) para 450.

[322] *Prosecutor v Katanga & Ngudjolo Chui* (Partly Dissenting Opinion of Judge Anita Usacka to the Confirmation of Charges Decision) ICC-01/04-01/07 (30 September 2008) para 31.

[323] B Kuschnik, 'Humaneness, Humankind and Crimes against Humanity' (2010) 2 *Goettingen Journal of International Law* 501.

[324] Boas, Bischoff and Reid (n 295) 99.

[325] See also: JP Pérez-León Acevedo, 'The Close Relationship Between Serious Human Rights Violations and Crimes Against Humanity: International Criminalization of Serious Abuses' (2017) 17 *Anuario Mexicano de Derecho Internacional* 145.

[326] *Ongwen* (CoC Decision) (n 23) para 90.

[327] See also Erb (n 50) 416.

Analogical reasoning under this category has focused mainly on whether forced marriage is comparable to sexual slavery.[328] The *Ongwen* PTC analysed whether the conduct '(i.e. to have forced women to serve as "conjugal partners" to himself and other LRA fighters in the Sinia brigade)' constituted another inhumane act or whether it is subsumed by the crime of sexual slavery.[329] For that purpose, it relied first on the SCSL case law because of the 'very similar factual allegations' and 'identical legal question'.[330] Despite the different fact pattern, it nonetheless also referred to the ECCC.[331] The Chamber cautiously concluded that such conduct *may*, in the abstract, qualify as an 'other inhumane act', and added that forced marriage 'will generally be committed in circumstances in which the victim is also sexually or otherwise enslaved'.[332]

This paragraph reveals a conceptual inconsistency. If forced marriage is defined by its non-sexual, conjugal nature rather than ownership, comparing it chiefly to sexual slavery is misplaced. Although Chambers note both sexual and non-sexual aspects, their reasoning stresses the latter. From a legality standpoint, it would have been more coherent to assess its similarity to enslavement or clarify why it could not fall under that crime.[333]

c. The Requirement of a Materially Distinct Element: the Imposition of Marriage, Exclusivity, and Social Stigma

Lastly, but most importantly, the other inhumane acts can only be used when the conduct is not captured by the other listed acts. Although the Elements do not list this as a separate material element, the case law has consistently recognised this constituent element.[334] A textual reading of '*other*' implies this category applies only when no other provision captures the conduct. The *Al Hassan* Chamber confirmed its distinct nature in terms of conduct, harm, and purpose.[335]

Several elements are used to prove the distinctiveness of the phenomenon.

The first consists of the imposition of marriage. In *Ongwen*, the Pre-Trial Chamber explained this as 'the imposition, regardless of the will of the victim, of duties that are associated with marriage, as well as of a social status of the perpetrator's 'wife'.[336] The practice of forced marriage was understood to violate 'the basic to consensually marry and establish a family'.[337] The judges

[328] C Eboe-Osuji, 'Forced Marriage – an International Crime?' in C Eboe-Osuji (ed), *International Law and Sexual Violence in Armed Conflicts* (Martinus Nijhoff, 2012) 245ff.

[329] *Ongwen* (CoC Decision) (n 23) para 88.

[330] ibid para 89.

[331] ibid para. 90.

[332] ibid para 91.

[333] *Al Hassan* (TC Judgment) (n 156) para 1188.

[334] *Prosecutor v Muthaura, Kenyatta & Ali (Decision on the Confirmation of Charges) ICC-01/09-02/11 (23 January 2012)* para 269.

[335] *Hassan* (CoC Decision) (n 150) para 553.

[336] *Ongwen* (CoC Decision) (n 23) para 93.

[337] ibid para 94.

claimed that '[t]his basic right is indeed the value distinct from e.g., physical or sexual integrity, or personal liberty'.[338] In the *Al Hassan case,* the Pre-Trial Chamber added that the marital status had to be assessed, taking into account the social dimension and how the victim was portrayed as a spouse.[339] The *Al Hassan* Pre-Trial Chamber almost copied the wording of the *Ongwen* Pre-Trial Chamber and articulated this element in terms of violating the right to marry.[340]

This raises how such unions were viewed culturally and how they differ from arranged marriages. Both Chambers held that legal recognition was unnecessary; what mattered was the victim's perception and the perpetrator's intent, with cultural traditions serving as indicators of marriage.[341]

The *Ongwen* Trial Chamber defined marriage as creating 'a status based on a consensual and contractual relationship – it is an institution and also an act or rite'.[342] This is difficult to square with another passage of the judgment in which the judge simply found that '[n]o traditional rituals of marriage were observed'.[343] The judgments offer little on what constitutes a marriage, linking its existence mainly to victim harm and stigma. A fuller explanation of how forced marriage distorted the institution – beyond mere arranged marriage – would have clarified matters.[344] Most wives described no ceremony, only being ordered to share a commander's bed.[345] Rituals like the shea butter smearing were general initiations, not marital rites, leaving unclear how marriage itself was perverted in *Ongwen.*[346] Although the informal label of wife attached to this forced conjugal association is treated as distinct from labels such as slave or child soldier, the *Ongwen* Trial Chamber did not clarify how this distinction operates. As noted, all returnees were stigmatised and consequently suffered similar harm. This makes the imposition of marriage as a distinct element unconvincing. Calling the girls 'wives' does not make these marriage practices. On appeal in *Ongwen*, the Appeals Chamber further confirmed that forced marriage protects a distinct interest – the right freely to choose one's spouse and to found a family – and upheld the permissibility of cumulative convictions with sexual slavery because the crimes have 'materially distinct' elements.[347]

[338] ibid para 94.

[339] *Hassan (*CoC Decision) (n 150) para 553.

[340] ibid para 554.

[341] *Ongwen* (CoC Decision) (n 23) para 93; *Hassan (*CoC Decision) (n 150) paras 556–58.

[342] *Ongwen* (TC Judgment) (n 23) para 2748; *Hassan (*TC Judgment) (n 156) para 1187.

[343] ibid para 2035.

[344] G Gangoli and others, 'Understanding Forced Marriage: Definitions and Realities' in AK Gill and S Anitha (eds), *Forced Marriage: Introducing a Social Justice and Human Rights Perspective* (Zed Books, 2011); Scharf and Mattler (n 103) 21–22.

[345] *Ongwen* (TC Judgment) (n 23) para 2042.

[346] ibid paras 906–15 and para 2103.

[347] *Prosecutor v Ongwen* (Judgment on the Appeal of Mr Ongwen against the Decision of Trial Chamber IX of 4 February 2021 entitled 'Trial Judgment') ICC-02/04-01/15 A (15 December 2022) paras 1678–84.

The discussion of the marriage practices in the *Al Hassan case* in relation to precisely the markers of marriage, is much more convincing.[348] The Pre-Trial Chamber elaborately explained how a system of temporary marriages unfolded, for which often a dowry was offered.[349] Furthermore, the judges explained the role of both the Islamic Police as well as the Islamic Tribunal in setting and controlling the matrimonial rules. It also set out how divorces were easy to obtain by the man unilaterally stating to the Police that he wanted to end the marriage.[350] The decision also explained how some local men took advantage of this religious regime being installed to complain to the Islamic Police that their wives had left them. Particularly, Hassan pressured women into returning to their husbands as he would otherwise have to bring them before the court, which self-evidently scared them.[351] This connection to pre-conflict marriage reinforces the proof of a system of marriages taking place.

The second element that is considered to make forced marriage a distinct crime is the exclusivity of the conjugal relationship, which is understood as the characteristic aspect absent from any other crime. Unlike 'sexual slavery, forced marriage implies a relationship of exclusivity between the "husband" and "wife", which could lead to disciplinary consequences for breach of this exclusive arrangement and, therefore, is "not predominantly a sexual crime"'.[352] The Trial Chamber confirmed that 'Ongwen's so-called "wives" had to maintain an exclusive conjugal relationship with him'.[353] It was described how this exclusivity was enforced and how a violation could result in severe punishment or even death.[354] In legal terms, this exclusivity was connected to 'the duties that are associated with marriage'.[355] It is interesting to note that 'assertion of exclusivity' is also understood as one of the factors indicative of enslavement. This, nevertheless, did not bring the Chamber to qualify the practice as enslavement.

Remarkably, the *Al Hassan* Pre-Trial Chamber qualified exclusivity as a factor from which a forced marriage can be inferred in a similar vein as the system of factors developed for enslavement.[356] The 2024 *Al Hassan* Trial Judgment only briefly referred to the 'exclusivity of the forced conjugal union imposed on the victim' without developing it further, which might signal that this aspect played a lesser role in the Chamber's analysis of forced marriage.[357] It remains vague whether this is or is not an element distinguishing it from the listed labels.

Lastly, throughout these cases, the judges have concluded that this conjugal union results in a harm that is different from the harm done by other crimes. The

[348] *Hassan (*CoC Decision) (n 150) paras 564–82.
[349] ibid para 577ff.
[350] ibid para 581.
[351] ibid para 581.
[352] *Ongwen* (CoC Decision) (n 23) para 93.
[353] *Ongwen* (TC Judgment) (n 23) para 206.
[354] ibid paras 2037–39.
[355] ibid para 2748.
[356] *Hassan (*CoC Decision) (n 150) para 558.
[357] *Hassan* (TC Judgment) (n 156) para 1188.

Ongwen Trial Judgment held that this harm 'can consist of being ostracised from the community, mental trauma, the serious attack on the victim's dignity, and the deprivation of the victim's fundamental rights to choose his or her spouse'.[358] Women subjected to forced marriage arguably experience distinct stigma and reintegration challenges. Yet this claim appears grounded more in precedent than in evidence. In *Ongwen*, no distinct stigma was demonstrated, and in *Al Hassan*, the reasoning largely reiterated *Ongwen*.[359] This lack of clarity on how evidence supports this reasoning is problematic in light of Article 22. By focusing on the victim, it misconstrues the crime label in violation of the principle of strict construction. As the analysis of the principle of strict construction and fair labelling has demonstrated, the interpretative result can only, in the second order, consider the fairness towards the victims. While harm may be a relevant factor, it cannot override strict construction or justify a label that misrepresents the accused's conduct. In Ongwen, it remains unclear how the harm suffered by the "wives" differed from that of other SGBC victims. Given the explicitly residual nature of this category, such reasoning raises legality concerns and calls for a more restrained approach.

ii. An Alternative Interpretation of the Category of Other Inhumane Acts

There are several problems with the way in which forced marriage has been approached by the ICC judges, but one of the most essential is the disconnect between the facts and the legal assessment. The *Ongwen* and *Al Hassan* Chambers have consequently relied on external precedents, where it should have been explained how a certain element is supported by the evidence. As a result, it is difficult to understand how these crimes are *materially distinct*.

To establish this, judges should assess the cultural meaning of marriage and how the forced marriage phenomenon interacts with pre-conflict marital practices. The ECCC carefully examined how the Khmer Rouge's state-imposed marriage policy distorted pre-existing traditions. In contrast, it remains unclear how the LRA reshaped marriage customs or whether 'wives' were viewed as such upon return. Evidence indicates that the term *wife* was largely nominal, masking a reality closer to slavery. The claim that bush wives faced greater stigma than other SGBV victims is similarly unpersuasive. The label *wife* does not constitute a materially distinct element, and the residual category of other inhumane acts should thus not have applied in *Ongwen*.[360] The so-called conjugal duties and exclusivity can equally be understood as flowing from the perpetrator's ownership over the victim. In *Ongwen*, these women were effectively slaves of their commanders and are better described as conjugal slaves.

[358] *Ongwen* (TC Judgment) (n 23) para 2749.
[359] *Ongwen* (CoC Decision) (n 23) para 93; *Hassan* paras *(*CoC Decision) (n 150) 555, 558; *Ongwen* (TC Judgment) (n 23) paras 2748–49.
[360] *Prosecutor v Ongwen* (Amici Curiae Brief on Forced Marriage) ICC-02/04-01/15 A A2 (22 December 2021) para 19.

While concern for victims' harm is understandable, it cannot override the principle of legality. The residual category should apply only when no listed crime fits, and cumulative convictions with it should be avoided. A stricter approach – using enslavement to encompass both sexual and non-sexual exploitation – would better respect legality and fair labelling.

D. Other Forms of Sexual Violence

Article 7(1)(g) holds at the end of the enumeration of sexual crimes, a residual category of 'other forms of sexual violence'. The Rome Statute is the first international instrument to develop such a second residual category. In a similar way to the other inhumane acts category, it is delineated by only encompassing acts of a similar gravity. A second material element of this crime is that the act needs to be sexual in nature.

Two ICC cases have analysed this residual crime. In *Bemba*, forced undressing was charged, but the Pre-Trial Chamber did not include this charge in the arrest warrant because it was not of comparable gravity.[361] The judge did say that it could be qualified as outrage upon personal dignity in the future.[362] In *Kenyatta et al*, forcible circumcision was viewed as ethnic rather than sexual.[363] These cases create the impression of a certain resistance to using this category. Whether it is because the category is new in its kind, or not, this category features in only a few of the ICC cases, even when there are accounts of sexual violence. These cases also show that violence labelled sexual by other courts,[364] is preferably labelled as an outrage upon human dignity or as another inhumane act. Both the *Al Hassan* and the *Ongwen cases* concern a wide range of SGBC use these categories, but have not included 'other forms of sexual violence'.

The SCSL case law made clear how this specific residual category could be relevant for future forced marriage practices.[365] In the *CDF case*, the Trial Chamber found it 'impermissible to allege acts of sexual violence' under the other inhumane acts category as the latter 'must logically be restrictively interpreted as covering only those acts of a non-sexual nature amounting to an affront to human dignity'.[366] Judge Boutet dissented and found that the other inhumane acts also cover acts of a sexual nature.[367] Judge Sebutinde returned to the distinc-

[361] *Prosecutor v Bemba* (Decision on the Prosecutor's Application for a Warrant of Arrest against Jean-Pierre Bemba Gombo) ICC-01/05-01/08 (10 June 2008) paras 39–40.

[362] ibid paras 39–40.

[363] *Muthaura, Kenyatta & Ali* (CoC Decision) (n 334) paras 260–66.

[364] See, eg, *Akayesu (TC Judgment) (n 33)* para 688.

[365] *Prosecutor v Norman et al (CDF Case)* (Trial Chamber Reasoned Majority Decision on Prosecution Motion for a Ruling on the Admissibility of Evidence) SCSL-04-14-PT (24 May 2005) para 19.

[366] ibid para 19.

[367] *Prosecutor v Norman et al (CDF Case)* (Dissenting Opinion of Justice Pierre Boutet on Decision on Prosecution Motion for a Ruling on the Admissibility of Evidence) SCSL-04-14-P (24 May 2005) paras 7–9.

tion between the residual categories and, in two dissenting opinions, explained what is at stake in applying these residual categories to a forced marriage fact pattern.[368] In the first opinion, she considered 'the sexual element inherent in' the bush wives phenomenon 'tends to dominate the other elements therein, such as forced labour and other forced conjugal duties', and that it should be qualified as a 'a form of sexual violence'.[369] She clearly separated the two residual categories and found that other inhumane acts are only for non-sexual acts, and other forms of sexual violence should encompass sexual acts only.

This clarification is absent at the ICC.[370] If it is accepted that each category has its role to play and that the acts not listed are categorised under their respective categories, then qualifying forced marriage as both sexual slavery and other inhumane acts is problematic. Either forced marriage is seen as predominantly sexual, justifying the labelling as sexual slavery, or it is predominantly non-sexual, justifying the label of other inhumane acts. It cannot be both.

This, in turn, lays bare another issue in relation to the concurrence of crimes and residual categories. The question here is whether the use of the residual categories is allowed where there is a listed crime with two elements – consists of elements a + b – and the residual category is argued to have an extra element – consists of elements a + b + c. By allowing for the qualification of sexual slavery and thus arguing that the crime encompasses acts of sexual violence (element a) and the exercise of the rights of ownership under the conjugal association with elements of coercion and control identical to enslavement (element b), what is left is the *additional* element of harm that comes from the marriage (element c). The *Celibici Judgment* held that in this particular form of concurrence, the more specific crime must be applied.[371] Following this reasoning, the residual category of other inhumane acts should be used and not that of sexual slavery. This, however, contradicts the finding that the LRA bush wives were the victims of sexual violence. This study finds the *Ongwen* Trial Chamber convicting for the practices against the LRA bush wives as sexual slavery, thereby acknowledging the sexual nature of the crime, difficult to square with the cumulative conviction as other inhumane acts. This reveals a need for a more thorough examination of the potential of the residual category of other forms of sexual violence. This discussion triggers yet another question, and that is, if the cumulative conviction with residual categories is allowed, why not combine the label of enslavement with that of sexual violence? It remains to be seen whether this will be put to the test in future case law, but overall, there is no doubt that this residual category must be applied conservatively, and the principle of strict construction supports limiting it to sexual crimes.

[368] *Prosecutor v Brima et al (AFRC Case)* (Separate Concurring Opinion of Justice Sebutinde) (n 112).
[369] *ibid* para 19.
[370] See further J Gong-Gershowitz, 'Forced Marriage: A "New" Crime Against Humanity?' (2009) 8 *Northwestern Journal of International Human Rights* 53, 60.
[371] *Čelebići case* (Appeals Judgment) (n 22) para 413.

E. Gender-Based Persecution

Persecution is a crime with considerable history and has been listed since the time of Nuremberg.[372] It has been understood as standing at the 'core of crimes against humanity'.[373] The definition of this crime has expanded over the years and is now generally considered to consist of a severe deprivation or gross denial of fundamental rights, contrary to international law (*actus reus*) on the basis of one of the discriminatory or persecutory grounds (*mens rea*).[374] The Rome Statute requires persecutory acts to be linked to other crimes within the Court's jurisdiction. This entails analogical reasoning and inevitably leads to concurrence, as those underlying crimes often evidence the discriminatory policy itself.[375]

The crime of persecution has created considerable disagreement amongst experts.[376] The Rome Statute is the first of its kind to include gender as a recognised ground for persecution.[377] And to make matters more complicated, gender as a persecutory ground has created considerable qualification difficulties.[378] Gender is the only persecutory ground defined.[379] As mentioned before, the proposition is to understand gender to mean a 'constructed and contingent set of assumptions *about* female and male roles'.[380]

Gender-based persecution was charged for the first time in relation to marriage practices in the Al Hassan case.[381] The Prosecutor specified the charge of persecution based on religious and gender grounds in the Document Containing the Charges (DCC), listed the rights violated, and established that the violations of rights were analysed as a whole.[382] The Prosecutor set out a range of persecutory practices. It was described how Timbuktu women were the victims of violent practices of arbitrary detentions and sanctions, were severely

[372] Art 6(c)Agreement for the Prosecution and Punishment of the Major War Criminals of the European Axis (London Charter) (8 August 1945) UNTS No 251; Art II(c)Control Council Law No. 10 Punishment of Persons Guilty of War Crimes, Crimes against Peace and against Humanity (December 20, 1945) 3 Official Gazette. See further on the historical development of the crime: Fausto Pocar, 'Persecution as a Crime Under International Criminal Law' (2006) 2 Journal of National Security Law & Policy 355 and for some tribunal case law on this crime: *Kupreškić* (Trial Judgment) (n 273) para 621.

[373] WA Schabas, *The International Criminal Court: A Commentary on the Rome Statute, 2nd edn* (Oxford Public International Law, OUP, 2016) 194.

[374] see *Ntaganda* (TC Judgment) (n 185) para 992.

[375] Article 7(1)(g) RS.

[376] L Davis, 'Dusting Off the Law Books: Recognizing Gender Persecution in Conflicts and Atrocities' (2021) 20 *Northwestern Journal of Human Rights* 1, 5.

[377] Article 7(1)(g) RS.

[378] The *Mbarushimana case* is the first to charge gender-based persecution, but given the lack of evidence, this charge was not confirmed. See also: Kateřina Uhlířová, 'Contribution of the International Criminal Court to the Prosecution of Sexual and Gender-Based Crimes: between Promise and Practice', *The Rome Statute of the ICC at Its Twentieth Anniversary* (Brill Nijhoff, 2018) 101–102; Oosterveld (n 51).

[379] Oosterveld (n 51) 56.

[380] Charlesworth (n 53) 394.

[381] *Hassan* (CoC Decision) (n 150) para 563.

[382] *Procureur c Al Hassan* (Version publique expurgée de la 'Version amendée et corrigée du Document contenant les charges contre M Al Hassan Ag Abdoul Aziz Ag Mohamed Ag Mahmoud') ICC-01/12-01/18-335-Conf-Corr (11 Mai 2019) para 972.

limited in their movement, could not mix with persons of the other sex, and had to conform to very strict vestimentary rules.[383] Also, the sexual enslavement and the forced marriage deprived these girls and women of their fundamental rights. Amongst the list of rights violated, the right to choose a partner of their choice and to marry and found a family featured.[384]

In the *Confirmation of Charges Decision,* the judges examined the different objectives of the marriage policy established by Ansar Dine.[385] The first objective of this practice was a religious one, namely, to create a new generation.[386] The second was to reward the men and allow them to fulfil their sexual needs.[387] Ansar Dine encouraged men to marry, even when they were already married, and despite the marriage often only being temporary.[388] The Pre-Trial Chamber also found that there was an ethnic objective implicit in these marriages, as the men were often of a lighter skin and the women often of a darker skin.[389] The Pre-Trial Chamber reiterated the definition of gender in the Statute and found,[390] correctly so, that the violence against women because they are women or which affects women disproportionately, is qualified as gendered violence.[391]

The Pre-Trial Chamber gave a detailed analysis of persecution. It first relied on the internal sources and cited a range of external precedents to set out how the crime of persecution is an *ensemble* of crimes that, taken together, consist of a grave violation of fundamental rights with the goal of excluding a certain group from society.[392] These fundamental rights can be the right to life, the right to be free from arbitrary detention, freedom of expression, the right to education, and so forth.[393] The women of Timbuktu were subjected to a strict dress code and not allowed to go outside without being accompanied by a man, nor to be alone with men other than their husbands.[394] The detentions and rapes of women were also proof of a policy of persecution.[395]

Most importantly, the judges articulated that, in the context of forced marriages, women were detained, subjected to sexual violence and rape.[396] The Pre-Trial Chamber found that this constituted persecution on grounds of gender, as these women were treated like objects and suffered because the persecution resulted in the loss of their social status, being marginalised within society, as well as facing stigma from their families.

[383] *Hassan* paras (CoC Decision) (n 150) 945ff.
[384] ibid paras 878-884.
[385] ibid paras 564-569.
[386] ibid para 570.
[387] ibid para 571.
[388] ibid para 571.
[389] ibid para 572.
[390] ibid para 666.
[391] ibid para 667.
[392] ibid paras 662–63.
[393] ibid para 664.
[394] ibid paras 698.
[395] ibid paras 676–82, 699.
[396] ibid 700.

It is clear from the reasoning that the judges did not isolate the right to marry and establish a family from this list, and it is doubtful whether this practice in and of itself constitutes a *severe* deprivation of fundamental rights as required by article 7(1)(h).[397] This is also entirely unnecessary because persecution is, by definition, a crime that assembles conduct, often criminal in nature, together to demonstrate a persecutory policy. As a result, it is also a crime that is likely to concur with other crimes. Contrary to the finding in relation to the residual categories, however, concurrence here is the essence of the crime rather than contradicting its nature. Cumulative conviction should therefore not be restricted in the same sense as in relation to the other inhumane acts category.

Lastly, and returning to the issue of harm in the context of this label, the *Al Hassan* case presents some interesting avenues, given that the charge of both religious and gender-based persecution is included.[398] Given that the marriage practices have a religious and gendered side, this means that these persecutory grounds potentially *intersect*. Persecution is an interesting label from the perspective of fair labelling to the extent that the judges can reflect these intersecting grounds in the label and express the intersecting harm done to the victims by combining the label of religious and gender-based persecution. While the *Al Hassan* Trial Chamber acknowledged that the Timbuktu jihadi marriages reflected gendered oppression and harm, it ultimately declined to qualify them as gender-based persecution, finding insufficient proof of a discriminatory intent or policy.[399]

V. CONCLUSION

This chapter demonstrated that not every fact pattern referred to as forced marriage should logically be given the same legal qualification. Interpretative divergence is not, in and of itself, a bad thing. Facts matter, which is why when labels are moulded to the fact pattern at hand, it can only be lauded. Unfortunately, this chapter found sufficient evidence that this is not always the case. In the *Ongwen case,* no legal gap justified applying *other inhumane acts* to the LRA *bush wives* phenomenon. Expert testimony in *Ongwen* did not portray that there were any marks of a marriage practice being present. lacking formal markers. As Gong-Gershowitz noted, the distinction between forced marriage and sexual slavery lies only in the label wife which is insufficient to justify the need for the use of a residual category.[400]

[397] Suhr (n 72) 189–90.

[398] AM Beringola, 'Intersectionality: A Tool for the Gender Analysis of Sexual Violence at the ICC' (2017) 9 *Amsterdam Law Forum* 84, 103; R Grey and others, 'Gender-Based Persecution as a Crime against Humanity: The Road Ahead' (2019) 17 *Journal of International Criminal Justice* 957.

[399] *Al Hassan* (TC Judgment) (n 156).

[400] Gong-Gershowitz (n 370) 68.

The judges' reasoning to use the other inhumane acts category seems to be driven by a desire to fairly label the phenomenon. Underpinning its use is the expressivist wish to call something by its name. This expressivist wish has also been connected to intersectionality. Violence is often the result of sexual, political, ethnic, gendered, and cultural reasons, and all these reasons frequently intersect to bring about a certain fact pattern and instance of violence. To respond to violence adequately and fairly, thus means that the label has to be intersectional. This is precisely where the category of 'other inhumane acts' steps in, as this category can encompass a set of harms. The question is whether these intersectional, expressivist motivations can be squared with the principle of legality.

The principle of strict construction requires a conservative approach to the residual categories and understands cumulative conviction of the residual category and other listed crime categories to be contradictory to the residual nature of these crimes. Driven by a desire to capture a different harm not included under other crimes, the majority opinion seems to be that recourse to the other inhumane acts is needed to qualify forced marriage. There is one fundamental problem with this reasoning, and that is that it assumes that other crime labels are not capable of capturing this non-sexual harm. In that regard, this chapter noted that the potential of enslavement remains underexplored. The LRA bush wives were subjected to conjugal slavery, and given that only the label of wife is what marks it as a marriage, the Trial Chamber in the *Ongwen case* should have labelled the conduct as enslavement. The relationships of control and coercion can only be understood as a relationship of ownership.[401]

The Court's tendency to classify forced marriage as an inhumane act prioritises interpretative breadth over conceptual precision, leaving the potential of enslavement – often the more accurate label for describing the ownership and control at the heart of these practices – largely underexplored. Reports from ongoing conflicts show that forced marriage persists and may soon reappear before international courts.[402] Among Rohingya women in Myanmar, for instance, violence within or outside marriage reflects patterns reminiscent of both African bush wives and Cambodian mass marriages.[403] In navigating the profound complexity of translating religious, local, and cultural practices into fixed legal concepts that aspire to be universal, the Court should acknowledge that something is always lost in that process of categorisation and that existing labels such as enslavement remain fully capable of capturing these harms and warrant consistent application.

[401] Sellers and Kestenbaum (n 197) 181.

[402] UNSC, *Report of the Secretary-General on conflict-related sexual violence*, 2018) reporting on the phenomenon occurring in Bangladesh, the Central African Republic, Iraq, Mali, Myanmar, Somalia and Syria.

[403] WA Schabas and J Powderly, 'Crimes against Humanity in Western Burma: The Situation of the Rohingyas' (*Irish Centre for Human Rights* 2010) 129ff.

Legality-Centred Conclusions on International Crime Interpretation

> Impatient in the face of continued atrocities and states' dogged unwillingness to align law with morality and justice better, and pressed with the need to take principled action, modern international judges have sacrificed the strict application of [the legality principle] to fashion the moral universe for the future international order that was envisioned during the momentous postwar period.[1]

AT THE HEART OF this book lies the conviction that legality, as the manifestation of the rule of law in criminal law, should be re-appreciated and taken seriously as a normative and structural guide in the interpretation of crimes in the international criminal justice sphere. Since its emergence in Beccaria's 1764 writings,[2] the principle has evolved from a blunt safeguard against an untrustworthy judiciary into a complex, multifaceted tool that both limits judicial discretion and guides interpretation. While its core rationale remains the protection against arbitrary power and governance,[3] it is now a much more comprehensive principle, composed of sub-principles that together discipline the interpretative act.

By way of discussing the *Radbruch formula*, this book revealed the tension between following the law and the pursuit of justice, a debate which in legal theory has been framed as the debate on law and morality. This debate, as reflected in the exchanges between Hart and Fuller, exposed the core divide between positivists and naturalists on the relationship between law and morality. For Hart, the validity of law does not depend on its moral content; law derives its authority from its sources, not from its moral worth. Fuller, by contrast, argued that law cannot be separated from an inner morality, that legality itself requires a certain moral coherence. This discussion set the stage

[1] B Van Schaack, 'Judicial Lawmaking: The Intersection Between Law and Morals' (2008–09) 97 *Georgetown Law Journal* 119, 191.

[2] C Beccaria, *On Crimes and Punishments and Other Writings* (first published 1764, CUP, 1995) 14–16.

[3] See KS Gallant, *The Principle of Legality in International and Comparative Criminal Law* (CUP, 2009) 15; C Stahn, *A Critical Introduction to International Criminal Law* (CUP, 2019) 11; Van Schaack (n 1) 121–22.

for understanding how interpretative boundaries are drawn and stretched. This book followed Hart's thinking in this regard because it shows that legality can function not in opposition to justice, but as a means through which justice is achieved by ensuring that judicial reasoning remains grounded in law rather than in subjective moral conviction. Based on his notion of primary and secondary rules and the rule of recognition as the key secondary rule in the context, this book offered a legality-centred approach to crime interpretation in line with Hartian positivism.

The historical analysis offered in this book traced how the limits of judicial interpretation were understood at Nuremberg, where concerns of legality were countered through a relaxed legality theory. Interpreting the legality principle as a principle of substantive justice – and not as a limitation of sovereignty[4] – allowed for challenges pertaining to the Nuremberg Charter's retroactivity to be countered. By invoking broad external sources, it had to be demonstrated that novel crime categories (ie, crimes against humanity and crimes against peace) in fact already existed. Expansive interpretative methods were not deemed problematic and were used to justify the entire enterprise. In the Nuremberg context, the legality principle shifted away from its original function of constraining the judge, opening the door to readings which would be impermissible today.[5]

After Nuremberg, the legality principle evolved further as a human right. Focusing on the case law of the ECtHR, this study showed how the principle took on new contours through the standards of accessibility and foreseeability. While these standards required that crimes be prescribed by law, the ECtHR did not impose a strict source doctrine or a rigid legality theory. The Court accepted broad approaches, particularly under the Nuremberg Clause, which sought to preserve the legitimacy of the Nuremberg proceedings. Consequently, international crimes were considered 'prescribed by law' where their criminalisation could be supported by reference to a broad range of sources.

These human rights developments became highly influential in the ICTs understanding of the legality principle through the standards of accessibility and foreseeability.[6] Furthermore, the ICTY reied on expansive notions such as the 'dictates of public conscience' to justify the existence of customary crimes, revealing that a relaxed legality theory persisted. Although the first references to strict construction emerged in this period, the dominant understanding of legality remained one of substantive justice. The dominant view

[4] *France et al v Göring et al* (Judgment and Sentence, 1 October 1946) *Trial of the Major War Criminals before the International Military Tribunal* 219.

[5] See, eg, A Cassese, 'From Nuremberg to Rome: International Military Tribunals to the International Criminal Court' in A Cassese, P Gaeta and JRWD Jones (eds), *The Rome Statute of the International Criminal Court*, vol 1 (OUP, 2002) 22ff.

[6] *Prosecutor v Vasiljevic* (Judgment) IT-98-32-T (29 November 2002) para 193.

was that the 'hydra-headed elusiveness of human conduct' necessitated a purposive approach to customary law, as the failure to adopt such a method would hinder the pursuit of justice too greatly.[7]

As a reaction to some of these creative interpretations handed down by the Tribunal judges, the drafters of the Rome Statute found it necessary to curb judicial discretion.[8] In that regard, there is no doubt that the adoption of Article 22 signals a departure from a relaxed legality theory towards a strict legality doctrine. The legality principle is no longer a principle of justice nor a monolithic concept,[9] but rather has grown into a complex interpretative framework, with three major sub-principles, impacting in different ways on crime interpretation. By way of introducing a second paragraph to the prohibition of retroactive criminalisation, this provision puts forth a set of legality requirements imposed upon the judge to take into account when interpreting crimes. Article 22(2) and its three sub-principles – principle of strict construction, ban on analogy, *in dubio pro reo* – have a complex way of regulating the interpretation of crimes. These sub-principles together shape a normative architecture that both empowers and limits the international judge.

This book's central ambition has been to move legality from the margins to the centre of interpretative theory. To accomplish this, the book proposed a two-dimensional, legality-centred model that distinguishes between the process of interpretation – the ascertainment of the applicable law and methods – and its result – the construction and labelling of crimes. The first dimension concerns the law's determination: what is the valid law, which sources can legitimately be invoked, and in what hierarchy must they be considered. The second dimension concerns law's interpretation: how these sources may be construed and which interpretative methods are appropriate. By separating these two dimensions, the interaction between sources and methods is revealed and allows for the categorisation of interpretative results into four quadrantal outcomes. Outcomes in the left bottom quadrant are broadly constructed and unfairly labelled and are self-evidently both in violation of the principle of legality as well as the principle of fair labelling. The upper right quadrant is the most desired outcome, offering both an interpretation that is strict and fair. The two remaining quadrants are where it becomes more difficult because the outcome is either in violation of the principle of fair labelling or the principle of strict construction. This model is visualised as such:

[7] *Prosecutor v Delalić et al* (Appeals Judgment) IT-96-21-A (20 February 2001) para 170.

[8] D Hunt, 'The International Criminal Court: High Hopes, "Creative Ambiguity" and an Unfortunate Mistrust in International Judges' (2004) 2(1) *Journal of International Criminal Justice*.

[9] Borrowing the term monolithic from: WT Worster, 'On the Purposes of Legality and Its Applicability to International Law' (2011) 9(4) *Journal of International Criminal Justice* 974.

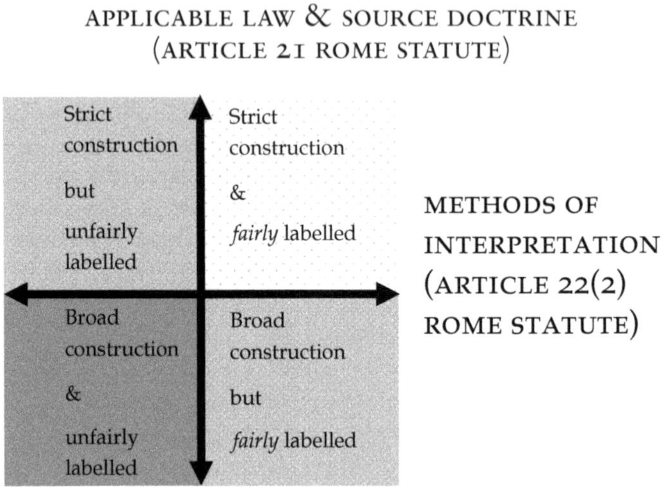

Understood through the legality-centred lens proposed in this book, and by conceiving Article 21 as a Hartian rule of recognition,[10] this study arrived at several key findings in relation to the **Rome Statute's source doctrine and applicable law.**

The first finding is that ICC judgments often fail to clarify which sources underpin their interpretations. From the perspective of legal certainty, judicial decisions must indicate clearly which sources inform the reasoning. While it is unnecessary to read Article 21 exhaustively – unlisted sources, such as academic writings, may inform interpretation – these must remain subsidiary and well-motivated.[11] The case study on organisational policy showed how the reliance on potentially irrelevant or minority scholarly opinions leads to unsubstantiated broad readings, which undermine the legitimacy of the interpretation.[12]

A second, central finding is that **the primacy of the internal sources** (**the Statute and the Elements of Crimes**) **must be strictly upheld** in crime interpretation.[13] This study proposed replacing the narrow *irreconcilable-contradiction* test[14] with an *inconsistency* test inspired by Article 9(3).[15] The broader concept of inconsistency allows conflicts between the Statute and the Elements to be resolved in favour of the Statute.

Third, the second tier of the hierarchy in **Article 21(1)(b) Rome Statute** is to include **treaties and customary law** as secondary sources.[16] Treaties rarely endanger legality and can clarify statutory provisions in light of their antecedents,

[10] See ch 3, ss I and II.
[11] See ch 3, s VIII and Conclusion.
[12] See Case Study 1, s II(B)(i).
[13] See ch 3, s IX and Conclusion.
[14] See ch 3, s III(B).
[15] See ch 3, s III(C).
[16] See ch 3, s IV(A).

such as the historical treaty background of enslavement, which the Court overlooked in addressing forced marriage. These treaties were insufficiently used in constructing the crime, which led to the incorrect assumption that they could not be used for the qualification of forced marriage patterns.[17] Customary law, by contrast, poses greater legality risks because of its unwritten nature. Judges must properly ascertain custom through state practice and *opinio juris*, rather than relying solely on the jurisprudence of other courts.[18] The organisational-policy case study showed that by uncritically adopting tribunal jurisprudence – some of which treated policy as merely evidentiary – the ICC judges disregarded the hierarchy of sources and thereby undermined legality.

This study also found that **general principles** do not belong under Article 21(1)(b) but under **paragraph** (c), where they have a strictly subsidiary role to custom.[19] Their abstract character prevents them from forming an autonomous basis for criminalisation. The risk of such broad reasoning is illustrated by the *Ongwen* Pre-Trial Chamber's reliance on human dignity to qualify forced-marriage practices as other inhumane acts, holding that victims forced into conjugal relationships endured a serious attack on human dignity comparable in gravity to other crimes against humanity.[20]

Another finding is that reliance on **internal precedent under Article 21**(2) strengthens consistency, whereas reference to external jurisprudence is justified only in cases of mirroring statutory provisions and when the case law is consistent and settled. Importing interpretations from tribunals that lacked comparable statutory elements, such as the policy requirement,[21] remains legally unsound.

Finally, **Article 21**(3), requiring consistency with **internationally recognised human rights**, cannot be used to reintroduce a relaxed legality doctrine.[22] While it rightly guides procedural fairness, it cannot expand criminalisation beyond the Statute's internal sources. Human-rights-inspired notions – such as dignity or fundamental freedoms – may inform evaluations of gravity or harm but must not replace the legality constraints firmly established in Article 22. Human rights–inspired reasoning has repeatedly influenced the interpretation of crimes: judges have, for instance, read the organisation requirement as referring to entities capable of infringing basic human values, [23] and used the residual category of 'other inhumane acts' to cover serious human rights violations not specifically enumerated.[24]

In relation to the **second dimension** of the interpretative process and the **interpretative methods**, the central argument developed in Chapter Four has

[17] See Case Study 2, s IV(A).
[18] See ch 3, s IV(B).
[19] See ch 3, s V.
[20] See Case Study 2, s IV(C)(i).
[21] See ch 3, s VI.
[22] See ch 3, s VII.
[23] See Case Study 1, s II(B)(i).
[24] See Case Study 2, s IV(C).

been that the uncritical transplantation of the Vienna Convention's methods has obscured the ICC's legality-oriented architecture.[25] The VCLT's crucible approach, designed for the interpretation of inter-state agreements, privileges flexibility, purposiveness, and systemic integration. These virtues, while laudable in public international law, are ill-suited to criminal law, where the stakes are individual liberty and where the foreseeability of the norm is paramount. The principle of effectiveness, the good-faith obligation, and the teleological method, all cornerstones of the VCLT paradigm, carry within them an expansive logic incompatible with strict construction. The danger of adopting them uncritically lies not only in doctrinal incoherence but in a normative inversion: an interpretative tool designed to preserve coherence in international law becomes, in the criminal sphere, a source of unpredictability. Given that the tensions between the VCLT and the Rome Statute are too abundant to solve, the central proposition is to understand the ICC as a self-contained system.[26] The level of self-containment, together with the concept of functional differentiation, supports the proposition that interpretative problems must be addressed through methods specifically developed for criminal law purposes and thus be **guided by the legality principle.**[27] For too long, the principle of legality has been an afterthought overshadowed by the VCLT; one of this study's key objectives was therefore to demonstrate that an interpretative methodology can be **built directly upon the three principles in Article 22(2) of the Rome Statute.**

The first interpretative principle set out in Article 22(2) is the **principle of strict construction.**[28] In relation to this principle, this study first debunked two central misconceptions. One, this principle does not require that the strictest construction is adopted. It only requires that the interpretation stays sufficiently close to the text. Two, this principle only relates to vagueness and not to ambiguity. Given that the judge's role is to make the law more precise by means of interpretation, strict construction only opposes too broad interpretations and requires vagueness to be rendered more specific. The principle of strict construction is therefore the prime reason for excluding broad and victim-oriented purposive approaches.

The second novel sub-principle is the **ban on analogy.**[29] This method does not bar contextual reasoning but bans the court from finding a substantially new crime. The ban on analogy means that the stretching of a crime definition to more than what a textual analysis allows for violates the principle of legality. Contextual reasoning that requires analogy should, therefore, be confined to the residual crime categories of 'other inhumane acts' and 'other sexual violence'. Both these *ejusdem generis* categories specifically necessitate an analogical

[25] See ch 4, ss II and III.
[26] See ch 4, s V(D).
[27] See ch 4, s V(E).
[28] See ch 5, s II(A).
[29] See ch 5, s II(B).

interpretative exercise, and were inserted to allow for some flexibility to respond to new criminal phenomena. Their built-in restrictions requiring comparable gravity to the other listed crimes facilitate adherence to legality.

The **in dubio pro reo principle** is the final sub-principle added to Article 22 Rome Statute.[30] Contrary to what some of the discussed cases have suggested, this principle is not merely relevant for evidentiary purposes but must be seen as a proper interpretative technique. The scope of the principle should nonetheless not be conflated, as it has a rather narrow playing field. First, the structure of Article 22(2) reveals that an interpretation in favour of the accused only occurs in case of an ambiguity. This principle thus only comes into play in case of an ambiguity. Second, it operates at the end of the interpretative process and should only be used when the use of Article 21's sources and the legality-approved methods of interpretation have not been helpful in solving an ambiguity.

As the two-dimensional model indicated, after the interpretative process, the **interpretative result** or crime interpretation still requires an evaluation in terms of its adherence to the legality principle. This study proposed to conduct this evaluation on the basis of the principle of strict construction on the one hand, and the principle of fair labelling on the other hand.

The **principle of strict construction** requires that *the result stays close to the text*. It has to be assessed whether the crime is *prescribed by law* – this requirement has been largely covered in the analysis of Article 21 – and whether the crime is strictly construed. To ensure adherence to the principle, this study adopts the foreseeability standard developed by the ECtHR and employed by the ICTs and the ICC, as further refined through Davidson's work. The first step is to assess whether the interpretation remains within the boundaries of the law by determining whether an existing provision, containing all the essential ingredients, can be applied to the case at hand. Where such a provision exists, it must be applied; the judge cannot resort to residual categories or external sources to construct new crimes. The second step is to evaluate whether the chosen label is foreseeable, applying an objective standard based on the perspective of a 'reasonable accused'. A mere foreseeability test would not, in itself, preclude qualifying forced marriage as another inhumane act, given its prior labelling by other courts. However, adding the further requirement that the interpretation must remain within the boundaries of the law and apply only labels containing all the essential ingredients, reveals that a legality problem does arise from using other inhumane acts in the context of some forced marriage practices.[31]

When this test is met, there is room to introduce the fair labelling perspective. The **principle of fair labelling** allows, within the confines of the law, an assessment of whether the chosen label accurately reflects the **wrongfulness, harmfulness, and blameworthiness** of the conduct. By introducing these three dimensions, this study operationalises the principle of fair labelling to

[30] See ch 5, s II(C).
[31] See ch 5, s III(A).

accommodate concerns of fairness towards the accused – proportionally reflecting the wrongfulness of the conduct –, towards victims – adequately capturing the harm done –, and towards the international community – expressing the blameworthiness of the events. In this way, the principle of fair labelling can temper the rigidity of strict construction while keeping the rights of the accused at the centre of crime interpretation. Considerations of fairness cannot justify treating the principles of fair labelling and strict construction as equals, since fairness cannot entail labelling conduct beyond the law. The judge must avoid falling into what has been termed the *balancing consciousness* – the flawed assumption that the interests of victims and accused in the context of crime interpretation can be weighed on equal footing – so that the principle of fair labelling operates only in a secondary, subordinate manner to the principle of strict construction. This approach does not deny the symbolic or communicative function of crime labels, but insists that their use remains, first and foremost, legally anchored. By foregrounding the principle of fair labelling alongside strict construction, this book has sought to re-insert questions of justice and meaning into the legality discourse. Legality without fairness risks formalism; fairness without legality risks arbitrariness.[32]

The application of this two-dimensional model in the context of the **organisational policy element** showed that we should not be guided by the logic of 'you know it when you see it'. Crimes against humanity suffer from **ontological haziness**, particularly due to interpretative uncertainty surrounding the contextual element of organisational policy. Broad definitions, some allowing even unconnected individuals to commit crimes against humanity, were rejected as incompatible with strict construction. Victim-oriented and purposive approaches, invoking goals such as ending impunity, cannot justify expanding the crime's scope. Similarly, abstract definitions based on human rights or humanitarian variants were too unconstructed to provide legal certainty and blurred what it means to prove versus constitute the element. Narrower interpretations proved more consistent with legality. The most concrete judicial attempt was by Judge Ozaki, who, drawing on the UN Convention against Transnational Organized Crime, proposed organisational features. Building on and refining this approach, this study identified four core properties of an organisation: (i) a collectivity of at least three persons, (ii) a common and identifiable purpose, (iii) some degree of stability over time, and (iv) a structure exceeding ad hoc collaboration.[33] These properties, supported by three types of inferences – reach and power, organisational capacity, and capability inferences – ensure that the notion of organisation captures entities capable of orchestrating collective violence without overextending the category. This balance preserves both legality and fair labelling.

[32] See ch 5, s III(B).
[33] See Case Study 1, ss III and IV.

In relation to the complex phenomenon of **forced marriage** and the delicate exercise of labelling this phenomenon, which is highly coloured by culture and local practices, the main argument developed in the second case study was to debunk the use of other inhumane acts when a listed act can be applied. The *Ongwen* case should have recognised that the enslavement label already encompassed all essential elements of the bush wives phenomenon, leaving no basis to resort to the residual category of other inhumane acts, which should apply only to conduct not covered by the listed crimes. The Trial Chamber's reliance on the elements of marriage, exclusivity, and social stigma to distinguish this conduct from sexual slavery is unconvincing, as no evidence established a genuine marriage or distinct stigma, and exclusivity is already captured within the exercise of ownership inherent in enslavement.[34] In the *Al Hassan* case, the fact pattern differed fundamentally from the bush-wives phenomenon: the presence of religious and cultural markers shaping the imposed marriages justified a more defensible recourse to the *other inhumane acts* category, as slavery-like practices were not central to the violence that occurred in Timbuktu. Despite these stronger legal arguments, the accused was acquitted and the label ultimately failed. As for gender-based persecution, although it did not lead to a conviction, its introduction marked a significant development, the full potential of which remained unexplored due to the limited evidentiary foundation in the *Al Hassan* case.

These case studies are indicative of a broader problem within international criminal law: a field still torn between moral ambition and legal discipline, between the aspiration to end impunity and universal justice claims and the obligation to remain within the boundaries of the law. The legality-centred framework proposed here does not claim to resolve this tension altogether, but it aspires to make crime interpretation less riddled with inconsistency and indeterminacy. It is also an invitation to test, challenge and refine the model in other settings. International criminal justice is an ever-changing field, confronted with constant demands to apply its categories to new phenomena that trigger their own interpretative questions – for example, the expanding field of environmental crimes, domestic prosecutions of international crimes in which national courts navigate the interpretation of the Rome Statute's crime categories through domestic legal constraints.

As the quote at the beginning of this conclusion indicates, judges have at times shown impatience, but the question is whether such impatience remains necessary. The law has evolved since Nuremberg, and the tools for labelling conduct have grown immensely. Unfortunately, the ICC Appeals Chamber has continued to send mixed messages regarding the legality principle, as the *Abd-Al-Rahman* case shows.[35] While the Appeals Chamber applied the foreseeability standard

[34] See Case Study 2, s V.

[35] *Prosecutor v Abd-Al-Rahman* (Judgment on the Appeal Against the Pre-Trial Chamber II's "Decision on the Defence 'Exception d'incompétence'") ICC-02/05-01/20-302 (1 November 2021).

and considered the flagrantly unlawful nature of the crimes relevant to its assessment – thereby echoing an older understanding of legality as a principle of substantive justice[36] – it simultaneously required that the conduct was criminalised under recognised sources of law, including customary law. [37] By reinforcing the 'prescribed by law' requirement, this last part raises the threshold of legality and gestures toward a stricter doctrine, one that should, in this study's view, guide the Court's interpretative practice.

To move beyond this mixed storyline, the key proposition is to understand legality as a deontic principle. As the case studies showed, judges sometimes adopt consequentialist positions guided by perceived justice, bending the law to reach morally attractive outcomes. The price paid—in legitimacy, predictability and fairness—often exceeds the perceived gain. A principled, rather than consequentialist, approach should be embraced not merely as a limit but as a guide—one that can reduce interpretative divergence and, paradoxically, lead to more just and consistent outcomes. Legality should be embraced as something positive: a guiding tool rather than merely a brake. Properly applied, it can steer interpretation away from divergence and inconsistency and, in that way, yield more just outcomes than broader, purposive approaches.

The arguments advanced in this book also speak to broader debates on judicial authority and discretion. While interpretation is inherently creative, that creativity must be channelled through the procedural and substantive constraints of legality. In this sense, legality reaffirms a separation-of-powers logic at the international level: it secures judicial legitimacy not by shrinking competence but by clarifying method. When judges interpret, they should do so transparently, foreseeably, and faithfully to the rule of law. The legality-centred model delineates the boundaries within which discretion can legitimately operate. The principle of legality in that way serves as the field's ethical backbone. In a system often driven by the desire to close impunity gaps and respond to atrocity, it is precisely its restraint that preserves the moral authority of international criminal justice. The rule of law does not promise perfect justice; it promises lawful justice. Its strength lies not in its capacity to punish all wrongs but in its refusal to punish without law. The international criminal judge, entrusted with unprecedented authority, operates in a field where moral urgency often tempts interpretative overreach. To resist this temptation is not to renounce justice; it is to pursue it through law. Legality offers precisely this path. It reminds us that the credibility of international criminal justice depends less on the breadth of its moral claims than on the coherence of its legal reasoning.

This book also contributes to the ongoing debate on the nature of international criminal law itself. Is it an extension of public international law, a branch of human rights law, or a form of criminal law with its own logic? The answer offered here is unequivocal: whatever its hybrid origins, international criminal

[36] ibid para 85.
[37] ibid para 89.

law must ultimately remain criminal law. Its legitimacy depends on adherence to principles that define criminal justice as a liberal enterprise – foreseeability, non-retroactivity, and the presumption of innocence. To the extent that ICL borrows from other branches, it must do so without betraying these foundational commitments. The legality-centred model offers a method for preserving this identity amidst inevitable cross-fertilisation.

Coming to the end of the book, the core message is simple: legality is not a constraint to be endured, but a craft to be practised. If international criminal law is to speak with authority in the decades ahead, it must do so disciplinedly in the language of law. Crime interpretation must be clearly embedded in its sources, strictly elucidated through its methods, and fairly communicate what lies behind the label. Only with this deontic approach can international criminal law maintain its legitimacy as a system governed by law rather than by moral impulse.

Bibliography

Aarnio A, Alexy R and Peczenik A, 'The Foundation of Legal Reasoning' (1981) 12 *Rechtstheorie* 133.

Acevedo JPP-L, 'The Close Relationship Between Serious Human Rights Violations and Crimes Against Humanity: International Criminalization of Serious Abuses' (2017) 17 *Anuario Mexicano de Derecho Internacional* 145.

Acquaviva G, 'At the Origins of Crimes against Humanity: Clues to a Proper Understanding of the *Nullum Crimen* Principle in the Nuremberg Judgment' (2011) 9 *Journal of International Criminal Justice* 811.

Adams A, 'Sexual Slavery: Do We Need This Crime in Addition to Enslavement?' (2018) 29 *Criminal Law Forum* 279.

Adolphe J, 'Gender Wars at the United Nations' (2012) 11 *Ave Maria Law Review* 1.

Akande D, 'Sources of International Criminal Law' in Cassese A (ed), *Oxford Companion to International Criminal Justice* (Oxford, Oxford University Press, 2005).

Allain J, *Slavery in International Law: Of Human Exploitation and Trafficking* (Martinus Nijhoff, 2012).

Allain J, *The Law and Slavery: Prohibiting Human Exploitation* (Leiden, Brill | Nijhoff, 2015).

Allain J and Hickey R, 'Property and the Definition of Slavery' (2012) 61 *International & Comparative Law Quarterly* 915.

Anitha and A Gill, 'Introduction: Framing forced marriage as a form of violence against women' in S Anitha and A Gill (eds), *Forced Marriage: Introducing a Social Justice and Human Rights Perspective* (Zed Books, 2011).

Alexy R, 'Law, Morality, and the Existence of Human Rights' (2012) 25 *Ratio Juris* 2.

Allum F and Gilmour S (eds), *Handbook of Organised Crime and Politics* (Cheltenham, Edward Elgar, 2019).

Ambos K, 'Punishment without a Sovereign? The *Ius Puniendi* Issue of International Criminal Law: A First Contribution Towards a Consistent Theory of International Criminal Law' (2013) 33 *Oxford Journal of Legal Studies* 293.

Ambos K, 'The Overall Function of International Criminal Law: Striking the Right Balance Between the *Rechtsgut* and the Harm Principles – A Second Contribution Towards a Consistent Theory of International Criminal Law' (2015) 9 *Criminal Law and Philosophy* 301.

Ambos K, 'The First Judgment of the International Criminal Court (*Prosecutor v Lubanga*): A Comprehensive Analysis of the Legal Issues' (2012) 12 *International Criminal Law Review* 115.

Ancel M, *Social Defence: A Modern Approach to Criminal Problems*, vol 14 *The Sociology of Law and Criminology* (London, Routledge, 1998).

Arajärvi N, *The Changing Nature of Customary International Law: Methods of Interpreting the Concept of Custom in International Criminal Tribunals* (Abingdon, Routledge, 2014).

Arajärvi N, 'The Role of the International Criminal Judge in the Formation of Customary International Law' (2007) 1 *European Journal of Legal Studies* 1.

Arajärvi N, 'Between *Lex Lata* and *Lex Ferenda*: Customary International (Criminal) Law and the Principle of Legality' (2010–11) 15 *Tilburg Law Review* 163.

Arendt H, *Eichmann in Jerusalem: A Report on the Banality of Evil* (rev and enlarged edn, New York, The Viking Press, 1964).

Argibay CM, 'Sexual Slavery and the Comfort Women of World War II' (2003) 21 *Berkeley Journal of International Law* 375.

Arsanjani MH, 'The Rome Statute of the International Criminal Court' (1999) 93 *American Journal of International Law* 22.

Ashworth A, *The Elasticity of Mens Rea* in Tapper C (ed), *Crime, Proof and Punishment: Essays in Memory of Sir Rupert Cross* (London, Butterworths, 1981).

Ashworth A, 'Robbery Re-assessed' (2002) *Criminal Law Review* 851.

Ashworth A and Horder J, *Principles of Criminal Law*, 7th edn (Oxford, Oxford University Press, 2013).

Ashworth A and Wasik M (eds), *Fundamentals of Sentencing Theory: Essays in Honour of Andrew von Hirsch* (Oxford Monographs on Criminal Law and Criminal Justice, Oxford, Clarendon Press, 1998).

Askola H, 'Responding to Vulnerability – Forced Marriage and the Law' (2018) 41 *UNSW Law Journal* 977.

Askin KD, *War Crimes against Women: Prosecution in International War Crimes Tribunals* (Martinus Nijhoff, 1997).

Askin KD, 'Sexual Violence in Decisions and Indictments of the Yugoslav and Rwandan Tribunals: Current Status' (1999) 93 *American Journal of International Law* 97.

Appazov A, 'International Criminal Court and the Decision-Making Heritage of the Ad Hoc Tribunals: A Study of Judicial Activism' (2016) 3 *Journal of Global Justice and Public Policy* 1.

Arnold J, Karsten N and Kreicker H, 'The German Border Guard Cases before the European Court of Human Rights' (2003) 11 *European Journal of Crime, Criminal Law and Criminal Justice* 67.

Baetens F, '*Ejusdem Generis* and *Noscitur a Sociis* in Municipal and International Law: Interpretative Cross-Fertilisation?' in Klinger J, Parkhomenko Y and Salonidis C (eds), *Between the Lines of the Vienna Convention? Canons and Other Principles of Interpretation in Public International Law* (Alphen aan den Rijn, Wolters Kluwer, 2019).

Baines E, 'Forced Marriage as a Political Project: Sexual Rules and Relations in the Lord's Resistance Army' (2014) 51 Journal of Peace Research 405.

Bales K and Robbins PT, '"No One Shall Be Held in Slavery or Servitude": A Critical Analysis of International Slavery Agreements and Concepts of Slavery' (2001) 2 *Human Rights Review* 18.

Barak A, *Judicial Discretion* (New Haven, Yale University Press, 1989).

Bartels R, *The Interplay between International Human Rights Law and International Humanitarian Law during International Criminal Trials* (Amsterdam Law School Legal Studies Research Paper, 2018).

Bassiouni C, *The Legislative History of the International Criminal Court: Introduction, Analysis and Integrated Texts* (1st edn, Ardsley NY, Transnational Publishers, 2003).

Bassiouni C and Schabas WA, *The Legislative History of the International Criminal Court*, vol 2 *International Criminal Law Series* (Leiden, Brill, 2016).

Bassiouni C, *Crimes against Humanity: Historical Evolution and Contemporary Application*, 2nd edn (Cambridge, Cambridge University Press, 2013).

Bassiouni C, 'The Penal Characteristics of Conventional International Criminal Law' (1983) 15 *Case Western Reserve Journal of International Law* 27.

Bassiouni C, 'International Recognition of Victims' Rights' (2006) 6 *Human Rights Law Review* 203.

Battaglini G, 'Fascist Reform of the Penal Law in Italy' (1933–34) *American Institute of Criminal Law and Criminology* 278.

Beccaria C, *On Crimes and Punishments and Other Writings* (Cambridge Texts in the History of Political Thought, Cambridge, Cambridge University Press, 1764).

Beccaria's original Italian title is implicit in the edition; you keep the English one as in your text.

Bedont B and Hall-Martinez K, 'Ending Impunity for Gender Crimes under the International Criminal Court' (1999) 6 *Brown Journal of World Affairs* 65.

Belair K, 'Unearthing the Customary Law Foundations of "Forced Marriages" during Sierra Leone's Civil War: The Possible Impact of International Criminal Law on Customary Marriage and Women's Rights in Post-Conflict Sierra Leone' (2006) 15 *Columbia Journal of Gender and Law* 551.

Benedetti F, Bonneau K and Washburn JL, *Negotiating the International Criminal Court: New York to Rome, 1994–1998* (Leiden, Brill, 2014).

Beringola AM, 'Intersectionality: A Tool for the Gender Analysis of Sexual Violence at the ICC' (2017) 9 *Amsterdam Law Forum* 84.

Bix B, 'HLA Hart and the Hermeneutic Turn in Legal Theory' (1999) 52 *SMU Law Review* [page not given in your text].

Bix B, 'Radbruch's Formula and Conceptual Analysis' (2011) 6 *American Journal of Jurisprudence* 45.

Bix BH, 'Robert Alexy, Radbruch's Formula, and the Nature of Legal Theory' (2006) 37. *Rechtstheorie* 139.

Blackstone W, *Commentaries on the Laws of England in Four Books* (London, Routledge–Cavendish, 1753).

Boas G, Bischoff JL and Reid NL, *International Criminal Law Practitioner Library, vol 2: Elements of Crimes under International Law* (Cambridge, Cambridge University Press, 2009).

Bohlander M, 'Criminalising LGBT Persons under National Criminal Law and Article 7(1)(h) and (3) of the ICC Statute' (2014) 5 *Global Policy* 401.

Bookbinder E, 'Crimes Committed Against Civilian Population by Transnational Criminal Organizations Should Be Considered Crimes Against Humanity and Leaders Prosecuted by ICC' (2016) 23 *Willamette Journal of International Law and Dispute Resolution* 255.

Boon K, 'Rape and Forced Pregnancy under the ICC Statute: Human Dignity, Autonomy, and Consent' (2000) 32 *Columbia Human Rights Law Review* 625.

Boister N and Currie RJ (eds), *Routledge Handbook of Transnational Criminal Law* (Abingdon, Routledge, 2015).

Borda AZ, 'Appraisal-Based and Flexible Approaches to External Precedent in International Criminal Law' (2015) 28 *Leiden Journal of International Law* 643.

Borgers MJ, 'De communicatieve strafrechter' in *Controverses rondom legaliteit en legitimatie* (Handelingen Nederlandse Juristen-Vereniging, Deventer, Kluwer, 2011).

Borrelli G, 'Foreword: Organised Crime and Its Relationship with Politics as Seen from Italy' in Allum F and Gilmour S (eds), *Handbook of Organised Crime and Politics* (Cheltenham, Edward Elgar, 2019).

Bradley MM, ''Protracted Armed Conflict': A Conundrum. Does Article 8(2)(f) of the Rome Statute Require an Organised Armed Group to Meet the Organisational Criteria of Additional Protocol II?' (2019) 32 *South African Journal of Criminal Justice* 291.

Brölmann C, 'Specialized Rules of Treaty Interpretation: International Organizations' (Amsterdam Law School Legal Studies Research Paper, 2012).

Broomhall B, 'Nullum Crimen Sine Lege' in Ambos K and Triffterer O (eds), *The Rome Statute of the International Criminal Court: A Commentary*, 3rd edn (Munich/Oxford/Baden-Baden, CH Beck – Hart – Nomos, 2016).

Bunting, BN Lawrance and RL Robert, 'Introduction: Something Old, Something New? Conceptualizing Forced Marriage in Africa' in A Bunting, BN Lawrance and RL Robert (eds), *Marriage by Force? Contestation over Consent and Coercion in Africa* (Ohio, Ohio University Press, 2016).

Bunting A and Ikhimiukor IK, 'The Expressive Nature of Law: What We Learn from Conjugal Slavery to Forced Marriage in International Criminal Law' (2018) 18 *International Criminal Law Review* 331.

Burnet JE, 'Situating Sexual Violence in Rwanda (1990–2001): Sexual Agency, Sexual Consent, and the Political Economy of War' (2012) 55 *African Studies Review* 97.

Canals JM, 'Classicism, Positivism and Social Defence' (1960) 50 *Journal of Criminal Law, Criminology, and Police Science* 541.

Cassese A, *International Criminal Law*, 3rd edn (Oxford, Oxford University Press, 2013).

Cassese A, 'The Martens Clause: Half a Loaf or Simply Pie in the Sky?' (2000) 11 *European Journal of International Law* 187.

Cassese A, 'Balancing the Prosecution of Crimes against Humanity and Non-Retroactivity of Criminal Law' (2006) 4 *Journal of International Criminal Justice* 410.

Cassese A, 'From Nuremberg to Rome: International Military Tribunals to the International Criminal Court' in Cassese A, Gaeta P and Jones JRWD (eds), *The Rome Statute of the International Criminal Court*, vol 1 (Oxford, Oxford University Press, 2002).

Chalmers J and Leverick F, 'Fair Labelling in Criminal Law' (2008) 71 *Modern Law Review* 217.
Charlesworth H, 'Feminist Methods in International Law' (1999) 93 *American Journal of International Law* 379.
Chouliaras A, 'A Strategic Choice: The State Policy Requirement in Core International Crimes' (2015) 28 *Leiden Journal of International Law* 953.
Christensen MJ and Orina NM, 'The International Criminal Court as a Law Laboratory: Professional Battles of Control and the "Control of the Crime" Theory' (2022) 20 *Journal of International Criminal Justice* 699.
Clark RS, 'History of Efforts to Codify Crimes Against Humanity from the Charter of Nuremberg to the Statute of Rome' in Sadat LN (ed), *Forging a Convention for Crimes against Humanity* (Cambridge, Cambridge University Press, 2011).
Claes E, *Legaliteit en rechtsvinding in het strafrecht: een grondslagentheoretische benadering* (Samenleving, Criminaliteit & Strafrechtspleging, Leuven, Universitaire Pers Leuven, 2003).
Cossman B, 'Gender Performance, Sexual Subjects and International Law' (2002) 15 *Canadian Journal of Law & Jurisprudence* 281.
Coulter C, *Bush Wives and Girl Soldiers: Women's Lives through War and Peace in Sierra Leone* (Cornell University Press, 2009).
Copelon R, 'Gender Crimes as War Crimes: Integrating Crimes against Women into International Criminal Law' (2000) 46 *McGill Law Journal* 217.
Corliss C, 'Human Trafficking as "Modern Slavery": The Trouble with Trafficking as Enslavement in International Law' (2019) 71 *South Carolina Law Review* 603.
Coulter C, *Bush Wives and Girl Soldiers: Women's Lives through War and Peace in Sierra Leone* (Cornell University Press, 2009).
Clapham A, 'Extending International Criminal Law Beyond the Individual to Corporations and Armed Opposition Groups' (2008) 6 *Journal of International Criminal Justice* 899.
Crenshaw K, 'Demarginalizing the Intersection of Race and Sex: A Black Feminist Critique of Antidiscrimination Doctrine, Feminist Theory and Antiracist Politics' (1989) *University of Chicago Legal Forum* 139.
Cryer R, *Prosecuting International Crimes* (Cambridge, Cambridge University Press, 2005).
Cryer R, 'Royalism and the King: Article 21 of the Rome Statute and the Politics of Sources' (2009) 12 *New Criminal Law Review* 390.
Cryer R and others, *An Introduction to International Criminal Law and Procedure* (2nd edn, Cambridge, Cambridge University Press, 2010).
Cugat P, *Les crimes contre l'humanité dans le statut de la Cour internationale* (Zurich, Schulthess, 2006).
Damaska MR, *The Faces of Justice and State Authority: A Comparative Approach to the Legal Process* (New Haven, Yale University Press, 1986).
Davidson C, *Crimes Against Humanity: Historical Evolution and Contemporary Application* (JSTOR, 2012).
Davidson C, 'Explaining Inhumanity: The Use of Crime-Definition Experts at International Criminal Courts' (2015) 48 *Vanderbilt Journal of Transnational Law* 359.
Davidson C, 'How to Read International Criminal Law: Strict Construction and the Rome Statute of the International Criminal Court' (2017) 91 *St John's Law Review* 37.
Davis L, 'Reimagining Justice for Gender-Based Crimes at the Margins: New Legal Strategies for Prosecuting ISIS Crimes Against Women and LGBTIQ Persons' (2018) 24 *William & Mary Journal of Women and the Law* 521.
Davis L, 'Dusting Off the Law Books: Recognizing Gender Persecution in Conflicts and Atrocities' (2021) 20 *Northwestern Journal of Human Rights* 1.
De Baets A, 'The United Nations Human Rights Committee's View of the Past' (2017) 8 *Comparative Practice* 29.
deGuzman MM, 'Article 21 Applicable Law' in Triffterer O and Ambos K (eds), *The Rome Statute of the International Criminal Court: A Commentary* (3rd edn, Munich/Oxford/Baden-Baden, C H Beck – Hart – Nomos, 2016).

deGuzman MM, 'Crimes Against Humanity' in Schabas WA and Bernaz N (eds), *Routledge Handbook of International Criminal Law* (Abingdon, Routledge, 2010).
deGuzman MM, 'The Road from Rome: The Developing Law of Crimes Against Humanity' (2000) 22 *Human Rights Quarterly* 335.
De Langis T and others, *"Like Ghost Changes Body": A Study on the Impact of Forced Marriage under the Khmer Rouge Regime* (2014).
de Souza Dias T, 'Recharacterisation of Crimes and the Principle of Fair Labelling in International Criminal Law' (2018) 18 *International Criminal Law Review* 788.
Descheemaeker J, 'Le Tribunal militaire international des grands criminels de guerre' (1946) 1 *Revue générale de droit international public* 210.
Dinstein Y, 'Crimes Against Humanity' in Makarczyk J and Skubiszewski K (eds), *Theory of International Law at the Threshold of the 21st Century: Essays in Honour of Krzysztof Skubiszewski* (The Hague, Kluwer Law International, 1996).
Dinstein Y, 'Case Analysis: Crimes Against Humanity after Tadić' (2000) 13 *Leiden Journal of International Law* 372.
Donnedieu de Vabres H, 'Le jugement de Nuremberg et le principe de légalité des délits et des peines' (1946–47) *Revue de droit pénal et de criminologie.*
Dotto G-P, 'Gender and Sex – Time to Bridge the Gap' (2019) 11 *EMBO Molecular Medicine.*
Drumond P, 'What about Men? Towards a Critical Interrogation of Sexual Violence against Men in Global Politics' (2019) 95 *International Affairs* 1271.
Dubber M, 'The Legality Principle in American and German Criminal Law: An Essay in Comparative Legal History' in Martyn G, Musson A and Pihlajamäki H (eds), *From the Judge's Arbitrium to the Legality Principle: Legislation as a Source of Law in Criminal Trials* (Berlin, Duncker & Humblot, 2013).
Dubler SCR and Kalyk M, *Crimes against Humanity in the 21st Century: Law, Practice and Threats to International Peace and Security* (Leiden, Brill Nijhoff, 2018).
Dworkin R, *Taking Rights Seriously* (London, Bloomsbury Academic, 1978).
Dyzenhaus D, 'The Grudge Informer Case Revisited' (2008) 83 *New York University Law Review* 1000.
Eboe-Osuji C, 'Forced Marriage – an International Crime?' in C Eboe-Osuji (ed), *International Law and Sexual Violence in Armed Conflicts* (The Hague, Martinus Nijhoff, 2012).
Edwards J and Simester A, 'Crime, Blameworthiness, and Outcomes' (2019) 39 *Oxford Journal of Legal Studies* 50.
Ehard H, 'The Nuremberg Trial Against the Major War Criminals and International Law' (1949) 43 *American Journal of International Law* 223.
Elander M, 'Prosecuting the Khmer Rouge Marriages' in L Kent and M Demian (eds), *Transitional Justice in Law, History and Anthropology* (Abingdon, Routledge, 2020) 160.
Enright M, 'Choice, Culture and the Politics of Bel ongoing: The Emerging Law of Forced and Arranged Marriage' (2009) 72 *The Modern Law Review* 331.
Erb NE, 'Gender-Based Crimes under the Draft Statute for the Permanent International Criminal Court' (1998) 29 *Columbia Human Rights Law Review* 401.
Eskauriatza JS, '"Complete Labelling" and Domestic Prosecutions for Crimes Against Humanity' (2021) *Criminal Law Forum.*
Fausto-Sterling A, *Sex/Gender: Biology in a Social World* (Abingdon, Routledge, 2012).
Ferme MC, *The Underneath of Things: Violence, History, and the Everyday in Sierra Leone* (Oakland, University of California Press 2001).
Feinberg J, *Doing and Deserving: Essays in the Theory of Responsibility* (Princeton NJ, Princeton University Press, 1970).
Fernández RAA and Estapà JS, 'Towards a Single and Comprehensive Notion of "Civilian Population" in Crimes Against Humanity' (2017) 17 *International Criminal Law Review* 47.
Ferri E, *La sociologie criminelle*, 2nd edn (Paris, Alcan, 1914).
Fletcher GP, *Basic Concepts of Criminal Law* (Oxford, Oxford University Press, 1998).
Fletcher GP, 'Two Kinds of Legal Rules: A Comparative Study of Burden-of-Persuasion Practices in Criminal Cases' (1967) 77 *Yale Law Journal* 880.

Fletcher GP and Ohlin JD, 'Reclaiming Fundamental Principles of Criminal Law in the Darfur' (2005) 3 *Journal of International Criminal Justice* 539.
Finnis JM, *Natural Law and Natural Rights*, 2nd edn (Oxford, Oxford University Press, 2011).
Finnis JM, 'Natural Law and Legal Reasoning' (1990) 38 *Cleveland State Law Review* 1.
Finnis JM, 'Law, Morality, and Sexual Orientation' (1993) 69 *Notre Dame Law Review*.
Fitzmaurice M, 'The Practical Workings of the Law of Treaties' in Evans MD (ed), *International Law* (Oxford, Oxford University Press, 2003).
Franck TM, *The Power of Legitimacy among Nations* (Oxford, Oxford University Press, 1990).
Frulli M, 'Advancing International Criminal Law: The Special Court for Sierra Leone Recognizes Forced Marriage as a "New" Crime against Humanity' (2008) 6 *Journal of International Criminal Justice* 1033.
Fuller LL, *The Morality of Law* (New Haven, Yale University Press, 1969).
Fuller LL, 'Positivism and Fidelity to Law: A Reply to Professor Hart' (1958) 71 *Harvard Law Review* 630.
Gaeta P, 'Does President Al Bashir Enjoy Immunity from Arrest?' (2009) 7 *Journal of International Criminal Justice* 315.
Gallant KS, *The Principle of Legality in International and Comparative Criminal Law* (Cambridge, Cambridge Universitiy Press, 2009).
Galand AS, 'The Systemic Effect of International Human Rights Law on International Criminal Law' in Scheinin M (ed), *Human Rights Norms in "Other" International Courts* (Cambridge, Cambridge University Press, 2019).
Galand AS, 'Approaching Custom Identification as a Conflict Avoidance Technique: *Tadić* and *Kupreškić* Revisited' (2018) 31 *Leiden Journal of International Law* 403.
Gangoli G et al, 'Understanding Forced Marriage: Definitions and Realities' in AK Gill and S Anitha (eds), *Forced Marriage: Introducing a Social Justice and Human Rights Perspective* (Zed Books, 2011).
Garibian S, 'Crimes against Humanity and International Legality in Legal Theory after Nuremberg' (2007) 9 *Journal of Genocide Research* 93.
Gardiner RK, *Treaty Interpretation* (Oxford, Oxford University Press, 2008).
Garfinkel P, *Criminal Law in Liberal and Fascist Italy* (Cambridge, Cambridge University Press, 2019).
Geiger R, 'The German Border Guard Cases and International Human Rights' (1998) 9 *European Journal of International Law* 540.
Geras N, *Crimes Against Humanity: Birth of a Concept* (Manchester, Manchester University Press, 2011).
Glaser S, '*Nullum Crimen Sine Lege*: A Contribution' (1942) 24 *Journal of Comparative Legislation and International Law* 29.
Glasius M, *Who Is the Real Civil Society? Women's Groups versus Pro-Family Groups at the International Criminal Court Negotiations* (Abingdon, Routledge, 2004).
Goldenberg SL, 'Crimes Against Humanity – 1945–1970' (1971) 10 *Western Ontario Law Review* 1.
Gong-Gershowitz J, 'Forced Marriage: A "New" Crime against Humanity?' (2009) 8 *Northwestern Journal of International Human Rights* 53.
Goodfellow NA, 'The Miscategorization of Forced Marriage as a Crime against Humanity by the Special Court for Sierra Leone' (2011) 11 *International Criminal Law Review*.
Ginsburg T, *International Judicial Lawmaking* (Tübingen, Mohr Siebeck, 2006).
Grey R, 'Conflicting Interpretations of "Sexual Violence" in the International Criminal Court' (2014) 29 *Australian Feminist Studies* 273.
Grey R et al, 'Gender-Based Persecution as a Crime against Humanity: The Road Ahead' (2019) 17 *Journal of International Criminal Justice* 957.
Grewal KK, 'International Criminal Law as a Site for Enhancing Women's Rights? Challenges, Possibilities, Strategies' (2015) 23 *Feminist Legal Studies* 149.
Grewal KK, 'Using War to Shift Peacetime Norms: The Example of Forced Marriage in Sierra Leone' in R Shackel and L Fiske (eds), *Rethinking Transitional Gender Justice* (London, Palgrave Macmillan, 2019).

Grover L, *Interpreting Crimes in the Rome Statute of the International Criminal Court* (Cambridge, Cambridge University Press, 2014).
Grover L, 'A Call for Arms: Fundamental Dilemmas Confronting the Interpretation of Crimes in the Rome Statute of the International Criminal Court' (2010) 21 *European Journal of International Law* 543.
Haenen I, *Force & Marriage: The Criminalisation of Forced Marriage in Dutch, English and International Criminal Law* (Antwerp, Intersentia, 2014).
Haenen I, 'The Parameters of Enslavement and the Act of Forced Marriage' (2013) 13 *International Criminal Law Review* 895.
Hafner G, 'Subsequent Agreements and Practice: Between Interpretation, Informal Modification, and Formal Amendment' in Gardiner RK (ed), *Treaties and Subsequent Practice* (Oxford, Oxford University Press, 2013).
Halley J, 'Rape at Rome: Feminist Interventions in the Criminalisation of Sex-Related Violence in Positive International Criminal Law' (2008) 30 *Michigan Journal of International Law* 1.
Hall J, *Principles of Criminal Law* (Indianapolis, The Bobbs-Merrill Company, 1947).
Hall CK, Powderly J and Hayes N, 'Article 7(3)' in K Ambos and O Trifferer (eds), *The Rome Statute of the International Criminal Court: A Commentary*, 3rd edn (CH Beck–Hart–Nomos, 2016) 216.
Halliday MA, 'Language and Knowledge: The "Unpacking" of Text' in *Text in Education and Society* (1998) 157.
Halling M, 'Push the Envelope, Watch It Bend: Removing the Policy Requirement and Extending Crimes against Humanity' (2010) 23 *Leiden Journal of International Law* 821.
Hansen TO, 'The Policy Requirement in Crimes against Humanity: Lessons from and for the Case of Kenya' (2011) 43 *Washington International Law Review* [page not specified].
Haque AA, 'Group Violence and Group Vengeance: Toward a Retributivist Theory of International Criminal Law' (2005) 9 *Buffalo Criminal Law Review* 273.
Hart HLA, *The Concept of Law*, 2nd edn (Oxford, Clarendon Press, 1994).
Hart HLA, 'Positivism and the Separation of Law and Morals' (1958) 71 *Harvard Law Review* 593.
Hayes N, 'Creating a Definition of Rape in International Law: The Contribution of the International Criminal Tribunals' in Darcy S and Powderly J (eds), *Judicial Creativity at the International Criminal Tribunals* (Oxford, Oxford University Press, 2010).
Heinze A and Dittrich VE (eds), *The Past, Present and Future of the International Criminal Court* (Nuremberg Academy Series, 2021).
Heller KJ, *The Nuremberg Military Tribunals and the Origins of International Criminal Law* (Oxford, Oxford University Press, 2011).
Hernández GI, 'Interpretation' in Kammerhofer J and d'Aspremont J (eds), *International Legal Positivism in a Post-Modern World* (Cambridge, Cambridge University Press, 2014).
Hernández GI, 'Interpretative Authority and the International Judiciary' in Bianchi A, Peat D and Windsor M (eds), *Interpretation in International Law* (Oxford, Oxford University Press, 2015).
Hochmayr G, 'Applicable Law in Practice and Theory: Interpreting Article 21 of the ICC Statute' (2014) 12 *Journal of International Criminal Justice* 655.
Hoffmann T, 'The Gentle Civilizer of Humanitarian Law' in Stahn C and van den Herik L (eds), *Future Perspectives on International Criminal Justice* (2010).
Horder J, 'Rethinking Non-Fatal Offences against the Person' (1994) 14 *Oxford Journal of Legal Studies* 335.
Hunt D, 'The International Criminal Court: High Hopes, "Creative Ambiguity" and an Unfortunate Mistrust in International Judges' (2004) 2 *Journal of International Criminal Justice* 56.
Hwang P, 'Defining Crimes against Humanity in the Rome Statute of the International Criminal Court' (1998) 22 *Fordham International Law Journal* 457.
Ingold T, 'Introduction to Social Life' in T Ingold (ed), *Companion Encyclopedia of Anthropology* (Abingdon, Routledge, 1994).
Irving E, 'The Other Side of the Article 21(3) Coin: Human Rights in the Rome Statute and the Limits of Article 21(3)' (2019) 32 *Leiden Journal of International Law* 837.

Jain N, 'Forced Marriage as a Crime against Humanity' (2008) 6 *Journal of International Criminal Justice* 1013.
Jain N, 'Going Beyond Prosecutorial Discretion: Institutional Factors Influencing Thematic Prosecution' in M Bergsmo and CW Ling (eds), *Thematic Prosecutions of International Sex Crimes* (Torkel Opsahl Academic Epublisher, 2012).
Jain N, 'Interpretive Divergence' (2017) 57 *Virginia Journal of International Law* 45.
Jalloh CC, 'Situation in the Republic of Kenya' (2012) 106 *American Journal of International Law* 118.
Jalloh CC, 'What Makes a Crime against Humanity a Crime against Humanity?' (2012) 28 *American University International Law Review* 381.
Jacobs D, 'Positivism and International Criminal Law: The Principle of Legality as a Rule of Conflict of Theories' in d'Aspremont J and Kammerhofer J (eds), *International Legal Positivism in a Post-Modern World* (Cambridge, Cambridge University Press, 2014).
Joseph JH, 'Gender and International Law: How the International Criminal Court Can Bring Justice to Victims of Sexual Violence' (2008) 18 *Texas Journal of Women and the Law* 61.
Joseph S and Castan M, *The International Covenant on Civil and Political Rights: Cases, Materials and Commentary*, 3rd edn (Oxford, Oxford University Press, 2013).
Johnston I, 'Treaty Interpretation: The Authority of Interpretative Communities' (1991) 12 *Michigan Journal of International Law*.
Jyrkkiö ST, 'Other Inhumane Acts as Crimes against Humanity' (2011) *Helsinki Law Review*.
Kafedžić S, 'Determining Modes of Liability in International Criminal Law: Why the Common Purpose Doctrine Is the Strongest Legal Response to Mass Atrocity Crimes' in Burke CR and Burke R (eds), *New Zealand Yearbook of International Law* (Leiden, Brill Nijhoff, 2018).
Kalra MS, 'Forced Marriage: Rwanda's Secret Revealed' (2001) 7 *UC Davis Journal of International Law & Policy* 197.
Karkazis K, 'The Misuses of "Biological Sex"' (2019) 394 *The Lancet* 1898.
Keating A, *Jurisprudence* (London, Thomson Reuters, 2011).
Kelsen H, *Pure Theory of Law*, 2nd edn (Berkeley, University of California Press, 1970).
Kelsen H, 'The Rule Against Ex Post Facto Laws and the Prosecution of the Axis War Criminals' (1945) *Judge Advocate Journal*.
Kelsall T, *Culture under Cross-Examination: International Justice and the Special Court for Sierra Leone* (Cambridge, Cambridge University Press, 2009).
Kelsen H, 'Will the Judgment in the Nuremberg Trial Constitute a Precedent in International Law?' (1947) 1 *International Law Quarterly* 153.
Kerr VM, 'Should Forced Marriages Be Categorized as "Sexual Slavery" or "Other Inhumane Acts" in International Criminal Law?' (2020) 35 *Utrecht Journal of International and European Law* 1.
Kestenbaum JG and Sellers PV, 'The International Crimes of Slavery and the Slave Trade: A Feminist Critique' (2020) *Cardozo Legal Studies Research Paper* 54.
Klabbers J, 'Virtuous Interpretation' in Fitzmaurice M, Elias O and Panos M (eds), *Treaty Interpretation and the Vienna Convention on the Law of Treaties: 30 Years On*, vol 1 (Leiden, Martinus Nijhoff, 2010).
Klatt M, *Making the Law Explicit: The Normativity of Legal Argumentation* (Oxford and Portland OR, European Academy of Legal Theory Monograph Series, 2008).
Klingers and conference-type working papers already excluded.
Koskenniemi M, *From Apology to Utopia: The Structure of International Legal Argument* (Cambridge, Cambridge University Press, 2006).
Kreß C, 'Nulla Poena Nullum Crimen Sine Lege' in Ambos K and Triffterer O (eds), *The Rome Statute of the International Criminal Court: A Commentary*, 3rd edn (Munich/Oxford/Baden-Baden, C H Beck – Hart – Nomos, 2016).
Kreß C, 'On the Outer Limits of Crimes Against Humanity: The Concept of Organization within the Policy Requirement' (2010) 23 *Leiden Journal of International Law* 855.
Kreß C, 'The Procedural Law of the International Criminal Court in Outline: Anatomy of a Unique Compromise' (2003) 1 *Journal of International Criminal Justice* 603.

Kuschnik B, 'Humaneness, Humankind and Crimes against Humanity' (2010) 2 *Goettingen Journal of International Law* 501.
Lamond G, 'The Rule of Law' in Marmor A (ed), *The Routledge Companion to Philosophy of Law* (Abingdon, Routledge, 2012).
Langenbucher K, 'Argument by Analogy in European Law' (1998) 57 *Cambridge Law Journal* 481.
Lauterpacht H, 'Restrictive Interpretation and the Principle of Effectiveness in the Interpretation of Treaties' (1949) 26 *British Yearbook of International Law* 48.
Le Cour Grandmaison R, 'Mexico: Politics, Cartels and Violence' in Allum F and Gilmour S (eds), *Handbook of Organised Crime and Politics* (Cheltenham, Edward Elgar, 2019).
Lehr-Lehnardt R, 'One Small Step for Women: Female-Friendly Provisions in the Rome Statute of the International Criminal Court' (2002) 16 *BYU Journal of Public Law* 317.
Leiter B, 'Explaining Theoretical Disagreement' (2009) 76 *University of Chicago Law Review* 1215.
Linderfalk U, *On the Interpretation of Treaties: The Modern International Law as Expressed in the 1969 Vienna Convention on the Law of Treaties* (Heidelberg, Springer, 2007).
Lombroso C, *Criminal Man* (Durham NC, Duke University Press, 2006).
Lugano G, 'Counter-Shaming the International Criminal Court's Intervention as Neocolonial: Lessons from Kenya' (2017) 11 *International Journal of Transitional Justice* 9.
Luban D, 'A Theory of Crimes Against Humanity' (2004) 29 *Yale Journal of International Law* 85.
Luban D, 'Beyond Moral Minimalism' (2006) 20 *Ethics & International Affairs* 353.
MacCormick N and Summers RS, *Interpreting Statutes: A Comparative Study* (Dartmouth Publishing, 1991).
MacCormick N, 'Argumentation and Interpretation in Law' (1993) 6 *Ratio Juris* 16.
MacKay D, 'The Ejusdem Generis Principle of Interpretation' (1920) 90 *Central Law Journal* 285.
Mahmood F, 'Prosecuting Human Trafficking for the Purpose of Sexual Exploitation under Article 7 of the Rome Statute: Enslavement or Sexual Slavery' (2019) 35 *Journal of Trafficking and Human Exploitation* 35.
Majola BC, 'Cumulative Charges under International Criminal Law: Issues and Perspectives' in M Bergsmo and others (eds), *Promoting Accountability under International Law for Gross Human Rights Violations in Africa* (Leiden, Brill | Nijhoff, 2015).
Mälksoo L, '*Kononov v Latvia*' (2011) 105 *American Journal of International Law* 101.
Markovic M, 'Vessels of Reproduction: Forced Pregnancy and the ICC' (2007) 16 *Michigan State Journal of International Law* 439.
Marmor A, *Interpretation and Legal Theory* (Oxford, Clarendon Press, 2005).
Marmor A, *The Routledge Companion to Philosophy of Law* (Abingdon, Routledge, 2012).
Marmor A, *The Language of Law* (Oxford, Oxford University Press, 2014).
Mariniello T, 'The "Nuremberg Clause" and Beyond: Legality Principle and Sources of International Criminal Law in the European Court's Jurisprudence' (2013) 82 *Nordic Journal of International Law* 221.
Mariniello T and Lobba P, 'The Cross-Fertilisation Rhetoric in Question: Use and Abuse of the European Court's Jurisprudence by International Criminal Tribunals' (2015) 84 *Nordic Journal of International Law* 363.
May L, *Normative Account of Crimes Against Humanity* (Cambridge, Cambridge University Press, 2004).
McDade PV, 'The Effect of Article 4 of the Vienna Convention on the Law of Treaties 1969' (1986) 35 *International and Comparative Law Quarterly* 499.
McGonigle Leyh B, *Procedural Justice? Victim Participation in International Criminal Proceedings* (Cambridge, Intersentia, 2011).
McGonigle Leyh B, 'Pragmatism over Principles: The ICC and a Human Rights-Based Approach to Interpretation' (2018) 41 *Fordham International Law Journal* 697.
Meron T, 'War Crimes Law Comes of Age' (1998) 92 *American Journal of International Law* 462.
Meron T, 'The Humanization of Humanitarian Law' (2000) 94 *American Journal of International Law* 239.

Miers S, *Slavery in the Twentieth Century: The Evolution of a Global Problem* (Altamira Press, 2003).
Moore CB, 'Embracing Ambiguity and Adopting Propriety: Using Comparative Law to Explore Avenues for Protecting the LGBT Population under Article 7 of the Rome Statute of the International Criminal Court' (2016) 101 *Minnesota Law Review* 1287.
Morsink J, *The Universal Declaration of Human Rights: Origins, Drafting, and Intent* (Philadelphia, University of Pennsylvania Press, 1999).
Moshan BS, 'Women, War, and Words: The Gender Component in the Permanent International Criminal Court's Definition of Crimes against Humanity' (1998) 22 *Fordham International Law Journal* 154.
Mowbray A, *The Development of Positive Obligations under the ECHR* (Oxford, Hart Publishing, 2004).
Mueller SD, 'Kenya and the International Criminal Court: Politics, the Election, and the Law' (2013).
Murphy SD, *Fourth Report on Crimes against Humanity* (ILC, 2019).
Murray R, *The African Charter on Human and Peoples' Rights: A Commentary* (Oxford, Oxford University Press, 2019).
Naucke W, 'Interpretation and Analogy in Criminal Law' (1986) *Brigham Young University Law Review* 535.
Nersessian DL, 'Comparative Approaches to Punishing Hate: The Intersection of Genocide and Crimes Against Humanity' (2007) 43 *Stanford Journal of International Law* 221.
Niv A, 'The Schizophrenia of the "No Case to Answer" Test in International Criminal Tribunals' (2016) 14 *Journal of International Criminal Justice* 1121.
Nowrojee B, *Shattered Lives: Sexual Violence during the Rwandan Genocide and its Aftermath* (Human Rights Watch, 1996).
Nyabola N, 'The Legal Challenge of Civil Militia Groups in Kenya' (2009) 18 *African Security Review* 90.
Obokata T, *Organised Crime in International Law* (Oxford, Hart Publishing, 2010).
Ohlin JD, 'Joint Intentions to Commit International Crimes' (2011) 11 *Chicago Journal of International Law* 693.
Ohlin JD, Van Sliedregt E and Weigend T, 'Assessing the Control Theory' (2013) 26 *Leiden Journal of International Law* 725.
Olásolo H, 'Is ICL an Appropriate Mechanism to Deal with Organised Crime?' in Van der Wilt H and Paulussen C (eds), *Legal Responses to Transnational and International Crimes* (Cheltenham, Edward Elgar, 2017).
Oosterveld V, 'Sexual Slavery and the International Criminal Court: Advancing International Law' (2003) 25 *Michigan Journal of International Law* 605.
Oosterveld V, 'The Definition of Gender in the Rome Statute of the International Criminal Court: A Step Forward or Back for International Criminal Justice?' (2005) 18 *Harvard Human Rights Journal* 55.
Oosterveld V, 'Gender-Sensitive Justice and the International Criminal Tribunal for Rwanda: Lessons Learned for the International Criminal Court' (2005) 12 *New England Journal of International and Comparative Law* 119.
Oosterveld V, 'The Special Court for Sierra Leone's Consideration of Gender-Based Violence: Contributing to Transitional Justice?' (2009) 10 *Human Rights Review* 73.
Oosterveld V, 'Gender-Based Crimes against Humanity' in LN Sadat (ed), *Forging a Convention for Crimes Against Humanity* (Cambridge, Cambridge University Press, 2011) 80.
Oosterveld V, 'The ICC Policy Paper on Sexual and Gender-Based Crimes: A Crucial Step for International Criminal Law' (2017) 24 *William & Mary Journal of Women and the Law* 443.
Oosterveld V, 'Force Marriage: Terminological Coherence and Dissonance in International Criminal Law' (2019) 27 *William & Mary Bill of Rights Journal* 1263.
O'Regan F, 'Prosecutor v Jean-Pierre Bemba Gombo: The Cumulative Charging Principle, Gender-Based Violence, and Expressivism' (2012) 43 *Georgetown Journal of International Law* 1323.

Orentlicher DF, 'Settling Accounts: The Duty to Prosecute Human Rights Violations of a Prior Regime' (1991) 100 *Yale Law Journal* 2537.

Orentlicher DF, 'Criminalizing Hate Speech: A Comment on *Nahimana*' (2005) 13 *Human Rights Brief*.

Orlova AV and Moore JW, 'Umbrellas or Building Blocks? Defining International Terrorism and Transnational Organized Crime in International Law' (2004) 27 *Houston Journal of International Law* 267.

Ortner D, 'The Merciful Corpus: The Rule of Lenity, Ambiguity, and Corpus Linguistics' (2016) 25 *Boston University Public Interest Law Journal* 101.

Park ASJ, '"Other Inhumane Acts": Forced Marriage, Girl Soldiers and the Special Court for Sierra Leone' (2006) 15 *Social & Legal Studies* 315.

Paoli L and Vander Beken T, 'Organized Crime: A Contest Concept' in Paoli L (ed), *The Oxford Handbook of Organized Crime* (Oxford, Oxford University Press, 2014).

Pappe HO, 'On the Validity of Judicial Decisions in the Nazi Era' (1960) 23 *Modern Law Review*.

Pearson Z, 'Non-Governmental Organizations and the International Criminal Court: Changing Landscapes of International Law' (2006) 39 *Cornell International Law Journal* 243.

Pellet A, 'Applicable Law' in Cassese A, Gaeta P and Jones JRWD (eds), *The Rome Statute of the International Criminal Court: A Commentary*, vol 2 (Oxford, Oxford University Press, 2002).

Pérez-León Acevedo JP, 'The Close Relationship Between Serious Human Rights Violations and Crimes against Humanity: International Criminalization of Serious Abuses' (2017) 17 *Anuario Mexicano de Derecho Internacional* 145.

Petersen N, 'Customary Law without Custom: Rules, Principles, and the Role of State Practice in International Norm Creation' (2008) 23 *American University International Law Review* 275.

Pin X, *Droit pénal général*, 10th edn (Paris, Dalloz, 2019).

Pinzauti G, 'The ECtHR's Incidental Application of International Criminal Law and Humanitarian Law: A Critical Discussion of *Kononov v Latvia*' (2008) 6 *Journal of International Criminal Justice* 1043.

Porat I, 'The Dual Model of Balancing: A Model for the Proper Scope of Balancing in Constitutional Law' (2006) 27 *Cardozo Law Review* 1393.

Poscher R, 'Ambiguity and Vagueness in Legal Interpretation' in Tiersma PM and Solan LM (eds), *The Oxford Handbook of Language and Law* (Oxford, Oxford University Press, 2012).

Powderly J, 'The Rome Statute and the Attempted Corseting of the Interpretative Judicial Function' in Stahn C (ed), *The Law and Practice of the International Criminal Court* (Oxford, Oxford University Press, 2015).

Preuss L, 'Punishment by Analogy in National Socialistic Penal Law' (1935) 26 *American Institute of Criminal Law & Criminology* 847.

Prins A, *Science pénale et droit positif* (Brussels, Bruylant, 1899).

Provost R, 'Interpretation in International Law as a Transcultural Project' in Bianchi A, Peat D and Windsor M (eds), *Interpretation in International Law* (Oxford, Oxford University Press, 2015).

Quirk J, 'Defining Slavery in All Its Forms: Historical Inquiry as Contemporary Instruction' in J Allain (ed), *The Legal Understanding of Slavery* (2012).

Raab D and Bevers H, 'The International Criminal Court and the Separation of Powers' (2006) 3 *International Organizations Law Review* 93.

Radbruch G, 'Gesetzliches Unrecht und übergesetzliches Recht' (1946) 1 *Süddeutsche Juristen-Zeitung* 105.

Radbruch G, Paulson BL and Paulson SL, 'Statutory Lawlessness and Supra-Statutory Law' (2006) 26 *Oxford Journal of Legal Studies* 1.

Rauter T, *Judicial Practice, Customary International Law and Nullum Crimen Sine Lege* (Heidelberg, Springer, 2017).

Ratner SR, *The Thin Justice of International Law: A Moral Reckoning of the Law of Nations* (Oxford, Oxford University Press, 2015).

Raz J, *The Authority of Law: Essays on Law and Morality* (Oxford, Oxford University Press, 1979).

Raz J, 'Legal Principles and the Limits of Law' (1972) 81 *Yale Law Journal* 823.
Raz J, 'Why Interpret?' (1996) 9 *Ratio Juris* 349.
Renzo M, 'Crimes Against Humanity and the Limits of International Criminal Law' (2012) 31 *Law and Philosophy* 443.
Roberts C, 'On the Definition of Crimes Against Humanity and Other Widespread or Systematic Human Rights Violations' (2017) 20 *University of Pennsylvania Journal of Law and Social Change* 1.
Robinson D, *Justice in Extreme Cases: Criminal Law Theory Meets International Criminal Law* (Cambridge, Cambridge University Press, 2020).
Robinson D, 'The Identity Crisis of International Criminal Law' (2008) 21 *Leiden Journal of International Law* 925.
Robinson D, 'A Cosmopolitan Liberal Account of International Criminal Law' (2013) 26 *Leiden Journal of International Law* 127.
Robinson D, 'Defining "Crimes Against Humanity" at the Rome Conference' (1999) 93 *American Journal of International Law* 43.
Rödenhäuser T, *Organizing Rebellion: Non-State Armed Groups under International Humanitarian Law, Human Rights Law, and International Criminal Law* (Oxford, Oxford University Press, 2018).
Rooney E, 'Intersectionality: Working in Conflict' in Aoláin FN and others (eds), *The Oxford Handbook of Gender and Conflict* (Oxford, Oxford University Press, 2015).
Rosenne S, 'The Temporal Application of the Vienna Convention on the Law of Treaties' (1970) 4 *Cornell International Law Journal* 1.
Rude-Antoine E, *Forced Marriages in Council of Europe Member States: A Comparative Study of Legislation and Political Initiatives* (Council of Europe Publishing, 2005).
Russell CC, 'The Chapeau of Crimes Against Humanity: The Impact of the Rome Statute of the International Criminal Court' (2011) 8 *Eyes on the ICC* 25.
Sadat LN and Carden RS, 'The New International Criminal Court: An Uneasy Revolution' (2000) 88 *Georgetown Law Journal*.
Sadat LN and Jolly JM, 'Seven Canons of ICC Treaty Interpretation: Making Sense of Article 25's Rorschach Blot' (2014) 27 *Leiden Journal of International Law*.
Sadat LN, 'Crimes Against Humanity and Customary International Law' (Washington University in St Louis Legal Studies Research Paper 25-03, 2025).
Saland P, 'Chapter 7 International Criminal Law Principles' in RS Lee (ed), *The International Criminal Court: The Making of the Rome Statute: Issues, Negotiations, Results* (Kluwer Law International, 1999).
Schabas WA, 'Commentary on Judgement, Prosecutor v Furundžija' in A Klip and G Sluiter (eds), *Annotated Leading Cases of International Criminal Tribunals, vol III: The International Criminal Tribunal for the Former Yugoslavia, 1997–1999* (Antwerp, Intersentia, 2001).
Schabas WA, 'Interpreting the Statutes of the Ad Hoc Tribunals' in LC Vohrah and others (eds), *Man's Inhumanity to Man: Essays on International Law in Honour of Antonio Cassese* (Leiden, Brill Nijhoff, 2003).
Schabas WA and Powderly J, *Crimes against Humanity in Western Burma: The Situation of the Rohingyas* (Irish Centre for Human Rights, 2010).
Schabas WA, *The International Criminal Court: A Commentary on the Rome Statute* (Oxford Commentaries on International Law, Oxford University Press, 2010).
Schabas WA, 'Strict Construction and the Rome Statute' in S Dewulf (ed), *Liber Amicorum Chris Van den Wyngaert* (Maklu, 2017).
Schabas WA, 'General Principles, Nullum Crimen and Accountability for International Crimes' in P Acconci and others (eds), *International Law and the Protection of Humanity: Essays in Honour of Flavia Lattanzi* (Leiden, Brill Nijhoff, 2017).
Scarpa S, 'The Nebulous Definition of Slavery: Legal versus Sociological Definitions of Slavery' in B Winterdyk and J Jones (eds), *The Palgrave International Handbook of Human Trafficking* (New Jersey, Springer, 2020) 3.

Scharf MP and Mattler S, *Forced Marriage: Exploring the Viability of the Special Court for Sierra Leone's New Crime against Humanity* (Case Research Paper Series in Legal Studies, 2005).
Schindler D, 'The Different Types of Armed Conflicts according to the Geneva Conventions and Protocols' (1979) 2 *Recueil des Cours* 117.
Schloenhardt A, 'Transnational Organised Crime and the International Criminal Court: Developments and Debates' (2005) 24 *University of Queensland Law Journal* 93.
Schloenhardt A, 'Transnational Organised Crime' in N Boister and RJ Currie (eds), *Routledge Handbook of Transnational Criminal Law* (Abingdon, Routledge, 2015).
Schwelb E, 'Crimes against Humanity' (1946) 23 *British Yearbook of International Law* 178.
Sellers PV, 'Wartime Female Slavery: Enslavement' (2011) 44 *Cornell International Law Journal* 115.
Sellers PV, *The Prosecution of Sexual Violence in Conflict: The Importance of Human Rights as Means of Interpretation* (WRGU, 2007).
Shahabuddeen M, 'Does the Principle of Legality Stand in the Way of Progressive Development of Law?' (2004) 2 *Journal of International Criminal Justice* 1007.
Siefert R, 'War and Rape: A Preliminary Analysis' in A Stiglmayer (ed), *Mass Rape: The War against Women in Bosnia-Herzegovina* (Lincoln, University of Nebraska Press, 1994) 54.
Siller N, '"Modern Slavery": Does International Law Distinguish between Slavery, Enslavement and Trafficking?' (2016) 14 *Journal of International Criminal Justice* 405.
Silving H, 'Analogy and Extensive Interpretation' (1967) 36 *Revista Jurídica de la Universidad de Puerto Rico* 311.
Sinn A, 'Transnational Organised Crime: Concepts and Critics' in P Hauck and S Peterke (eds), *International Law and Transnational Organised Crime* (Oxford, Oxford University Press, 2016).
Slater R, 'Gender Violence or Violence against Women? The Treatment of Forced Marriage in the Special Court for Sierra Leone' (2012) 13 *Melbourne Journal of International Law* 732.
Sluiter G, '"Chapeau Elements" of Crimes Against Humanity in the Jurisprudence of the UN ad hoc Tribunals' in LN Sadat (ed), *Forging a Convention for Crimes Against Humanity* (Cambridge, Cambridge University Press, 2011).
Smith JM, 'An International Hit Job: Prosecuting Organized Crime Acts as Crimes against Humanity' (2009) 97 *Georgetown Law Journal* 1111.
Spaak T, 'Meta-Ethics and Legal Theory: The Case of Gustav Radbruch' (2009) 28 *Law and Philosophy* 261.
Stahn C, *A Critical Introduction to International Criminal Law* (Cambridge, Cambridge University Press, 2019).
Stahn C, 'Between Consolidation and Innovation: The International Criminal Court's Trial Chamber Judgment in the Lubanga Case' in TD Gill and others (eds), *Yearbook of International Humanitarian Law*, vol 15 (The Hague, TMC Asser Press, 2012).
Stahn C and van den Herik L, '"Fragmentation", Diversification and "3D" Legal Pluralism: International Criminal Law as the Jack-in-the-Box?' in C Stahn and L van den Herik (eds), *The Diversification and Fragmentation of International Criminal Law* (The Hague, Martinus Nijhoff, 2012).
Steains C, 'Gender Issues in the Statute of the International Criminal Court' in RS Lee (ed), *The International Criminal Court: The Making of the Rome Statute* (Alphen aan den Rijn, Kluwer Law International, 1999) 367.
Steer C, 'Legal Transplants or Legal Patchworking? The Creation of International Criminal Law as a Pluralistic Body of Law' in E van Sliedregt and S Vasiliev (eds), *Pluralism and Harmonization in International Criminal Law* (Oxford, Oxford University Press, 2013).
Stern DG, *Wittgenstein's Philosophical Investigations: An Introduction*, vol 2 (Cambridge, Cambridge University Press, 2004).
Stiglmayer A (ed), *Mass Rape: The War against Women in Bosnia-Herzegovina* (Lincoln, University of Nebraska Press, 1994).
Stuckenberg C-F, 'Cumulative Charges and Cumulative Convictions' in C Stahn (ed), *The Law and Practice of the International Criminal Court* (Oxford, Oxford University Press, 2015) 840.

Suhr VV, *Rainbow Jurisdiction at the International Criminal Court: Protection of Sexual and Gender Minorities under the Rome Statute* (The Hague, Asser Press–Springer, 2021).

Swart M, 'Judicial Lawmaking at the ad hoc Tribunals: The Creative Use of the Sources of International Law and "Adventurous Interpretation"' (2010) *Zeitschrift für ausländisches öffentliches Recht und Völkerrecht (ZaöRV)*.

Toy-Cronin BA, 'What Is Forced Marriage? Towards a Definition of Forced Marriage as a Crime against Humanity' (2010) 19 *Columbia Journal of Gender and Law* 539.

Uhlířová K, 'Contribution of the International Criminal Court to the Prosecution of Sexual and Gender-Based Crimes: Between Promise and Practice' in H von Hebel and others (eds), *The Rome Statute of the ICC at Its Twentieth Anniversary* (Leiden, Brill | Nijhoff, 2018).

Ullrich L and Hoyle C, 'New Court, New Justice? The Evolution of Justice for Victims at Domestic Courts and at the ICC' (2014) 12 *Journal of International Criminal Justice* 681.

Usprich SJ, 'A New Crime in Old Battles: Definitional Problems with Sexual Assault' (1987) 29 *Criminal Law Quarterly* 202.

Van der Wilt H, 'Nullum Crimen and International Criminal Law: The Relevance of the Foreseeability Test' (2015) 84 *Nordic Journal of International Law* 515.

Van der Wilt H, 'Legal Responses to Transnational and International Crimes: Towards an Integrative Approach?' in Van der Wilt H and Paulussen C (eds), *Legal Responses to Transnational and International Crimes* (Cheltenham, Edward Elgar, 2017).

van den Herik L, 'Using Custom to Reconceptualize Crimes Against Humanity' in Darcy S and Powderly J (eds), *Judicial Creativity in International Criminal Tribunals* (Oxford, Oxford University Press, 2010).

Van Schaack B, 'Judicial Lawmaking: The Intersection Between Law and Morals' (2008–09) 97 *Georgetown Law Journal* 119.

Van Schaack B, 'The Definition of Crimes Against Humanity: Resolving the Incoherence' (1998) 37 *Columbia Journal of Transnational Law* 787.

Vasiliev S, 'General Rules and Principles of International Criminal Procedure: Definition, Legal Nature, and Identification' in Sluiter G and Vasiliev S (eds), *International Criminal Procedure: Towards a Coherent Body of Law* (The Hague, TMC Asser Press, 2009).

Vasiliev S, 'International Criminal Tribunals in the Shadow of Strasbourg and the Politics of Cross-fertilisation' (2015) 84 *Nordic Journal of International Law* 371.

Vittorio M, 'Italy: Politics, Local Government and Mafias' in Allum F and Gilmour S (eds), *Handbook of Organised Crime and Politics* (Cheltenham, Edward Elgar, 2019).

Villiger ME, 'The Rules on Interpretation: Misgivings, Misunderstandings, Miscarriage?' in Cannizzaro E (ed), *The Law of Treaties Beyond the Vienna Convention* (Oxford, Oxford University Press, 2011).

Vierdag EW, 'The Law Governing Treaty Relations Between Parties and Non-Parties to the VCLT' (1982) 76 *American Journal of International Law* 779.

Vité S, 'Between Consolidation and Innovation: The ICC's Judgment in *Lubanga*' in Gill TD and others (eds), *Yearbook of International Humanitarian Law*, vol 15 (The Hague, TMC Asser Press, 2012).

Von Hebel H and Robinson D, 'Crimes within the Jurisdiction of the Court' in Lee RS (ed), *The International Criminal Court: The Making of the Rome Statute* (The Hague, Kluwer Law International, 1999).

Waibel M, 'The Origins of Interpretive Canons in Domestic Legal Systems' (Research Paper).

Weißer B, 'Transnational Organised Crime and Terrorism' in Hauck P and Peterke S (eds), *International Law and Transnational Organised Crime* (Oxford, Oxford University Press, 2016).

Werle G and Burghardt B, 'Do Crimes Against Humanity Require the Participation of a State or a State-Like Organization?' (2012) 10 *Journal of International Criminal Justice* 1151.

Williams G, 'Convictions and Fair Labelling' (1983) 42 *Cambridge Law Journal* 85.

Williams P, 'Transnational Criminal Networks' in Arquila J and Ronfeldt D (eds), *Networks and Netwars: The Future of Terror, Crime and Militancy* (Santa Monica CA, RAND, 2001).

Williams S and Palmer E, 'The Extraordinary Chambers in the Courts of Cambodia: Developing the Law on Sexual Violence?' (2015) 15 *International Criminal Law Review* 452.

Wittgenstein L, *Philosophical Investigations* (Oxford, Blackwell Publishing, 1986).
Worster WT, 'On the Purposes of Legality and its Applicability to International Law' (2011) 9 *Journal of International Criminal Justice* 973.
Zabyelina Y, 'Unpacking Pandora's Box: Defining Transnational Crime and Outlining Emerging Criminal Trends' (2010) 4 *Central European Journal of International and Security Studies* 124.
Zawati HM and Doherty TA, *Fair Labelling and the Dilemma of Prosecuting Gender-Based Crimes at the ICTs* (Oxford, Oxford University Press, 2014).
Zalewski M, 'Gender/s' in LJ Shepherd (ed), *Handbook on Gender and Violence* (Cheltenham, Edward Elgar, 2019).
Zeegers K, *International Criminal Tribunals and Human Rights Law: Adherence and Contextualization*, vol 5 (International Criminal Justice Series, Springer, 2016).
Zoller E, 'La définition des crimes contre l'humanité' (1993) 120 *Journal du droit international* 549.

Index

References are to page number.

www.ingramcontent.com/pod-product-compliance
Ingram Content Group UK Ltd.
Pitfield, Milton Keynes, MK11 3LW, UK
UKHW020241290926
15470UKWH00002B/663

9 781509 985173